caring for
infants &
toddlers

second edition

Derry G. Koralek

with Amy Laura Dombro and Diane Trister Dodge

Teaching Strategies Inc.

Washington, DC

Editors: Laurie Taub, Sherrie Rudick
Cover, book design, and computer illustrations: Carla Uriona
Production: Jennifer Love King
Illustrations: Mary Ross

Teaching Strategies, Inc.
P.O. Box 42243
Washington, DC 20015
www.TeachingStrategies.com
ISBN 13: 978-1-879537-49-1
ISBN 10: 1-879537-49-4

Teaching Strategies and *The Creative Curriculum* names and logos are
registered trademarks of Teaching Strategies, Inc., Washington, DC.

The publisher and the authors cannot be held responsible for injury,
mishap, or damages incurred during the use of or because of the
information in this book. The authors recommend appropriate and
reasonable supervision at all times based on the age and capability
of each child.

Library of Congress Cataloging-in-Publication Data
Koralek, Derry Gosselin.
 Caring for infants & toddlers / Derry G. Koralek with Amy Laura Dombro and Diane Trister Dodge.-- 2nd ed.
    p. cm.
 Includes bibliographical references.
 ISBN 1-879537-49-4
 1. Child care--Study and teaching. 2. Early childhood education. I. Title: Caring for infants and toddlers. II. Dombro,
Amy Laura, 1953- III. Dodge, Diane Trister. IV. Title.
 HQ778.5.K68 2005
 649'.122--dc22

                        2005007594

Printed and bound in the United States of America
2010   2009   2008   2007   2006
10 9 8 7 6 5 4 3 2

Acknowledgments

This completely updated and redesigned second edition of *Caring for Infants & Toddlers* builds on the original training program developed for the U.S. Navy and the U.S. Army Child Development Services Programs. Carolee Callen, former head of the Navy Child Development Services Branch, and M.-A. Lucas, Chief of Child Development Services in the U.S. Army, were both instrumental in the development of the original work, which was then adopted by all branches of the military. We thank M.-A. Lucas for urging us to update these materials for a new generation of early childhood educators.

Our deep appreciation goes to Laurie Taub, Editor, for her careful and thoughtful review of every module and to Sherrie Rudick, Director of Infant and Toddler Initiatives, for jumping in when the project was underway to help in the review process. Carla Uriona, Creative Director, designed the book and kept us moving forward. Without the copyediting, layout work, tracking of modules, and overall attention to detail of Jennifer Love King, our Production Specialist, this project would not have been finished on time. Thanks also to Judy F. Wohlberg for her final editing help.

It is our hope that this second edition of *Caring for Infants & Toddlers* will have a positive impact on the quality of early childhood programs by giving staff developers and teachers a practical and comprehensive tool to support their important work.

Table of Contents

Orientation

Welcome to *Caring for Infants & Toddlers*, a personalized training program designed for teachers who work with infants and toddlers. Whether you are new to the profession or have years of experience, this program offers practical information about topics central to your work. The training program consists of two books: *Caring for Infants & Toddlers* and a *Skill-Building Journal*. This book, *Caring for Infants & Toddlers*, contains all of the readings for the 13 modules in the training program. It also includes a glossary of terms used throughout the training, a list of references, and a bibliography of additional resources. The *Skill-Building Journal* is a personal record of your learning. It includes the instructions and forms for the activities you will do to apply what you have read about each topic and to reflect on your practice.

Early childhood educators who work with infants and toddlers refer to and think of themselves in many ways. They may be called *teacher*, *caregiver*, *care provider*, or even *educarer*. We use the term *teacher* to mean any adult who works with young children in a classroom setting, including mentor teachers, lead teachers, teacher aides, teacher assistants, caregivers, care providers, and volunteers. We use the term *trainer* to refer to the individual who is guiding your participation in this training program.

Several features of *Caring for Infants & Toddlers* make it unique:

- The materials are appropriate for both **new and experienced** teachers.

- You take **responsibility** for your progress through the training program, with **guidance and feedback** provided by a trainer.

- The training program is **individualized**. You work independently, according to your own schedule and at your own pace.

- The information presented in the modules is **practical** and of **immediate use** in your daily work with children.

- Many of the learning activities ask you to **observe** children to learn about their skills and interests. Observation is a key way to get to know children and to plan a program that responds to each child's individual skills, needs, interests, and other characteristics.

- Your completed learning activity forms become a **professional resource** and a record of your growth and competence.

How the Training Program Can Help You

Caring for Infants & Toddlers is designed to help you gain the knowledge and skills to provide a high-quality program for infants and toddlers. The modules describe the typical developmental stages of children from birth to age three and include many examples of how you can apply this knowledge every day in your work. Once you begin this training program, you will discover that you already have many skills and that completing the modules will let you extend your skills and knowledge. The training will help you to meet the profession's standards and to become a more competent teacher.

Completing *Caring for Infants & Toddlers* can help you meet the requirements for achieving a nationally recognized credential that acknowledges your skills as a teacher of infants and toddlers. The training program is based on the Child Development Associate (CDA) Competency Standards defined by The Council for Professional Recognition (the Council) in Washington, DC. The 13 CDA functional areas define the skills and knowledge base of competent teachers.

Functional Areas of the Child Development Associate (CDA) Competency Standards

Safe
Provide a safe environment to prevent and reduce injuries.

Healthy
Promote good health and nutrition and provide an environment that contributes to the prevention of illness.

Learning Environment
Use space, relationships, materials, and routines as resources for constructing an interesting, secure, and enjoyable environment that encourages play, exploration, and learning.

Physical
Provide a variety of equipment, activities, and opportunities to promote the physical development of children.

Cognitive
Provide activities and opportunities that encourage curiosity, exploration, and problem-solving appropriate to the developmental levels and learning styles of children.

Communication
Communicate with children and provide opportunities and support for children to understand, acquire, and use verbal and nonverbal means of communicating thoughts and feelings.

Creative
Provide opportunities that stimulate children to play with sound, rhythm, language, materials, space, and ideas in individual ways to express their creative abilities.

Self
Provide physical and emotional security for each child and help each child to know, accept, and take pride in himself or herself and to develop a sense of independence.

Social
Help each child to feel accepted in the group, help children learn to communicate and get along with others, and encourage feelings of empathy and mutual respect among children and adults.

Guidance
Provide a supportive environment in which children can begin to learn and practice appropriate and acceptable behaviors as individuals and as a group.

Families
Maintain an open, friendly, and cooperative relationship with each child's family, encourage their involvement in the program, and support the child's relationship with his or her family.

Program Management
Use all available resources to ensure an effective operation.

Professionalism
Make decisions based on knowledge of early childhood theories and practices, promote quality in child care services, and take advantage of opportunities to improve competence both for personal and professional growth and for the benefit of children and families.

Each of the modules in *Caring for Infants & Toddlers* addresses one of the CDA functional areas. Teachers may apply for a CDA credential from the Council when they have completed 120 clock hours of training and can demonstrate that they have acquired the skills and knowledge outlined in the CDA Competency Standards. Contact the Council at www.cdacouncil.org or 1-800-424-4310 for more information about the requirements for a CDA credential.

Working With Your Trainer

An important part of the training process is the feedback and support you receive from a trainer. Your trainer might be a colleague, mentor teacher, supervisor, education coordinator, college instructor, or other individual who can observe you working with children and provide meaningful feedback to support your professional development. Although the modules are meant to be self-instructional, you will benefit most if an experienced trainer reviews and discusses your responses to learning activities, answers questions, and comments on your interactions with children and families. Your trainer can provide feedback on-site at the program, during a phone conference, via electronic mail (e-mail), or in a group meeting.

Beginning the Program

After reading this *Orientation*, your next step is to complete the *Self-Assessment* in your *Skill-Building Journal* (section 0-1). The *Self-Assessment* lists the three major areas of competence related to the topic of each module. You read each item and check the box that describes your current level of implementation. You will want to respond as objectively as possible, so you can identify your strengths and interests as well as areas that need strengthening. Afterward, you discuss your responses with your trainer and choose three modules to work on first.

You and your trainer will also develop a tentative schedule for completing the entire training program. You can expect to spend about 4–6 weeks on each module. It generally takes 12–18 months to complete the entire training program.

You might begin with a module of particular interest precisely because you think you have already acquired many of the relevant skills. Alternatively, you might begin with a module that addresses a training need identified through the *Self-Assessment* or your trainer's observations. If this training program is part of a course or seminar, your trainer might ask you to begin with a particular module so you can participate in group meetings with others working on the same module. Your program director might ask you to begin with a module that addresses a program need, such as improving partnerships with families.

Completing Each Module

Each of the 13 modules follows a consistent format using both books. The chart that follows shows how the sections of the books are related.

Section	Caring for Infants & Toddlers	Skill-Building Journal
Overview	An introduction to the topic addressed in the module, identification of three major areas of competence, related strategies, and three brief examples of how teachers apply their knowledge and skills to support children's development and learning.	Questions about each of the examples and sample answers.
Your Own Experiences	A short discussion of how the topic applies to adults.	A series of questions about personal experiences related to the topic.
Pre-Training Assessment (presented only in the *Skill-Building Journal*)		A checklist of how often teachers use key strategies and a question about skills to improve or topics to learn more about.
Learning Activities (4–5 per module)	Objectives for each *Learning Activity* and several pages of information about the topic.	Instructions for applying the reading to classroom practices. This may involve answering questions; observing children and using the information to address individual needs and interests; completing a checklist; trying new teaching strategies; or planning, implementing, and evaluating a new activity. When appropriate, *Answer Sheets* are provided.
Reflecting on Your Learning (presented only in the *Skill-Building Journal*)		An opportunity to consider how the topic relates to curriculum implementation and building partnerships with families. Questions help teachers summarize what they learned.

As you can see from the chart, the two books are coordinated. Each section of a *Caring for Infants & Toddlers* module includes an instruction that directs you to the corresponding section of the *Skill-Building Journal*. Look for the *what's next?* box at the bottom of the page. Similarly, each section of the *Skill-Building Journal* explains whether to continue with the next section of the *Journal* or to return to your reading of *Caring for Infants & Toddlers*.

When you are directed to a section of the *Skill-Building Journal*, you can identify the correct forms by finding the corresponding section numbers in the upper right-hand corner of the pages. The first part of the section number (to the left of the hyphen) indicates the number of the module. The second part of the number (to the right of the hyphen) indicates the step of the module that you are working on. If the step has more than one form, a lowercase letter has been added.

Although the content and activities in the modules vary, you will follow the same process for completing each module. That process is described in the following paragraphs and illustrated in the diagram on page xi. As you complete each step, be sure to record your feedback sources in section 1 of each *Skill-Building Journal* module.

Overview

You will read a short introduction to the topic addressed in the module. For each related area of competence, you also review strategies that teachers use and three stories about how they apply their knowledge and skills. Then you answer questions about each story and compare your answers to those on the *Answer Sheet* at the end of the module in the *Skill-Building Journal*.

Your Own Experiences

Next, you will read about how the topic relates to adults and answer questions about how it relates to your own experiences, both on and off the job. You examine how personal experiences affect your approach to your work with children and families and your choice of teaching strategies.

Pre-Training Assessment

The next step is to complete the *Pre-Training Assessment*—a list of the strategies that competent teachers use—by indicating whether you do these things regularly, sometimes, or not enough. Then you will review your responses and identify 3–5 skills you want to improve or topics you want to know learn more about. You may refer to the *Glossary* at the end of *Caring for Infants & Toddlers* for definitions of the terms used.

Next, you will want to schedule a meeting with your trainer to discuss your responses to the *Overview* questions and *Pre-Training Assessment*. After your discussion, you will be ready to begin the learning activities for the module.

Learning Activities

Each module includes four or five learning activities. After reading several pages of information about the topic, you will apply your knowledge while working with children and families. For example, you might answer questions related to the reading and to your own teaching practices; complete a checklist; try out suggestions from the reading and report the results; plan, implement, and evaluate an activity; or observe and record children's behavior and interactions and then use your observation notes to individualize the program. Examples of completed forms, summaries, and charts are provided, when needed, to demonstrate the activity.

Your trainer will be an important source of support as you complete the learning activities. Your trainer might observe the way you implement an activity, conduct a co-observation of a child, review your plans and help you collect materials, or discuss and answer your questions about the content.

After you have completed a learning activity, schedule a time to meet with your trainer, individually or with a group of teachers who completed the same activity. This will be an opportunity to discuss the content of the module, report what you did and learned, and voice your concerns. For some activities, you will also meet with colleagues or a child's family, or review an *Answer Sheet* at the end of the module. It is always best to discuss your work on a learning activity while it is fresh in your mind, so it is important to let your trainer know when you are ready for a feedback conference. A full understanding of each activity is particularly important when an activity builds on the knowledge and skills addressed in the previous one.

Reflecting on Your Learning

After completing all of the learning activities, take time to summarize your progress. Review your responses to the *Pre-Training Assessment* and describe your increased knowledge and skills. For some modules, you will also review and add examples to a chart created in one of the learning activities.

After summarizing your progress, you will meet with your trainer to review your learning and to discuss whether you are ready for the knowledge and competency assessments. When you are ready, schedule a time to complete the *Knowledge Assessment* and set another time for your trainer to conduct the *Competency Assessment* observation. If you need more time to learn about the knowledge and skills addressed in the module, your trainer can suggest supplemental strategies and resources. *Caring for Infants & Toddlers* also includes a bibliography of resources for early childhood professionals.

Assessing Knowledge and Competence

There is a *Knowledge Assessment* for each module and a *Competency Assessment* for modules 1-12. The *Knowledge Assessment* is a short written test about information presented in the modules. For the *Competency Assessment*, your trainer will conduct a focused observation of how you apply your knowledge and use key skills in your work with children. You will need to achieve a score of 80% or higher on each assessment before starting another module. Your trainer will discuss the assessment process in greater detail.

Documenting Progress

As you successfully complete each section and assessment for a module, you can record your progress on the Individual Tracking Form that your trainer will provide and sign.

---

what's next?

Read "The Training Process" chart.
Go to *Skill-Building Journal*, section **0-1** (*Self-Assessment*).

The Training Process

Complete the Orientation

Read about the training program
Complete the Self-Assessment
Develop a module-completion plan

Feedback and Discussion

Complete a Module

Overview

Read about the topic and three related areas of competence
Review examples of what teachers do
Answer questions

Your Own Experiences

Relate topic to own experiences
Answer questions

Pre-Training Assessment

Assess own use of strategies
List skills to improve or topics to learn about

Learning Activities

Read about topic
Apply knowledge
Answer questions

Reflecting on Your Learning

Review responses to Pre-Training Assessment
Summarize skills and knowledge gained
Discuss readiness for assessments

Feedback and Discussion

Not ready for assessment
Review or repeat activities

Ready for assessment
Schedule times

Assessments

Knowledge Assessment
Competency Assessment

Feedback and Discussion

Did not demonstrate competence
Review or repeat activities

Demonstrated competence
Document progress
Begin next module

Overview

Maintaining Practices and Environments That Prevent and Reduce Injuries

Planning for and Responding to Emergencies

Showing Children That They Are in a Safe Place

Your Own Need for Safety

Learning Activities

A. Using Your Knowledge of Infants and Toddlers to Ensure Their Safety

B. Creating and Maintaining a Safe Environment

C. Preparing for and Handling Emergencies

D. Introducing Safety Practices to Children

1. Safe

Safety is freedom from danger, harm, and loss. Adults feel safe when they are in control of situations, know how to prevent and handle injuries, and know what to do during emergencies. Our sense of security grows when we can do something to reduce the risk of harm.

Promote safety by minimizing risk.

You and your colleagues are risk managers whose thoughtful actions prevent injuries. Your program supports your risk management efforts through policies and procedures that reduce hazards and promote safe practices. Recommended adult-child ratios prevent injuries because you and your colleagues can work as a team to supervise all children at all times and in all areas. Safety checklists help you identify and address potential environmental hazards. Children are less likely to hurt themselves when you provide age-appropriate equipment.

You have a professional responsibility to protect infants and toddlers.

As stated in the Code of Ethical Conduct of the National Association for the Education of Young Children, child safety is your professional responsibility.

> *Above all we shall not harm children. We shall not participate in practices that are disrespectful, degrading, dangerous, exploitative, intimidating, psychologically damaging, or physically harmful to children.*[1]

Infants and toddlers depend on you to keep them safe.

Teachers use three key safety strategies. First, create and maintain indoor and outdoor spaces that are free from hazards so children can safely explore and learn. Second, learn your program's procedures for ensuring children's safety every day and during emergencies. Follow them calmly during drills and actual emergencies. Third, show children, through your words and actions, that they are in a safe place. This will foster a sense of security that encourages exploration and supports development and learning.

You can keep children safe by

- maintaining practices and environments that prevent and reduce injuries

- planning for and responding to emergencies

- showing children that they are in a safe place

Maintaining Practices and Environments That Prevent and Reduce Injuries

1. **Check indoor and outdoor areas, toys, materials, and equipment daily and address identified hazards.** Cover unused electrical outlets with safety caps, remove broken play materials, place cushioning under indoor climbers, and lock the outdoor storage shed.

2. **Keep potentially dangerous items and substances out of children's reach at all times.** Stow adult purses and bags out of children's reach and store cleaning materials in locked cabinets.

3. **Check safety equipment monthly to ensure that it is in good condition and easy for adults to reach.** Notify the appropriate person if there are problems.

4. **Arrange the room with clear exits, pathways, and areas where children can move without bumping into anything.** Rearrange the room as needed when new children join the group and as children develop new skills.

5. **Work with colleagues to supervise all children at all times.** Follow recommended adult-child ratios and group sizes throughout the day.

Ms. Gonzalez Acts Quickly

As you read the following story, pay attention to the way Ms. Gonzalez responds to a risky situation. Also think about what the child, Zora, learns from the experience.

Mr. Lewis: Ms. Gonzalez, look at Zora! We forgot to put the box of balls away.

Ms. Gonzalez: Thanks, Mr. Lewis. I'll take care of it.

Ms. Gonzalez: I'm going to help you climb down. The box isn't strong enough to hold you. It might break.

Ms. Gonzalez: We need to put this box of balls in the closet. Would you like to help?

Ms. Gonzalez: Now, who would like to climb on the climber? It's a safe place to climb.

Planning for and Responding to Emergencies

6. **Maintain current medical information for all children.** Be prepared to handle children's unique needs and update this information several times a year.

7. **Respond quickly and calmly to children in distress.** "You bumped your head when you stood up. Let's get some ice."

8. **Develop and post injury and emergency procedures and evacuation routes.** Keep them in a prominent place.

9. **Make sure that a telephone is easy to reach and working properly.** Know where to find families' emergency telephone numbers.

10. **Check the first-aid kit and safety devices regularly and restock or repair them as needed.** "We are running low on disposable nonporous gloves in the first-aid kit, so we need to restock it immediately."

11. **Know and follow established procedures for taking children to safety during fire and other hazard drills and in real emergencies.** Work as a team to make sure every child gets out of the building to a safe place.

Rolling to Safety

As you read the following story, pay attention to the way Ms. Bates and Mr. Lewis work together to take infants out of the building quickly.

2:12 p.m.

Mr. Lewis: We're going outside for a few minutes.

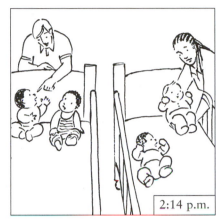

2:14 p.m.

Ms. Bates: I'm sorry, Sammy. I'll help you in a minute, when we're safe outside.

2:15 p.m.

Mr. Lewis: I have all of mine. How about you?

Ms. Bates: I do, too. Let's go.

2:16 p.m.

2:18 p.m.

Ms. Bates: Okay, Sammy. Now I can see what you need.

Mr. Lewis: Peek-a-boo, Peter.

2:25 p.m.

Showing Children That They Are in a Safe Place

12. **Explain to children what you are doing while taking safety precautions.** "Justine, I'm snapping the seat belt on your stroller so you won't slip out and hurt yourself."

13. **Use positive guidance strategies to redirect children from unsafe to safe activities.** Show them where they can crawl, walk, ride, jump, and climb without getting hurt.

14. **Model ways to stay safe throughout the day.** Use a step stool to reach a high shelf and ask for help in carrying something heavy.

15. **Introduce a few important safety rules to toddlers.** "We take turns on the slide so that we don't bump into each other. Wait until your friend stands up and moves away."

16. **Share information with families so they can promote their children's safety.** "Terrie tried to climb out of her crib today. Let's talk about whether it's time for her to use a cot."

Ms. Bates Helps Adam Learn About Safety

As you read the following story, pay attention to the way Ms. Bates assures the children that the program is a safe place. Also think about what the children learn to do to keep themselves safe.

Adam: Me knock down.

Ms. Bates: Are you okay?

Ms. Bates: The children got hurt when the blocks fell on them. Next time, before you knock down the blocks, I'll help you politely ask the others to move. Then everyone will be safe.

Ms. Bates: Adam, ask us to get out of the way, please. After we move, you can knock it down.

what's next?

Skill-Building Journal, section **1-2** (*Overview*), section **1-10** (*Answer Sheets*), and section **1-1** (*Feedback*).

Your Own Need for Safety

Feeling safe is a basic human need.

Everyone needs to feel protected from harm in order to function well. Safe environments help us feel secure, relaxed, confident, and able to enjoy ourselves. When people do not feel protected, they are often fearful and anxious.

The increasing violence in many communities—especially random, unpredictable violence—makes many of us feel unsafe. We see violence on television and might also experience it in our homes and neighborhoods. A sense of security is important for everyone.

When you are in charge of your environment, you can keep it free from hazards most of the time. You have probably done things that were potentially dangerous, but you took steps to make these activities safer. Do you remember when you

- climbed a ladder while someone held it to keep it stable
- parked your car at night in a well-lit area of the shopping mall
- carefully unplugged a lamp with a frayed cord and had the wiring replaced

Learning about safety begins in childhood.

Your life experiences have taught you how to stay safe. When you were a child, the important adults in your life may have covered the electrical outlets to keep your bedroom safe and helped you develop safety habits, such as wearing a helmet when you rode your bike. As you grew older, you learned what to do to minimize danger in a variety of situations.

what's next?

Skill-Building Journal, section **1-3** (*Your Own Need for Safety*), section **1-1** (*Feedback*), and section **1-4** (*Pre-Training Assessment*).

Learning Activities

LEARNING ACTIVITY

A. Using Your Knowledge of Infants and Toddlers to Ensure Their Safety

In this activity you will learn to

- recognize some typical behaviors of infants and toddlers

- use what you know about infants and toddlers to ensure their safety

The infants and toddlers in your care rely on you to keep them safe as they gain new skills. Their families depend on you to maintain a safe environment and practices that prevent injuries. To carry out these important responsibilities, you must be aware of infant and toddler behaviors that affect their safety, and you must have up-to-date information about each child's abilities. You and your colleagues need to be aware of who is doing what and always to expect the unexpected. Your role includes sharing in children's pleasure as they grow and develop, while always staying alert and anticipating how their growing skills support new exploration that could lead to injuries.

Young infants (birth–8 months) explore by touching, tasting, and beginning to move.

- Sammy (3 months) puts things in his mouth.

- Jon (6 months) rolls from one side of his blanket to the other.

- Luci (8 months) reaches for toys and other things that she sees.

Young infants begin to investigate the world as soon as they are born. They touch and taste everything they can, as soon as they can. When they begin to roll over and sit up and see and reach for things, they discover exciting new things to see and do. They may also come across new dangers, such as electrical outlets, sharp corners, or a pen that fell out of your purse.

Mobile infants (8–18 months) move and explore.

- Malou (9 months) crawls all over the room.

- Peter (12 months) likes to pick up and throw his toys.

- Zora (16 months) can follow simple directions.

Learning to move from one place to another literally expands the world of mobile infants. Standing up and walking gives them visual and physical access to all parts of the room or play yard. They can see and reach things they never noticed before. At the same time, their language and thinking skills are growing. When they hear you say, "No," they might stop for a moment before returning to what they were doing. You and your colleagues must always watch and be ready to step in to protect them from harm.

Toddlers (18–36 months) move more competently.

- Lovette (20 months) helps her grandma wipe up a spill.

- Ricky (28 months) runs toward the slide.

- Jessica (34 months) can walk up stairs with ease.

Toddlers are explorers on the move: walking, climbing, running, shaking, pouring, collecting, and dumping. They concentrate on what they are doing at the moment, rarely planning where to go or what to do next. For toddlers, walking forward and backward; pushing chairs across the room; and climbing over, around, and into boxes are interesting activities. Toddlers tend to have strong feelings and sometimes express themselves by hitting, pushing, or shoving other children. To keep toddlers safe, you have to try to think as they do and predict what they might do. You must also work as a team with colleagues to provide constant supervision in all areas of the room and outdoors.

Children begin to learn safety practices through everyday experiences.

One of the best ways to introduce safety practices is to explain what you are doing as you model them. Children learn from your simple explanations and reminders, e.g., "Let's use a sponge to wipe up the spilled water so no one slips," and "I'm using the hammer to fix the nail that is sticking out of the shelf." When they feel cooperative and competent, they will gladly help you pick up toys that someone might trip over. These everyday experiences teach toddlers that they can help make their world a safer place, which is an important lesson. You can introduce a few clear safety rules to toddlers, such as "Walk in the room," but keep in mind that they will not always be able to remember them.

The following list summarizes key characteristics of young infants, mobile infants, and toddlers that affect their safety.

Development of Infants and Toddlers

Young infants (birth–8 months)

- put almost everything they hold into their mouths

- wiggle and squirm, sometimes unexpectedly

- roll over, from back to stomach and stomach to back

- sit on a blanket or rug, propped at first and then without external support

- touch, pat, and then hold their bottles

- reach for things they see

Mobile infants (8–18 months)

- move by creeping and crawling

- explore objects by grabbing, throwing, shaking, dumping, and dropping

- understand many words and follow simple directions

- pull themselves up to a standing position

- enjoy taking part in daily routines and activities

- begin to walk on their own

Toddlers (18–36 months)

- love to run but cannot always stop or turn

- understand rules but need to be reminded to follow them

- enjoy climbing—on anything and everything

- act on their curiosity by manipulating, poking, handling, twisting, and squeezing objects

- push, pull, and ride wheeled toys

- like to imitate their favorite grown-ups

what's next?

Skill-Building Journal, section **1-5** (*Learning Activity A*), section **1-10** (*Answer Sheets*), and section **1-1** (*Feedback*).

LEARNING
ACTIVITY

Learning Activities

B. Creating and Maintaining a Safe Environment

In this activity you will learn to

- maintain safe indoor and outdoor spaces for infants and toddlers

- develop and use daily and monthly safety checklists to assess the indoor and outdoor environment, toys, and equipment

One of the most effective ways to promote safety is to use what you know about infants and toddlers—how they are likely to explore, move, and behave—to create and maintain safe spaces. A curious young child is likely to think that an exposed outlet, a dangling wire, and a can of cleanser on the bathroom floor are interesting things to poke, pull, and taste. Sit on the floor so that you see the room from a child's level. Do you spot potential dangers you did not notice before? Infants and toddlers cannot think ahead and predict the results of their actions. It is up to us to think about what each child can and might do and respond accordingly to ensure their safety.

Many people play a role in creating and maintaining a safe environment.

Creating and maintaining a safe environment for infants and toddlers is a shared responsibility. Architects and builders consider safety as they select flooring, paint, and plumbing fixtures, and as they decide where to locate windows and doors. With input from teachers and families, the program director orders toys, furniture, and equipment that meet voluntary industry standards for safety. (For current information about child safety standards, visit the American Society for Testing and Materials Web site, www.astm.org) The custodial staff repairs damaged toys, furniture, and equipment, and they keep hallways, stairs, and outdoor play areas free of clutter and debris. Keeping materials and equipment in good repair means keeping them free from protruding nails, splinters, cracks, chipped paint, and lead paint and making sure that all nuts, bolts, and screws are fastened securely.

Teamwork allows you to supervise every child and area, all day, every day.

No matter how many precautions are taken, the environment is never completely safe for children. Teachers must discuss safety practices and plan ways to work as a team to provide constant supervision of every child and area, all day, every day. For example, you can take turns sweeping slippery sand and picking up toys that someone could trip over. While one of you changes a diaper, the other can watch the rest of the room. Get in the habit of giving each other cues. You might nod, glance, and point to possible hazards. Remember how, in the *Overview* example, Mr. Lewis alerted Ms. Gonzalez when he saw Zora standing on the cardboard box?

When activities require close supervision, conduct them with small groups.

Some activities require closer supervision than others. You might divide the group and do an activity with a few children while another teacher supervises the rest of the children. You must also notice how children are feeling. Frustrated and tired children are more likely to fall or get hurt. Brief, simple activities are most appropriate for this age group.

In addition, you must always be alert for hazards such as spilled water, splintered wood, and worn-out safety straps. The chart that follows describes the characteristics of a safe environment for infants and toddlers and summarizes your responsibilities for preventing and reducing injuries.

A Safe Environment for Infants and Toddlers [2]

Characteristics of a Safe Environment	Your Responsibility
All children are supervised at all times, in all areas.	At all times, maintain appropriate adult-child ratios and watch children in all indoor and outdoor areas, including bathrooms. If you work with a partner, position yourselves in different parts of the room or outdoor area. Arrange indoor and outdoor areas so children are always in view.
There are standard procedures for responding to injuries quickly, effectively, and without alarming the children.	Follow your program's procedures for responding to an injured child. Complete injury reports promptly; notify families immediately, if appropriate.
Children are released only to family members and authorized designees for whom families provide written consent. Family members, or their authorized designees, must sign a child in and out of the program by noting the date, time, child's name, and their name.	Release children only to family members and authorized designees for whom families have provided written consent. Make sure a family member or authorized designee signs the child in and out of the program in a daily log.
The center is well-lit, well-maintained, and free from clutter.	Make sure stairs and hallways are lighted and free of clutter. Report problems promptly so they can be addressed.
Infant and toddler rooms provide 35' sq. of available floor space per child. (With typical furnishings, this usually means 50' sq. per child, from wall to wall.)	Arrange the room so infants and toddlers can move freely without bumping into anything. Create clear pathways and exits.
Venetian blind cords are replaced with plastic rods or secured out of children's reach. Cords long enough to encircle a child's neck are not accessible to children.	Replace cords or blinds with safe models. Contact the U.S. Consumer Product Safety Commission for more information about strangulation from window coverings.

A Safe Environment for Infants and Toddlers, *continued*

Characteristics of a Safe Environment	Your Responsibility
Electrical systems are inspected regularly and appliances are used with care.	Report problems promptly so they can be addressed. Cover unused electrical outlets with child-resistant caps. Unplug small appliances when not in use. Make sure electrical cords are not frayed or damaged; keep them out of children's reach. Use extension cords only when absolutely necessary and follow safety guidelines for their use. Do not place cords under carpeting or near water.
Heating and cooling systems are inspected regularly; pipes and radiators are covered or insulated.	Report problems promptly so they can be addressed.
Water temperature is set at 120° F or less (manually or with scald-resistant faucets).	Check the water temperature often to make sure that children will not be scalded. Report problems immediately.
There is sufficient space for storing hazardous items out of children's reach in locked cabinets or closets.	Place sharp objects (pins, needles, knives, adult scissors) out of children's reach in locked cabinets or closets. Put adult purses, tote bags, and all plastic bags out of children's reach. Keep medicine in the original, labeled, childproof containers in locked cabinets or a refrigerator, per labels.
Cleaning supplies are stored out of children's reach.	Store cleaning supplies and poisonous substances in original, labeled containers in locked cabinets. Rinse empty cleaning product bottles before disposal; then place them in trash receptacles that are out of children's reach.

Toys, Furniture, and Equipment

Characteristics of a Safe Environment	Your Responsibility
All toys, furniture, and equipment meet voluntary industry standards for safety, are age-appropriate, sturdy, have no loose parts with a diameter of less than 1 1/4". Balls must be larger than 1 3/4" in diameter. If any object appears to fit entirely into a child's mouth, keep it away from the child.	Keep up with Consumer Product Safety Commission (CPSC) recalls and advisories (www.cpsc.gov). Check to make sure toys and equipment are in good repair. Make sure unsafe items are removed immediately in order to be fixed or thrown away. Display toys on open shelves, with heavier items at the bottom. Place cushioning, such as mats, under indoor climbers.
High chairs, strollers, swings, infant seats, car seats, and similar equipment have safety straps in good repair.	Buckle safety straps every time you use such equipment because children can slip, fall, or climb quickly and unexpectedly. Check straps regularly; arrange for repairs if needed.
Changing tables have easily accessible drawers or shelves for supply storage.	Never leave a child unattended. Make sure supplies are in place at the start of each day; restock during the day, as needed.
Shelves and other furniture with sharp edges have protective corners or edge bumpers.	Make sure all sharp edges are protected; help mobile infants and toddlers slow down so that they do not bump into corners.
Cribs have latches and locks on dropsides, so babies cannot fall or climb out. To prevent suffocation and head entrapment, cribs have firm, tight-fitting mattresses with less than 2" clearance on all sides; slats or spindles no more than 2 3/8" apart; and corner posts of 1/16" or less. Cribs are spaced at least 3' apart to allow easy access to each child.	Make sure cribs are in good repair and at least 3' apart. When infants sleep in cribs • raise the sides of the crib after placing the baby down • place babies under 12 months on their backs, to decrease the risk of sudden infant death syndrome (SIDS) • remove pillows, comforters, fluffy blankets, stuffed animals, rattles, and squeeze toys • make sure babies' heads are uncovered while they sleep[3]
Mats or cots are available for older mobile infants and toddlers who can climb out of cribs. They are spaced at least 3' apart to allow easy access to each child.	Observe children so you know when they are able to climb out of their cribs; share this information with families and transition children to mats or cots.
Tables and chairs used by older mobile infants and toddlers are child-size, sturdy, and stable.	Supervise children to make sure that they do not stand on tables or chairs or use them in unsafe ways.
Safety gates are at least 3/4 of children's height (so they cannot climb over). They also have a straight top edge and a rigid mesh screen or openings too small for a child's head to enter. Pressure gates and accordion gates should not be used.	Place safety gates at the tops and bottoms of stairs and across other areas that are off-limits to children, in accordance with local fire codes. Always use the latching devices.

Emergency Preparedness

Characteristics of a Safe Environment	Your Responsibility
Emergency exits are marked and unlocked from the inside; evacuation procedures are posted in a visible place so all staff and visitors can get children out of the building quickly and safely during an emergency.	Post emergency plans and exit routes. Conduct monthly emergency drills. Make sure emergency exits are kept clear and unlocked from the inside.
Smoke detectors are installed on the ceiling, or on the wall 6" to 12" below the ceiling, every 40' of each level of the building. (Smoke detectors are not installed above suspended ceilings or behind acoustic walls.)	Check smoke detector batteries monthly; replace, or make sure they are replaced, every 6 months.
Poison control numbers are posted in a visible place near a phone.	Check numbers periodically to make sure they are current.
A-B-C-type fire extinguishers are installed and maintained. The size, number, and placement of extinguishers are determined after a survey by the fire marshall or by an insurance company representative. Instructions for use are posted next to each extinguisher.	Learn how to use fire extinguishers correctly; make sure they are refilled after use.

Transportation

Characteristics of a Safe Environment	Your Responsibility
All vehicles used to transport children are licensed, registered, and well-maintained.	Practice emergency evacuation of vehicles with the children.
A first-aid kit and copies of children's emergency identification and contact information must be carried in every vehicle when children are being transported.	Make sure children's emergency data is up to date and first-aid kits are supplied.
Drivers have valid and appropriate licenses. Because they must focus on driving, they may not use cell phones, play loud audio equipment, or wear earphones while driving with children, and they are not included in child-adult ratios.	Maintain appropriate child-adult ratios in vehicles. Keep children from sticking their heads, hands, limbs, or objects out of vehicle windows. Make sure children enter and leave vehicles only on the curbside of the road or driveway.
All passengers use safety devices: infant safety seats for children weighing less than 20 lbs., toddler safety seats for children weighing 20 lbs. or more (who can sit by themselves), and seat belts for adults.	Use the correct seat for a child's weight. Install infant seats in the back seat, facing the rear, in a semi-reclining position; secure the strap. Install toddler safety seats in the back seat, facing forward, using the vehicle's seat belt. Wear your own seat belt.

Outdoors

Characteristics of a Safe Environment	Your Responsibility
The outdoor play area accommodates a variety of developmentally appropriate infant and toddler activities.	Check daily for glass, splintered wood, and debris; arrange for prompt removal, as needed. Check steps and walks for ice and snow. Make sure children ride wheeled toys and tricycles on flat surfaces only and wear helmets if the wheel base is more than 20" in diameter.
The play area is enclosed with a natural barrier or a fence at least 4' high, and the bottom of the fence is no more than 3 1/2" aboveground; fences have at least two gates with latches out of children's reach.	Check the fence for openings, splinters, and sharp edges; latch both gates when using the area.
The play area is well-drained; there are no toxic plants; the soil is free from hazardous levels of chemicals or toxins.	Check the area for standing water before use; sweep or drain puddles before children enter the area.
The outdoor play equipment meets voluntary industry standards, has no lead or chipped paint, and is securely anchored with 6' of clearance around each item. Stationary equipment with moving parts, such as swings, must have clear space to the front and rear that is equal to at least twice the height of the equipment.	Check equipment (sandbox, climbers, slides, swings, etc.) for sharp corners, rust, rot, cracks, splinters, protruding nails or bolts, and loose fasteners; arrange for prompt repairs, as needed. Cover play equipment during hot weather so slides and climbers do not overheat.
There is adequate shock-absorbing cushioning (large wood chips, mulch, sand, or safety-tested mats) under and around equipment to reduce and prevent injuries.	Check regularly to make sure there is sufficient cushioning under and around equipment. The depth of the material depends upon the type. Report problems so more cushioning can be installed.
Storage sheds are locked and off-limits to children.	Put away equipment and lock storage sheds when equipment is not in use.
Children use sprinklers, hoses, or water tables instead of portable wading pools.	Fill water tables with no more than 2" of water; empty and sanitize daily; turn over or store when not in use. Closely supervise children playing in or near water.
Teachers take a first-aid kit and copies of each child's emergency identification and contact information on walks and trips.	Carry first-aid and emergency information in a tote bag, backpack, or fanny pack. Keep the first-aid kit stocked with needed items and current emergency information.

Some practices are prohibited.

The following chart lists things you should **never** do because they can cause suffocation, strangulation, choking, or other serious injuries. Review your program's materials, equipment, and practices with your colleagues, so that unsafe practices can be corrected immediately. Make and post a chart of the prohibited practices—the "nevers"—as a reminder for yourself, your colleagues, and children's families. Your regional poison control center or Cooperative Extension Service will be able to provide a complete list of poisonous plants.

Remember the "Nevers" [4]

To prevent poisoning, NEVER

- grow poisonous plants indoors or outdoors (e.g., azaleas, daffodils, dieffenbachia)

- use toxic art materials that children could swallow or inhale

To prevent falls and injuries, NEVER

- use walkers, unless indicated by a child's Individual Family Service Plan (IFSP)

- use trampolines

- hold a child on your lap in a moving vehicle, because, in an accident or sudden stop, the child could fly out of your arms

To prevent choking, NEVER

- feed children small solid foods such as hot dogs (unless cut into very small cubes or strips), hard candy, whole grapes, gum, popcorn, and peanuts

- have toys and materials smaller than 1 1/4" diameter or with detachable small parts (balls must be at least 1 3/4" in diameter)

- have coins, marbles, Styrofoam® objects, or safety pins where children can reach them

- prop a baby's bottle

- leave infants and toddlers unsupervised at meal- and snack times

To prevent strangulation, NEVER

- allow children to wear hoods with drawstrings (ask parents to remove the drawstrings)

- have toys with attached cords longer than 12"

- hang rattles or pacifiers around children's necks

- allow children to wear long scarves when climbing or jumping

- tie toys to any part of a crib

To prevent suffocation, NEVER

- have plastic bags within children's reach, except to line trash cans in supervised areas

- place a baby to sleep on pillows or a soft covering shift

To prevent burns, NEVER

- heat bottles in a microwave oven, because heating is uneven

- drink hot beverages while holding or standing near children

Daily and monthly checklists help you identify safety hazards.

As you know, you do a lot to help keep children safe. Daily and monthly safety checklists that list potential hazards can help you manage your safety-related responsibilities. Using checklists lets you step back for a few minutes to focus on things you might otherwise overlook because you are so involved with the children. A daily checklist helps you make sure the room and outdoor play area are ready for the children each day. A monthly checklist helps you review items that need attention less frequently.

what's next?

Skill-Building Journal, section **1-6** (*Learning Activity B*) and section **1-1** (*Feedback*).

Learning Activities

C. Preparing For and Handling Emergencies

In this activity you will learn to

- prepare for emergencies

- follow the program's established procedures for responding during emergencies

Even the most safety-conscious and well-prepared teacher will have to deal with emergencies from time to time. How would you respond if a toddler swallowed a toxic substance?...if the building lost power during a rainstorm?...if you smelled smoke? Would you get flustered and panic, or would you remain calm and collected while caring for an injured child or taking the children from the building?

Emergency plans explain how to respond to injuries and conduct evacuations.

Your program's emergency plan explains what to do if a child is injured and how to evacuate the entire group from the building if there is a fire, gas leak, or natural disaster. Some plans include step-by-step instructions for handling specific kinds of emergencies and injuries, such as responding when a child is choking, has suffered burns, or has swallowed poison. No matter how detailed the emergency plan, however, you must do more to prepare than simply read the plan. It is important to have ongoing training to keep your skills current and to conduct monthly evacuation drills so you and the children can stay calm in a real emergency.

- Have you read your program's emergency plan? How often is it revised?

- Would you be able to act quickly and effectively in an emergency?

- What do you do to keep your skills current?

Responding to Children's Injuries

Most injuries in an infant/toddler program are minor—bumped heads and scraped knees—requiring only soothing words and perhaps a bandage. For minor injuries such as cuts and bruises, your program probably has a standard injury report form. You should complete the form promptly, while you recall what happened clearly. At pick-up time, inform the child's family member of the incident and ask him to read and sign the form. In addition, let your supervisor know what happened and what you did in response.

Follow your program's policies and procedures for determining when and how to seek medical care for a child. Although every injury and illness is different, some common sense practices apply to all situations. To help you assess a situation, your program might have standard procedures such as these.

Emergency Procedures List [5]

1. **Find out what happened.**
   Who was injured?
   Does the scene present hazards to other children?
   Who can help?

2. **Check for life-threatening problems using the ABCs.**
   A = open the **a**irway
   B = check for **b**reathing
   C = check for **c**irculation (pulse)

3. **Call local emergency medical services—911 or an ambulance—if the child's condition is serious, even if you are not entirely sure about the seriousness of the child's condition.**
   Use good judgment and common sense to decide if a child has a better chance of survival if you call for an ambulance before or after you administer emergency first aid. If you call first, the ambulance will be on its way while you are tending to the child. Ideally, one person can make the call while another administers first aid.

4. **Check for injuries, starting at the head and working down.**
   Give information about injuries to the medical personnel as soon as they arrive.

5. **Calm the other children.**
   If the injured child needs your undivided attention, ask a colleague or other staff member to care for the other children.

6. **Contact the child's parents or guardian as soon as possible.**

7. **Follow the program's procedures for filing an injury/incident report.**

THINK
- Have you ever had to deal with a serious injury or illness? What did you do? How did you feel?

- If you could go back in time, would you change anything about your response? What would you do differently?

Sometimes a sick or injured child must go to the hospital.

When children's injuries or illnesses are serious, you must seek emergency assistance at once. Urgent situations that you might encounter as a child care provider are listed in the boxes that follow.

Getting Immediate Medical Help [6]

Call Emergency Medical Services (EMS) immediately if a child

- is at risk for permanent injury

- is acting strangely, is much less alert, or is much more withdrawn than usual

- has difficulty breathing or is unable to vocalize

- has discolored skin or lips that look blue, purple, or gray

- has a seizure (rhythmic jerking of arms and legs and a loss of consciousness)

- is unconscious

- is less and less responsive

- after a head injury has a decreased level of alertness, confusion, headache, vomiting, irritability, or difficulty walking

- has increasing or severe pain anywhere

- has a cut or burn that is large, deep, or will not stop bleeding

- is vomiting blood

- has a severe stiff neck, headache, and fever

- is significantly dehydrated (sunken eyes, lethargic, not making tears, not urinating)

After you have called EMS, remember to call the child's legal guardian.

Notify parents or guardians and accompany the child to the hospital.

Your program should have a plan for emergency transportation to the closest hospital or health care facility. If you must accompany a child in the ambulance, bring the child's signed medical history and emergency authorization forms. Most programs ask parents or guardians to complete forms at enrollment that authorize emergency medical care and give the names and phone numbers of emergency contacts. The director or a colleague should contact the child's parents and ask them to meet you at the hospital as soon as possible.

Sometimes children need urgent medical attention even when the situation does not require an ambulance. If a child has one of the conditions listed below, inform the child's legal guardian immediately. If you or the guardian cannot reach a physician within one hour, the child should be taken to a hospital.

Getting Other Urgent Medical Attention [7]

Get medical attention within one hour for

- fever in any child who looks more than mildly ill

- fever in a child less than 2 months (8 weeks) of age

- a quickly spreading purple or red rash

- a large volume of blood in the stools

- a cut that may require stitches

- any medical condition specifically included in a child's care plan as requiring parental notification

---

First aid helps manage the situation until medical care can be given.

While waiting for an emergency team to respond, it may be appropriate to administer first aid to manage the situation until the child can get additional medical care. For example, in cases of drowning, electric shock, or smoke inhalation, a teacher or other staff member would use cardiopulmonary resuscitation (CPR) to clear the throat and help the victim to breathe. Many state licensing agencies require teachers and other staff to have first-aid and CPR training and to update their skills and knowledge annually. If you are not certified in first aid and CPR, we strongly recommend that you take this training.

Recommended Emergency Management Training

Experts recommend that every adult who works with young children learn to manage

- bleeding

- burns

- poisoning

- choking

- injuries, including insect, animal, and human bites; splinters; other puncture wounds

- shock

- convulsions or nonconvulsive seizures

- musculoskeletal injury (such as sprains and fractures)

- dental emergencies

- head injuries

- allergic reactions

- eye injuries

- loss of consciousness

- electric shock

- drowning

- emergencies related to illness[8]

When giving first aid, remember these important rules:

- Do not move a child who may have a serious head, neck, or back injury, except to save a life. Moving the child might cause further injury.

- Do no harm. Harm might occur if you fail to treat an injury, as well as if you make an injury worse.

Maintain well-stocked first-aid kits.

Early childhood programs should have a number of well-stocked first-aid kits that are stored where adults—but not children—can reach them easily. For every group of infants and toddlers, there should be a first-aid kit to keep inside and another kit in a tote bag, back pack, or fanny pack to take on walks and field trips. All vehicles used to transport children must have first-aid kits and emergency identification and contact information for every child. Restock first-aid kits after each use and check them once a month to make sure all items are still included. A basic first-aid kit includes the following items.

Contents of a Basic First-Aid Kit [9]

- Emergency contact information for all children, including parents' home and work phone numbers (usually written on a card or form completed at enrollment and updated regularly)

- Coins for pay phones and/or a fully charged cell phone

- Index cards or note pad and pens (to write instructions or keep notes for medical staff)

- Current first-aid guide or chart (American Academy of Pediatrics or equivalent)

- Fresh water (small plastic bottle)

- Liquid soap

- Disposable, nonporous latex gloves

- Unbreakable pediatric thermometer (nonglass)

- Scissors

- Tweezers

- Splints (small, plastic or metal)

- Sterile, nonstick guaze pads (one box each of 2" and 4" sizes)

- Flexible roller gauze

- Assorted adhesive strip bandages (extras of the 1" size; not for use where an infant or child can remove them)

- Triangular muslin bandages (2)

- Safety pins

- Bandage tape

- Eye dressing

- Cold pack

- Plastic bags for ice packs, for wrapping soiled clothes, and for isolating used gauze and other materials used in handling body fluids

- Poison Control Center phone number

- Supplies prescribed for children with special health needs (e.g., antihistamine for a child with severe allergies, glucose tablets or insulin for a diabetic child, an inhaler for an asthmatic child)

Preparing for Emergency Evacuations

In a highly visible place, post evacuation plans in English and children's home languages.

Evacuation plans state the procedures for getting children out of the building to a safe place. Write the plan in both English and children's home languages, as appropriate, and include photos or pictures to provide further clarity. Post it in a highly visible place so all adults can work as a team to lead children to safety. Many infant and toddler programs have one or more wheeled evacuation cribs positioned near an exit door. They are used to hold several infants at a time while an adult rolls them to safety. (The *Overview* of this module includes a story about evacuation cribs.)

Hold emergency drills every month.

You and your colleagues must hold an emergency evacuation drill every month. Time yourselves so you will know how long it takes to get everyone outside. After each drill, document the date and time of day and discuss what happened. Note what went well and what you need to improve. With plenty of practice, teachers and children will be more likely to respond effectively in a real emergency.

To ensure teamwork, it is helpful to agree on specific staff responsibilities in advance. For example, you could designate specific individuals to administer first aid if needed, to oversee the evacuation of the building, to account for all children and adults, and to call 911.

- How do you and your colleagues handle emergency evacuations as a team?

- Do your evacuation drills go smoothly? How do the children respond?

- Is there anything you would like to change about your evacuation drills? If so, discuss your ideas with your colleagues.

Know when—and when not—to fight a fire.

It is important to know when—and when not—to use a fire extinguisher to fight a fire. You might be able to put out a small fire in some situations, but, if it gets out of control or threatens to block an exit, you must leave the building immediately.

Never use a fire extinguisher

- until all the children are safely out of the area and in the care of a responsible person

- to fight a fire that has spread beyond the spot where it started

Only use a fire extinguisher if you

- can get out quickly if your efforts do not work

- are nearby when the fire starts or discover the fire soon after it has started

- know the fire is small and confined to one place, such as a trash can or small appliance

- can fight the fire with your back to an exit

To use the extinguisher, stand back about 8 feet and aim at the base of the fire, not at the flames or smoke. Squeeze or press the lever while sweeping from the sides of the fire to the middle.

If in doubt, get out!

If you have the slightest doubt about whether to fight the fire or get out, leave the building and call the fire department. Your safety is more important than the property you might save.

Learn how to respond during natural disasters typical to your area.

Some geographic areas have a history of specific weather-related emergencies and other natural disasters, such as blizzards, ice storms, floods, hurricanes, lightning storms, earthquakes, and tornadoes. It is important to learn about those likely to happen in your area and to have an up-to-date plan for responding to such events. If you know what to do, you can act swiftly and prevent injuries. Resources for learning how to prepare for weather emergencies include local agencies, the American Red Cross, the National Weather Service (NWS) (http://www.nws.noaa.gov), and the Federal Emergency Management Agency (FEMA).

Before taking children on walks and trips away from the center, it is a good idea to get a current weather report. Listen to a radio or television weather channel or to a weather radio that receives NWS warnings of severe weather conditions. Such warnings begin with a tone alert that is followed by current information about fast-moving storms.

During any weather-related emergency, administer first aid if necessary and try to keep the children calm. Turn on a transistor radio so you can listen for emergency instructions.

- What kinds of weather emergencies are typical in your area?

- How does your program plan to keep children safe during these emergencies?

- How will the program care for children who must stay overnight at the center?

what's next?

Skill-Building Journal, section **1-7** (*Learning Activity C*) and section **1-1** (*Feedback*).

Learning Activities

D. Introducing Safety Practices to Children

In this activity you will learn to

- model and talk about safety practices with infants and toddlers throughout the day

- introduce toddlers to a few simple safety rules

Throughout this module you have learned about ways to protect the infants and toddlers in your care. It is also important to help young children gradually learn what they can do to keep themselves safe. It will be many years before they can be completely responsible, but they can begin the learning process.

Model safe practices while caring for infants and toddlers.

Introduce safety concepts to infants and toddlers by showing them how you—an important person in their lives—take steps to prevent injuries. Let them see you model good habits such as these:

- Walk—do not run—in the room.

- Sit—do not stand—on chairs.

- Use a step stool to reach a high cupboard.

- Buckle safety straps on high chairs, strollers, swings, car seats, and similar equipment.

- Put broken toys away until they can be mended.

Talk about what you are doing and how it promotes safety.

When handling a potentially dangerous item, taking a calculated risk, or doing something to prevent injuries, talk to the children about what you or your colleagues are doing and how it helps to prevent injuries. For example, you might offer explanations like these:

Scissors are sharp. When I'm finished using them, I will put them back in the cupboard and lock the door.

Mr. James is going to change the light bulb. He's moving the table to set up the ladder right under the light. Now he's fastening the safety latches to keep the ladder steady as he climbs. Ms. Kim is standing nearby to hand him the new bulb and to be ready if he needs help.

Seth, I'm putting you on your back so you can breathe easily. Now I'll check the crib sides. Yes, they are up and latched. Everything's okay. Have a restful nap.

Introduce safety practices during daily activities such as a walk in the neighborhood.

Infants and toddlers may not understand everything you say, but they will begin to understand that you think safety is important. When they get older, they are likely to do similar things to keep themselves safe.

Every day, there are many opportunities to explain and demonstrate safe practices. As you read the following guidelines for taking walks in the neighborhood, think about the many ways you introduce safety to children on walks and throughout the day.

At enrollment and throughout the year

- Recruit additional help from family members, senior citizens, or early childhood students from local high schools or colleges.

- Ask families to sign permission slips at enrollment so they will know that taking walks is a regular part of the program.

- Provide a list of the places to which you will walk (e.g., to the end of the block and to a park around the corner).

Before each walk

- Schedule the walk for when extra adults will be available to help supervise (both the children taking a walk and the children who stay at the center).

- Plan where you will go and for how long.

- Decide who will be going and maintain appropriate adult-child ratios (for example, one adult per three children, with one child in a stroller or backpack).

- Review a few simple rules, such as these:

  We all stop when we get to the curb.

  When everyone is ready to cross the street, we hold hands or hold onto the buggy.

- Review the rule for crossing the street safely, e.g., *Look to the left, look to the right, look to the left again, and wait for the green light.*

- Bring the portable first-aid kit and emergency phone numbers.

- Collect bottles, diapers, snacks, sweaters, and outerwear that children might need.

- Leave a sign on the door that states the time you left, where you went, and the time you expect to return.

During each walk

- Walk in small groups so you can get quickly across busy streets.

- Keep strollers and buggies on the sidewalk when getting ready to cross the street. Never push a stroller or child cart into the street until it is safe for everyone to cross.

- Make sure every child is in a backpack, stroller, or carriage, or has an adult hand to hold when crossing streets.

- Have fun while you walk: sing songs, take giant and tiny steps, talk about what you see and hear along the way and what you expect to see and do at your destination.

- Remind children of the rules discussed before the walk. Follow rules consistently and expect that children will need help to follow them.

- Pay attention to children's moods and behavior. Return to the program if children seem tired or frustrated, or if they are behaving in unsafe ways.

- Make sure all children are accounted for at all times.

Introduce a few simple and important safety rules to toddlers.

The toddlers in your care are probably ready to begin learning a few important safety rules for equipment, materials, and activities. As you talk with toddlers about safety rules, use simple language. Soon they will start to understand that they can do things to keep themselves safe. It is important, however, to have appropriate expectations for toddlers' behavior. They do not understand the meaning of danger and have not yet developed the thinking skills and self-control needed to follow rules consistently. You must continue to remind them often.

Even when toddlers do follow rules, you cannot count on their doing so all the time. For example, a child might one day proudly follow the rule about wearing a helmet when riding tricycles, because she thinks that is a grown-up thing to do. The next day she might be more interested in asserting her independence than in following the rule, and she might want to ride without a helmet. You will need to remind her. It is helpful to explain what she may do, rather than what she may not. "Jana, everyone must wear a helmet when riding a trike. If you don't want to wear a helmet, you may play in the sandbox or on the climber."

When you see a child in a potentially dangerous situation, think quickly about the best way to respond. Sometimes a look or a few words suffice, e.g., "Jeremy, slow down a little so you won't trip and fall." Other times it is best physically to help a child stop what he is doing and then explain the reason. "Jeremy, I'm going to hold you for a minute until you calm down. You were running so fast that you might have fallen and been hurt."

Toddlers will find it easier to remember safety rules if you work as a team with colleagues and families to apply a few rules consistently. They are also more likely to follow the rules when you reinforce their safe behavior with a smile or positive comment.

what's next?

Skill-Building Journal, section **1-8** (*Learning Activity D*), section **1-1** (*Feedback*), and section **1-9** (*Reflecting on Your Learning*).

Healthy

Overview

Creating and Maintaining Indoor and Outdoor Environments That Promote Wellness

Using Daily Routines to Introduce Good Health and Nutrition to Infants and Toddlers

Recognizing and Reporting Child Abuse and Neglect

Your Own Health and Nutrition

Learning Activities

A. Using Your Knowledge of Infants and Toddlers to Promote Good Health and Nutrition

B. Creating and Maintaining a Hygienic Environment

C. Introducing Health and Nutrition to Infants and Toddlers

D. Recognizing and Reporting the Signs of Child Abuse and Neglect

2.   Healthy

Healthy people feel good about themselves.

Good health is a state of physical, mental, social, and emotional well being, not simply the absence of disease. Healthy people generally are rested and energetic, eat the right foods, feel competent, and get along well with others.

Hygienic environments promote wellness and reduce the spread of disease.

Teachers play a key role in keeping infants and toddlers healthy. Children under age three have more illnesses related to infection than any other age group. Infants and toddlers who attend child care programs tend to be exposed to more diseases than children cared for at home. Teachers need to maintain hygienic environments that promote wellness and reduce the spread of disease. They start each day by checking the health of children as they arrive. Throughout the day, they wash and disinfect the diapering area after each change, place soiled diapers and clothes in closed containers, and wash their hands and the children's often.

Model and talk about healthy practices during routines.

During daily routines—diapering, toileting, brushing teeth, washing hands, preparing foods, and more—teachers can introduce good health and nutrition to children. You can model and talk about healthy practices and encourage mobile infants and toddlers to develop and use self-help skills. When feeding a baby, sit in a quiet corner of the room where the two of you can relax and enjoy being together. Invite older infants and toddlers to help you wipe the table, and offer a simple explanation of why it needs to be cleaned. Encourage toddlers to learn about nutrition by such activities as rinsing blueberries and then stirring them into a bowl of yogurt.

Sometimes teachers are the only witnesses to the signs of abuse and neglect.

This module also addresses an important but disturbing aspect of keeping children healthy: recognizing the signs of possible abuse and neglect and reporting them to appropriate authorities. Other than the children's families, teachers may be the only people who have daily contact with infants and toddlers. Because you know the children well, you are likely to notice unusual changes in their behavior and/or unexplained injuries. All teachers have the ethical and legal responsibility to report suspected child abuse and neglect.

You can promote children's health by

- creating and maintaining indoor and outdoor environments that promote wellness

- using daily routines to introduce good health and nutrition to infants and toddlers

- recognizing and reporting child abuse and neglect

Creating and Maintaining Indoor and Outdoor Environments That Promote Wellness

1. **Check the room daily for adequate ventilation and lighting, comfortable temperatures, and sanitary conditions.** While teachers typically do not have direct responsibility for controlling the classroom temperature and air circulation and for replacing light bulbs, you need to be aware of environmental conditions and report problems to your supervisor.

2. **Arrange the diapering area so it is easy to sanitize.** Keep latex or vinyl gloves and cleaning supplies within adult reach; use a covered, washable trash container with a foot pedal.

3. **Provide tissues and paper towels where mobile infants and toddlers can reach them.** When children use these supplies, they help prevent the spread of germs.

4. **Complete daily health checks and stay alert to symptoms of illness throughout the day.** Follow the program's policies and procedures for notifying families when you suspect that a child is ill.

5. **Wash and disinfect toys and surfaces daily.** Use a bleach solution to disinfect washable items touched and mouthed by children.

6. **Use the handwashing methods recommended by the American Academy of Pediatrics (AAP) and the American Public Health Association (APHA) to help prevent the spread of germs.** Wash your hands and help children wash their hands frequently throughout the day.

Lovette Wipes Her Own Nose

As you read the following story, pay attention to what Ms. Gonzalez does to maintain a healthy environment.

Ms. Gonzalez (thinks): "We need some fresh air…"

Ms. Gonzalez (thinks): "…and a new box of tissues."

Ms. Gonzalez: Good morning. I see you have the sniffles today, Lovette. Let's wipe your nose. A box of tissues is next to the sink.

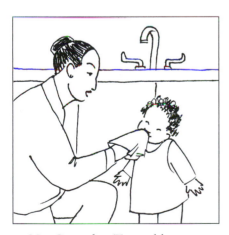

Ms. Gonzalez: Try to blow your nose.

Ms. Gonzalez: Okay, Lovette. Now we need to wash our hands.

Ms. Gonzalez: Now the germs are gone.

Using Daily Routines to Introduce Good Health and Nutrition to Infants and Toddlers

7. **Help children gradually gain self-help skills for toileting, handwashing, toothbrushing, and eating.** Give a baby a spoon to hold and use while you feed her with another.

8. **Model and talk about healthy habits such as handwashing, using tissues, eating nutritious foods, and washing and disinfecting materials and surfaces.** "Uh-oh, here comes a big sneeze! I'd better get a tissue."

9. **Tell families how you and your colleagues promote wellness.** Provide copies of snack and meal menus; share an article about preventing colds through frequent handwashing; and post a chart on the symptoms of common childhood diseases.

10. **Exchange information with families about their child's health and nutrition.** Maintain individual daily logs so you and the families can tell each other about each child's routines and activities at the center and at home.

Crunchy Apples and Shiny Teeth

As you read the following story, pay attention to the way Mr. Lewis helps the children develop healthy habits. Also think about the children's use of self-help skills.

Mr. Lewis: Jessica, will you please pass the apples to me?

Mr. Lewis: Thank you. I like crunchy apples.

Mr. Lewis: Remember to brush up and down.

Jessica: Me brush teeth.

Recognizing and Reporting Child Abuse and Neglect

11. **Respond to children in caring ways while avoiding situations that might be questioned by others.** Work with your supervisor to make sure that all staff and family members are aware of appropriate ways for teachers to nurture children, so that the program supports staff members in doing their jobs.

12. **Know the definitions of physical abuse, physical neglect, sexual abuse, and emotional abuse and neglect.** If you are unclear about the definitions of abuse and neglect, talk with your supervisor.

13. **Recognize and be alert to the physical and behavioral signs that a child might be a victim of abuse or neglect.** The signs of abuse and neglect include, but are not limited to, bruises and marks (often covered by clothing), dizziness, and talking about being beaten or sexual acts.

14. **Report suspected child abuse and neglect to authorities according to applicable laws and program policies.** Your program should provide information about teachers' responsibilities as persons who are required to report suspected abuse and neglect.

15. **Support families by helping them get the services they need.** Talk with your supervisor and other colleagues about agencies and organizations your program uses for referrals.

Noticing Some Unexplained Bruises

As you read the following story, think about why Ms. Bates suspects possible child abuse and neglect. Also pay attention to how the center director supports Ms. Bates as she handles her concerns.

Ms. Bates: You are soaked. I'm going to pick you up and change your diaper.

Ms. Bates: That's the second time I've seen a bad bruise on her inner thigh. Her mom has been rushing out of here lately. She used to stop and share stories about Loretta.

Ms. Bates: I need to talk to you about some unexplained bruises.

Ms. Collier: Are you ready to report your observations? If so, I can stay with you while you make your call.

Ms. Bates: I would like you to stay. I'm ready to call Child Protective Services.

Ms. Collier: It's our job to report your suspicions. Now CPS will try to find out what caused the bruises.

what's next?

Skill-Building Journal, section **2-2** (*Overview*), section **2-10** (*Answer Sheets*), and section **2-1** (*Feedback*).

Your Own Health and Nutrition

Staying healthy improves your life.

We all know that good health and proper nutrition are important. The public focus on staying fit has provided much useful information about how staying healthy improves the quality of life and can actually prolong life. To maintain wellness, perhaps you have

- begun walking or jogging more often

- joined a gym or taken an exercise class

- quit smoking or vowed never to start

- added more vegetables, fruits, and whole-grain foods to your diet

- maintained an appropriate weight using a sensible eating plan

- begun eating more fibrous foods and less sugar, fats, and salt

- used healthy strategies to manage stress

- experienced the positive effects of relaxation techniques

You may have discovered, though, that changing too much, too quickly can lead to discouragement and failure. Have you found yourself saying these things?

I tried to quit smoking, but I felt like I was going crazy and couldn't stop eating.

I don't have time to run and still work, care for my family, and do the gardening.

I'd like to serve healthier meals, but they take too long to plan and prepare.

Change your health and nutrition habits one step at a time.

It can be hard to change health and nutrition habits. We may know what to do, without actually doing it. It can help to think of change in terms of more and less. Try to develop more good habits, such as

- exercising

- eating foods that are low in fats, salt, and sugar

- drinking plenty of water

- getting enough sleep

- spending time with family and friends

The *Dietary Guidelines for Americans*, developed by the U.S. Department of Agriculture (USDA) and the U.S. Department of Health and Human Services (DHHS), provide recommendations for maintaining good health and nutrition habits. The *Guidelines* also include special advice for children about such matters as exercise, milk consumption, and the amount and sources of fats.

The USDA and DHHS jointly update and publish these guidelines every five years. You can obtain the *Dietary Guidelines* online (http://www.health.gov/dietaryguidelines/dga2005/document). A booklet that explains the guidelines may also be viewed and downloaded from the Internet (http://www.healthierus.gov/dietaryguidelines) or ordered by calling 888-878-3256.

what's next?

Skill-Building Journal, section **2-3** (*Your Own Health and Nutrition*) and section **2-4** (*Pre-Training Assessment*).

LEARNING ACTIVITY

Learning Activities

A. Using Your Knowledge of Infants and Toddlers to Promote Good Health and Nutrition

In this activity you will learn to

- recognize some typical behaviors of infants and toddlers

- use what you know about infants and toddlers to promote good health and nutrition

Teachers should work as a team to minimize germs in the environment.

Infants and toddlers depend on you to keep them healthy. They explore and learn by touching and by putting fingers and other things in their mouths. As a result, germs can enter and infect their bodies, and they can pass infections to others. You and your colleagues must work as a team to minimize the germs in the room through frequent handwashing, by disinfecting surfaces and play materials, and by following sanitary diapering and toileting procedures. These skills are discussed at length in *Learning Activity B, Creating and Maintaining a Hygienic Environment*.

Feeding and eating routines are a major part of caring for infants and toddlers. Teachers provide relaxed bottle feedings of formula or breast milk for infants and offer nutritious snacks and meals for older infants and toddlers. Many of our attitudes about food and nutrition are based on our early experiences. By introducing new foods, serving and eating meals family-style, and inviting older children to help prepare food, you can help them begin to develop eating habits that will keep them healthy throughout their lives.

Young infants (birth–8 months) need to follow individualized routines.

- Sammy (3 months) drinks a bottle of his mother's expressed breast milk, mid-morning and mid-afternoon.

- Jon (6 months) is getting his first tooth.

- Luci (8 months) puts anything and everything she can hold into her mouth.

Young infants have their own rhythms for playing, eating, sleeping, and eliminating. The healthiest way to meet their needs is to individualize routines. Talk and laugh with a child when he is awake and interested in playing, feed him when he is hungry, let him sleep when he is tired, and change his diaper when it is wet or soiled. To reduce the spread of germs that cause illness, always follow feeding, diapering, and sanitizing procedures recommended by health professionals. These include frequent washing of your hands and babies' hands.

Babies have different burping needs.

To create a relaxed atmosphere for feeding a young infant, sit in a comfortable place, such as a glider or overstuffed chair. Hold her partially upright, support her head, and position her so you can see each other's eyes. Stop for burping every 3–5 minutes or each time she takes 2–3 ounces of formula or milk. Taking a brief rest lets her slow down and prevents her from taking in too much air. If she does not burp, place her in an upright position for 10–15 minutes after the feeding, to prevent spitting up. Ask the family what burping technique their baby prefers. For example, you might

- hold her upright on your shoulder and gently pat her back

- sit him on your lap and pat his back while supporting his head and neck

- rest her over your lap, tummy down; lift and support her head so it is higher than her chest; and pat her back

Work with families to comfort babies with colic.

About 10–20 percent of young infants in Western cultures develop colic, a condition that can last through the fourth month.[10] Babies with colic tend to cry loudly, uncontrollably, and for a long time; extend or pull their legs up to their stomachs; have enlarged stomachs; and/or pass gas. Some pediatricians recommend soy-based formulas for children with colic. There is often no apparent cause for colic, but most children grow out of the condition. Work with families to find ways to calm and comfort a colicky infant. For example, you might

- swaddle her in a light blanket with arms at her side, to help her stay calm

- wear him in a front carrier so he can be close to you and soothed by your movements

- rock her to sleep by putting her in a stroller and gently pushing it back and forth

- place him stomach-down over your lap and softly rub his back

- offer a pacifier, if parents agree, so she can try to calm herself

Between 4–8 months of age, many infants are ready for their first solid food, usually cereal. Many families prefer to introduce it at breakfast so they can participate in this milestone. When you feed a baby at the center, always work in partnership with the family. Communicate daily about what the child eats at home and at the center. It is important to add new foods one at a time, in case the infant has an allergic reaction such as diarrhea, rash, or vomiting. Depending on the families' preferences, you may offer fresh or prepared foods.

Mobile infants (8–18 months) begin to take part in routines.

- Malou (9 months) drinks from a sippy cup.

- Peter (12 months) puts his arm in the sleeve as his teacher helps him change his shirt.

- Zora (16 months) is learning to eat oatmeal with a spoon.

Mobile infants use their rapidly developing small muscle skills to take more active roles during routines. At mealtime a baby might reach out and grab the spoon you are holding, scoop up a handful of applesauce, or hold and shake juice from her sippy cup. Mobile infants can pick up and eat finger foods that are soft, easy to swallow, and broken into small pieces so they will not choke. You might serve well-cooked peas or carrot slices, pieces of banana, toast strips, and cereal. Be aware of foods that can cause choking. **Never** give infants large pieces of raw carrots, hot dog chunks, popcorn, nuts, whole grapes, cherries with pits, spoonfuls of peanut butter, or any other foods that could get stuck in their throats.

At this age, infants begin to take off their clothes (socks are a favorite item to remove), and they may cooperate when you dress and undress them. To keep infants healthy, wash their hands if they touch soiled clothing. They may be eager to take off coats, hats, mittens, and even shoes, because they don't know that these items keep them warm on cold days. Your gentle encouragement will help them keep outerwear on when playing outdoors.

In addition, mobile infants are rapidly developing large muscle skills. They move around the room, pull themselves up to standing, and climb on furniture and equipment. It's part of your job to minimize the spread of germs by washing and disinfecting floors and other surfaces and items that they are likely to touch, put in their mouths, or sit on with wet diapers.

Toddlers (18–36 months) are beginning to learn self-help skills.

- Lovette (20 months) feeds herself macaroni and cheese by using her fingers.

- Ricky (28 months) watches Adam (30 months) use the toilet.

- Jessica (34 months) pours juice from a small pitcher into her cup.

Toddlers are movers and doers. Their growing physical skills take them to new places, levels, and activities. They need active indoor and outdoor play to release energy and to exercise their developing muscles. Of course, toddlers need to rest, too. Your program should offer daily naps and a balance of active and quiet times and indoor and outdoor activities.

Toddlers' small muscle skills and desire to be independent set the stage for beginning to learn many self-help skills. They are learning to put on jackets, use the toilet, brush their teeth, wash their hands, and blow their noses. By encouraging these skills, you can help toddlers learn to keep themselves healthy.

Many toddlers like to copy the important people in their lives. They want to help prepare food, wipe the table, serve themselves, and eat finger foods independently. Some toddlers have strong preferences for familiar foods; others are eager to try new things. Toddlers are still learning to chew and swallow solids, so you need to withhold foods on which children choke easily.

The following list summarizes key characteristics of young infants, mobile infants, and toddlers that can affect their health.

Development of Infants and Toddlers

Young infants (birth–8 months)

- have individual schedules for eating, sleeping, and eliminating
- soil and wet their diapers and clothes
- get much of their nutrition by breastfeeding or drinking from bottles
- are developing secure attachments with families and teachers
- use their senses (touch, hearing, sight, taste, and smell) to learn about the world
- have weak neck muscles that cannot immediately support their large, heavy heads

Mobile infants (8–18 months)

- pick up small objects by using thumb and forefinger (pincer grasp)
- begin to take off hats, shoes, and socks and cooperate when being dressed
- hold toys, cups, and other objects with two hands
- crawl and pull themselves up by holding onto furniture and railings
- understand a few words and simple phrases and sometimes follow simple instructions
- enjoy water play

Toddlers (18–36 months)

- learn self-help skills and use them during routines
- gain large motor skills, e.g., running, jumping, kicking, climbing, and throwing
- begin to learn about health and nutrition
- may have strong opinions about foods they like and dislike
- begin to gain some bowel and bladder control
- like to do things for themselves, most of the time

what's next?

Skill-Building Journal, section **2-5** (*Learning Activity A*), section **2-10** (*Answer Sheets*), and section **2-1** (*Feedback*).

LEARNING ACTIVITY

Learning Activities

B. Creating and Maintaining a Hygienic Environment [11]

In this activity you will learn to

- create indoor and outdoor spaces that promote wellness and reduce disease

- follow procedures recommended by health professionals for handwashing, sanitation, diapering, and toileting

Germs can spread easily in infant/toddler rooms.

Caregiving environments for infants and toddlers can be germ-filled places where illnesses are passed among children and adults. When you think about typical scenes in infant and toddler rooms, it is easy to understand why germs might spread easily.

- Ms. Bates holds a baby at arm's length as she carries him from his crib to the diapering area. He is soaked from armpit to knees. She carefully lays him on a piece of paper that covers the diapering surface and removes his shirt and pants. He coos and gurgles, then pats his bare tummy.

- An 8-month-old chews on a ring of large pop beads while sitting on the rug facing another child. She drops the pop beads and coughs for a few seconds. The other child picks up the beads, waves them in the air, and then puts them down. Next, he rubs his eyes with his hands.

- A toddler sneezes, wipes his nose with his hand, picks up a ball, and tosses it in the air. Another toddler picks up the same ball, carries it across the yard, puts it down, sucks his thumb, and then kicks the ball.

It is a major part of your job to work with your colleagues to make sure your cozy, comfortable setting also promotes wellness and minimizes illness and disease. You can eliminate disease-producing germs and preserve everyone's good health through daily practices such as keeping the room clean and uncluttered; disinfecting surfaces and toys; washing hands frequently; following recommended diapering and toileting procedures; refrigerating human milk, formula, and foods; and cleaning spills as they occur.

Germs can be passed from one person to another.

Germs can be left on tables, materials, and equipment, and they can grow on perishable foods. Most childhood illnesses are contagious, so it is very likely that, when one child in your room gets sick, the germs can be passed to others. Germs can be spread from a child's saliva, mucus, urine, and stool. Each time a child sneezes or coughs, shares food, or does not wash her hands after using the toilet, disease-causing germs can be transmitted. You cannot always tell who has a contagious illness by whether he looks sick. Some diseases are contagious even when the child appears healthy. Most illnesses, such as flu and chicken pox, are contagious in the several days before symptoms appear. Some, such as giardia, hepatitis B, and HIV, can be carried for a long time without any symptoms. That is why it is essential to follow universal precautions—handwashing, cleaning and disinfecting, and using gloves for contact with body fluids—to prevent the spread of diseases among children and adults.

Handwashing Procedures

Handwashing reduces germs for children and adults.

Health professionals agree that frequent, thorough handwashing can reduce the spread of disease in child care by 50 percent and protect adults and children from serious illnesses. Handwashing is for everyone. Teachers should wash their own hands and those of infants, and watch and help toddlers wash

- upon arrival and departure for the day or when moving from one child care group to another

- before and after preparing and feeding bottles

- before and after preparing, serving, and eating food

- before and after giving or applying medication

- before and after playing in water that was used by more than one person or that was standing for more than a few hours

- after diapering and helping a child use the toilet or after using the toilet, yourself

- after handling body fluids or soiled clothes

- after caring for a child who may have a contagious illness

- after handling pets, cages, or pet supplies

- after removing disposable gloves

- after cleaning the room, bathroom surfaces, or toys

- after cleaning or changing the plastic bag in a trash can

- after playing outdoors and in sandboxes[12]

Handwashing Procedures for Adults [13]

- Make sure a clean paper towel is available.

- Remove rings (because they can hide germs).[14]

- Turn on warm water. Wash and dry rings and set them aside on a clean paper towel.

- Moisten hands with water and apply liquid soap.

- Rub hands together vigorously until lather appears; continue rubbing for at least 10 seconds.

- Wash all surfaces: backs of hands, wrists, palms, fingers, between fingers, areas that were covered by jewelry, and under fingernails.

- Rinse your hands well. Leave the water running.

- Dry your hands with a paper towel. Replace rings.

- Turn off the water using a paper towel instead of bare hands. Throw away the towels.

Helping Children Wash Their Hands [15]

- Hold infant and place her hands under running water. Apply liquid soap to infant's hands; rub lather on all hand surfaces; rinse under running water; dry with a clean paper towel; discard the towel.

- If a child is too heavy to hold but is unable to stand,

  - wipe the child's hands with a damp paper towel on which you have placed a drop of liquid soap; discard the towel

  - wipe all of the soap from the child's hands with a clean, wet paper towel; discard the towel

  - dry the child's hands with a clean paper towel; discard the towel

- Have older children stand on a step stool so they can place their hands under the running water.

- Show older children how to follow the handwashing steps described above.

- Wash your own hands when the children's hands are clean and dry.

Use a bleach solution to disinfect surfaces and materials.

Washing and Disinfecting Surfaces, Toys, and Equipment

Children and adults can leave bacteria, parasites, and viruses on tables, materials, toys, equipment, and clothing. Your best defense is to wash surfaces, toys, and equipment thoroughly with soap and water, and then disinfect them to kill germs. Some programs disinfect washable toys in a washing machine or in the hot cycle of a dishwasher, separately from dishes. Otherwise, use the following bleach solutions to disinfect surfaces and other items in an infant and toddler room effectively.

Surface **Bleach Solution**	**Cleans**
1/4 cup of liquid chlorine bleach to 1 gallon of water or 1 tablespoon of liquid chlorine bleach to 1 quart of water	All surfaces, including the diapering area and bathroom; tabletops and counters; feeding chair trays; walls; door frames and doorknobs; floors; mops, brooms, and dustpans used to clean up body fluids
Mild **Bleach Solution**	**Cleans**
1 tablespoon of liquid chlorine bleach to 1 gallon of water or 1 teaspoon of liquid chlorine bleach to 1 quart of water	All play materials, and other objects that children have put in their mouths.
Dishwashing **Bleach Solution**	**Cleans**
1 1/2 teaspoons of liquid chlorine bleach to 1 gallon of water	Dishes and utensils during the third step of dishwashing when these items are not washed and dried in a dishwasher

Make fresh bleach solutions every day.

One of your daily tasks is to mix new batches of both bleach solutions. Pour *surface* bleach solution into labeled spray bottles and place them in the food preparation, diapering, and toileting areas. Pour the *mild* bleach solution and the *dishwashing* bleach solution into separate labeled containers. Store all solutions away from direct sunlight and out of children's reach. Discard unused bleach solutions at the end of the day because they weaken and lose effectiveness very quickly.

Cleaning and Disinfecting Surfaces

- Wash the surface with soap and water. Rinse with clear water.

- Coat the surface with bleach solution (dispensed from a spray bottle).

- Let the surface air dry, unless it is likely to be mouthed by children. If so, wait for two minutes, wet a fresh towel with tap water, and use it to wipe the surface.

Cleaning and Disinfecting Toys and Other Washable Objects Mouthed and Handled by Children

- Place mouthed items in a designated container, out of children's reach, during the day.

- Clean toys and other items with soap and water. Scrub with a brush to reach all parts.

- Rinse in clear water.

- Coat the surface with bleach solution and place in a rack or on a clean towel to air dry. Dishes and utensils that are not disinfected in a dishwasher should be placed in dishwashing bleach solution for at least one minute before air drying in a clean rack.

Keep pets and cages clean.

If your program has pets, be sure to clean their cages frequently. Program pets need to be up-to-date on their shots and checked regularly to ensure that they are healthy and free from diseases. The animals need food and clean water daily to stay in good health. Children can begin to learn important health concepts by helping to care for pets.

Hygienic Feeding and Eating Practices

Teachers usually prepare bottles and baby food, while the food services staff prepares and serves snacks and meals for mobile infants and toddlers. Germs can contaminate foods, so the kitchen and/or food preparation area should be located near a sink and used only for preparing bottles and food. The following strategies will help everyone keep breast milk, formula, and foods fresh and safe for use.

Feeding bottles and baby foods

- Label breast milk, formula, and perishable baby foods with the child's name and date. (Use labels that will not come off or become illegible in water or when handled.)

- Refrigerate bottles and baby food at 40° F or cooler.

- Warm bottles in warm water; never warm bottles in a microwave oven.

- Hold babies during bottle feedings; never prop a bottle.

- Discard the remains of any bottle that was fed over a period that exceeds one hour from the beginning of the feeding.

- Refrigerate unused breast milk during the day and send it home at the end of the day. Do not use it the next day.

- Mix formula according to the family's or health professional's instructions and refrigerate. Discard unused mixed formula after 48 hours.

- Use a new bottle of formula for each feeding. Discard formula left in a bottle.

- Transfer baby food to a clean bowl before feeding; discard the leftovers.

Serving snacks and meals

- Make sure food from home is in containers labeled with the child's name, the date, and contents.

- Refrigerate food at 40° F or cooler, or keep warm food at 140° F or hotter.

- Use only cooking equipment, dishes, and utensils that can be washed and disinfected.

- Store leftover food immediately; do not cool leftovers at room temperature.

- Make sure children use their own plates, cups, and utensils, and do not share food they have touched or started to eat.

Cleaning up

- Wash counters, feeding chair trays, and table tops with soap and water; disinfect with surface bleach solution.

- Scrape food off dishes and utensils into a trash container and place the dishes and utensils in a basin to be returned to the kitchen for washing and disinfection.

Diapering and Toileting Practices

Minimize the spread of germs during diapering and toileting.

Teachers spend much of their days changing diapers and helping older children use the toilet. The changing table should be at least 3' above the floor (to prevent spread of infectious diseases) and have a waterproof surface (e.g., vinyl or plastic) with no tears or cracks. It should be located near a sink that is not used for any other purpose, supply shelves or cupboards within easy reach, and a plastic-lined trash container with a cover and foot pedal.

To minimize the spread of germs during diapering

- change wet and soiled diapers only in the diapering area

- use the diapering area only for changing diapers

- check diapers at least hourly and change them as needed

As with all routines, it is important for you to become an expert on the health and safety aspects of diapering and toileting. Carefully following procedures for diaper changing and handwashing is one of the most important things you can do to prevent the children you care for—and yourself—from getting many illnesses. Stool carries germs that cause gastrointestinal diseases with diarrhea and vomiting, as well as some more serious diseases, such as hepatitis A.

It is a good idea to practice diaper changing until it becomes second nature to you. These are the key things to remember:

Have everything you need at hand before you start diapering. This way, you can focus on the child, and you will not have to ask a busy colleague to assist you or risk leaving the child to get something you need.

While diapering, you want to make sure that you are not contaminating any clean surfaces with soil from diapers. Always separate soiled things from clean things. For example, be careful not to hold a baby with a soiled diaper close to your body as you carry her to the diaper-changing station, so you don't soil your own clothing. Use a step-on diaper can, and use your elbows or a paper towel to turn on the water faucet when you wash your hands after diapering.

Keep a hand on the child at all times. That is the only way to guarantee the child's safety. Never leave a child alone, even for a minute. You cannot rely on straps to keep the child safe, and straps would slow you down if you needed to respond to an emergency.

Learn your program's policies. For instance, does your program use disposable or cloth diapers? What are your program's policies on the use of gloves or diaper creams? To follow universal precautions, you must use gloves for blood. Some programs recommend or require gloves for routine diapering as well. If you do use gloves, you must know when to put them on and how to take them off to avoid contamination.

The American Academy of Pediatrics and the American Public Health Association describe detailed procedures that you should follow to minimize the spread of disease when you diaper children or help them with toileting.[16] Here are the most important parts of the procedures:

Get organized.

- Wash your hands.

- Verify that all supplies are on hand. These include

    - nonabsorbent paper to cover the diaper-changing surface from the child's shoulders to beyond the child's feet

    - fresh diapers

    - clean clothes if needed

    - wipes

    - plastic bag for soiled clothes

    - bleach solution, made fresh daily

Begin the process.

- Bring the child to the changing table and lay him down.

- Remove the child's shoes and socks to keep them clean.

- Remove the child's soiled clothes and put them in a securely tied plastic bag to send home. (Don't rinse them or empty the stool.)

Change the diaper.

- Unfasten the diaper, but leave the soiled diaper under the child.

- Lifting the child's legs, use disposable wipes, wiping front to back, to clean the child's soiled bottom. Use a fresh wipe for each swipe.

- Remove the soiled diaper and fold the paper table liner if necessary to maintain a clean surface. Lower the child's legs back onto the clean paper. Be very careful not to contaminate any clean surfaces with the soiled diaper. Fold the diaper inward and then put it in a covered, plastic-lined, hands-free covered can.

- Clean your hands with a disposable wipe, and then clean the child's hands with another disposable wipe. Put the wipes into the diaper can.

- Put on the clean diaper.

- Dress the child.

- Wash the child's hands with soap and water.

Clean and sanitize the diaper-changing surface.

- Dispose of the liner in the diaper can.

- Clean any visible soil with detergent and water, and rinse with water.

- Wet the surface with a sanitizing solution. If a bleach solution is used, let it remain on the surface for at least two minutes. A bleach solution of 1/4 cup chlorine bleach in a gallon of water, made fresh daily, is an effective and cost-effective way to sanitize the surface.

- Wash your hands with soap and water.

Document the diaper change.

- Record the time; what was in the diaper; and any problems such as loose stool, unusual odor, blood in the stool, or any skin irritation.

Toddlers need your support during toilet learning.

Some of the older toddlers in your care may be learning to use the toilet. The bathroom is a major source of germs. Handles, sinks, toilet seats, and the floor should be washed and disinfected with surface bleach solution, at least once a day and more often if visibly soiled. Line the trash container with a plastic bag. Replace the bag, at least twice a day and more often if needed.

To support toilet learning, your program should have child-size toilets, seats that attach to adult-size toilets (with a washable step stool nearby), or potty chairs placed on the bathroom floor. The use of potty chairs is discouraged, and centers should only use potty chairs if there is a utility sink that is used only for cleaning these chairs.

Although they are eager to be independent, toddlers need your support to learn healthy practices such as washing their hands thoroughly after using the toilet. Offer a step stool so they can reach the sink, hang paper towels where they can reach them, and provide a plastic-lined trash container with a pedal-operated lid. When children have accidents, help them clean themselves and change into clean clothes. Use disposable gloves in accordance with your program's procedures. Wash your hands and make sure children wash theirs. (See module 8, *Self*, for a detailed discussion of working with families to support children who are learning to use the toilet.)

Promoting Wellness While Children Sleep at the Center

Good hygiene can minimize the spread of germs while children sleep.

Even while children are sleeping, germs can pass from one person to another. When a sick child sleeps right next to another child, both may end up with the same illness. Sharing beds and linens can also spread disease. Hygienic practices can minimize the spread of germs while children are sleeping.

- Set up cribs, mats, or cots at least 3 feet apart. (If cribs have Plexiglas® partitions, they can be placed closer together.)

- Assign a specific crib, mat, or cot to each child who attends the program four hours or more per day.

- Label each assigned crib, mat, or cot with the child's name.

- Make sure children sleep in assigned places. (If a child accidentally sleeps in another child's crib, mat, or cot, disinfect it and change the linens before the assigned child uses it again.)

- Store sleeping mats and cots so sleeping surfaces do not touch each other.

- Cover crib mattresses, mats, and cots with nonabsorbent, washable covers (if they are not already covered that way).

- Clean and disinfect beds weekly and whenever soiled or wet.

Ask families to provide several sets of bedding.

In addition, have children use their own sheets and washable blankets. Label each child's linens and store them separately so that they do not touch another child's bedding. Ask families to provide several sets, because you will need to change the linens often. Any item that is soiled or wet should be replaced immediately. When changing beds, place soiled linens in a plastic bag, seal it, and store it out of children's reach until it can be sent home to be laundered. Wash your hands after handling soiled linens.

Recognizing the Symptoms of Common Childhood Illnesses

Even in a seemingly spotless and sanitary environment, there will be germs. Young children typically get sick 5–12 times a year. On any given day, several of the children in your care are likely to arrive feeling ill. Most of the time, the illnesses are not serious.

Very few illnesses necessitate sending a child home.

Few illnesses require a child's exclusion from a program. Some typical childhood illnesses are not contagious, and many contagious illnesses—such as the common cold—begin to spread before symptoms appear. By the time you know a child is sick, the others in the group may have already been exposed to the germs. If the child is coughing uncontrollably, feverish, or unable to participate in daily activities, or if he requires greater care than the teacher can give without compromising the care of the other children, he should be cared for outside the program.[17]

Most children with mild illnesses can safely attend your program, although the program might have policies regarding specific symptoms (such as a fever over a specified temperature). Because you know the children in your care, you can determine whether a mildly ill child can participate in activities and whether you and your colleagues can adequately care for the child without hindering the care of other children. When sick children remain at the center, they need extra attention. For example, depending on the illness, a child might need

- additional time to rest or sleep

- appropriate food and drinks, especially to prevent dehydration

- medication (dispensed according to program policy, written physician's instructions, and written permission from the parents or guardians)

- close supervision and comfort

Obtain written permission to administer medication.

The family may ask the program to administer medication. Complete training in proper procedures before giving medicine to any child. You must have the parents' or guardians' written permission, and the medication must be in the original dated container with a child-protective cap. Medications must include instructions for use and disposal, and they must be labeled with the child's name and that of the health care provider. Refrigerate medications when appropriate, storing them away from food and out of children's reach.

When administering medication, follow licensing procedures and your program's policies and procedures. Use standard measuring devices and be sure to read the instructions carefully so you understand the required dosage. Never administer one child's medication to another. Keep accurate records noting the child's name, the date and time, and the name and amount of medication administered. Be alert to possible side effects of the medicine.

Conduct daily health checks.

There are times, however, when an ill child should not be cared for at the center. You and your colleagues should conduct daily health checks to look for specific signs of more serious illnesses. A daily health check upon arrival will help you identify infants and toddlers who might be ill.

As you take attendance and greet children, be alert for the following symptoms:

- difficulty breathing
- yellowish skin or eyes
- unusual spots or rashes
- feverish appearance
- difficult or rapid breathing
- mouth sores with drooling
- severe coughing (red or blue in the face, high-pitched croup or whooping sound)
- pinkeye (tears, redness of eyelid lining, irritation, swelling, discharge of pus)
- infected skin patches or crusty, bright-yellow, dry, or gummy skin areas
- unusual behavior (child is cranky, less active, or more irritable than usual; child feels general discomfort or just seems unwell)

Be alert for signs of illness.

During the day, be alert for the signs just listed and these additional signs of illness

- diarrhea not associated with a diet change or medication

- sore throat or trouble swallowing

- headache or stiff neck

- nausea and vomiting

- loss of appetite

- frequent scratching of the scalp or body

Sometimes children need to be excluded from the program.

Your state licensing agency has specific policies that identify diseases that require a child to go home and remain out of care until he or she is no longer contagious. The following chart summarizes information about the symptoms of contagious illnesses transmitted through direct contact, the intestinal tract, and the respiratory system, and guidance about when it is safe for a child to return to the program. This information is provided as a general guide. For information about when a child may return to the program after being ill, refer to the most recent edition of *Caring for Our Children: National Health and Safety Performance Standards: Guidelines for Out-of-Home Child Care Programs* (available online from http://nrc.uchsc.edu/CFOC/XMLVersion/NewTOCwoSubs.xml). Also check with your supervisor.

Contagious Illnesses [18]

Diseases Spread by Direct Contact	Symptoms	When Child May Return to the Program
Chicken pox	Fever, runny nose, cough, rash (pink/red blisters)	When sores have dried and crusted (typically 6 days after onset of blisters)
Head lice	Whitish-gray nits (eggs) attached to hair shafts or presence of adult lice	After treatment and removal of nits, and child's clothes and bedding are washed in hot water (130° F) and dried in a hot dryer to destroy lice and eggs
Herpes (mouth or cold sore)	Sores on lips or inside mouth	No need for exclusion if sores are covered
Impetigo	Red oozing sore capped with a golden yellow crust that appears stuck on	Twenty-four hours after treatment has begun
Measles	Fever, runny nose, cough, and red-brown blotchy rash on the face and body	Four days after the rash appears
Mumps	Swelling of the glands at the jaw angle accompanied by cold-like symptoms.	Nine days after swelling begins
Pertussis (Whooping Cough)	Cold-like symptoms that develop into severe respiratory disease with repeated attacks of violent coughing	Five days after antibiotic treatment has been completed
Purulent Conjunctivitis (Pinkeye)	Eyes are pink/red, watery, itchy, lid swollen, sometimes painful, and pus is present	Twenty-four hours after treatment has begun (not all pinkeye is contagious)
Ringworm	**Skin:** reddish scaling, circular patches with raised edges and central clearing or light and dark patches on face and upper trunk or cracking, peeling skin between toes **Scalp:** redness, scaling of scalp with broken hairs or patches of hair loss	No need to exclude the child; advise family that treatment is needed
Scabies	Crusty, wavy ridges and tunnels in the webs of fingers, hand, wrist, and trunk	After treatment has been completed
Shingles	Blisters in a band or patch	No need for exclusion if sores are covered

Contagious Illnesses, *continued*

Diseases Spread Through the Intestinal Tract	Symptoms	When Child May Return to the Program
Diarrheal diseases	Increased liquid and number of stools in an 8-hour period.	Diarrhea has stopped (if caused by *Salmonella typhi* or other infection, may require that a stool culture be taken by a physician)
Vomiting (as a symptom)	Abdominal pain, digested/undigested stomach contents, refusal to eat, headache, fever.	When vomiting has stopped or when a health care provider determines that the cause of the vomiting is not contagious or serious and that the child is not in danger of dehydration
Hepatitis A	Fever, loss of appetite, nausea, yellowish skin and whites of the eyes, dark brown urine, light-colored stool.	One week after illness begins, if fever is gone, or as directed by the health department when preventive measures have been taken to protect other children and staff members

Diseases Spread Through the Respiratory Tract	Symptoms	When Child May Return to the Program
Bacterial meningitis	Fever, vomiting, unusual irritability, excessive crying with inability to be comforted, high-pitched crying, poor feeding, and activity levels below normal.	After fever is gone and child has completed a closely supervised program of antibiotics The Health Department may recommend preventive medicine for exposed children and staff
Colds and flu	**Colds:** stuffy or runny nose, sore throat, sneezing, coughing, watery eyes, and perhaps a fever **Flu:** sore throat, fever, muscular aches, and chills	When coughing has subsided, fever is gone, and child can participate in daily activities
Strep throat	Red and painful throat, often accompanied by fever.	Generally when fever subsides and child has been taking antibiotics for at least 24 hours

Isolate the ill child in a comfortable area.

When you see any symptoms of an illness that requires the sick child to be away from the program, isolate the child in a quiet, comfortable, supervised area until a family member arrives. Inform your supervisor so you can discuss how to notify other families of the contagious illness.

Share the information in the contagious illness chart with families. Encourage them to tell you when their child has been exposed to one of these illnesses so you can take precautions to keep the illness from spreading.

Facts About HIV

HIV is not transmitted through casual contact.

HIV (human immunodeficiency virus) is the cause of AIDS (acquired immune deficiency syndrome). HIV attacks the immune system that normally protects the body from viruses and bacteria. This makes it hard for the body to fight infection. HIV is not transmitted through casual contact or from simply being around someone who is infected. It cannot be transmitted by mosquitoes or pets. The virus does not live by itself in the air. You **cannot** get HIV by

- being in the same room with someone who has the virus
- sharing drinks or food
- being near when someone coughs or sneezes
- hugging, shaking hands, or kissing as friends do
- sharing a swimming pool, bath, or toilet

HIV is transmitted through blood, semen, and vaginal secretions.

A person can be infected with HIV

- **from mother to child (perinatal) during pregnancy or delivery.** If the mother has HIV infection, her blood can transmit the virus to the baby during pregnancy or delivery. Most children under age 13 with HIV are infected in this way. Because HIV has been found in breast milk, mothers with HIV infection are discouraged from breastfeeding.
- **through sexual intercourse with a man or woman who has HIV disease.** Sexually abused children are at risk for HIV infection.
- **by sharing or being stuck with intravenous needles that contain infected blood from a previous user.**
- **from blood and blood product transfusions given before 1985, before donated blood was tested for HIV.** Many people were infected this way as children, including those with hemophilia.

Children with HIV infection can remain healthy for long periods of time. They develop AIDS when the virus has severely damaged the immune system. Because children with HIV infection are more susceptible to illnesses, good hygiene is very important.

Always take universal precautions when handling blood.

Because you and your colleagues might not know that a child has HIV and because HIV is carried in the blood, **always** take universal blood precautions. Wear disposable, nonporous gloves to create a barrier between yourself and any person's blood when giving first aid or cleaning up spills. The federal government defines *hazardous exposure to blood* as direct contact by blood or blood-containing body fluids with the employee's eyes, mouth, or non-intact skin.[19] Federal regulations require the following measures:

- Wash the exposed body part.

- Clean and disinfect spills.

- Report to your supervisor.

- Document the exposure.

- Have a medical exam within 24 hours.

- Follow up and receive treatment as necessary.

Children with HIV infection may have special nutrition and therapy needs. Encourage parents and guardians to share pertinent medical information so you can provide the best care for their child. If a child has HIV disease or any other medical condition, programs should have a special care plan outlining medications, emergency procedures, and measures to prevent and recognize illness. If you care for a child with HIV infection, get specific training so you will know how to meet the child's needs.

A Hygienic Environment for Infants and Toddlers

What Is It Like?	What Is Your Responsibility?
Center-Wide	
Air temperature is kept between 65° and 72° F.	Check the air temperature each morning and throughout the day.
Caregiving rooms have windows.	Open windows to let in fresh air, unless the air conditioning is on. Make sure air conditioners are cleaned frequently to remove dust and mold.
Food preparation, diapering, and toileting areas have metal or plastic trash containers.	Line containers with large, sturdy plastic bags. Tie, remove, and replace bags daily, and more often if needed.
There are individual storage containers for each enrolled child.	Keep each child's clothes and personal belongings separate to avoid the spread of germs.
Teachers wear washable clothing.	Have a change of clothing on hand in case the clothes you are wearing get wet or soiled. Launder clothes frequently.
Teachers use a clean cloth to wipe the gums of babies who do not have teeth, and they clean teeth that have erupted. Teachers and older children brush their teeth at the center.	Store toothbrushes so they can air dry without touching. Make sure children use toothbrushes that are clearly labeled with their names. Discard toothbrushes that children use by mistake and when brushes touch. Do not disinfect them; provide new ones. Notify the parents or guardians of a child who uses the brush of a child who is ill.
The outdoor sand-play area has a cover.	Cover the sand when it is not in use, so animals cannot go in the area.
Cigarette smoking is not permitted in the center.	Follow the center's non-smoking policy.
Handwashing	
The program follows health experts' recommendations for **when** to wash hands.	Wash your hands and the children's before and after specified daily routines and activities.
The program follows health experts' recommendations for **how** to wash hands.	Wash your hands and the children's thoroughly by following the Center for Disease Control's recommended procedures.

A Hygienic Environment for Infants and Toddlers, *continued*

What Is It Like?	What Is Your Responsibility?
Disinfecting Surfaces, Toys, and Equipment The program follows health experts' recommendations for using a bleach solution to disinfect surfaces likely to be touched and mouthed by children.	Make fresh **surface** bleach solution daily (1/4 cup of liquid chlorine bleach per 1 gallon of water, or 1 tablespoon per 1 quart of water). Store in labeled spray bottles in kitchen, toileting, and diapering areas, out of direct sunlight and children's reach. Discard unused portions daily. Use throughout the day to disinfect all surfaces except play materials. Use to disinfect mops, brooms, and dustpans that are used to clean up body fluids.
The program follows health experts' recommendations for washing, rinsing, and disinfecting hard toys, utensils, and other items children mouth, and for cleaning cloth toys in hot water in a washing machine.	Make fresh **mild** and **dishwashing** bleach solution daily. Store in labeled containers out of direct sunlight and children's reach. Discard unused portion daily. Put toys and other items mouthed by children in a container during the day. Clean and disinfect them at the end of the day. Wash cloth toys and books at least once a week.
Feeding and Eating Food preparation areas are located near a sink and used only for food.	Transfer baby food to a bowl before feeding; discard leftovers (do not save them for later). Disinfect tabletops, counters, and high chair trays with **surface** bleach solution.
Refrigerators are in or near the food preparation area.	Check daily to make sure the refrigerator is working and the temperature is less than 40° F. Label breast milk, formula, and perishable foods with child's name and date. Refrigerate at 40° F or cooler. Discard formula left in a bottle after a feeding (do not save for later), and discard unused mixed formula after 48 hours. Refrigerate unused breast milk during the day; send it home at the end of the day. Do not use it the next day.
There is a dishwasher or three-compartment system for washing, rinsing, and disinfecting dishes.	Have children use their own bottles, bowls, and utensils. Use **dishwashing** bleach solution to disinfect dishes and utensils. Place older children's dirty dishes and utensils in a container for transfer to the center's kitchen.
There are child-size tables and chairs in each caregiving room.	Use **surface** bleach solution to clean tables after snacks, meals, and messy activities.

A Hygienic Environment for Infants and Toddlers, *continued*

What Is It Like?	What Is Your Responsibility?
Diapering The changing table is at least 3' above the floor (to prevent spread of infectious diseases) and has a waterproof surface (e.g., vinyl or plastic) with no tears or cracks. The diapering area is near a sink that is not used for any other purpose. The program follows health experts' recommended diapering practices.	Repair any tears or cracks in the diapering surface. Change wet and soiled diapers in the diapering area but nowhere else. Use the diapering area for changing diapers but nothing else. Check diapers at least hourly and change them as needed. Follow recommended practices for diapering, handwashing, and disinfecting the area.
The diapering area has a place to store supplies within easy reach.	Store individual supplies in containers labeled with the child's name. Keep the area well-stocked with disposable gloves (if used), diapers, wipes, paper towels, soap, small and large plastic bags, and **surface** bleach solution. Have supplies ready before bringing a child to the area for a diaper change.
The diapering area has a container with a cover and foot pedal.	Line the container with large plastic bags. Place soiled diapers, wipes, and gloves in the container. Empty the container and replace the plastic bag at least twice a day and more often if needed.
Toileting There is one child-size sink (22" high) for every 10 toddlers.	Wash faucet handles, sinks, and the floor at least once a day and when soiled. Disinfect with **surface** bleach solution.
There is one child-size toilet (11" in height) per 10 toddlers, seats that attach to adult toilets, or potty chairs. If potty chairs are used, there is a nearby utility sink that is not used for food preparation or dishwashing.	Wash toilet seats at least once a day and when soiled. Disinfect with **surface** bleach solution. Flush potty chair contents in the toilet; then rinse in the utility sink. Wash chairs twice with soap, water, and paper towels; disinfect with **surface** bleach solution; and air dry. After sanitizing the potty chair, sanitize the utility sink and then wash your hands.
There is a trash container with a pedal-operated lid in the bathroom.	Line the trash container with large plastic bags. Empty and replace the plastic bag at least twice a day and more often if needed.
The program supports toddlers learning to use the toilet independently.	Provide a step stool. In the bathroom, place disposable wipes, toilet paper, paper towels, and soap within toddlers' reach. Make sure toddlers wash their hands, dry them with paper towels, and discard towels in the trash container. Show them how to turn off the water with a towel.

A Hygienic Environment for Infants and Toddlers, *continued*

What Is It Like?	What Is Your Responsibility?
Sleeping Children who attend four hours or more per day have separate, assigned cribs, mats, or cots.	Make sure children sleep in their assigned places. Place cribs without Plexiglas® partitions at least 3' apart and/or lay infants head to toe in separate cribs, to prevent the spread of germs. Set up mats or cots used by older children at least 3' feet apart and/or place children head to toe on separate mats, to prevent the spread of germs.
Crib mattresses, mats, and cots have nonabsorbent, washable covers.	Use **surface** bleach solution daily to disinfect crib rails mouthed by infants. Use **surface** bleach solution to disinfect covers on crib mattresses, mats, and cots at least weekly and when soiled or used by another child.
Families provide several sets of washable sheets and blankets.	Wash sheets at the center (if there are laundry facilities) or send them home to be laundered at least once a week. Change sheets and blankets when soiled or if used by another child. Seal soiled linens in plastic bags until laundered or sent home. Remind families to return washed linens as soon as possible.

what's next?

Skill-Building Journal, section **2-6** (*Learning Activity B*) and section **2-1** (*Feedback*).

LEARNING
ACTIVITY

Learning Activities

C. Introducing Health and Nutrition to Infants and Toddlers

In this activity you will learn to

- model and talk about healthy practices with infants and toddlers throughout the day

- introduce a few simple health and nutrition concepts to toddlers

Earlier in this module, you read about ways to keep the infants and toddlers in your care healthy, and then you applied your knowledge on the job. It is also important to help young children gradually learn to take care of their own health and nutrition. It will be many years before they can be completely responsible for their physical, mental, social, and emotional well-being, but the learning process begins now.

Model healthy practices while caring for infants and toddlers.

You can introduce health and nutrition to infants and toddlers by showing them how you—an important person in their lives—use healthy practices. Young children learn from your good habits.

- Store bottles and perishable foods in the refrigerator.

- Serve and eat healthy foods during snacks and meals.

- Drink fresh water throughout the day and offer it to children frequently.

- Wash your hands and children's hands frequently throughout the day.

- Wear a hat on cold days.

- Sneeze into your elbow if you do not have a tissue handy, not your hand.

- Wash fruits and vegetables well before serving them.

Talk about what you are doing and why it ensures good health and nutrition.

When munching on a pear, tossing a tissue in the trash can and then washing your hands, or placing a baby in her assigned crib, talk to the children about what you and your colleagues do and why it supports wellness. Infants and toddlers may not understand everything you say, but they will learn that you think good health and nutrition are important. When they are older, they will do similar things to take care of themselves.

Here are examples of what you might explain:

Lucy, you drank almost all of your mom's milk. She's coming at lunch time to feed you.

Ms. Bates changed her shirt, because Danny's diaper was wet and she got wet too. She put it in a bag until she can wash it. Now she's washing the germs off her hands.

We've been sitting for a long time. I need to stretch my arms and legs. Who wants to stretch with me?

Young children are learning health habits from you.

Your use of healthy practices is the first step in helping young children develop their own good health and nutrition habits. This is true for several reasons:

Young infants are building a foundation for learning to take good care of themselves. When their families and teachers respond to infants' need for food, rest, diapering, and company, they feel valued. As they grow older they will be more likely to use their self-help skills to meet their own health and nutrition needs.

Mobile infants want to be like the important people in their lives. When mobile infants see parents, older siblings, and teachers wash their hands, brush their teeth, and eat fresh fruits, they want to copy them. Although they don't know about germs, cavities, and vitamins, they do know they want to be like the people they love.

Toddlers are developing self-help skills and a desire to do things for themselves. Offer small utensils, pitchers, dishes, and other props in the water table, sandbox, and dramatic play area so toddlers can pretend and practice mealtime behaviors and self-help skills. Encourage them to take part in feeding themselves, dressing, handwashing, toileting, and toothbrushing so they can begin to develop lifelong healthy habits.

Introducing Health and Nutrition Throughout the Day

You do not have to plan special activities to introduce health concepts and practices to infants and toddlers. There are natural opportunities every day to help children begin to understand what you do to keep them healthy and how they can participate. Here are some suggestions:

Feeding and Eating

- Make sure that bottle feeding or nursing times are **quiet and relaxed** so infants will have pleasant associations with feeding.

- Offer fresh drinking water to all children frequently throughout the day.

- Use a **small spoon** when introducing solid foods so a baby can take a little bite, taste it, and pause before taking another. This helps a baby begin learning to tell when he is full.

- Give a mobile infant her **own spoon** so she can practice holding it, dipping into food, and getting the food into her mouth.

- Serve **soft, easy-to-swallow finger foods** that are broken into small pieces, so infants can begin to learn to feed themselves.

- Use **sippy cups** with lids and spouts. At first, put a little water in the bottom; then gradually add more water and eventually juice or milk. Expect infants to explore this interesting new item.

- Invite toddlers **to help prepare healthy snacks and meals** so they can learn what foods are good for them. With your guidance, toddlers can rinse apples, mash potatoes, tear lettuce leaves, sprinkle cheese on a muffin pizza, spread apple butter on a cracker, or whisk egg and milk together for French toast. Set up food preparation activities with plenty of room and utensils so children don't have to share or wait for too long to take part.

- Serve **family-style meals** using large bowls or platters. Provide serving utensils and small, covered pitchers so that toddlers can serve their own foods and drinks. Eat with children to model healthy eating practices. Talk about the foods being served: how they look, taste, and smell, and how they build strong bodies.

- **Accept messes,** because they are unavoidable when infants and toddlers are learning to eat and drink. Provide mobile infants and toddlers with materials (paper towels and sponges, for example) and encouragement so they can help clean up spills.

Toothbrushing

- **Brush your teeth** while children brush theirs. Explain in simple terms how to brush up and down and why brushing helps teeth stay strong and healthy.

- Wipe babies' gums with a clean cloth; brush teeth that have erupted with a soft brush and a pea-sized dot of toothpaste.

- Have older children **use their own brushes** and store them so they can air dry without touching each other. Explain why this keeps them healthy.

Diapering

- In simple terms, describe your actions and explain how you are keeping children healthy. Infants may not understand everything you say, but **they will learn that what you are doing is important.**

- Let toddlers **participate,** by such things as holding and handing you a clean diaper, telling you what to do next, and washing their hands.

Toileting

- Let children **do as much as they can on their own.** For example, they might decide when they need to use the toilet, pull their pants up and down, wipe with toilet paper, and wash and dry their hands.

Going outdoors

- Let older children **use their self-help skills** to put on and take off outdoor clothing.

- In simple terms, explain that **dressing appropriately for the weather** helps people stay healthy. Discuss how hats, gloves, and coats help us stay warm on cool days, and point out that boots keep feet dry and cozy on wet days.

- Encourage children to **drink plenty of water** and **play in the shade** as much as possible on hot days.

Playing

- Provide baby dolls, blankets, bottles, and related props so older infants and toddlers can **pretend and practice self-help skills.** Engage children in conversations about what they are doing.

- Lead children in handwashing **before and after water play.** Offer dolls and rubber animals to wash with soap and water. Talk about parts of the body.

Reading and writing stories

- **Read books** about healthy practices with children. Here are a few examples:

    - going to the doctor: *Going to the Doctor* by Ann Civardi

    - exercising: *From Head to Toe* by Eric Carle

    - toothbrushing: *Brush Your Teeth Please* by Leslie McGuire

    - eating: *Breakfast Time* by Julia Noonan

    - toilet learning: *Uh Oh! Gotta Go!: Potty Tales from Toddlers* by Bob McGrath

- **Write and illustrate** a book or make laminated photo cards about a daily routine or activity, such as *The Day We Made Fruit Salad* or *Step by Step, We Wash Our Hands*.

Involving families

- Tell families about what you do to keep children healthy. Focus on **practices they can do at home**, such as handwashing, caring for gums and teeth, and serving finger foods.

- Share information with families about their child's **growing self-help skills** so they can encourage the child to use them at home.

what's next?

Skill-Building Journal, section **2-7** (*Learning Activity C*) and section **2-1** (*Feedback*).

Learning Activities

LEARNING ACTIVITY

D. Recognizing and Reporting the Signs of Child Abuse and Neglect

In this activity you will learn to

- recognize the signs of possible child abuse and neglect

- report suspected cases of child abuse and neglect in accordance with state and local laws

Child abuse and neglect are any behavior of an adult who is responsible for the care and well-being of a child or youth under age 18 that causes physical or emotional harm to the child. Abuse and neglect can result from an act—doing something to cause harm—or an omission—not taking action to protect a child. Abuse and neglect can involve a single incident, such as burning a toddler's hand, or a pattern of behavior that continues over time, such as failing to give a child sufficient food or love and attention.

Teachers play a key role in identifying signs of possible abuse or neglect.

It is very likely that, at some time in your career, you will care for a child who has been abused or neglected. Teachers play two key roles in preventing and stopping child abuse and neglect. First, because they care for children daily, they may identify signs of possible abuse or neglect that would otherwise go unnoticed. Second, all states require teachers to report their suspicions of abuse and neglect in accordance with state and local laws.

There is no typical profile of adults who mistreat children. They live in cities, suburbs, and rural areas. They are of both genders and come from a variety of cultures, ethnic backgrounds, and socioeconomic groups. They may be relatives, neighbors, family friends, teachers, support staff, and strangers.

There are physical and behavioral signs of child abuse and neglect.

Children may exhibit physical and/or behavioral signs of their abuse and neglect. Physical signs, whether mild or severe, are those you can actually see, such as bruises or broken bones. Behavioral clues, ranging from subtle changes to extreme withdrawal or fear, may by present with or without physical signs. Clues may be found in the way a child looks and acts, what a parent or other responsible adult says, or how she relates to the child. They may be seen in the way a child and adult behave when they are together. No single sign or clue proves abuse or neglect, but repeated signs or several signs together indicate the **possibility** of abuse or neglect.

In federal, state, and local laws, most definitions of child abuse and neglect cover four types of maltreatment. Descriptions and signs of each type follow.

Physical Abuse

Physical abuse includes nonaccidental physical injuries caused by an adult in single or repeated episodes. Sometimes physical abuse is intentional, such as when an adult burns, kicks, bites, punches, hits, twists, shakes, or otherwise harms a child. Such injuries can be the result of inappropriate physical punishment, such as when an angry or frustrated adult lashes out at a child. Physical abuse can cause minor injuries such as cuts and bruises, or major injuries such as brain damage and broken limbs. It can hinder a child's healthy social/emotional development and leave emotional problems that last into adulthood.

Notice where the injury is located on the child's body.

Active young children sometimes fall down and bump into things. These accidents may cause injuries to their elbows, chins, noses, foreheads, and other bony areas. Bruises and marks on the soft tissue of the face, back, neck, buttocks, upper arms, thighs, backs of legs, or genitals, however, are more likely to be the result of physical abuse. Another sign to look for is bruises at various stages of healing, as if they resulted from more than one incident. When changing a diaper or helping a child take off a shirt, you might see bruises or burns that were covered by clothing. An adult might try to cover the signs of abuse by dressing the child in long sleeves or long pants, even when lightweight clothes are appropriate for the weather.

Injuries to a young child's abdomen or head, which are particularly vulnerable spots, are often undetected until symptoms appear. Abdominal injuries can cause swelling, tenderness, and vomiting. Head injuries can cause swelling, dizziness, blackouts, retinal detachment, and even death. Shaken baby syndrome results when an infant or young child is shaken violently. Very young children have large heads, weak neck muscles, and fragile brains and blood vessels. Shaking can cause hemorrhaging of the brain and eyes and lead to mental retardation, blindness, deafness, and even death.

Young children might also exhibit behavioral signs of physical abuse. Here are some examples:

- When a 6-month-old wakes up in his crib, he always lies quietly for a long time and never cries or seeks attention.

- The parents of a 17-month-old take turns picking him up from the center. When his mother arrives, he is excited to see her. When his father comes, he screams and hides his face.

- Every time a toddler hears another child crying, she runs to get her blanket. She clutches it and rocks back and forth, saying, "No hitting. No hitting."

- Why might a baby lie quietly in his crib, instead of seeking attention?

- Why might a mobile infant scream and hide when his father picks him up?

- Why might a toddler get upset when another child cries?

Sexual Abuse

Sexual abuse includes a wide range of contacts or interactions in which a child is used for the sexual stimulation of an adult or older child. It includes intercourse, rape, sodomy, fondling a child's genitals, exhibitionism, incest, and commercial exploitation through pornographic pictures or films.

Signs of possible sexual abuse can be physical and/or behavioral.

The physical signs of sexual abuse include some that a teacher would notice during diapering or toileting. For example, while helping a child use the bathroom, you might see torn, stained, or bloody underclothing, or bruised or bleeding genitals or anal area. If a child says it hurts to walk or sit, or complains of pain or itching in the genital area, take note and watch to see if this is a recurring condition.

Children who have been sexually abused may also show behavioral signs. They might be very afraid of specific places, such as the bathroom or a bed; show excessive curiosity about sexual activities; or repeatedly touch adults on the breast or genitals. Sometimes children act out their abuse using dolls or talk with others about sexual acts. Their premature sexual knowledge can mean they have been exposed to sexual activity.

Here are some examples of signs that a young child might be a victim of sexual abuse:

- For several weeks, an older toddler has had trouble settling down at nap time. When she does fall asleep, she sometimes wakes up crying about monsters. Today, she whispers to her teacher, "Gary says we have a secret. I don't want to have a secret." Gary is her 12-year-old brother.

- A child who has just turned two years old says she has to go to the bathroom. When a new teacher offers to take her, the child asks, "Will you take a picture of my bottom?" The adult responds, "What do you mean?" The child says, "Like Mr. B. did."

- Why might a toddler have trouble sleeping or talk about secrets?

- Why might a toddler ask someone if she will take a picture of her bottom?

Physical Neglect

Physical neglect is failing to provide a child with adequate or proper food, shelter, clothing, health care, supervision, or education, when the responsible person has resources to meet these needs. Neglect tends to be chronic, an ongoing pattern of behavior, but it can also be a single incident, such as being deliberately scalded by hot water. The National Child Abuse and Neglect Data System reported that, in 2002, more than one-third (38 percent) of child maltreatment fatalities were associated with neglect alone.[20] Some neglected children suffer from malnutrition, chronic illness, or high levels of stress. Neglectful families often appear to have many problems that they cannot handle.

Signs of neglect include poor hygiene, inappropriate clothing for weather conditions, and inattention to health needs. Also, developmental disorders, such as being extremely small for his or her age, might indicate that a child is neglected.

Neglect can be an ongoing pattern of behavior.

When considering the possibility of neglect, it is important to look for patterns. Do the signs of neglect occur rarely or frequently? Are they chronic (present almost every day), periodic (after weekends or absences), or episodic (for example, seen twice when the child's mother was in the hospital)?

Here are some examples of signs that a young child might be a victim of physical neglect:

- A teacher talks with the mother of a 4-month-old about her son's severe diaper rash. The mother says, "I'll bring you some of that greasy ointment. If you have time to use it, go ahead." The teacher applies the ointment all week, and the rash goes away. She sends the tube home over the weekend. On Monday, the child arrives with the rash again, so the teacher asks the mother to send more ointment. This pattern is repeated for several weeks.

- A toddler falls down and badly scrapes her knee. The center's nurse cleans and bandages it and prepares an accident report for the child's parents. Four days later, the child complains that her knee hurts. When the nurse rolls up the child's pants, she sees that the bandage has not been changed and the wound is now infected.

- Why might an infant's untreated diaper rash be a sign of possible neglect?

- Why might a toddler's uncared-for wound be a sign of possible neglect?

Emotional Abuse or Neglect

Emotional abuse or neglect includes intentionally blaming, belittling, ridiculing, and disparaging a child so as to cause low self-esteem, undue fear or anxiety, or other damage to the child's psychological well-being. It also includes passive or passive-aggressive inattention to emotional needs, nurturing, or psychological well-being. It is the most difficult form of maltreatment to identify because the signs are rarely physical and the effects may not show up for years. Also, the signs of emotional abuse are similar to those for emotional disturbance. Emotional abuse is almost always present with other types of maltreatment. The effects can last a lifetime.

Emotional abuse and neglect are the most difficult to identify.

Here are some examples of signs that a child might be a victim of emotional abuse or neglect:

- Each day when a mother comes to pick up her toddler, she makes fun of his efforts, saying such things as, "Another red picture? Is that the only color you can use?" and "How come you can't climb the ladder? Are your legs too short?"

- On a home visit, a teacher rings the doorbell and waits for someone to come to the door. She hears lots of noise inside: loud music, adults arguing, and children crying. She rings again, thinking they might not have heard her. Finally the door opens, and a man rushes past her. Inside, she sees a woman bent over and holding her stomach. Three young children stand in a doorway looking very scared.

- Why might a mother's repeated unkind comments about her child's efforts be a sign of possible emotional abuse or neglect?

- Why might spousal abuse in front of children be a sign of possible emotional abuse or neglect?

Picking Up Clues From Observations and Conversations

At daily drop-off and pick-up times, be alert for clues about possible abuse or neglect.

Early childhood programs are generally family-oriented, encouraging a great deal of formal and informal communication between teachers and families. You can gather important information from routine conversations with children and families. Young children enjoy talking about their families, so they may also share information about life at home. During daily drop-off and pick-up times and at scheduled conferences, family members describe family life, discuss discipline methods, or ask for help with problems. Conversations can provide clues to how a family member feels about a child. Be alert to possible signs of child abuse and neglect if the family member constantly

- blames or belittles the child ("You look like an idiot, sucking your big, fat thumb.")

- considers the child as being very different from his or her siblings ("His big sister Terry never caused me these problems. She always did exactly what I told her to do.")

- describes the child as being "bad," "evil," or a "monster" ("He's out to get me. He's just like his mother, and she was really evil.")

- finds nothing good or attractive about the child ("Some kids are just a pain in the neck. You can see this one doesn't have much going for her.")

- seems unconcerned about the child ("He was probably having a bad day. I don't have time to talk about it.")

- fails to keep appointments or refuses to discuss problems the child is having in the program ("That's what I pay you for! It's your job to make her behave.")

- misuses alcohol or other drugs

Isolation and extreme stress can lead to child abuse and neglect.

When you know a family well, you are in a better position to evaluate the seriousness of a problem. You can figure out whether it is a chronic condition or a temporary situation, a typical childhood problem the program and family can handle, or one that requires intervention. Family circumstances may also provide clues. The risk of abuse or neglect increases when families are isolated from friends, neighbors, and other family members, or if there is no apparent support system to which a family can turn in a crisis. Marital, economic, emotional, or social crises are among the causes of family stress that can lead to abuse or neglect.

Abuse and neglect can occur in a child care program.

You may find it hard to imagine that child abuse and neglect can take place at a child care center, but it does happen. Thinking about this possibility might make you feel as though you are suspicious of your colleagues or that your supervisors will be spying on teachers. However, you are responsible for keeping children safe and healthy. One important way to do this is to be alert to the possibility of child abuse and neglect right at your center.

Many of the physical and behavioral signs described earlier also apply to abuse and neglect in child care. The examples below are additional signs that warn of possible abuse or neglect in a child care setting:

A child

- refuses to participate in activities supervised by a particular teacher

- shows extreme fear of a particular staff member

- states that he or she has been hurt by a teacher

A teacher

- spends long periods of time out of sight with one child

- takes unscheduled breaks without telling his or her colleagues

- says a child is "bad," "spoiled," or "needs to be taught a lesson"

- shows favoritism and gives one child special attention and treats

- holds a child often, although the child seems tense and tries to get away

If you see any of these signs or others that cause you to suspect the possibility of child abuse or neglect, discuss your observations with your supervisor.

Understand the difference between nurturing children and possible child abuse.

There are situations in which teachers fear that hugging a child or letting a child sit on his or her lap could be viewed as child sexual abuse. Children's safety in the program is certainly the most important concern. However, program supervisors must support staff members' ability to perform their jobs, and that includes comforting and nurturing children in appropriate ways. All staff and family members should be aware of program policies regarding child nurturance. Talk with your supervisor if you have questions or concerns about how you may respond to children in caring ways.

Reporting Child Abuse and Neglect

All teachers are legally obligated to report suspected abuse and neglect.

In every state and the District of Columbia, teachers are mandated reporters, which means that you have a legal obligation to report suspected child abuse and neglect. In addition, you have an ethical and professional responsibility to know, understand, and follow the reporting requirements and procedures of your state, community, and program.

Each state law specifies one (or more) agencies to receive reports of suspected child abuse and neglect. Often reports are made to the Department of Social Services; the Department of Human Resources; the Division of Family and Children's Services; or Child Protective Services of the city, county, or state government. In some states, the police department also receives reports. Some states require either a written or an oral report. Others require an immediate oral report, followed by a written report within 24–48 hours. Check your state law for specific requirements. The National Clearinghouse on Child Abuse and Neglect Information (http://nccanch.acf.hhs.gov/) maintains current online reports on state statutes.

Most states require reporters to provide the following information:

- child's name, age, and address

- the location where the child can be found (for example, at the center)

- parent's or guardian's name and address

- nature and extent of the injury or condition observed

- reporter's name and location (sometimes not required but very useful for the agency conducting the investigation)

Most programs have established policies defining the duties and responsibilities of all staff members in reporting child abuse and neglect. If you don't have a copy of your program's child abuse and neglect reporting procedures, ask your director for one.

Overcoming Barriers to Reporting

You do not have to prove your suspicions.

When you suspect child abuse or neglect, you may be very reluctant to file a report. Some teachers find that their personal feelings are a barrier to reporting child abuse or neglect. They prefer not to get involved or convince themselves that there is a perfectly good explanation for the child's injuries or behavior. They may fear that parents, their supervisor, and their colleagues will think that they are incompetent or alarmist.

Another potential barrier to reporting is the special relationship between a teacher and a family or between two colleagues. When teachers observe signs of abuse or neglect, they may give family members or colleagues the benefit of the doubt. Sometimes, they expect the family member or colleague to be hostile, indignant, or distressed, or to retaliate by filing a lawsuit. People who are required by law to report their suspicions are not responsible for legal damages if they made the report with good intentions, even if investigators decide that abuse and neglect are not involved. If you are sued, the case will be dismissed when the court learns that you are required by law to file a report.

Your primary responsibility is to protect children.

Regardless of why you might feel uneasy about reporting, you have legal and professional responsibilities to protect children and to support their families. By reporting your suspicions to the appropriate authorities, you are actively protecting children and beginning the helping process. In addition, you are helping families (or your colleagues) get the assistance they need to change their behavior. Focus on your responsibility to report your suspicions. Remember, your report is not an accusation and you are not required to have proof or to conduct an investigation.

Getting Ready to Report

When you suspect that a child is being abused or neglected, file your report as soon as possible. Obviously, this is not a pleasant task. You will probably feel at risk, confused, and generally uncomfortable. It helps to organize your thoughts and secure the support you will need when the report is filed. Here are steps to follow as you prepare to report.

Reporting Child Abuse and Neglect

Document your suspicions:

1   Review your observation notes and anecdotal records.

2.   Identify what caused you to suspect abuse or neglect. List the physical and behavioral signs you have observed.

3.   Describe the interactions you observed between the family member (or a colleague) and the child. Include examples of the person's lack of interest in the child or of the adult's speaking badly of the child, if observed.

4.   Discuss with your colleagues the physical and behavioral signs you have documented. If they suspect abuse or neglect, discuss their reasons.

Secure support:

5.   Ask your supervisor what support he or she will provide after you file the report and what the program will do if the family tries to remove the child.

6.   Set up a support system so you can talk with others about your feelings and concerns without breaching confidentiality.

File the report:

7.   Review the program's reporting policy.

8.   Collect the information needed to file the initial report.

9.   Look up the phone number and address of the agency to which you will report (or ask your director for the information).

10.   Obtain forms or use letterhead or blank paper, if a written report is required.

11.   Make your oral and/or written report.

12.   Notify your supervisor that you have filed the report.

13.   Consult with your supervisor about whether and how to notify the child's parents or guardians that you have filed a report.

14.   Use your support system.

In some cases, you will not be able to complete all of these steps because the seriousness of the case requires you to report your suspicions immediately.

Offer support to the child and family.

You and your program might decide to notify the child's parents or guardians that you filed a report. The conversation will be difficult. Maintain a professional tone while describing **what** you reported ("repeated incidences of cigarette burns on Carl's arm"), **when** ("this morning"), and **to whom** ("Child Protective Services"). Explain that you have carried out your legal, professional, and ethical responsibilities to report your suspicions and are not involved in investigating or proving the case. In addition, offer the family support as they deal with this difficult situation. They may not accept your gesture immediately, but it is important to let them know you are not judging anyone. Instead, you have reported signs of possible abuse so their child and the family can get the help they need.

Your report might not receive a response.

In some states and local jurisdictions, the agency that receives reports of child abuse and neglect is so overwhelmed that they cannot respond to every case. Internal agency policies may require the staff to respond first to cases that are life-threatening or extremely clear-cut. You may not see action after you file a report. If this happens, continue supporting the child and family and advocating for them to receive needed services. Stay alert to physical and behavioral signs of abuse or neglect. If necessary, file a second or even third report. Some states have a child abuse and neglect hotline. Find out if there is one in your state, and use it if necessary.

what's next?

Skill-Building Journal, section **2-8** (*Learning Activity D*), section **2-10** (*Answer Sheets*), section **2-1** (*Feedback*), and section **2-9** (*Reflecting on Your Learning*).

3

Learning Environment

Overview

Creating Indoor and Outdoor Spaces That Support Relationships and Encourage Exploration

Selecting and Arranging Equipment and Materials That Promote Development and Learning

Planning Daily Routines and a Flexible Schedule That Meet Each Child's Needs

Your Own Responses to the Environment

Learning Activities

A. Using Your Knowledge of Infants and Toddlers to Create a Responsive and Supportive Environment

B. Creating and Maintaining the Caregiving Environment

C. Selecting and Displaying Toys and Materials

D. Planning Daily Routines and a Flexible Schedule

3. Learning Environment

A well-designed environment helps you get to know and respond to children.

An early childhood environment includes the indoor and outdoor spaces where you care for children; the schedule and routines; and the teachers and children who spend their days together. When it is well-designed, attractive, comfortable, and flexible, the environment allows you and the children to enjoy being together. A supportive environment encourages play and learning and assures children that what they do is important to you.

Both indoors and outdoors, it is important to furnish and organize the environment to meet the needs of children and adults. A room for infants and toddlers might have such things as a comfortable chair for feeding and relating to infants, a low table and chairs for using crayons or eating, cribs and cots or mats for sleeping, open areas for pushing and pulling wheeled toys, and a four- or six-seat wagon for taking trips to the park.

A good outdoor environment has hard and soft surfaces, shady and sunny areas, and safe places to play. Ideally, the outdoor area is easy to get to: right outside your room or adjacent to the center. It is a place where children can stretch their muscles; breathe fresh air; take in the sunshine; and enjoy the smells, sights, and sounds of nature.

A variety of play materials supports development in all areas.

Infants and toddlers need a variety of play materials to support all areas of development. Materials include some typically found at home, such as plastic dishes; some made by staff, such as jingle-bell socks; and some from a reputable supplier, such as washable rattles and clutch balls. See *Learning Activity C, Selecting and Displaying Toys and Materials*, for a list of good toys and play materials for infants and toddlers.

Adjust your schedule and routines when necessary to meet the needs of each child.

The days tend to go more smoothly when you follow a simple, flexible schedule and plan routines based on children's needs and abilities. Many events, such as arrival and going outdoors, typically occur at about the same time each day, but a strict schedule will not allow you to meet children's needs. You and your colleagues can adjust the way you do things to meet the needs of individual children and the group.

You can establish and maintain a responsive and supportive environment by

- creating indoor and outdoor spaces that support relationships and encourage exploration

- selecting and arranging equipment and materials that promote development and learning

- planning daily routines and a flexible schedule that meet each child's needs

---

Creating Indoor and Outdoor Spaces That Support Relationships and Encourage Exploration

1. **Establish areas for different kinds of play and for diapering, feeding, and other routines.** Arrange each area so that teachers can address children's needs and support exploration and development.

2. **Create a relaxed, homelike atmosphere.** Personalize the space with family photographs; colorful, textured curtains; washable throw rugs with non-skid backing; a vase with fresh flowers; and small lamps in place of overhead fluorescent lights.

3. **Include open areas where children can safely move and explore.** Provide soft surfaces for crawling and washable floors for painting and eating areas, ramps and vinyl-covered foam wedges that offer different heights, and sturdy furniture and railings to support infants as they practice standing and walking.

4. **Make changes to the environment, if necessary, to support children with disabilities.** For example, widen pathways to accommodate the special equipment of a child with an orthopedic disability.

5. **Arrange the outdoor area to support a variety of activities.** Designate separate places for activities such as running and kicking balls, experiencing the world while lying on blankets, riding tricycles, and digging in sand.

It's Time to Get Organized

As you read the following story, pay attention to what Mr. Lewis and Ms. Bates learned by observing the children outdoors and how they reorganized the outdoor play area.

Mr. Lewis: Whoops! I'll help you fill the watering can again. I think we need more space here.

Ms. Bates: I think it's time to reorganize the outdoor shed. The children are frustrated because they can't get the toys and equipment.

Mr. Lewis: I agree. Let's also rearrange the area so children don't get in each other's way.

Ms. Bates: Our outdoor play area is much more fun now. We can do lots of different things.

Selecting and Arranging Equipment and Materials That Promote Development and Learning

6. **Provide materials that include the cultures and languages of the children and their families.** These might be such things as books, pictures, and music.

7. **Provide a variety of open-ended materials that can be used safely in different ways.** Offer books, pots and pans, blocks, rattles, trucks, dolls, balls, push toys, and other items that support a range of skill levels and promote various kinds of play and learning.

8. **Offer materials that encourage children to use their senses.** Supply texture balls and books to touch; bells, rattles, and music to hear; and mirrors and mobiles to look at.

9. **Arrange play materials so children can find and return them on their own.** Store toys on low, open shelves that are labeled with pictures and words to show where things belong.

10. **Display materials so children can choose them without being overwhelmed or frustrated.** Place toys on shelves with space between each item, and provide duplicates of favorite items.

The Wonder of Everyday Materials

As you read the following story, pay attention to the way Ms. Bates involves Zora's family in the program by inviting them to share household play materials.

Ms. Bates: Hi, Ms. Trent. Zora had a great day. She filled the shopping cart with pretend food and strolled around the room.

Ms. Trent: That sounds like fun! Do you need more throwaways for the children to play with?

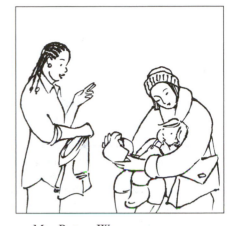

Ms. Bates: We can use some replacements. Do you have any egg cartons?

Ms. Trent: I'll check when we get home.

Ms. Bates: Goodbye. See you tomorrow.

Mr. Trent: We found some egg cartons at home.

Ms. Bates: Thank you. The children will enjoy these.

Planning Daily Routines and a Flexible Schedule That Meet Each Child's Needs

11. **Allow ample time for completing daily routines.** Use feeding, diapering, dressing, and other routines as opportunities for building relationships with individual children and for encouraging self-help skills.

12. **Follow a consistent but flexible schedule that can be adapted to respond to individual and group needs.** "Adam is still sleepy. Should I stay with him and some of the other children while you take the others for a walk?"

13. **Plan time each day for the children to be outdoors.** Take the children outdoors at least twice a day, for 30–45 minutes each time.

14. **Help each child relax and feel comfortable at naptime.** "Thank you for your suggestion. Lovette has a much easier time going to sleep now that I softly sing her special song."

15. **Communicate often with families about their children.** Every day, share information with families about what their child explored and noticed, as well as the child's patterns for sleeping, eating, diapering/toileting, and playing.

Jon and Peter Take a Nap

As you read the following story, pay attention to how Ms. Gonzalez and Mr. Lewis adapt the daily schedule to respond to Jon and Peter.

10:15 a.m.

Mr. Lewis: Jon often rubs his eyes when he is tired.

Ms. Gonzalez: His dad said they were up several times last night.

10:20 a.m.

Mr. Lewis: Peter is usually the first one ready to go.

Ms. Gonzalez: That's right. Maybe he is tired, too.

10:30 a.m.

Ms. Gonzalez: Have a good walk, everyone. I'm going to stay here today so Jon and Peter can sleep.

10:45 a.m.

Ms. Gonzalez: Hush, little Peter, don't say a word.

11:00 a.m.

11:30 a.m.

what's next?

Skill-Building Journal, section **3-2** (*Overview*), section **3-10** (*Answer Sheets*), and section **3-1** (*Feedback*).

Your Own Responses to the Environment

We are not always aware of how our environment is affecting us.

We all respond to our environments. Our surroundings affect our feelings, comfort level, behavior, and ability to accomplish tasks. Consider how you feel and act in the following situations.

- You are standing in a hot, crowded bus or subway, sandwiched between strangers. Perhaps you pull your shoulders in, try to avoid any contact with others, and count the minutes until you get off.

- You are eating in a special restaurant with a favorite friend. The lights are low, and the noise level is muffled. The food smells delicious, and photographs of beautiful places hang on the walls. You are probably relaxed, enjoying the conversation, and savoring each bite.

- You are preparing a meal in an unfamiliar kitchen. You may be very frustrated, because you cannot figure out how the kitchen is organized. You spend lots of time looking for the things you need. You may not cook as well as usual.

It is easy to see in these examples how our environment can affect actions and feelings, but the influence of our surroundings is not always so clear. Your work environment should help you provide high quality care. An effective environment makes your job easier and more enjoyable. When people describe their favorite place, they often identify

- a quiet place to be alone

- a soft and comfortable place to stretch out

- a place where music is playing or only the sounds of nature are heard

- a bright and sunny place with clean air

- a colorful and attractive place

Try to find ways to incorporate the features you like best, inside and outdoors. A comfortable environment for young children makes them want to be there and engages them in learning.

what's next?

Skill-Building Journal, section **3-3** (*Your Own Responses to the Environment*), section **3-1** (*Feedback*), and section **3-4** (*Pre-Training Assessment*).

Caring for Infants & Toddlers

Learning Activities

LEARNING ACTIVITY

A. Using Your Knowledge of Infants and Toddlers to Create a Responsive and Supportive Environment

In this activity you will learn to

- recognize some typical behaviors of infants and toddlers

- use what you know about infants and toddlers to create a responsive and supportive environment

Young infants (birth–8 months) use their senses to explore the world.

When people think of an environment for infants and toddlers, they often envision an arrangement that is similar to a preschool room. However, children of this age group have unique needs because of their typical developmental characteristics. Knowing what infants and toddlers are like at each stage of development will help you create a safe, comfortable environment that supports and challenges them.

- Sammy (3 months) reaches for the terrycloth bunny when his teacher makes it dance near his hands.

- Jon (6 months) creeps across the carpet and pats his image in the safety mirror mounted near the bottom of the wall.

- Luci (8 months) waves bye-bye when her daddy leaves for work.

Adults and other children are much more interesting to an infant than expensive toys. Infants and toddlers depend on you to respond to their efforts to communicate and to appreciate their growing skills. When they smile, you smile back. When they coo and gurgle, you join in. When they wave their arms or kick their legs, you share their excitement. When infants roll over, you notice, share this accomplishment with colleagues and family members, and remember to place them in protected places where they can safely practice moving.

Young infants are active explorers who use their senses to learn about the world. They look, listen, touch, and put everything they can reach in their mouths. Hang a tinkling wind chime over the changing table, touch it lightly, and watch a young infant track and respond to its movements. It is easier for young infants to focus on objects if they are placed on a plain background. For example, it is easier for a young infant to focus on a rattle when it is placed on a solidly colored blanket instead of a plaid blanket.

Once infants can hold objects and explore more actively, their toys and materials should be chewable, washable, and easy to grasp. To encourage exploration and learning, offer toys and materials that infants can move or use to make noises. As you observe infants, you will see them experiment to see what effect they can have on people and things. "If I smile at Ms. Bates, will she smile at me?" "If I kick my legs, will the bell jingle again?"

Mobile infants (8–18 months) are developing and using new motor skills.

- Malou (9 months) bangs two small blocks together.

- Peter (12 months) pushes a shopping cart in the outdoor play area.

- Zora (16 months) points to a familiar object in a picture book and asks, "Puppy?"

Mobile infants can move around on their hands and knees and may be learning to walk and climb. This ability to crawl and then walk from one place to another opens up their world. They are eager to investigate and explore everything they can reach.

Mobile infants often move by pulling themselves up and holding onto furniture or railings. When standing, they can see what is on top of shelves and tables. If items look interesting or are just in the way, mobile infants are likely to push them to the floor. It is essential to keep the environment safe so that mobile infants are free to explore and learn.

Mobile infants are also developing other new motor skills. You can support these skills by offering things to stack, fill and dump, push and pull, and fit together. When their standing and walking abilities develop, they will be ready for ride-on toys, low climbers, and large trucks.

As they get older, mobile infants develop many complex skills. They learn to hold a crayon and scribble on paper, build a tower of three or four blocks, say several words and understand many more, pretend to talk on the phone, and cooperate when getting dressed. As they gain and refine small motor skills, they begin to feed themselves by picking up finger foods, holding and drinking from sippy cups, and eventually grasping spoons.

Toddlers (18–36 months) are expanding skills in all areas.

- Lovette (20 months) bangs on a drum while listening to a snappy march.

- Ricky (28 months) and Adam (30 months) crawl through a tunnel their teacher made from cardboard boxes.

- Jessica (34 months) plays a simple homemade lotto game with Ms. Ellie, the foster grandmother who volunteers in her program.

Young toddlers (about 18–24 months) are by far the most mobile children in your care. They move very quickly and try to get into all areas of the environment. Everything they do is an opportunity for learning. They continue to learn through their senses, explore and manipulate objects with their hands, and watch what others are doing. All of this movement supports learning, as toddlers expand their understanding of cause and effect and begin to make sense of concepts such as size, shape, and weight.

Between 30–36 months, toddlers slow down a bit and expand their ability to sustain what they are doing. They are likely to stop for a while in their travels to thumb through a storybook, play dress-up, or put pegs in a pegboard. Toddlers' fine motor skills are quite well-developed. They like to explore and create with art materials such as playdough, paint, and crayons. Sand and water play are other favorite activities.

In addition, toddlers' language skills are growing. Most toddlers understand more than they can say. Nevertheless, they can make themselves understood with words and actions when interacting with adults and peers.

Toddlers enjoy pretend play, whether conducting an imaginary phone conversation with grandma or moving a block across the floor while saying, "Vrroom. Vrroom." As they get older, they engage in dramatic play using simple props such as hats, tote bags, and dolls.

The following list summarizes key characteristics and events in the development of young infants, mobile infants, and toddlers. These aspects of development affect the way you create a responsive and supportive environment.

Development of Infants and Toddlers

Young infants (birth–8 months)

- feel most secure at home with their families

- use all of their senses to learn about the world

- coo, babble, and smile on their own initiative and in response to others

- reach for and pick up objects

- distinguish familiar from unfamiliar things and events

- stretch their legs and kick

- sit, at first using their hands for support and then without support

- begin creeping and crawling

Mobile infants (8–18 months)

- creep and then crawl, from one place to another

- pull up to standing, cruise by holding furniture or railings, and eventually begin to walk

- sit on the floor or ground and in chairs

- put things in and take them out of containers

- learn about objects by handling them and watching other use them

- sometimes need to get away from the group to be alone or with a special person

- begin simple forms of pretend play

- understand and practice using language

Toddlers (18–36 months)

- walk steadily and smoothly

- try to throw and catch

- run, jump, and hop

- manipulate objects with hands and fingers and are developing eye-hand coordination

- become increasingly aware of possessions and may struggle with sharing

- make simple decisions

- are learning to use the toilet on their own

- enjoy playing with other children

what's next?

Skill-Building Journal, section **3-5** (*Learning Activity A*), section **3-10** (*Answer Sheets*), and section **3-1** (*Feedback*).

LEARNING
ACTIVITY

Learning Activities

B. Creating and Maintaining the Caregiving Environment

In this activity you will learn to

- organize separate areas for different routines and activities

- arrange the environment to support each child's development and interests

Form follows function.

When architects design a building, they begin by thinking about the *function*: what people will do in the space. Next, they apply their artistic and engineering expertise to create the *form*: how the building will be organized, what it will look like, and how it will make people feel. Louis Sullivan, a famous American architect, coined the phrase "form follows function" to describe this approach to design. It is a useful way to think about creating an environment for infants and toddlers.

You considered the function of an infant/toddler environment in *Learning Activity A* while reviewing typical developmental characteristics of infants and toddlers and describing how teachers respond. You probably noticed that much of your day is spent in routines: saying hello and goodbye, preparing and eating food, napping, diapering and toileting, and dressing. During the rest of the day, infants and toddlers engage in simple activities such as moving from one place to another, exploring toys and materials, and playing with a teacher.

A well-planned environment benefits children, families, and teachers.

The next step is to think about form: How can you create an environment that supports children, families, and teachers? Children, families, and teachers benefit from a well-planned environment:

- Children with a range of developmental skills, varied interests, and specific abilities and disabilities gain a sense of trust and security, which encourages exploration and learning.

- Families feel welcome and are reassured because they find a warm, inviting place that respects their cultures and each child's unique characteristics.

- Teachers have a pleasant and efficient work environment that supports them as they provide individualized care for infants and toddlers.

The entrance area welcomes children and families.

You can start by thinking about the rooms in a home where infant and toddler routines and activities take place. Then arrange your infant/toddler environment with comparable spaces: an entrance area, a place for sleeping, areas for diapering and toileting, and indoor and outdoor play areas. Including as many homelike touches as possible will help create a relaxed atmosphere. A description of this type of arrangement follows.

Many infant/toddler rooms have an **entrance area** with cubbies; a counter; a low bench; adult-size chairs; hooks and storage for adult belongings; and displays that welcome families, such as an attractive bulletin board or other message center with information in the families' home languages and English. Located near the door, it is where unhurried transitions take place as children, teachers, and families say hello and goodbye each morning and afternoon.

In the entrance area, you might observe

- families and teachers exchanging information through written daily logs stored on top of a counter

- adults helping children take off and put on their jackets, hats, and boots

- a father admiring a display of toddlers' fingerpainting

- a toddler taking his well-worn blanket out of his cubby

- a parent volunteer signing in and storing her coat and tote bag

- a teacher watering a plant placed on the top of a counter, out of children's reach

- children blowing kisses to their loved ones as they leave the room

The eating area is like a kitchen at home.

Teachers and children need an **eating area** with a washable floor, sink, counter, refrigerator, microwave oven (not used to heat bottles), 2–3 high chairs, a child-size table and chairs, and a private space with a comfortable chair where mothers may nurse their babies. Cupboards and drawers offer storage for clean-up tools, pots and pans, plastic bowls, spoons, pots, measuring cups, and child-size utensils. It is the place where teachers, often with children's help, store, prepare, eat, and clean up snacks and meals.

In the eating area, you might observe

- a mother putting labeled bottles of expressed milk in the refrigerator

- an infant seated in her high chair, squishing and tasting a piece of banana

- several toddlers stirring, peeling, pouring, and mixing while helping their teacher trying out a snack recipe provided by a child's grandmother

- children playing with pots and pans they found in a low cupboard

- a teacher warming a small bowl of strained apricots

- a toddler getting some paper towels to help wipe up a spill

The sleeping area is where children take naps during the day.

Infants and toddlers need a **sleeping area** with cribs and cots or mats, a comfortable chair, and pictures on the walls. The cribs are set up all the time because each infant has a personal schedule for sleeping. Cribs might have safety mirrors, family photographs, and mobiles (hung out of children's reach). Teachers bring out the cots or mats when needed by older mobile infants and toddlers and then store them during the rest of the day. This leaves plenty of room for active play. There is a place to store extra sheets and blankets.

In the sleeping area, you might observe

- several infants placed on their backs to sleep in assigned cribs

- a teacher rocking a fussy infant to sleep

- toddlers taking afternoon naps on their assigned cots

- a teacher helping a child relax by gently patting his back before putting him in his crib

The diapering/ toileting area encourages communication between children and adults.

Every day, children and teachers spend a lot of time in the **diapering/toileting area**. It is designed and equipped to meet the safety and health standards described in modules 1 and 2 and to allow teachers to use these routines to build relationships with individual children. There is a large, sturdy diapering table with interesting things to look at hanging overhead and nearby. The table has built-in steps, or there is a step stool, so toddlers can climb up when they need a diaper change. Bleach solution and other supplies are stored on a high shelf or in a closed cupboard, within reach of adults but out of the reach of children. Individual storage containers, labeled with each child's name, hold diapering supplies and extra clothes. Covered trash containers hold soiled throwaways.

This area, or a nearby bathroom, has child-size sinks to encourage handwashing and child-size toilets so older toddlers can learn to use them. Soap, paper towels, and waste baskets are placed within children's reach.

In the diapering/toileting area, you might observe

- a teacher pointing to an infant's image in a nearby mirror and then singing a made-up song to her while changing her diaper, "Feliz tiene ojos grandes color café y pelo ondulado color café" ("Feliz has big brown eyes and curly brown hair")

- an infant looking at herself in a large unbreakable mirror mounted on the wall behind the diapering table

- two toddlers standing on stools at the sink, their hands covered in soapsuds, while they discuss a nearby picture of a child washing his hands

- a mobile infant pulling off his socks and handing them to a teacher, who retrieves a clean pair from a labeled container nearby

- a toddler climbing the stairs to the diapering table, while a teacher stands next to him

- a teacher helping an older toddler change clothes after a toileting accident, "After we wash our hands, you may crawl through the tunnel with Kelli again"

The play area encourages exploration, relaxation, and learning.

Most of the time that children are awake, they are in a large **play area**. In this area, a large open section supports gross motor play and exploration. Other sections are arranged for children to spend time alone, in small groups, or with a teacher. Low, open shelves divide the area and provide space to display books, toys, and materials within children's reach. This area might double as the sleeping area for older mobile infants and toddlers. There are a few adult-size chairs so family members can observe and visit with their children.

Much of the area is carpeted, and there are mats and protected areas where infants can safely use their senses to take in their surroundings; kick their legs and wave their arms; and gradually learn to roll over, creep, and crawl. Ramps, carpeted platforms, or firm foam cushions take mobile infants to new levels. Strategically placed railings give mobile infants something to hold onto while learning to stand and walk. Toddlers have room and equipment for climbing, sliding, and stepping up and down; riding wheeled toys; crawling through cubes or boxes; tumbling on mats; and moving to music. Clear pathways are wide enough to accommodate a child who uses a wheelchair or other special equipment. Pathways lead children from one defined area to the next so they are less likely to get in each other's way.

For quiet activities there is a sofa or an overstuffed chair where children cuddle with adults or listen to a story. A large, comfortable chair is also ideal for feedings and one-on-one activities such as singing, reading stories, or doing fingerplays.

It is best if part of the play area has a washable floor and a small table and chairs. Older mobile infants and toddlers enjoy simple activities such as poking holes in playdough, scribbling on a piece of paper taped to the table, painting with one or two colors at low easels, filling and dumping containers with sand and water, and putting pegs in a pegboard.

For older toddlers, part of the play area might have a few simple interest areas such as housekeeping and blocks. A two-level play house or loft with stairs or a ramp sets the stage for many different kinds of toddler play. They feel powerful and strong when they climb to the top, even if the play house is only as high as the eye-level of a teacher. They also enjoy seeing the room and watching people from a different height.

In the play area, you might observe

- an infant leaning on his elbows and pushing himself up to look at a laminated photograph of his family

- a teacher saying, "These pretty pink roses are from my grandma's garden," as she lifts an infant so he can see and smell a vase of flowers on a high shelf

- a teacher reading to two toddlers sitting with her in a large, comfortable chair

- two toddlers putting their dolls to bed

- a mobile infant touching the textured panels on a "feely" wall

- several seated children, including a child in an Educube® chair, using combs, cups, scoops, and other props in individual dish pans filled with sand

- a visiting dad reading a sign that explains what he might see children doing and learning in the area

- a teacher and several toddlers dancing to music

The outdoor play area is used every day.

An **outdoor play area** is an essential part of an environment for infants and toddlers. Outdoors, children and adults feel free to move, make noise, climb, run, and use their large muscles. In addition, many activities enjoyed indoors can also be taken outdoors. An infant can lie on a blanket and reach for her toes or have a bottle while older children eat a picnic-style snack or lunch under a shady tree. Older mobile infants and toddlers can paint the side of the building with water. Everyone can sing a song or listen to a story. A good outdoor play area for infants and toddlers includes

- some natural materials such as trees, bushes, grass, vegetables, and flowers (all must be nonpoisonous)

- areas shaded by trees or shelters where children are protected from the sun

- different textures for children to touch and different levels on which to crawl and climb (small hills, ramps, flat areas, low climbers with platforms at different heights)

- a grassy, open area

- a variety of exploration and play opportunities for children with different skills, interests, and abilities

- safe places for young infants that are out of the way of children who crawl and walk

- smaller defined areas for activities such as sand and water play

- a lockable storage area large enough to hold wheeled toys, balls, and other outdoor materials and equipment

- a safe, hard surface for riding, pushing, and pulling wheeled toys such as tricycles, wagons, and doll carriages

In the outdoor play area, you might observe

- older mobile infants and toddlers reaching for colorful streamers tied to the fence and waving in the wind, and infants sitting nearby to watch the action

- a teacher giving three mobile infants a ride in a wagon

- a teacher and several children of various ages blowing, chasing, catching, and watching bubbles, each in her own way

- toddlers drawing with chalk on low easels

- a teacher rocking a child in a hammock swing

Teachers are the most important part of the environment. Like the family members who share a home, you and your colleagues are the most important part of the program environment. Infants and toddlers are building trusting relationships with the important adults in their lives. Your supportive interactions with individual children help them feel valued and loved. Your timely response in meeting their basic needs helps them learn that they can count on you and other people. This sense of security supports them as they experiment and explore.

what's next?

Skill-Building Journal, section **3-6** (*Learning Activity B*) and section **3-1** (*Feedback*).

LEARNING ACTIVITY

Learning Activities

C. Selecting and Displaying Toys and Materials

In this activity you will learn to

- select toys and materials that correspond to the families, cultures, languages, needs, skills, abilities, and interests of the infants and toddlers in your care

- display toys and materials in ways that invite infants and toddlers to explore and play

Choosing Toys and Materials

Toys and materials must be safe, healthy, interesting, and developmentally appropriate.

The toys and materials you provide for infants and toddlers must be safe and healthy. This means that they are free of hazards and durable enough to withstand frequent cleaning and sanitizing. Check the room daily and remove items with broken parts, missing pieces, chipped paint, splinters, or jagged edges. (See module 1, *Safe*, and module 2, *Healthy*, for more information on safe and healthy toys and materials.)

In addition, when selecting toys and materials for infants and toddlers, you and your colleagues can ask the following questions.

Will it interest and be developmentally appropriate for the infants and toddlers in our care? Good play materials offer challenges, but they are not so hard to use that they lead to frustration and distress. Because you must offer toys and materials for children with a wide range of abilities, you will need to observe closely to make sure individual children have access to toys that are appropriate for them. For a child with special needs, consult with the family and specialists to make sure you are providing toys and materials that support the child's involvement in the program and promote growth and development.

Does it relate to the children's families, cultures, and home languages? Include tapes and CDs, books, posters, photographs, dress-up clothes, dolls, wooden figures to use with blocks, and other items that let children and families feel valued and secure. Make sure the toys and materials reflect the diversity of our society and show people with disabilities engaged in meaningful, everyday activities. Families are a good resource to help you address this question.

Can it be used in many different ways? The term *open-ended* describes toys and materials that can be used in many different ways. There is no right or wrong way to explore items such as blocks, crayons and paper, and nesting cups, so they can be used by children with a wide range of interests and skill levels. As children build skills and discover new interests, they find new ways to use familiar toys and materials. For example, a young infant mouths the edge of a nesting cup, a mobile infant tries to fit the cups inside each other, and a toddler dumps and fills the cup with clothespins.

Does it help children feel secure? As discussed in the previous learning activity, infants and toddlers enjoy playing with familiar items that remind them of their families. Unbreakable measuring cups, plastic dishes and flatware, dress-up clothes, and homemade books and play materials help to create a familiar, comfortable environment.

Will it encourage children's growth and development? Infants and toddlers learn about their world by using their senses and moving from one place to another. Make sure your inventory of toys and materials introduces a variety of sounds, colors, and textures; lets children make their own discoveries; and encourages them to move their small and large muscles in different ways.

Collecting Play Materials

Provide a wide variety of toys and materials.

Although most early childhood programs work with limited budgets, you can provide a rich inventory of toys and materials. We have all heard about the child who opened a gift, ignored the expensive toy, and played with the box. Teachers and families can collect many good play materials for infants and toddlers. Young children will enjoy such things as

- dress-up clothes (clothing outgrown by older children is often just the right size)

- simple props for dramatic play (tote bags, phones, plastic dishes, pots and pans)

- household furnishings (plastic bottles, cups, bowls, and flatware)

- large cardboard boxes (children can push a box across the floor, climb in and out of a box, and crawl through several boxes taped together to form a tunnel)

- paper scraps (children build small motor skills by tearing paper and making collages)

- fabric pieces (invite a young infant to explore the textures of a collection of felt, corduroy, velveteen, wool, and cotton fabric scraps; make a "feely" panel to hang on a wall at children's height; provide small fabric scraps for collages)

Responding to Children's Changing Interests and Growing Skills

Observe continuously in order to respond to children's changing interests and skills.

Young children develop and change very quickly. A toy that was challenging last month might seem boring today. A piece of equipment that was safe in the past can become unsafe as children who crawl, walk, and climb become more skilled at moving around the room. You must observe continuously to see how children use toys and to determine whether they are still developmentally appropriate.

Choose toys and materials that provide both continuity and variety. Children need to find some items in the same place every day so they can build a sense of trust and security. It is also true that, without variety, children can become bored and they will have fewer opportunities to learn about new things. Add or rotate toys and materials in response to children's changing interests and growing skills and when you want to give children new experiences.

When you notice that particular toys are being ignored, try rotating some play materials. Put unused toys away and replace them with items that have been in storage. Chances are that the children will rediscover the fun of the toys that were in storage. After a few weeks, rotate some toys again. When you bring back the toys that were being ignored, the children will probably explore them as if they were brand new.

Providing Play Materials for Children With Special Needs

You may need to adapt toys and materials for children with special needs.

Your inventory of play materials should be appropriate for the abilities of the infants and toddlers in the group, including children with special needs, such as visual, hearing, or mobility impairments; developmental delays; or other conditions that affect their participation. Many toys that are developmentally appropriate for this age group are also appropriate for a child with special needs. However, you may need to adapt toys or provide items designed for children with a particular need.

Typically, a child with special needs receives the services of an early intervention specialist from the local school system. The child's family and the specialist can help you learn what items to purchase and how to make or adapt toys and materials to support the child.

A specialist such as an occupational or physical therapist might make suggestions such as these:

- Use bolsters, wedges, or platforms to increase the comfort of children with mobility impairments so they can stack blocks, roll small trucks, make marks on paper, and play with other toys.

- Thicken brush handles and crayons by applying Velcro® strips or several layers of masking tape to help a child who has trouble grasping and holding them.

- Adjust the height of tables and easels so a child in a wheelchair can use them.

- Mount a planter on legs and provide hand tools so a child with mobility impairments can participate in gardening activities.

- Make tapes of interesting sounds—meowing cats, ocean waves, trucks rolling by, chirping birds—to provide sensory stimulation.

- Glue spools or short pieces of dowels to puzzle pieces so they are easier to grasp.

- Glue foam pieces to the corners of pages, to make them easier to turn.

- Glue magnetic strips on toys; then put them on a metal cookie tray where they will stay in place.

Organizing and Displaying Toys and Materials

Organizing and displaying toys and materials are important parts of creating an environment for infants and toddlers. Children can make choices when they are able to see what is available, and they can begin to help clean up when it is clear where things belong.

Arrange toys and materials so that children can make choices and begin to help clean up.

Here are some suggestions:

- Display toys and materials on low, open shelves so children can play with them safely and independently.

- Limit the number of toys and materials displayed at one time so children can make selections without being overwhelmed by too many choices.

- Display toys on a surface with a single, neutral color and leave space between each item. This allows children easily to see what is available so they can make choices.

- Label shelves and containers with pictures and words. Use photographs or catalog pictures, or draw them on cardboard. This shows children that everything has a place. They can refer to the labels when helping to put toys away.

- Provide duplicates of favorite items to prevent disagreements and minimize waiting time. Sharing is difficult for this age group because they are still developing concepts about ownership.

Suggested Toys and Materials for Infants and Toddlers

Assess your inventory of toys and materials.

The list that follows suggests a variety of toys and materials for infants and toddlers. You probably have many of these items already. You can use the list as a guide when assessing your inventory of play materials and making decisions about what to add. Remember, a good environment for infants and toddlers provides toys and materials that match the characteristics of the children in your group. Take time to review the information on toy safety in module 1, *Safe*. Also keep these ideas in mind as you review the toys and materials list:

- Furniture and equipment should be appropriately sized for this age group and free from splinters and other hazards.

- You can make some of the suggested toys and materials.

- Child development areas are interrelated. Most good toys and materials support development across these areas.

- Children may need adult supervision when using some of the items on the list.

Some Good Toys and Materials for Infants and Toddlers [21]

To encourage children to use their senses

- Washable toys for sucking, chewing, and teething
- Items with simple, contrasting designs
- Wall hangings (textured, touchable, securely fastened)
- Jack-in-the-box
- Clutch balls
- Rattles

- Mobiles (hung out of reach)
- Push-and-pull toys
- Stuffed animals and dolls
- Texture balls
- Music boxes
- Sand and water table or individual tubs or basins
- Tape or CD player; tapes or CDs (music, voices, other sounds)

- Sand and water play props (plastic cups, bowls, scoops)
- Cloth blocks
- Mirrors (unbreakable)
- Ribbons, scarves, fabrics
- Playdough
- Fingerpaint

To encourage small motor development

- Objects to grasp, hold, and shake
- Stacking rings with a straight post
- Containers to fill and dump
- Objects that fit together (large pop beads, blocks, rings)

- Large wooden beads and thick strings or laces
- Puzzles (wood, rubber, heavy cardboard) with 3–8 pieces
- Balls and baskets
- Dolls and doll clothes

- Containers in graduated sizes (e.g., plastic bowls and cups)
- Pegboards with large holes and large, colored pegs
- Cardboard boxes with lids

To encourage large motor development

- Tunnel
- Soft balls of various sizes
- Riding toys (without spokes and pedals)
- Cars and trucks
- Wagons
- Large cardboard boxes

- Shopping cart
- Rocking boat
- Climber with steps and slide
- Vinyl-covered foam ramps, cushions, and furniture
- Structures to climb into, out of, and around

- Low, carpeted stairs with hand rail
- Simple doll carriage
- Tumbling mats
- Push-and-pull toys

Some Good Toys and Materials for Infants and Toddlers, *continued*

To support language and literacy development

- Song and story tapes or CDs
- Puppets
- Dolls and animals
- Cloth, vinyl, and board books to explore
- Simple picture and story books to read with an adult

- Books with textures and pop-up tabs
- Pictures of families, familiar objects, animals
- Interesting things to talk about
- Simple games and items for sorting and matching

- Large paper for scribbling and painting
- Things to scribble and paint with (large crayons, brushes, paint)
- Low easel

To support pretending and dramatic play

- Dolls (soft, washable, male and female, multi-ethnic)
- Doll accessories (clothes, bottles, brushes)
- Doll beds, chairs, and carriages
- Simple dress-up clothes

- Purses and tote bags
- Hats
- Plastic dishes and utensils
- Large wooden or plastic spoons
- Pots and pans
- Child-size broom

- Telephones
- Puppets
- People and animal figures
- Full length, unbreakable mirror
- Empty product containers

To support exploration and discovery

- Large soft blocks
- Large cardboard blocks
- Hollow or unit blocks
- Small cars and trucks
- People and animal figures

- Aquarium and fish
- Toys that encourage a child to explore cause and effect (e.g., wrist bells, container with screwable lid)

- Natural items such as pine cones, shells, rocks, and leaves
- Simple gardening tools and equipment

what's next?

Skill-Building Journal, section **3-7** (*Learning Activity C*) and section **3-1** (*Feedback*).

LEARNING
ACTIVITY

Learning Activities

D. Planning Daily Routines and a Flexible Schedule

In this activity you will learn to

- use daily routines as opportunities to build responsive relationships with infants and toddlers

- plan a flexible schedule that allows teachers to meet the needs of each child

Daily Routines

Daily routines are opportunities to build relationships with children.

Daily routines are events that take place each day. As adults, we usually do not give much thought to our own daily routines. Day after day we take showers, cook meals, sweep floors, and fill our gas tanks. Often we approach routines as tasks to be completed so we can get on to what we really want to do.

For infants and toddlers, daily routines—arriving, eating, sleeping, diapering and toileting, cleaning up, and departing—are significant parts of the day. They are not chores to be completed quickly so children may get back to more important activities. Instead, routines are wonderful opportunities to build relationships with individual children and support their learning. By repeating the same things, often in the same way, children begin to make sense of the world.

During routines such as diapering and feeding, infants have your undivided attention as you focus on meeting their needs and getting to know them. Being changed means more to a 4-month-old than just getting a clean, dry diaper. She can look closely at your face, listen to your voice, and have a simple conversation. You might look at her and say, "I see you, Joni, Joni, macaroni." She might respond with a gurgle, causing you to comment, "That's right, Joni. I like you too." If you describe what you are doing, she will gradually learn the meaning of words such as *wet* and *dry*, *up* and *down*. Eventually she will begin to understand simple directions: "Please lift your legs so I can pull out the wet diaper. Thank you."

THINK

- How do you and your colleagues carry out routines?

- Do you look forward to spending time with individual children?

- What are children learning during routines?

Older mobile infants and toddlers can participate in routines as they gain new skills. Their involvement provides opportunities to develop

- small muscle skills as they pull off socks or brush their teeth

- large muscle skills as they push a chair across the floor to the table or help you carry a bag of balls outside

- social and language skills as they smile and listen to you during bottle feedings or tell you a story while getting ready to go home

- cognitive skills, such as matching, as they put toys in containers with picture labels

Some teachers are reluctant to let children do things for themselves because it takes a long time and often creates messes that they will have to clean up. It is important to recognize that all learning takes time, whether it's learning to use a computer or eat a banana. As you read the following example, think about what the child is learning as he eats a banana.

When Vinh eats a banana, he might . . .	He learns . . .
Pick up a piece and put it in his mouth.	*I can feed myself.*
Spit it out.	*I don't like bananas.*
Pick it up and try again.	*I was wrong. I do like bananas.*
Finish the pieces on his tray and bang the tray.	*I love bananas. I want more.*
Squish a piece against the tray.	*I can change this. I am powerful.*
Drop a piece on the floor and watch it fall.	*When I let go, it falls to the ground and I can't reach it.*
Try to feed some to his teacher, Mr. Lewis.	*Mr. Lewis really likes me, and he likes bananas, too.*
Hear his teacher say, "Banana."	*This thing has a name.*
Try to say, "Banana."	*I can communicate.*

THINK

- How do you respond when a child takes a long time to do something?

- What do you think and do when a child's independence results in a mess?

Repeating the same activities again and again helps toddlers master new skills. It takes a lot of practice to learn to pull up pants, buckle overall straps, and zip coats. When toddlers do things for themselves, they feel independent and competent. You can support the learning process by being patient and respectful. When you wait for Demian (28 months) to practice zipping his coat, you show respect for his efforts: "You are learning something important. There's no need to hurry. Take as much time as you need."

Daily routines support children's learning.

Here are some suggestions for making daily routines valuable learning experiences:

Keep groups as small as possible. When caring for infants, routines for eating, sleeping, and diapering are usually carried out one-on-one. For other activities and with older children, keep groups small. Small groups are less stressful for both children and adults.

Treat children as partners. Talk with infants and toddlers about what you are doing as you diaper, dress, and feed them. Observe what they are doing and let them participate as much as they are able.

Develop a system for each routine. It is easier to build a relationship with a child if you aren't interrupted by the need to find a misplaced item.

Relax and take your time. There is no hurry to finish in a set amount of time. You can talk, snuggle, tickle a tummy, or sing a song as you change a diaper or feed an infant. Give toddlers plenty of time to practice doing things for themselves.

The Daily Schedule

The daily schedule orders the events of the day. It shows how you expect the day's events and activities to flow, in what order, and for how long.

Flexibility helps you meet each child's needs.

When caring for infants, you are likely to have as many schedules as you have infants, because each child follows a personal schedule for eating, sleeping, diapering, and playing. Although you try to predict when the infants in your care are likely to get tired or hungry or need a diaper changed, you will need to be flexible. Flexibility is an important guiding principle when caring for infants.

For toddlers, you can plan the day—up to a point. For example, you do not know when an unplanned toddler exploration will cause you to reschedule a planned art activity. An impulsive toddler might decide to put her socks in the toilet, causing it to overflow onto the floor. Luckily, when the maintenance staff arrives to help, the huge water puddle, giant mops, and bucket with magic rollers will fascinate the children as they watch the cleanup. Later, you will need to talk about the event so the toddlers can begin to understand why you want them to keep their socks out of the toilet.

- How would you have reacted to the overflowing toilet?
- How do you feel when your plans must be adapted, changed, or abandoned?

Flexible schedules support children, teachers, and families.

You might wonder, "Why should we have a schedule if we're just going to change it?" Here are some reasons why a schedule is important:

Children learn that their world is safe, secure, and predictable. When children do some things at the same time and in the same order each day, they develop a sense of trust. They feel secure because they can predict that, for example, outdoor play comes before lunch and parents return after afternoon naps. This knowledge leads to feelings of security and confidence.

Teachers have a sense of order. Every day is different when caring for infants and toddlers. This can be wonderful, but a framework helps you plan and make good use of each day.

Families have an idea of what takes place each day. Families are reassured when they can imagine what their child is doing while they are gone. Knowing the time and order of events also helps them plan for special events like doctor appointments. Give each family a copy of the schedule and post it in the room where they can read it.

What is a good schedule for infants and toddlers? No single schedule will work for all groups and all teachers. Here are some characteristics of an appropriate schedule that may be changed to meet individual needs:

- Major events occur in the same order each day.

- There is sufficient time for daily routines and for transitions from one event to the next.

- There is a balance between active and quiet times.

- Children have opportunities to be alone or with a familiar teacher.

- Children have opportunities to spend time in small groups of 2–3 children.

- There is a balance between child-initiated and teacher-led activities.

- Children go outdoors twice a day (in full-day programs).

Consistency helps children feel secure.

Although your schedule needs to be flexible, it is important to be consistent from day to day and week to week. As noted earlier, children feel more secure when they can accurately predict the events of the day, e.g., "After lunch we wash our hands and get ready for naps." By knowing what comes next, they learn to trust the environment and their teachers.

Be flexible when it is best for the children.

When is it a good idea to be flexible? Suppose it is too windy for your regular walk outside or the children are having so much fun dancing to music that the activity is lasting longer than planned. Rather than going on the walk anyway or trying to cut the activity short, you may adapt the schedule. It is appropriate to abandon your plans completely to take advantage of "teachable moments," such as the appearance of a rainbow during a walk or the arrival of the maintenance staff when they come to solve a problem.

Adapt the schedule to meet the needs of individual children.

It is also appropriate to adapt the schedule for individual children. For example, if a child is thoroughly involved in finger painting, let him play a little longer while the rest of the group cleans up. Another child might get hungry and need a snack before lunch.

In summary, a daily schedule is a tool to help you. Use and bend it to meet your needs and those of the children.

what's next?

Skill-Building Journal, section **3-8** (*Learning Activity D*), section **3-1** (*Feedback*), and section **3-9** (*Reflecting on Your Learning*).

4

Physical

Overview

Creating Indoor and Outdoor Environments That Invite
Infants and Toddlers to Move and Explore

Offering Opportunities for Infants and Toddlers to Use
Their Muscles

Responding as Infants and Toddlers Practice and Gain New
Physical Skills

Taking Care of Your Body

Learning Activities

A. Using Your Knowledge of Infants and Toddlers to Support
Physical Development

B. Creating an Environment That Supports Physical Development

C. Responding as Infants and Toddlers Use Physical Skills

D. Supporting Physical Development Throughout the Day

4. Physical

Physical development involves the use and coordination of fine and gross motor skills.

Physical development includes the gradual gaining of muscle control. Children develop gross motor skills such as crawling, walking, and throwing, and fine motor skills such as holding, pinching, and flexing fingers and toes. Coordinating movement is an important part of physical development. During the first three years of life, most children begin to develop eye-hand coordination, the ability to direct finger, hand, and wrist movements. They can fit large pieces into wooden puzzles and thread jumbo beads on wide laces. With the help of their senses—especially sight, sound, and touch—infants and toddlers learn to coordinate the movement of their large and small muscles. They walk while pulling toys behind them and pick up small pieces of food and pop them in their mouths.

Most young children do not have to be reminded to move their bodies.

Infants and toddlers like to move their bodies. Infants gleefully kick their legs, reach for objects, and, as soon as they are able, try to roll over, crawl, and walk. Toddlers push, pull, shake, dump, and pour. They delight in running and climbing as well as building and knocking down. Building gross motor skills is a natural part of everyday activities.

We use fine motor skills throughout our lives.

As young children develop small muscle skills, they are able to accomplish many tasks. Writing and drawing require the coordination of hands, fingers, and wrists. Small-muscle strength and coordination are needed for cutting with scissors and using other tools. Control and dexterity are required for buttoning, zipping, snapping, and holding utensils.

Physical skills help infants and toddlers feel competent.

Infants and toddlers use their muscles, along with their senses, to explore and build their understanding of the world and their place in it. Greg (7 months) shakes a rattle and hears a sound. He shakes it again, and again hears the sound. Soon he realizes that the rattle produces the sound when he shakes it, that his action has an effect. Such experiences help children begin to think of themselves as competent individuals who can make things happen. Children who feel competent are more likely to experiment and use physical skills in new ways.

You can support physical development by

- creating indoor and outdoor environments that invite infants and toddlers to move and explore

- offering opportunities for infants and toddlers to use their muscles

- responding as infants and toddlers practice and gain new physical skills

Creating Indoor and Outdoor Environments That Invite Infants and Toddlers to Move and Explore

1. **Use furniture, platforms, and ramps to create multiple levels.** Arrange furniture and equipment so that children can pull themselves up and practice different ways of moving.

2. **Provide a variety of surfaces on which children can lie, roll, crawl, walk, and use wheeled toys.** Baby Emma sits on her blanket, watching two toddlers roll cars and trucks on the carpet.

3. **Offer safe and interesting objects and materials that invite children to explore with their senses.** "Here's a pinecone. How does it feel? How does it smell?"

4. **Provide toys and materials that invite children to use their hands and fingers, such as squeeze balls, rattles, and pop beads.** Nigel grasped a chunky crayon with a foam curler around it and made marks on butcher paper taped to the table. Then he laughed and patted the marks he had made.

5. **Provide a variety of equipment and materials that invite children to use their arms and legs.** Offer balls, pull toys, and low climbers with slides.

Zora Is on the Move

As you read the following story, pay attention to the way the indoor environment invites infants and toddlers to move and explore. Also notice how Ms. Gonzalez and Mr. Lewis support Zora's physical development.

Ms. Bates: Hello, Zora. Did you come to say hello to us?

Ms. Bates: Goodbye, Zora. I see you are on the move!

Mr. Lewis: Look who has come to visit! Hi, Zora.

Zora: Dow?

Mr. Lewis: Yes. You sat down.

Mr. Lewis: Bend your knees and jump.

Zora: Jup.

Offering Opportunities for Infants and Toddlers to Use Their Muscles

6. **Schedule outdoor play twice a day (in full-day programs).** "The toddlers may go for a walk today, while the other children stay in the play yard to blow and pop bubbles."

7. **Provide opportunities for indoor active play during bad weather.** On stormy days, rearrange the furniture to make room for an indoor climber and slide.

8. **Provide materials and activities for children with different levels of fine and gross motor skills.** Vinh's mom decorated plastic lids with tissue paper and yarn. They hang from the ceiling where young infants can see the pretty colors and older children can reach for them.

9. **Invite children to participate in routines so they can develop and use self-help skills.** "Do you want to hold your bottle, Annie? You hold the bottle while I hold you."

10. **Offer music and movement activities so children can move their bodies and become aware of rhythm.** Tommy is dancing and shaking a maraca in each hand.

Dancing Toddlers

*As you read the following story, pay attention to the ways in which
Mr. Lewis supports the children's physical development.*

Mr. Lewis: After we clean up,
let's play some music and
move our bodies.

Mr. Lewis: Let's dance.

Leonard: My scarves are
dancing.

Mr. Lewis: You are terrific
dancers!

Mr. Lewis: I see that Ricky is
shaking all over, and Jessica is
swaying! Leonard is bending
his knees!

Responding as Infants and Toddlers Practice and Gain New Physical Skills

11. **Observe, record, and exchange information with families about each child's physical abilities, interests, and needs.** "Joseph was trying to reach the water, so I asked, 'How can you make yourself taller?' He got a step stool and put it on the floor in front of the sink. Does he do that at home?"

12. **Share children's pleasure in their new accomplishments.** "Theresa, you pulled off your sock. You figured out how to do it!"

13. **Recognize and respect each child's individual rate of development.** Danny reaches for the toy puppy at the edge of his blanket. Instead of jumping in, Ms. Bates gives him a chance to get it himself.

14. **Ensure safety by adapting the environment and teaching practices as children gain new skills.** After several infants begin crawling, Mr. Lewis arranges some bolsters to make a safe area for the babies who are not yet ready to crawl.

Jon Rolls Over

As you read the following story, pay attention to the way Ms. Bates supports Jon's physical development. Also think about why she does not intervene when he tries to roll over.

Ms. Bates: I think you want to get down.

Ms. Bates: Look, there you are. There's Jon.

Jon: Ba, ba, ba.

Ms. Bates: It looks like you are going to roll over, all by yourself.

Ms. Bates: Hooray for Jon! This time you rolled over without any help.

Jon: Aaaah.

Ms. Bates (writes): Mon., 3/19, 10:00 a.m. Jon rolled over by himself.

what's next?

Skill-Building Journal, section **4-2** (*Overview*), section **4-10** (*Answer Sheet*), and section **4-1** (*Feedback*).

Taking Care of Your Body [22]

As a teacher, you are concerned about children's physical development. To do a good job, it is essential that you take care of yourself, too. How many times a day do you

- bend from the waist to lift up a baby?

- lean over a toddler-size sink to wash your hands?

- sit on the floor and lean forward to roll a ball back and forth with a baby?

- lift a toddler, even though he can climb up to the changing table himself?

Such actions are typical for teachers, and they often cause sore backs and limbs. Back problems are the most common cause of occupational injuries for early childhood teachers.

Try these suggestions to prevent back injuries:

Lifting, holding, and carrying

- Hold the child close to you and avoid twisting motions when lifting or lowering the child.

- Drop the sides of the crib before lowering or lifting an infant into or out of it. (Be sure to raise the sides again.)

- Bend your knees, tuck in your buttocks, and pull in your stomach muscles when lifting children and heavy objects.

- Avoid standing for long periods of time with a child on your hip.

- Use safe equipment to move children from one space to another. For example, put infants in a multi-seat carriage to take them outdoors.

Sitting

- Sit in adult-size chairs.

- Sit in a comfortable chair with good back support when feeding an infant or reading a story.

Diapering, toileting, and handwashing

- Make sure the changing table is a comfortable height for adults.

- Position the stairs next to the changing table so toddlers can climb up. Stand nearby to steady the children so they will not fall.

- Provide small, stable step stools so older children can reach the sink without being lifted.

Caring for infants and toddlers is physically demanding. Remember to take care of yourself.

what's next?

Skill-Building Journal, section **4-3** (*Taking Care of Your Body*), section **4-1** (*Feedback*), and section **4-4** (*Pre-Training Assessment*).

Learning Activities

LEARNING
ACTIVITY

A. Using Your Knowledge of Infants and Toddlers to Support Physical Development

In this activity you will learn to

- recognize typical large and small muscle skills of infants and toddlers

- use what you know about infants and toddlers to support physical development

It is important to know how children develop and how individual children approach physical tasks.

While infants and toddlers follow individual schedules for mastering new skills, their physical growth follows a general, predictable pattern. For most children, large muscle control begins with the head and progresses to the legs and feet. Infants need you to support their heads at first, but they soon develop the strength to do this themselves. Next, they raise their heads and chests and wave their arms. Then they kick their legs.

Physical development typically starts with the center of the body and moves outward to the fingers and toes. Skills involving the large muscles in a child's arms and legs—sitting, crawling, walking, running, and throwing—therefore develop before fine motor skills such as holding, pinching, and flexing fingers and toes.

As their physical abilities grow, children learn to use them to accomplish new tasks. For example, when a toddler develops strong leg muscles, she is ready to figure out how to use a riding toy. She watches other children and experiments to figure out where to place her feet and how to use her legs to make the toy move.

The following descriptions summarize the typical sequence of the gross and fine motor development of young infants, mobile infants, and toddlers. This information will help you plan ways to support the physical development of the children in your care. You also need to know the children as individuals: what they can already do, what they are learning to do, and what they are not yet ready for. Through regular observation and by sharing information with families and colleagues, you can keep up-to-date about each child's expanding skills.

Young infants (birth–8 months) begin to strengthen and control their muscles.

- Sammy (3 months) is beginning to lift his head.

- Jon (6 months) reaches for toys.

- Luci (8 months) likes to stand and stretch her legs while her daddy holds her hands.

Most of a newborn's first movements are reflexive; they happen automatically, without thought. For example, if you touch the area around an infant's lips or cheeks, the child will turn toward you and begin moving her mouth as if sucking. At first, young infants do not control their movements. Much of their kicking, squirming, and wiggling is random, without obvious purpose. As they grow, infants begin to gain control over how they move their bodies. They develop muscles and skills as, for example, they reach for the mobile hanging over the changing table or turn to get the rattle that rolled to the edge of the blanket.

Young infants use their fine motor skills and senses to learn about themselves and the people and objects around them. With their hands and mouths, they explore the properties of new foods. Eyes and ears collect information about the source of sounds, such as a wind chime. Jon uses his fingers, hands, and wrists to touch a soft stuffed animal and to shake a rattle.

Young infants are also working on eye-hand coordination. Once tightly-fisted newborns, they are on their way to being able to point, hold spoons, and scribble. These seemingly simple skills involve many prior accomplishments. Luci can hand a pop bead to her Grandma because she has already learned to reach, grasp, pick up, let go, and move things from hand to hand.

Mobile infants (8–18 months) use large and small muscles to explore and do things for themselves.

- Malou (9 months) crawls quickly across the floor.

- Peter (12 months) cruises while holding onto furniture.

- Zora (16 months) puts toys in a wagon and pulls it behind her.

Mobile infants are delighted with their developing large muscle skills and are eager to explore the world. Crawling infants feel the soft rug and hard floor as they move from one place to another. They pull themselves up on chairs, sofas, and people, and—to everyone's excitement—attempt their first steps. As children learn to walk around the room, they discover books and toys that they never noticed before. Outdoors, they learn to walk on grass and sidewalks. Soon children walk with ease and speed and begin to run, jump, and hop. As their coordination grows, they combine skills, for example, to push a buggy as they walk.

As their fine motor skills develop, mobile infants can take active roles in routines and play. Tasks that adults accomplish automatically, such as eating a cracker, involve complex skills with many steps. Before Malou can move her tongue, gums, and lips to eat a cracker, she must see it, reach for it, grasp it, bring it to her mouth, open her mouth, and put it in. Another baby is mastering her pincer grasp. She uses her thumb and forefinger to pick up small pieces of carrot from her plate. Peter helps his big sister turn the pages when she reads to him. Zora coordinates her small muscle movements to tear lettuce leaves.

Toddlers' (18–36 months) range and variety of movements help them learn about themselves and their world.

- Lovette (20 months) puts small blocks in a bucket and then dumps them out.

- Ricky (28 months) and Adam (30 months) climb to the top of the outdoor climber.

- Jessica (34 months) feels proud as she bounces to music the way she has seen her older sister do many times.

Most toddlers walk very steadily, and they can run, climb, squat, push, pull, and jump. As toddlers' physical skills grow, they use them to achieve their goals. Soon after a toddler learns to climb on a stool, she might carry it to the window, step up, and look outside. Toddlers need many opportunities to practice using their arm and leg muscles, in order to gain more control over their movements. Observe the toddlers in your group to determine who needs encouragement to try new gross motor activities and who needs support to increase motor competency.

Toddlers are also gaining and refining fine motor skills. Lovette can coordinate her eyes, arm, and hand movements well enough to make single marks. Ricky can coordinate his hand, arm, and wrist well enough to fill his paper with scribbles. Jessica can make circles. Toddlers gain the ability to coordinate their fine motor skills so they can reach for and pick up objects. They learn to eat using utensils, turn the pages of books, fit pieces into simple puzzles, build with blocks, and pour juice from a small pitcher. Because they can move about without using their hands for support, their hands are free to touch, lift, grasp, push, and so on.

The following lists summarize key characteristics and events in the physical development of young infants, mobile infants, and toddlers. They are followed by physical development alerts.

Development of Infants and Toddlers

Young infants (birth–8 months)

- gain control of their heads (raise and turn their heads from side to side)

- lie on their stomachs, raise their heads, and use their arms to raise their upper bodies

- reach for and grasp toys and other objects

- pick objects up, let them go, and pick them up again

- move objects from one hand to the other; bang objects together

- roll over (from back to stomach and stomach to back)

- sit on a blanket or rug, propped at first and then without external support

Mobile infants (8–18 months)

- feed themselves finger foods; use a spoon; drink from a sippy cup

- hold and handle toys such as small blocks, shape boxes, and cars and trucks

- make marks with crayons and markers

- creep or crawl from one place to another

- pull themselves up to standing and cruise by holding onto furniture, railings, or people

- pick up small objects using a thumb and forefinger (pincer grasp)

- walk steadily, but may still prefer crawling

Toddlers (18–36 months)

- walk well; walk on tiptoe; learn to run without falling

- pull and push things, such as boxes, chairs, and wheeled toys

- gain large muscle skills, such as throwing, catching, kicking, jumping, and hopping

- gain small muscle skills, such as turning pages, making marks, pouring, opening containers, and using scissors

- grip with thumb and forefinger (pincer grasp) effectively

- begin to coordinate eye and hand movements, e.g., threading beads on laces

- sit on and use their feet to propel riding toys

Children's physical development is associated with other major areas of development.

Development: It's All Connected

Because infants and toddlers learn by doing, their physical development is closely connected with every other aspect of their development. Here are a few examples:

Cognitive

Infants use their growing physical abilities and their senses to make discoveries about their world, such as when they focus their eyes to examine their hands.

Toddlers build their understanding of how things work, such as when they try to balance on one foot or build ramps for their cars to roll down.

Communication

Infants develop small muscle skills that will eventually allow them to hold writing tools.

Toddlers' scribbles are the start of many more literacy explorations that eventually lead to writing.

Self

Young infants feel good about themselves when they master rolling over, as do mobile infants when they stand and see the world from a new perspective.

Toddlers use their gross motor skills when they pull a friend in a wagon or share a rocking boat with another child.

Social

Infants learn that it is fun to play with other people, while rolling a ball back and forth with a teacher or another baby.

Toddlers learn about relationships with other people when they hold hands and dance to music with a friend or wait for a turn on a riding toy.

Some Physical Development Alerts [23]

It may be time to suggest that a family consult their health provider if, by

2 months, a child does not notice his hands

3 months, a child cannot support her head well

3 months, a child does not grasp and hold objects

4 months, a child does not

- push down with his legs when feet are placed on a firm surface
- reach for and grasp objects
- bring objects to her mouth
- turn his head to locate sound

5 months, a child does not roll over from front to back or back to front

6 months, a child

- cannot sit without help
- does not reach for objects

7 months, a child does not put some weight on her legs

9 months, a child

- cannot sit up without help or support
- does not use finger and thumb to pick up objects

18 months, a child cannot walk

2 years, a child

- cannot push a wheeled toy
- does not drink from a cup or use a spoon

3 years, a child does not

- walk down steps
- take part in getting dressed

what's next?

Skill-Building Journal, section **4-5** (*Learning Activity A*), section **4-10** (*Answer Sheets*), and section **4-1** (*Feedback*).

Learning Activities

B. Creating an Environment That Supports Physical Development

In this activity you will learn to

- set up indoor and outdoor spaces so infants and toddlers can gain fine and gross motor skills

- adapt the environment so each child can practice her new physical skills

A supportive environment for infants and toddlers encourages movement and exploration because it is safe, interesting, and challenging. Children can freely kick their legs and wave their arms, roll over and sit, creep and crawl, pull up and walk, run, hop, jump, and skip. There are interesting objects for children to touch, grasp, pick up, shake, mouth, and poke. Such an environment encourages children to practice skills they have mastered and to try new ones.

Characteristics of a Safe Environment That Supports Physical Development [24]

There is more time to build supportive relationships with individual children in a safe environment. The architectural features, furniture and equipment, and toys and materials meet established safety standards. They reflect knowledge of how infants and toddlers move and learn, and support the roles of teachers. (Creating safe environments for infants and toddlers is also addressed in modules 1 and 3.)

These are features of a safe environment:

Architectural features enhance children's safety.

Windows are located 26 inches off the ground. Shelves and play equipment (typically 24 inches high) are placed under some windows so that mobile infants and toddlers can see outside by pulling themselves up and standing at the window.

Low-pile carpet is used throughout most of the room because infants and toddlers spend a lot of time on the floor, lying on blankets, creeping, crawling, walking, pushing trucks, riding scooters, rolling balls, and playing with toys and materials. The entrance, diapering/toileting, and eating areas have washable flooring, and so does part of the play area. When it is easy to clean up spills and messes, teachers are more relaxed about letting infants and toddlers explore.

Levels created by ramps, platforms, and lofts allow infants and toddlers to see their world from various perspectives. It is fun to crawl up a ramp to look out a window, step up on a platform to read a book, and climb up and down the ladder to the loft.

Doors open by swinging away from areas where children play and move. This prevents injuries when a child is near a door.

Edges of counters, shelves, window sills, corners, lips, ledges, and equipment located at child height have rounded corners of at least a 1/4" radius. Infants and toddlers can move freely without bumping sharp corners.

A child-height sink allows older infants and toddlers to develop and use fine motor skills, as they take part in routines such as handwashing and toothbrushing.

Open spaces and clear pathways provide plenty of room for children to practice moving and to push, pull, and ride wheeled toys such as wagons and scooters.

Appropriate furniture and equipment support children's safety.

Tables and chairs should be sized for the ages of the children and so all children can sit, play, and eat comfortably.

Shelves should be secured to the floor, wall, or platform. A good shelf size for mobile infants and toddlers is 24" high x 48" long x 12" deep. This height allows children to hold onto the shelves to pull themselves up and move from one place to another. The depth is shallow enough for children to use their fine motor skills to pick up toys. Use shelves to create protected areas where young infants can watch and play without being in the way of children who crawl and walk.

Equipment such as cribs, high chairs, infant seats, and multi-seat carriages should have easy-to-use safety features such as locking sides, raised edges, or straps. Straps should not be used on diapering tables, however. Walkers, baby bouncers, and similar items are unsafe. You do not need these items to support development of large muscle skills, unless they are part of a child's Individual Family Service Plan (IFSP).

Cushioned mats that are placed under climbers provide an extra level of safety under climbers. Mats are also fun places to sit, tumble, and roll. Arrange shelves and mats to create soft, protected areas where infants can practice skills such as rolling over.

Simple adjustments encourage the participation of children with special needs.

If you care for a child with special needs, work with the family and specialists to create a safe, supportive, and challenging environment. Adaptive equipment, specially designed furniture, and simple changes allow children with special needs to play with toys and materials. Position children with bolsters and wedges so they can reach toys that they might otherwise not be able to reach. Glue corks and wooden knobs to puzzle pieces and other toys to make them easier to grasp. For more ideas, see "Adapting the Environment for Children with Special Needs" in *The Creative Curriculum® for Infants & Toddlers*.

Examples of Safe Toys and Materials That Support Physical Development

Safe and interesting objects and materials that support sensory explorations

- Mobiles (teacher-made or purchased)
- Finger paint
- Playdough and simple utensils
- Large, nontoxic crayons
- Sand and water table with containers and scoops
- Paper for scribbling and for tearing
- Wall hangings (textured, touchable, and securely fastened)
- Ribbons, scarves, and fabrics

Equipment and materials that encourage children to use their arms and legs

- Balls of different sizes
- Low climbers and slides
- Tunnel (purchased or made by taping cardboard boxes)
- Open cubes
- Riding toys (low, propelled by feet)
- Wagons
- Tractor tires
- Large cardboard boxes
- Push-and-pull toys
- Tumbling mats
- Cars and trucks
- Small pillows and baskets in which to toss them
- Low, carpeted steps
- Foam furniture covered with vinyl

Toys and materials that invite children to use their hands and fingers

- Grasping toys
- Balls to clutch and squeeze
- Rattles
- Boxes with lids
- Large pegs and pegboards
- Stacking rings with straight post
- Nesting cups
- Shape-sorting boxes
- Interlocking blocks
- Pop beads
- Large wooden beads and thick strings or laces
- Wooden and rubber puzzles (3–8 pieces)
- Dramatic play props
- Dress-up clothes

Offering Familiar Experiences and Providing New Challenges

Open-ended materials support a range of skill development.

The way you arrange the environment and the types of toys, materials, and equipment you provide should be appropriate for infants and toddlers and correspond to the strengths, needs, interests, and abilities of individual children. When the environment is familiar, children feel secure and are more likely to explore and learn. For example, Ruby (12 months) feels secure when the armchair that she used yesterday to cruise from the shelf to the table is still available today. To increase their physical abilities, however, infants and toddlers need gentle challenges that let them practice their skills and develop new ones. For example, if a baby in your care readily grasps a rattle you hold near her hand, place the rattle just out of her reach and see if she is ready to try to get it. When challenges are too difficult, however, children get frustrated. If you put the rattle too far away, the baby is likely to cry or simply give up.

Open-ended materials, such as nesting cups and balls, are ideal for supporting a range of skill development. Children find different ways to use them, depending on their skills and interests. A young infant can grasp a stacking ring and bang it on the floor, while an older child might try to order the rings on a post by size. A soft ball is an ideal grasping toy for an infant; a toddler can toss the ball into a basket. Such items offer challenges without causing frustration.

Infants and toddlers use their large and small muscles in many different ways.

Throughout the day, both indoors and outdoors, you are likely to see infants and toddlers using their large and small muscles in many different ways. Here are some examples.

- A 3-month-old lies on the diapering table. You reach up and set some chimes in motion. He turns his head toward the noise.

- An 11-month-old sits on the carpet with her knees raised. She moves her feet forward a little, pushes, and moves her bottom forward. Soon she has scooted across the rug and is banging two blocks together.

- A 20-month-old, propped with a bolster because of his physical disability, sits facing you. You roll a beach ball back and forth with him.

- A 2-year-old sits on a bench in the greeting area, taking her boots off. Her mother holds her backpack open and says, "Here you go. Your sneakers are right on top."

- A toddler pushes the buttons on a phone and lifts the receiver to his ear. You ask, "Who's there?" He smiles.

- Two toddlers crawl through a cardboard box tunnel. When they get through, they stand up, turn around, and crawl back.

Regular observation provides useful information about children's use of physical skills.

One of the best ways to learn about the effectiveness of your indoor and outdoor environments is to observe children engaged in routines and play. Your observation notes will provide useful information about how the environment supports children's use of physical skills. As you review your notes, you are likely to find clues about what the children need in order to develop new large and small muscle skills.

what's next?

Skill-Building Journal, section **4-6** (*Learning Activity B*) and section **4-1** (*Feedback*).

Learning Activities

LEARNING ACTIVITY

C. Responding as Infants and Toddlers Use Physical Skills

In this activity you will learn to

- recognize how your relationships with infants and toddlers support their physical development

- interact with infants and toddlers in ways that encourage them to feel competent and confident

Positive relationships with children enhance their physical development.

As you think about ways to support children's physical development, remember the importance of your relationships with them. Infants and toddlers need to feel safe and secure, in order to attempt the exploration and experimentation that are necessary to learning new physical skills. By building trusting, caring relationships, you help them feel comfortable in your care. Your interest in and encouragement of what they are doing—whether learning to grasp a toy or pull down their pants to use the toilet—promotes their physical development more than the activities or toys, themselves. Your primary task is therefore to be responsive to each child in your care.

Try these suggestions for responding to the physical skills of infants and toddlers:

Remember that children develop skills at different rates. Note a child's progress without making comparisons to other children. "Luis, I saw you balance on one foot for a long time."

Use what you know about each child to decide how to respond. Some examples follow:

- Encourage a child who is eager to accomplish a goal: "Tobey, you can reach so far! Stretch just a little more, and you'll have that rattle."

- Accept the feelings of a child who is frightened: "You don't want to go up the steps to the slide. That's okay. You'll try it when you are ready."

- Suggest a new activity for a child who is ready for a challenge: "Would you like to move like a snake?"

- Share a child's pleasure in gaining a new skill: "You are standing all by yourself!"

Keep track of every child's growing skills. Watch children carefully, maintain up-to-date records, and share information with families and colleagues. You can use what you learn to rearrange the environment and adapt your practices to ensure safety and promote physical development. "Mr. Pitt said J. T. rolled over last night. From now on, we'll have to be sure to put him on his blanket in a protected area."

Suggest how to overcome an obstacle or prevent a problem. Offer suggestions to help children cope with frustration that can hamper learning. For example, you might advise, "Hold your cup with both hands so your milk won't spill again," or "Let's tie your shoes so you don't trip on the laces while you are dancing."

Know when to step in and when to stand back. Use your knowledge of child development and individual children to decide whether to intervene or to let a child solve a problem independently. Here are some examples:

- You watch Kenny figuring out how to climb into a box. When he tries to climb into his crib, you intervene.

- You wait to see if Feliz can figure out how to climb down from the top of the climber. When it looks as though she might fall, you move nearby in case she needs help.

- You wait to see what happens when Carl turns the last puzzle piece around and around. You think, "If I rush to help, he won't enjoy the satisfaction of completing the puzzle on his own."

Set clear limits and offer reminders to help children learn about safety. Stand next to the rocking boat while telling two toddlers, "When you rock, hold onto the boat with two hands so you won't fall." Point to the protected area of the carpet while saying to a baby, "This is a safe place to crawl. The walking children will not bump into you here."

Teach skills directly, when appropriate. To help a toddler learn to catch, demonstrate and describe the steps for catching a ball before you throw it: "I'm ready to throw the ball to you. Put your arms out in front of you. Turn your hands so that your palms face up. Keep your arms stretched out. Here it comes."

Show children that moving is an enjoyable part of your life. Invite a child to hold your feet while you do sit-ups. He will have fun helping you, and you will get some exercise. Crawl, jump, and walk on tiptoe while playing "Follow the Leader" with a small group of toddlers. Chase bubbles, roll hoops, and do jumping jacks.

Physical development plays an important role in helping children feel good about themselves. When children master physical skills—holding a bottle, pulling up to standing, jumping down from a step, rolling a wheelchair—they feel good about their bodies and begin to see themselves as competent people who can accomplish meaningful tasks. Feeling competent and confident leads to emotional security and a willingness to attempt challenging cognitive tasks. Promoting the physical development of infants and toddlers is linked to encouraging growth and learning in all areas and situations.

what's next?

Skill-Building Journal, section **4-7** (*Learning Activity C*) and section **4-1** (*Feedback*).

Learning Activities

D. Supporting Physical Development Throughout the Day

In this activity you will learn to

- individualize daily routines to give each child opportunities to build and practice physical skills

- encourage play experiences that allow children to use their large and small muscles to explore, discover, and learn

Children can practice small and large muscle skills while dressing and undressing.

Individualizing Daily Routines

Each day you and the children spend much of your time together involved in the daily routines of dressing, toileting, and eating. It may be tempting to hurry through these activities, but they deserve the same care and attention as anything else you do with children. Each routine provides rich opportunities for supporting the development of fine and gross motor skills. As children gain new skills, they can practice them during daily routines.

Infants and toddlers of all ages can practice physical skills while getting dressed and undressed. While Ms. Bates pulls on his shirt, Jeremy (3 months) becomes more aware of his body and works on controlling his head. To the frustration of Mr. Lewis, Mike (15 months) likes to practice walking while he gets dressed. At 24 months, Jerry is coordinated enough to put his foot into his boots, while Minh Le (32 months) can zip her own jacket after Ms. Gonzalez gets it started.

- How is your approach to dressing a 3-month-old different from your approach to dressing a toddler? How is it the same?

- How do you know that a child is ready for a greater role in dressing and undressing?

As children gain physical skills, they can participate in diapering and toileting.

Every child develops at his or her own pace, but, typically between 24–30 months, children become aware of and are able to control their bladder and bowel muscles. This usually means that they are ready to begin using the toilet. Long before this time, however, children use both fine and gross motor skills during diaper changes. They gradually progress from complete dependence on adults to keep them dry and clean to greater and greater independence. Here are some examples:

- Danny (5 months) has discovered his feet, and he sucks his toes. You give him time to play with his feet before fastening his dry diaper.

- Kara (18 months) climbs the steps to the diapering table and lies down. She helps you pull down her pants and undo her diaper. You hand her a clean diaper to hold until you are ready for it. When the change is finished, she climbs down, walks to the sink, turns on the faucet, and stands next to you while you both wash your hands. She shakes the water off her hands, reaches for two paper towels, and hands one to you. After drying her hands, she steps on the foot pedal and drops the used towel in the trash can.

- Arnie (33 months) walks into the bathroom himself. He pulls his pants down, urinates, and pulls them up again on his own. He follows the directions displayed in simple pictures on the bathroom wall that remind him to flush the toilet and wash his hands.

- How is your approach to diapering a 6-month-old different from the way you diaper a 1-year-old? How is it the same?

- How did a child in your care let you know he was ready to begin using the toilet?

Children use hands and fingers while being fed and when they feed themselves.

Bottle feedings and meal- and snack times are wonderful opportunities for physical development. Children of different ages participate in different ways. Here are some examples:

- Carla (4 months) pats the bottle while you hold it for her.

- Dion (6 months) holds and waves a spoon while you use another spoon to feed him.

- Josie (9 months) sits up straight in her high chair and uses her pincer grasp to pick up a piece of toast. Whether she eats it or throws it on the floor depends upon her mood.

- Harry (14 months) insists on feeding himself. He gets a little applesauce on the spoon and into his mouth, although most of it ends up on his shirt. Sometimes he drops the spoon and digs in with his hands.

- John (22 months) loves to stir and pour when he helps make French toast for snack.

- How is your approach to feeding a 2-month-old different from your approach to feeding a 6-month-old? How is it the same?

- How do you feel when a child smears yogurt on her face, smooshes banana all over his feeding tray, drops crackers on the floor, or shakes juice out of her sippy cup? What do you do? Why?

Encouraging Play and Learning

Programs offer many daily opportunities for infants and toddlers to use their small and large muscles. As described above, you can invite children to use physical skills while participating in routines. Children also gain and practice physical skills as they move about and explore the environment. Although teachers sometimes respond by standing back to observe, they often introduce and guide children's play by joining in and by suggesting ideas that build on and enhance the children's experiences. Here are some examples:

Young infants...

- **use all their senses.** Put a baby on a blanket under a shady tree. When the wind makes the leaves flutter, listen to her coo.

- **explore their body parts.** Give infants plenty of time to suck on toes, hands, and fingers.

- **grasp and shake things.** Provide items such as rattles, measuring spoons, and squeeze balls.

- **enjoy swaying back and forth.** Turn on a lively tune, hold a baby against your chest and shoulder, and gently dance together.

Mobile infants...

- **pat and feel things.** Put out a collection of fabric squares and watch an infant explore each piece.

- **crawl and push.** Keep trucks and cars in a carpeted area of the room.

- **snap and unsnap.** Offer large pop beads to an infant who is ready for that challenge.

- **walk and push.** Provide cardboard boxes to push across the carpet and the grass.

- **reach for things.** Blow giant bubbles with the children so they can reach for and pop them.

Toddlers...

- **dig.** Expect toddlers to use shovels to fill buckets, dump them out, and start again.

- **hold objects.** Listen and jot down notes while a child holds a play telephone to his ear and talks to his dad.

- **pound.** Put out playdough and mallets so toddlers can use their large muscles.

- **move in different ways.** Invite toddlers to walk, run, skip, and hop with you.

- **use fingerpaint.** Show toddlers where to find smocks and how to scoop a little paint onto a tray.

- **enjoy fingerplays.** Sing a song and show older toddlers how to move their fingers to correspond with the verse.

Going outdoors is important for both children and adults.

Spending all day inside can be stressful for everyone. Both children and adults find it refreshing to go outside every day, to explore and learn in a different environment and to release pent-up energy. Outdoors, young infants take in new sights and sounds, and mobile infants and toddlers are free to move and use their bodies. You can play music outdoors and show children how to bounce and sway to the tunes they hear.

Most outdoor play areas offer many opportunities for gross motor development. There might be stationary slides, climbers, swings, and a sandbox. A ramp connecting the indoor and outdoor environments allows children in wheelchairs easily to enter and leave the building and enjoy playing outdoors. A shaded, grassy area provides a safe setting where a young infant can sit on a mat and reach out to touch the grass. Older infants and toddlers enjoy playing with push-and-pull toys, balls, tunnels, riding toys, wagons, and cardboard boxes that they are able to climb into and out of. (See module 3, *Learning Environment*, for more information on playing and learning outdoors.)

Try these suggestions during outdoor play times:

Pay attention to what the children are doing and participate with them. Talk with your colleagues before the children arrive, while on breaks, and after the children go home.

Position yourself at the children's level as much as possible. Sit on a blanket with an infant and talk to her about what she sees and hears. Kneel or crouch and roll balls to a one year old. Hold a toddler's hand while playing "Ring Around the Rosie."

Coordinate with colleagues to schedule short refreshment breaks. Use this time to move, stretch, or take a quick run around the yard. You will get some exercise and show the children that using large muscles is important to you, too.

what's next?

Skill-Building Journal, section **4-8** (*Learning Activity D*), section **4-1** (*Feedback*), and section **4-9** (*Reflecting on Your Learning*).

5

Cognitive

Overview

Creating an Environment That Invites Infants and Toddlers to Learn by Using Their Senses and Moving Their Bodies

Offering Opportunities for Infants and Toddlers to Explore and Begin to Understand Their World

Interacting With Infants and Toddlers in Ways That Encourage Them to Explore

Your Own Experiences as a Learner

Learning Activities

A. Using Your Knowledge of Infants and Toddlers to Support Cognitive Development

B. Creating an Environment That Encourages Exploration and Discovery

C. Supporting Infants' and Toddlers' Thinking Skills During Routines

D. Encouraging Cognitive Development Throughout the Day

5. Cognitive

Infants and toddlers think and reason.

Cognitive development is the process of learning to think and to reason. From birth, young children are ready to learn. They are curious, active investigators who use their senses, brains, and rapidly growing skills to explore and make sense of the world.

During the past 30 years, many scientists have observed and documented the behaviors of infants and toddlers. These researchers have concluded that very young children are capable of complex thinking and reasoning. Infants and toddlers have memories. They observe and try to make sense of cause and effect relationships. They also think about numbers and mathematical concepts, such as size and quantity.

Every important person in a child's life can have an impact on brain development.

New technologies such as brain scans have allowed scientists to expand our knowledge of how the brain works. Research confirms what parents, teachers, and others have known about the important learning that takes place during early childhood. Infants are born with about 100 billion brain cells, called neurons, which are connected into networks as the brain matures. As infants respond to people and experiences, their brain cells form networks that give them the capacity to think and learn. Every important person in the child's life can support brain development. Touching, holding, and stroking a baby stimulates the brain to release the hormones that allow growth. New connections are formed as children explore with their senses.

The early years include important windows of opportunity for brain development. However, scientists also remind us that the brain is a complex organ that continues to develop for many years. A child's interactions and experiences have a great impact on the development of social, emotional, intellectual, language, and physical skills, in early childhood and after.

You can support cognitive development by

- creating an environment that invites infants and toddlers to learn by using their senses and moving their bodies

- offering opportunities for infants and toddlers to explore and begin to understand their world

- interacting with infants and toddlers in ways that encourage them to explore

---

Creating an Environment That Invites Infants and Toddlers to Learn by Using Their Senses and Moving Their Bodies

1. **Organize the room to help children develop a sense of order.** Group items that are used together, such as dolls and blankets, on low, open shelves within children's reach.

2. **Include a variety of interesting things for children to touch, taste, see, hear, and smell.** Provide cushions covered with different textures for children to crawl or sit on; finger foods to touch, taste, see, and smell; bells, chimes, and musical instruments; and mobiles that make sounds and shadows on the wall.

3. **Offer open-ended materials that children can use in different ways according to their skills and interests.** Provide balls; blocks; dolls; and household items such as pots, pans, spoons, and measuring cups.

4. **Provide toys and materials that allow infants and toddlers to begin to understand that their actions cause results.** Offer rattles, pop-up toys, music makers, playdough, chunky crayons and paper, and similar items.

5. **Provide places and equipment that encourage infants and toddlers to move their bodies.** Offer a sheltered area where it is safe to roll over, a pile of cushions to crawl on, boxes to crawl in and out of, steps to go up and down, and a low climber with several levels.

Jon Uses His Senses to Learn About Beads

As you read the following story, pay attention to how
Ms. Gonzalez encourages Jon to learn about the beads by using his senses.

Jon: Aaaah.

Ms. Gonzalez: Jon, you are looking at my pretty beads. They are blue and pink and purple.

Ms. Gonzalez: I'll help you touch the beads. They feel cold and smooth.

Ms. Gonzalez: Do you hear the bells jingling?

Ms. Gonzalez: Look, Jon. That's you, wearing the beads.

Ms. Gonzalez: These aren't safe for you to play with on your own. I'll put them away. We can play with them another day.

Offering Opportunities for Infants and Toddlers to Explore and Begin to Understand Their World

6. **Invite children to participate in daily routines so they feel competent and learn how things work.** "Nadia, lift your arms so we can take off your shirt.""Kim, you can use a sponge to wipe up the spill.""Let's pick up the blocks so no one trips and falls."

7. **Take children outdoors and into the neighborhood.** Take a listening walk with a few children to hear different sounds; talk about the people, things, and events you observe outdoors.

8. **Create opportunities for children to touch, taste, see, hear, and smell.** Include children in simple food preparation activities, such as spreading cream cheese on bread or dipping fruit in yogurt.

9. **Encourage children to experiment, make discoveries, and think.** Put out basins of water with objects that sink and float; play peek-a-boo to help children learn that things exist even when out of sight; and ask questions that prompt children to recall past events, e.g., "What did we do at the park this morning?"

Luci Explores Her Crackers

As you read the following story, pay attention to the way Ms. Bates supports Luci's exploration of her crackers.

Ms. Bates: Would you like a cracker?

Ms. Bates: Does that taste good?

Ms. Bates: No, thank you, Luci. That's your cracker.

Ms. Bates: Are you ready for another cracker?

Interacting With Infants and Toddlers in Ways That Encourage Them to Explore

10. **Identify and respond to individual children's interests, needs, and learning styles.** Use observation, conversations with families, and other strategies to learn about each child's learning style and to maintain a current understanding of her skills.

11. **Talk with children about what they are touching, tasting, seeing, hearing, smelling, and doing.** "The fingerpaint feels smooth." "The snap on your jacket goes 'pop' when it opens." "These oranges smell delicious." "You put two circles in the box! Can you find any more?"

12. **Share in children's pleasure and excitement about their explorations, discoveries, and accomplishments.** "Dina, did you let go of your cracker? Look, it fell on the floor." "Jonathan, you worked hard to pick up that rattle. You're really holding it tightly now."

13. **Introduce words that describe children's experiences and discoveries.** "Thanh, you smashed your peach all over your nose. You must have liked the smell." "Omar is swinging up in the air—then down. Up and down." "I'm putting your arm in your sleeve."

14. **Recognize when to let children solve problems on their own and when to offer help.** "Gina makes little squeals when she's working hard to figure something out. When she cries loudly, it means, 'I'm frustrated. Please help me.'"

15. **Answer children's questions and encourage them to ask more.** "Maybe the playdough feels sticky because it's too wet. What do you think we could do to make it less sticky?"

16. **Tell families about their children's use of thinking skills.** "Omar put his arms up in the air to ask me to lift him up." "Luci lined up four blocks and said, 'Choo-choo.'"

Peter Takes His Time

As you read the following story, pay attention to how Mr. Lewis encourages Peter's curiosity while respecting his learning style.

Mr. Lewis: Peter likes to watch before doing new things. He might try it later.

Mr. Lewis: Zora, can you get the ball?

Mr. Lewis: Would you like a ball, Peter?

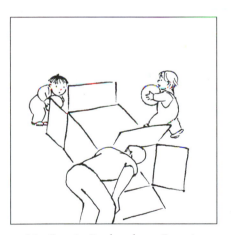

Mr. Lewis: Peek-a-boo, Peter!

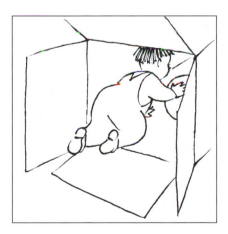

Mr. Lewis: Peek-a-boo, Peter! I see you!

---

what's next?

Skill-Building Journal, section **5-2** (*Overview*), section **5-10** (*Answer Sheets*), and section **5-1** (*Feedback*).

Your Own Experiences as a Learner

Learning is a lifelong experience.

People do not stop learning when they leave school; they continue to refine their thinking and reasoning skills. Think of people you know whom you consider to be good learners and thinkers. Would you say they are...

- willing to accept a challenge?

- curious and interested in learning new things?

- creative thinkers who can look at something and see several possibilities?

- eager to speak up and express their views and ideas?

- able to handle problems by trying different strategies until they find a solution?

We all know different things.

We do not all know the same things, and we do not need to. A computer specialist knows a lot about the inner workings and capabilities of computers. When a computer program has a problem, a specialist can figure out why and think of ways to get around it. If you know very little about how computers work, that doesn't make you less smart. You are probably an expert about other things, such as how to nurture infants and toddlers. What really matters is whether we have the knowledge and skills we need to function successfully in our work and home lives.

Many factors affect our ability to learn something new. Most important is whether the new information is useful or of interest to us. We tend to be most motivated to learn when we see a way to apply new information and skills, on or off the job. It helps if the information is related to something we already know or something we have wanted to know for some time.

Learning style refers to the way we learn best.

Each of us has our own style, or way of learning, that works best for us. If you were trying to acquire conversational skills in a new language would you...

- take a class?

- get a book and tape from the library and teach yourself?

- ask a native speaker to help you learn some words and phrases?

- use all of the strategies above?

Many factors affect our ability to learn.

Other factors that affect a person's ability to learn include how the information is presented, how it is organized, and whether the content is presented at an appropriate level. Readiness to learn is also affected by how we feel. It is a lot easier to learn when we know what is expected of us and when we are well-rested, focused, and comfortable.

This training program is designed to help you gain new knowledge and skills:

- Learning activities are short and focused.

- All the learning activities are related to your work, and you complete many of them while caring for children.

- The training program is self-paced.

- Examples in each module help you understand the content.

- Opportunities to receive feedback are built into the training program.

- Your *Skill-Building Journal* is an ongoing reference tool.

what's next?

Skill-Building Journal, section **5-3** *(Your Own Experiences as a Learner),* section **5-1** *(Feedback),* and section **5-4** *(Pre-Training Assessment).*

LEARNING
ACTIVITY

Learning Activities

A. Using Your Knowledge of Infants and Toddlers to Support Cognitive Development

In this activity you will learn to

- recognize some typical exploratory behaviors of infants and toddlers

- use what you know about infants and toddlers to support their cognitive development

At one time, people believed infants and toddlers were too young to learn very much because they couldn't talk or do things for themselves. They did not realize that, from birth, young children are learning all the time, during daily routines at home and at the center, while walking to the park, and when playing with a variety of interesting and challenging materials. As they drink a bottle, shake a rattle, look around, smell food, grab their toes, or move a chair across the room, young children are using their senses and motor skills to collect information and increase their understanding of the world.

Young infants (birth–8 months) use their senses to learn about the world.

- Sammy (3 months) looks at his hands as he turns them over and back again.

- Jon (6 months) has figured out that, when he smiles at people, they smile back at him.

- Luci (8 months) squeals as she mashes a piece of banana on her plate with her palm.

Young infants need to use their senses in order to learn. They focus on what they are sensing immediately. When lying on a blanket or resting slightly upright in an infant seat, they notice what's going on around them: the sound of a running faucet, the sight of two toddlers rolling a ball back and forth, or the taste of a new food.

Young infants learn something from every experience, whether a new event or a familiar routine. Think about what happens as you dress a 3-month-old in a clean stretch suit. What information might the child be collecting as you

- gently lift his arm and place it in a sleeve?

- smile and talk with him?

- lean over so your face is close to his?

Young infants spend a lot of time looking at their hands, grabbing their feet, sucking their toes, and stretching and kicking their legs. These explorations help infants figure out where their bodies begin and end.

Over time, young infants begin to construct an important understanding: Their actions can make something else happen. Their early explorations of cause and effect emerge from infants' relationships with favorite adults. They also learn as they move their bodies and discover things in the environment. If a young infant could use words to describe her learning, she might say,

> *When I babble at Mr. Lewis, he babbles back to me.*

> *When I shake my rattle, it makes noise.*

> *When I drop toys off my high chair tray, Mr. Lewis picks them up.*

When infants begin to understand cause and effect relationships, they gain a sense of power and competence. They begin to repeat actions that are enjoyable or bring a desired result.

Very young infants do not understand *object permanence*, the concept that people and objects still exist when they are out of sight. It takes most children about two years to develop this understanding fully. When a 4-month-old drops a toy from his crib, he does not look for it. Between 4–8 months, infants reach for a partially hidden object but stop if it disappears. They continue to develop an understanding of object permanence in the coming months.

Mobile Infants (8–18 months) continue to explore.

- Malou (9 months) raises her bottle as the level of milk drops.

- Peter (12 months) pulls on the string of a toy to bring it within reach.

- Zora (16 months) names familiar objects, including spoons, juice, and shoes.

As they have since birth, mobile infants use their senses to learn about the world. They also have a new skill: moving from one place to another. This literally takes them to new levels of learning. When Malou sees something interesting, she crawls over to explore it firsthand. She picks it up, puts it in her mouth, shakes it, bangs it on the floor, and then puts it aside when something else catches her attention.

Mobile infants can begin to recall past experiences and use what they know in new situations. For example, when Zora sees Ms. Bates sit down in the glider, it triggers pleasant memories. She walks to the chair, picks out a storybook from the basket on the floor, and puts the book in Ms. Bates's lap. Ms. Bates says, "Hi Zora. Would you like to read a story?" Peter turns his head when Ms. Gonzalez offers a spoonful of sweet potatoes. He remembers the look, taste, and smell of sweet potatoes. Peter did not like them before, so he does not want to eat them now.

Children in this age group are beginning to use objects purposefully. You might see a mobile infant tug on a string to bring a toy within reach or stack several small blocks to make a tower.

Mobile infants gain a lot from their relationships with special adults such as you and their family members. They watch and listen to you, then imitate your actions and language. They are also learning how to relate to other children. When you respond to their sounds, words, and actions, they deepen their understandings about relationships.

Children in this age group are also developing language skills. They know their names, understand many words and phrases, and begin to name things and use words and simple sentences to communicate. By combining words and actions, they can make themselves understood. A child might say, "Ball," while pointing to the closet where you keep the balls used outdoors. Another child might remark, "Mommy, go," while watching at the window as her mother walks to her car. The child might then tell you, "Up," and lift her arms.

Toddlers' (18–36 months) thinking and language skills develop rapidly.

- Lovette (20 months) hangs a bag over her shoulder and says she is going to the "oppice."

- Ricky (28 months) and Adam (30 months) say, "In," and, "Out," as they drive their toy cars in and out of a cardboard box garage.

- Jessica (34 months) can sort cars and trucks into two piles and say, "Cars go here."

Toddlers continue to use their senses to explore the world. They use their whole bodies to learn actively. While toddlers play, they make sense of concepts such as in and out, up and down, front and back.

Toddlers' behavior sometimes confuses adults. Toddlers tend to have short attention spans, frequently moving from one activity to another. However, they can also get very involved with an activity, staying with it for a long time. You probably know toddlers who would like to spend the whole morning lathering and rinsing their hands or filling a container with clothespins, dumping them out, and filling it again. They are eager to do things for themselves, yet they also want to continue being close to the important people in their lives: you and their families.

When you watch toddlers, you see them using their knowledge as they play:

- Steven reaches inside a bag without looking and says, "It's an orange." He knows how oranges feel.

- Lovette puts a bowl in a spoon and pretends to eat. She knows that spoons and bowls are used together.

- Adam pretends to read his favorite storybook. He remembers the simple story because he has heard it many times.

- Mika eats snack and says, "My daddy come soon." She knows going home comes after eating snack.

- Ricky picks up a block, holds it to his ear, and says, "Where are you?" He can use an object to represent something else.

Once toddlers begin to talk, their language skills expand rapidly. At first they speak in 2- to 3-word sentences. Soon they speak in longer sentences, describing yesterday's and tomorrow's events and talking with their friends. Talking becomes part of their pretend play. As Adam puts his stuffed bunny to bed, he covers him with a blanket and says, "See you in the morning," just as his daddy says to him.

Toddlers continue to explore cause and effect by experimenting to see what will happen as a result of their actions. They might turn over a cup of juice; put sand in the water table; pile blocks on top of each other; and test limits, e.g., "I'll climb on the table when Mr. Lewis isn't watching."

The following list summarizes key characteristics and events in the development of young infants, mobile infants, and toddlers that are related to their cognitive development.

Development of Infants and Toddlers

Young infants (birth–8 months)

- use their senses to gather information about people and things

- visually follow and respond to objects and faces as they move

- put almost everything they handle in their mouths

- hold and manipulate objects

- explore their bodies and how they move

- vocalize to themselves, people, and toys

- begin to understand that their actions have effects

Mobile infants (8–18 months)

- use their senses and movement to explore the world

- begin to understand that objects and people exist even when they are out of sight

- begin to remember past experiences and use the information in new situations

- imitate adult actions and language

- make choices between clear alternatives

- begin to solve problems on their own

- use actions and words to communicate

Toddlers (18–36 months)

- learn by moving and doing

- construct understandings about concepts such as size, shape, and weight

- concentrate for longer periods of time

- sometimes think about actions before performing them

- enjoy and learn through pretending and dramatic play

- often want to do things for themselves

- talk in simple sentences

- experiment to see what will happen as a result of their actions

Development: It's All Connected

Infants and toddlers learn by sensing, moving, and doing, and through their relationships with important adults. Their cognitive development is closely connected with every other aspect of their development. Here are some examples.

Physical

Young infants grasp and shake rattles and pick up finger foods, while curious mobile infants crawl to new parts of the room and find new things to explore.

Toddlers gain new information about height and direction by climbing up and down the stairs.

Communicaion

Infants begin to recall their favorite rhymes and songs.

Toddlers begin to make sense of time concepts, such as yesterday, today, and tomorrow, and before and after. For example, they talk about taking a nap after lunch and putting on a coat before going outside.

Self

Young infants gain a sense of who they are and what they can do as they play with their hands and kick their legs.

Young and mobile infants learn that they like being with other people, by cuddling with familiar adults.

Toddlers feel proud when they solve a problem or think of a new way to do something.

Social

Infants begin to understand object permanence while playing peek-a-boo with a teacher.

Toddlers have fun with other people when they play a game of lotto with a teacher and a peer.

Some Cognitive Development Alerts [25]

Note: Because cognitive development is very closely related to other areas of development, some of the following alerts are also listed in other modules.

It may be time to suggest that a family consult their health provider if, by

2 months, a child does not notice his or her hands or smile at the sound of a favorite adult's voice

2 to 3 months, a child does not visually follow moving objects

3 months, a child does not reach for, grasp, and hold objects

4 months, a child babbles but does not try to imitate sounds

4 months, a child does not

- bring objects to his or her mouth

- turn his or her head to locate sound

5 months, a child does not smile spontaneously

6 months, a child does not laugh or squeal or reach for objects

7 months, a child does not

- try to attract attention

- follow objects with both eyes at 1' and 6' ranges

8 months, does not show interest in playing peek-a-boo

12 months, a child does not

- search for objects hidden while he or she watches

- say any words

- use gestures such as hand waving or head shaking

- point to pictures or things

15 months, a child does not seem to know what household objects are used for

18 months, a child does not speak at least 15 words

2 years, a child does not

- use two-word sentences

- imitate actions or words

- follow simple instructions

3 years, a child

- cannot build a tower of more than four blocks

- does not engage in pretend play

- cannot copy a circle

what's next?

Skill-Building Journal, section **5-5** (*Learning Activity A*), section **5-10** (*Answer Sheets*), and section **5-1** (*Feedback*).

Learning Activities

LEARNING
ACTIVITY

B. Creating an Environment That Encourages Exploration and Discovery

In this activity you will learn to

- create an environment that encourages infants and toddlers to explore, discover, and gain new skills

- select and make materials that stimulate infants' and toddlers' curiosity

Environments that promote learning "provide ample opportunities for young children to be active agents in their own learning and to receive predictable responses from their surroundings."[26] They must be safe so children can explore freely. They should offer interesting objects to manipulate and include areas for moving, so children can use their senses and motor skills to learn. Learning environments must also include caring adults who talk with and respond to children's efforts to act and communicate.

Creating an environment that supports exploration and discovery starts with a review of the ways infants and toddlers get to know and make sense of the world. As described in the previous learning activity, young infants begin to think and reason while using their senses to learn about their world. Gradually, children expand their skills.

Infants and Toddlers Expand Their Skills as They...

- use their senses and small motor skills in combination (e.g., hold and suck a rattle)

- travel to different levels (e.g., pull up to standing) and from one place to another (e.g., crawl to reach a toy)

- remember their experiences and apply their understanding in new situations (e.g., look for a toy in the last place they saw it)

- learn by imitating what they see and hear

- solve problems on their own (e.g., try different approaches to reach a toy)

- begin to plan before acting (e.g., choose props for pretend play)

Selecting Toys and Materials That Support Cognitive Development

All of the toys and materials you provide for children's use should be safe, germ-free, and easy to sanitize. Module 3, *Learning Environment*, includes a list of toys and materials for infants and toddlers. Also consider the following suggestions for selecting toys and materials that invite children to explore, discover, and expand their thinking skills:

Provide toys and materials that react to the actions of infants and toddlers.

- Young infants can learn about their abilities to make things happen through bat-and-kick crib toys, grasp-and-shake rattles, and other noise-making toys.

- Mobile infants can discover the effects of their actions with pop-up toys, jack-in-the-boxes, and activity centers with dials, knobs, and push buttons.

- Toddlers can experiment with chunky crayons and paper, playdough and utensils, sand and water play props, musical instruments, and a collection of plastic containers with screwable tops.

Include items that stimulate children's senses.

- Seeing: colored scarves and ribbons hung on a fence in a shady outdoor area or suspended from the ceiling, an aquarium filled with fish or plants, hand-held safety mirrors, picture books, aluminum pie plates hung at different levels

- Touching: soft dolls and animals; feely toys, books, boxes, and wall panels made from fabrics with different textures (velvet, terrycloth, polyester, cotton, burlap); paper to crumple; sand, water, and related props

- Tasting: a variety of safe, washable toys to grasp and mouth; washable books; new foods for snacks and meals; foods prepared by the children

- Listening: soothing background sounds, such as soft music and a table-top fountain; wind chimes made with recycled items; bells to ring; pot lids to clang together; and drums to bang

- Smelling: cut flowers in a vase placed out of children's reach, an outdoor garden, fruits and snacks with distinctive aromas

Include items that encourage children to move their bodies.

- For young infants, provide a soft blanket or comfortable mat on which to lie.

- For mobile infants, offer push-and-pull toys, ride-on cars and trucks, wagons, and balls of different sizes and textures.

- For toddlers, provide tunnels, swings, riding toys, and climbers.

Include familiar items that support a sense of security and new items that offer challenges.

- **Offer household items similar to those children use with their families** (pots and pans, nesting bowls, dishes, dress-up clothes).

- **Display items in the same places every day** (books, dolls, blocks, crayons and paper) so children can find what they need.

- **Provide materials that invite children to increase their skills** but that are not so difficult to use that they are frustrating.

- **Include open-ended toys and materials** that can be used in different ways by children with varied skills and interests, such as blocks, pots and pans, and simple dress-up clothes.

Making Toys That Meet the Needs and Interests of Individual Children

Homemade toys are a wonderful way to respond to individual skills, interests, and needs while supporting cognitive development. When families see their children enjoying homemade toys at the center, they may want to make them at home. The following instructions suggest ways teachers and families can use inexpensive materials to make appropriate toys.

Simple pattern card

For:	Young infants
Materials:	Plain white 4" x 6" index card; thick, colored markers; tape
Make it:	Draw a simple shape on the card, using one or two colors.
Use it:	Place or tape the card where a young infant can see it (e.g., on the side of a crib, on the wall next to the diapering table, or securely propped on the floor in front of the child). Provide variety by making other cards with different shapes and colors.

Mobiles

For: Young infants

Materials: Clothes hangers; string; clothespins; thick, colored markers; glue; interesting things to hang from the mobile, such as plastic container lids, bells, keys, fabric scraps, colored ribbons, small paper plates, pictures of familiar objects, scarves, and aluminum foil

Make it: Use a clothes hanger as the frame for each mobile. Tie strings of different lengths to the hanger and attach clothespins to each string. Make interesting things by drawing simple faces on paper plates and gluing pictures to plates or container lids. Clip a drawing, picture, or another interesting item to each string. Make several mobiles at one time.

Use it: Hang mobiles at different heights so children can see but not reach them. Touch a mobile so it moves and makes noise. Lift an infant so he can touch it himself.

Puppet

For: Young and mobile infants and toddlers

Materials: White tube sock, polyester fiberfill, strong thread, felt or fabric, needles, scissors, yarn (optional)

Make it: Stuff the foot of the sock with fiberfill. Secure the opening with strong, tight stitches or a rubber band. Sew on felt or fabric eyes, nose, and mouth. Make sure your stitches are secure. (For toddlers, sew yarn hair on the puppet's head.)

Use it: Teachers and young infants can play with the puppet together, and mobile infants can play with it on their own or with an adult. Toddlers might talk to the puppet and pretend that the puppet talks to them.

Shape-sorting box

For: Mobile infants and toddlers

Materials: Empty container with a lid (e.g., oatmeal box or plastic wipes box), contact paper, small blocks, scissors

Make it: Cover container with contact paper. Cut openings in the lid, to match the shapes and sizes of the blocks.

Use it: Mobile infants might remove the lid and drop the blocks inside; older children might push the blocks through the openings.

Texture cards

For: Young and mobile infants and toddlers

Materials: Cardboard; shoe box or plastic basket; wallpaper; fabric, ribbon, sandpaper, wallpaper, and other scraps with a variety of textures; scissors; glue or self-adhesive Velcro® strips

Make it: Cut the cardboard, if necessary, to fit in the container. Use glue or Velcro® strips to secure a different scrap to each piece of cardboard. Store the texture cards in the box or basket. (Alternatively, you can bind the cards with laces to make a texture book or attach them to the wall at children's height to make a panel for them to feel.)

Use it: Teachers can share the texture cards with children or put them where children can touch them on their own. Talk with children about how the cards feel, e.g., "This is soft. This is smooth. This is scratchy."

Fill-and-dump set

For: Mobile infants and toddlers

Materials: One-gallon plastic milk jug, scissors, one-piece wooden clothes pins, poker chips, or other inexpensive items that are too large to swallow (i.e., too large to fit in an empty film container)

Make it: Clean the milk jug; then cut off the top, leaving the handle in place. Fill the jug with inexpensive items to dump.

Use it: Children feel competent as they fill the jug, dump it, and then do it again.

Lacing set

For: Toddlers

Materials: Empty thread spools; open container such as a shoe box or large yogurt container; several short, thick laces; 4" x 6" index card; colored markers; and tape

Make it: Knot one end of each lace or attach a spool to the end so that additional spools will not slide off. Put the spools and laces in the container. Use the card to make a label, by drawing a picture of spools on a lace. Tape the card to the outside of the container.

Use it: Toddlers can thread the spools on the laces.

what's next?

Skill-Building Journal, section **5-6** (*Learning Activity B*) and section **5-1** (*Feedback*).

Learning Activities

LEARNING ACTIVITY

C. Supporting Infants' and Toddlers' Thinking Skills During Routines

In this activity you will learn to

- recognize how your relationships with infants and toddlers support their cognitive development

- use routines to encourage infants and toddlers to explore and make discoveries

Positive relationships support cognitive development.

Infants and toddlers have much to learn about the world, but how they feel about themselves as learners is as important as what they learn. For an infant or toddler, learning and feelings go hand in hand. They need trusting, caring relationships with their teachers to feel safe and secure enough to explore and learn. This is one reason why it is important to interact with young children, individually and, as they get older, in very small groups. You and your colleagues can divide the group so each child has a primary teacher. This person builds a special, responsive relationship with several children and families. The primary teacher supports the cognitive development of assigned children in several ways. Here are some examples:

- Berthe (4 months) builds a sense of trust when Ms. Bates has her bottle ready before she cries to announce her hunger. Ms. Bates knows that, when Berthe starts to cry, she is very hungry and ready to eat. Because Berthe trusts Ms. Bates, she feels secure enough to get to know the world actively.

- Charles (10 months) can depend on Ms. Gonzalez to be as excited as he is when he learns something new, such as pulling himself up to standing. To let him know that she understands how hard he worked on this new skill, she claps her hands and says, "Charles, you are standing all by yourself. Congratulations!"

- Emily (26 months) feels competent when Mr. Lewis expresses confidence in her ability to make decisions. After they finish reading a book he says, "We can read another story or play lotto. Which would you like to do?"

When you respond to infants and toddlers during routines such as diapering, eating, and cleaning up, you encourage them to think and learn. Here are some simple things you might already do during routines to build relationships and support thinking skills.

While diapering children

- talk about softness as you take turns touching a clean diaper

- point to your images in the mirror

- touch a mobile to make it move or make a noise

- describe what you are doing and ask older children, "What's next?"

- play peek-a-boo with a clean diaper and patty-cake (after hands are clean)

- sing simple songs such as "Open, Shut Them"

- speak children's names and respond to their language

While feeding infants

- look at them so they know that they have your attention

- talk about what they are doing or might be feeling ("This tastes so good, you kicked your legs.")

- sing and recite rhymes

- talk about concepts such as full and empty

- relax and enjoy being together

While preparing and eating snacks and meals with older children

- invite them to participate before, during, and after eating

- point out smells, colors, and textures

- involve them in conversations about yesterday, today, and tomorrow

- discuss cause and effect ("What happened to the cheese on your pizza while it was in the toaster oven?")

When you engage with and respond to a child during a routine or at any other time, you encourage children to notice sights and sounds, sustain attention, and construct understandings about the world.

what's next?

Skill-Building Journal, section **5-7** (*Learning Activity C*) and section **5-1** (*Feedback*).

Learning Activities

LEARNING
ACTIVITY

D. Encouraging Cognitive Development Throughout the Day

In this activity you will learn to

- consider the situation and the child when deciding how best to support cognitive development

- plan simple, developmentally appropriate activities that correspond to individual children's skills and interests

In the previous activity, you focused on using routines to build relationships and support thinking skills. As discussed in *Learning Activity B, Creating an Environment That Encourages Exploration and Discovery*, infants and toddlers also make sense of the world while playing with a variety of interesting toys and materials. Older infants and toddlers make decisions, solve problems, and develop concepts while taking part in simple activities such as playing catch, drawing with chunky crayons, and blowing and chasing bubbles.

Think about the child and the situation before deciding to step in.

Children initiate most of their play. They don't need you to show them how to fit nesting cups together or push boxes and chairs around the room. Sometimes it is appropriate to get involved in their play, but, before you step in, think about the child and the situation. For example, you might place a toy slightly out of an infant's reach because you know she is curious and will want to creep on her tummy to find out what it is. You might see a toddler getting frustrated because the paper bag he is drawing on keeps moving around. If he is usually open to suggestions, you might ask, "Would you like to help me tape the bag to the table so it will stay in one place?" If he agrees, show him how to apply the tape. If not, respect his choice and let him continue what he is doing.

Sometimes it is supportive and respectful to give children the freedom to explore and make discoveries by themselves. As children develop, their attention spans grow and they learn how to focus on an activity such as completing a puzzle, pretending to rock a doll to sleep, or filling containers and pouring at the water table. When teachers interrupt children's concentration, they interfere with the learning process instead of enhancing it. Your ongoing observations will help you learn when and when not to step in to guide children's play and learning.

Be ready to step in immediately, however, if a child is in danger or getting too frustrated. A mobile infant needs help immediately when he stands on tiptoe and is about to pull a clipboard off the counter and onto his head. So does a toddler who begins throwing pieces of a puzzle because she can't get them to fit.

- How do you decide when and when not to step in to guide a child's play?

- How can you use your observation notes as a guide to recognizing when a child is too frustrated to continue with an activity?

Sometimes teachers improvise on-the-spot activities and experiences.

Many times during the day you improvise activities on the spot. You might lift your arms in the air to play "So Big" with an infant, or offer to toss a ball with a toddler. Over time, you will add more and more on-the-spot activities to your caregiving repertoire.

You might also involve infants and toddlers in problem-solving experiences, such as how to free a pull toy when the string is wrapped around a chair leg. Kneel down with the child and study the situation. Point out that the string is twisted around the chair leg. Although you may be the one who actually frees the toy, your calm demeanor and "can do" attitude will help the child learn to analyze and solve problems.

- What on-the-spot activities are in your caregiving repertoire?

- How do you model problem-solving skills?

Planning Activities That Promote Cognitive Development

Teachers also plan simple activities for individual children and for a very small group.

Most mobile infants and toddlers enjoy simple, hands-on activities that are planned with their skills and interests in mind. Activities for this age group are most successful when they are open-ended, i.e., when there is no right or wrong way to participate. Offer activities that allow children to make choices such as when to join and when to leave, and which materials to use and how to use them. Include opportunities for children to use their senses and thinking skills.

Here are some guidelines for offering simple activities to individual children or to a very small group:

- **Have clear goals.** Think about what children might do and learn from the activity.

- **Be ready.** Gather the materials you need ahead of time, so you can focus on and respond to the children.

- **Choose an appropriate setting.** Think about what the children will be doing, how they will use materials, and how much space they will need. For example, it's best to offer water activities outdoors or in an area of the room with a washable floor.

- **Consider the time of day.** Schedule the activity for a time when children are most likely to be interested and receptive. If an unexpected event disrupts your plan, reschedule the activity for another day.

- **Repeat the activity.** Learning takes time and practice. When children do an activity several times, they construct deeper understandings about what they experienced.

- **Give a brief, step-by-step explanation.** Tell the children what you and they are going to do, and in what order.

- **Encourage children to use their senses.** For example, on a walk outdoors, invite children to listen to the sounds of chirping birds or stop to watch a truck rolling down the road. While making muffins, let the children smell both cinnamon and nutmeg; then ask them to decide which spice to use in the recipe.

- **Be willing to change your expectations.** Children may have ideas that are different from yours about how to use materials or how to join in. Sometimes other things interest the children more than the planned activity. If you see a crew fixing a pothole while you are walking to the mailbox, accept that the event has captured the children's attention. You can walk to the mailbox another day.

Ask open-ended questions that encourage thinking.

You can help older children expand their thinking skills by asking open-ended questions that don't have simple *yes* or *no* answers. For example, you might ask questions to help children

- recall a past experience ("What happened the last time it snowed?")

- remember someone who is not present ("Where is Mr. Lewis today?")

- make a prediction ("What do you think will happen if you drop the rock in the puddle?")

- solve a problem ("Where can you put your wet boots?")

- When do you encourage children to use their senses to explore and discover?

- How do you respond as children answer your open-ended questions?

Keep in mind that the goal of these questions is not to receive a correct response. Listen and respond in ways that encourage thinking and help children feel confident in themselves as learners.

what's next?

Skill-Building Journal, section **5-8** (*Learning Activity D*), section **5-1** (*Feedback*), and section **5-9** (*Reflecting on Your Learning*).

6
Communication

Overview

Creating Places Where Infants and Toddlers Can Enjoy Sounds, Language, Pictures, and Print

Offering Opportunities for Infants and Toddlers to Explore Sounds, Language, Pictures, and Print

Encouraging and Responding to Infants' and Toddlers' Efforts to Communicate

Your Own Experiences With Communication

Learning Activities

A. Using Your Knowledge of Infants and Toddlers to Promote Communication Skills

B. Creating an Environment That Invites Infants and Toddlers to Enjoy Sounds, Language, Pictures, and Print

C. Encouraging the Language Development of Infants and Toddlers

D. Sharing Books With Infants and Toddlers

6. Communication

Communication is the sharing of ideas and feelings with others. People communicate in many ways: through gestures, facial expressions, touch, pictures, speech, and writing. They communicate in order to think, plan, solve problems, figure out what others think and feel, and build relationships with others. Effective verbal communication involves listening, speaking, reading, and writing.

The drive to communicate begins early in life.

Our strong drive to communicate begins soon after birth. A newborn's cries are reflexive, but soon a baby learns that crying will bring a trusted adult to meet her needs. Within a short time, infants smile and coo when they see a familiar face. When people respond, infants begin to learn about the give-and-take of conversations.

By the end of their first year, babies communicate intentionally, both verbally and nonverbally. They vocalize while pointing at objects or raising their arms to be picked up. By the time they are toddlers, children understand and begin to use conventional language to communicate. Their thinking skills grow, and they learn to identify concepts, such as up and down, and begin to talk about past and future events.

You play an essential role in supporting children's communication skills.

Young children learn a lot about language simply by interacting with adults who listen and talk with them. Daily interactions have enormous benefits for young children. For almost 2 1/2 years, researchers Betty Hart and Todd R. Risley observed and documented the language development of very young children.[27] Their study found that, by age 3 and when retested at age 9, the children whose parents spent the most time talking with them had much larger vocabularies than children who had fewer verbal interactions. The children who were exposed to the least language required 41 hours per week of language-rich interventions to catch up with their more verbal peers.

Singing, saying rhymes, talking about anything and everything, reading aloud, and modeling writing skills are among the many ways to support children's language development. Most importantly, by responding to each child's efforts to communicate, you indicate, "I received your message, and I think it is important. Please tell me more."

You can support the development of children's communication skills by

- creating places where infants and toddlers can enjoy sounds, language, pictures, and print

- offering opportunities for infants and toddlers to explore sounds, language, pictures, and print

- encouraging and responding to infants' and toddlers' efforts to communicate

---

Creating Places Where Infants and Toddlers Can Enjoy Sounds, Language, Pictures, and Print

1. **Provide pleasant sounds and music when children are likely to listen.** Eliminate continuous and disruptive noise and sounds. Turn off the tape or CD if nobody is paying attention.

2. **Include a variety of books that correspond to individual and group skills, interests, languages, cultures, and families.** Consult observation notes, families, and librarians when choosing books for the children in your group. Keep favorites on hand and update your collection regularly so there is always something familiar and something new to read.

3. **Make books about familiar people, objects, and events, and share them with children.** "This story is about the day we cooked French toast. Listen carefully to hear what happened."

4. **Provide inviting, comfortable, cozy spaces for communicating with one child or a small group.** Indoors, a glider, small couch, or pile of cushions are ideal settings for laughing, singing, talking, and reading together. Outdoors, you can sit and talk on a blanket, at a picnic table, or under a tree.

5. **Provide toys, materials, and equipment that encourage talking and playing together.** Two mobile infants or toddlers can rock and talk in a wooden rocking boat; several children can play in a house made from a cardboard box; two or more can play with balls.

6. **Share pictures and photographs of familiar objects, events, and people, including children's families.** Talk about the pictures and photographs, and ask mobile infants and toddlers to name what they see. Mount the pictures on cardboard and cover them with clear adhesive paper.

Lovette Says, "I Want to Read a Book"

As you read the following story, pay attention to how Ms. Gonzalez encourages Lovette to use language and to explore books.

Lovette: Book.

Ms. Gonzalez: Lovette, do you want the book?

Ms. Gonzalez: Here is the book. It's a big one.

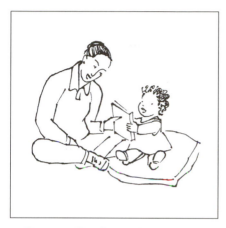

Lovette: Book.

Ms. Gonzalez: Would you like to read *Goodnight Moon*?

Ms. Gonzalez: "In the great green room…"

Ms. Gonzalez: Lovette said a new word today: *book*! Has she said any new words at home?

Offering Opportunities for Infants and Toddlers to Explore Sounds, Language, Pictures, and Print

7. **Use picture and word labels to show where toys and materials are stored.** Tape sturdy, laminated labels to shelves and containers. Refer to the labels when helping children find and put away materials.

8. **Encourage children to notice sounds in their indoor and outdoor environments.** "Do you hear the leaves crunching when you walk through them?"

9. **Provide a variety of papers and writing tools for children who are ready for them.** Beginners can use large brown paper bags and chunky crayons; children with more experience will enjoy different kinds of paper and non-toxic markers with wide tips.

10. **Introduce new and interesting sounds, words, and language patterns.** Make up rhymes, sing silly sings, and recite chants and fingerplays. Invite children to join, as they are able; teach older toddlers short poems and fingerplays.

11. **Read aloud every day, with individual infants and very small groups of toddlers.** Invite children to participate and talk about the pictures and stories.

12. **Encourage families to read aloud.** Share tips about reading aloud with infants and toddlers. Make arrangements with libraries and book distribution programs so every family has access to children's books.

13. **Model reading and writing during daily routines.** Invite toddlers to add their marks to a shopping list for snack supplies; read aloud a note to or from a family member.

Jessica and Adam Tell a Story

As you read the following story, pay attention to how Ms. Bates and Mr. Lewis encourage the children to use language and to explore writing.

Mr. Lewis: Welcome back! What did you see on your walk?

Adam: A big bird!

Jessica: We saw a bird's nest, too. The bird flew 'round and 'round. Then she sat on her nest.

Mr. Lewis: That's exciting!

Ms. Bates: Are you writing a story?

Jessica: My story says, "We saw a big bird flying. We saw a nest. The bird sat on her nest."

Adam: This is my story, and this is a picture of the mama bird.

Encouraging and Responding to Infants' and Toddlers' Efforts to Communicate

14. **Listen and respond to children's gestures, vocalizations, words, and phrases.** "I hear you saying 'Bah, bah, bah.'" "Are you saying you want to get down from my lap now?" "Geoff, do you want to know what that is? It's a duck."

15. **Talk with children about what they see and experience throughout the day.** "The fingerpaint feels cool and smooth." "Hannah is crying because she fell down. Mr. Lewis is helping her feel better."

16. **Learn a few important words in families' home languages so that the children know that their home language is important to you.** "Gracias, Josefina. Thank you for helping Raoul find his mitten."

17. **Share enjoyment of listening, talking, singing, reading, and writing.** "Let's sing the 'Eensy Weensy Spider.' It's one of my favorites." "There's Spot. What's that silly puppy going to do next?"

18. **Make comments and pose questions that encourage children to communicate.** "These are really crunchy carrots. What are some other crunchy things?"

Mr. Lewis and Sammy Have a Conversation

As you read the following story, pay attention to how Mr. Lewis encourages Sammy to babble. Also pay attention to how Mr. Lewis lets Sammy know that he is listening to him.

Mr. Lewis: Sammy, are you trying to touch the mobile?

Mr. Lewis: Would you like to touch the mobile?

Sammy: Ah-bah.

Mr. Lewis: Do you want to make it spin again?

Sammy: Ooooh.

Mr. Lewis: That's pretty exciting, isn't it?

Sammy: Ah-bah.

Mr. Lewis: Let's see what other interesting things we can find.

what's next?

Skill-Building Journal, section **6-2** (*Overview*), section **6-10** (*Answer Sheets*), and section **6-1** (*Feedback*).

Your Own Experiences With Communication

We use language skills all day, every day.

Communication requires listening, talking, reading, and writing well enough to send and receive messages. As lifelong learners, we use communication skills to increase our knowledge and understanding of the world, do our jobs, and explore special interests. We send and receive messages orally, nonverbally (by using facial expressions, body positions, and gestures), and in writing. You use language skills all day, every day, on and off the job. On a typical morning, you might

- listen to the voice of a radio announcer giving today's weather report

- talk with family members about what is happening that day

- read the instructions on a box of oatmeal to learn how to cook it in the microwave

- write a note to your trainer saying you are ready to discuss a learning activity

It is important to send clear messages.

To send clear verbal messages, it is important to say what you mean. If you want someone to help you choose books, you might say, "I'd like to order some new informational books. Will you help choose the titles?" An unclear message could be misinterpreted. For example, asking, "Do you think we have enough informational books for our group?" might not encourage anyone to help choose titles because it does not express a request for help. You also need to pay attention to your nonverbal communications. Make sure your body language matches your message.

Communication also involves receiving and interpreting messages from other people. Listen carefully to the sender's words and note nonverbal cues. To make sure you understand a message correctly, you sometimes have to ask for more information. To confirm your understanding, you might use questions and statements like the following:

- Are you saying that...?

- Do you mean...?

- Do I understand correctly that...?

- It sounds like you want...

Teachers communicate regularly through written messages such as notes, daily logs, and e-mails. Be sure to write clearly so colleagues and families receive accurate information that will not be misunderstood. Use a dictionary or style guide if you have questions about spelling, punctuation, or grammar.

Read for your own pleasure.

In addition to reading so you can learn more about caring for infants and toddlers, we hope you read for pleasure. Reading is a lifelong activity that introduces people, places, events, and experiences you might never encounter firsthand. Choose whatever you enjoy. It could be a newspaper or magazine, fiction or non-fiction, a short story or full-length novel.

what's next?

Skill-Building Journal, section **6-3** (*Your Own Experiences With Communication*), section **6-1** (*Feedback*), and section **6-4** (*Pre-Training Assessment*).

Learning Activities

A. Using Your Knowledge of Infants and Toddlers to Promote Communication Skills

In this activity you will learn to

- recognize some typical communication behaviors of infants and toddlers

- use what you know about infants and toddlers to support their communication skills

Infants develop communication skills when families and teachers respond to their coos and smiles, sing lullabies, and play games such as peek-a-boo. These daily interactions teach children about the pleasures and purposes of talking with other people. Young children continue to develop listening and speaking skills as they communicate their needs and wants through sounds and gestures, say their first words, and begin to use simple sentences, e.g., "Me go," or "Daddy back soon?" By the time they are three years old, children have progressed from using language to seek attention to using it to learn. They take part in conversations, talk about past and future activities, and tell stories about real and imaginary events.

The first five years are the most important time for learning language.

Scientists tell us that there are times when certain information can be learned more easily than at other times. The first five years are the prime time for learning language. This does not mean that children learn all there is to know about language by age five. Language learning continues to take place throughout life.

As they are gaining listening and speaking skills, infants and toddlers are also exploring print. Although it will be many years before the children in your care are readers and writers, they are already learning about books and print. When you read aloud with Savanna (3 months), she may not know what books are and she does not understand what you are reading, but she enjoys being with you and listening to the sound of your voice. These warm, comforting feelings will stay with her, and she will probably think of reading as a pleasant experience. Older infants and toddlers explore books on their own and listen as you read and tell stories. They can hold crayons and make marks on paper: the first step on the road to writing.

Young infants (birth–8 months) communicate by using facial expressions, body movements, cries, and other vocalizations.

- Sammy (3 months) raises his eyebrows and turns his head toward the speaker when he hears, "Hi, Sammy."

- Jon (6 months) coos as Mr. Lewis talks to him while changing his diaper.

- Luci (8 months) looks up when Ms. Bates points to the sky and asks, "See the bird?"

Long before they can understand or say a single word, young infants begin communicating. A hungry infant cries and moves her lips when picked up. An infant in pain cries and holds his body stiffly. Soon families and teachers learn the meaning of different cries and body language. One cry might mean, "I'm hungry," while another says, "I'm bored. Come pick me up and play with me!" Within a few months, most infants learn to laugh, coo, and gurgle, and their ability to communicate expands. Then they can express pleasure and affection. They can "talk" back and forth with other people, expressing needs and interests.

Each of the world's 6,000 languages has a different set of distinctive sounds. These sounds, known as phonemes, are used to form words. Infants are born with the ability to distinguish these sounds from other sounds in their environment. Their babbles include many more sounds than those used in their home languages. Beginning at about 6 months, infants begin to ignore the phonemes that are not used in their home languages. From this point on, their babbling includes only the sounds they hear most often. Although Sandy (5 months) does not know that "ma-ma-ma-ma" sounds like "Mama," she is learning to distinguish and repeat sounds that are similar.

As they get older, infants begin to respond to simple, familiar requests and to their own names. Raoul (8 months) understands Ms. Bates' gesture, and he might understand some of her words, when she holds out her arms and says, "Raoul, do you want to get up?" He responds by sitting up in his crib and raising his own arms.

Mobile infants (8–18 months) send messages with sounds and gestures.

- Malou (9 months) shakes her head and pushes the spoon away when she has had enough yogurt.

- Peter (12 months) takes a paper towel from Ms. Gonzalez as she says, "Here you go Peter. Dry your hands."

- Zora (16 months) turns the pages and repeats, "Night," while reading *Goodnight Gorilla* with Mr. Lewis.

Mobile infants have figured out that they can send messages to other people. They point, shake their heads, and look back and forth between an object and another person to ask questions, make requests, seek attention, say hello, and get someone to attend to what they are looking at. Although they do not express themselves with words yet, they begin to understand the meaning of words and phrases. For instance, Tommy (9 months) claps his hands when Ms. Gonzalez says, "Pat-a-cake."

After several months of babbling and making word-like sounds, an infant says a first word, usually one with personal meaning. For example, Andy, an active one-year-old, is always climbing into, over, under, and around things. His first word is *up*. Next comes *Bo* (his cat's name is Bones). Language gains are rapid as mobile infants learn the words that label familiar people, animals, body parts, toys, foods, and more. Soon infants use the same word to mean different things by varying their inflexion and adding gestures. A child might say, "Mama?" while pointing to the door. His teacher responds by using the child's word in a full sentence, "That's right. Your mama went to work. She'll be back soon." Another day, the child might exclaim, "Mama!" to greet his mother when she walks in.

Older mobile infants have the fine motor skills needed to hold large crayons. At first, they may explore crayons by smelling and tasting them. With a little guidance, they learn to grasp a crayon in their fist and make marks on paper. This is an exciting experience for mobile infants, who are most interested in the physical experience of moving their arms back and forth across the paper.

Mobile infants like books about people, things, and simple experiences. They begin to understand that pictures represent real things. Upon request, they point to details in pictures, e.g., pointing to the rabbit when someone asks, "Where's the bunny?" While listening to a story, a mobile infant might jump up to get an object like the one pictured in the book. Read-aloud sessions should be short, to match children's attention spans.

Mobile infants continue to enjoy playing with language. They brighten when a teacher invites them to sing and to recite rhymes and chants.

Toddlers (18–36 months) understand and use increasingly complex language.

- Lovette (20 months) points to her nose when Mr. Lewis says, "Lovette, where's your nose?"

- Ricky (28 months) tells Adam (30 months) "My hat!" when Adam tries to take it from him.

- Jessica (34 months) listens to Ms. Bates read aloud, "Chicka, chicka...," and joins in, "Boom, boom!"

Toddlers experience an explosion of language. An 18-month-old may have a speaking vocabulary of 10 or more words. Within six months, the same child will say as many as 300 words and combine two words in a simple sentence, e.g., "Go out." Between her second and third birthday, she will gain 600 more words, learn to speak in longer sentences, and begin to use different parts of speech: prepositions (*in, on*), plurals (add *s* to words), pronouns (*me, she, it*), articles (*the, a*), and conjunctions (*and, but*). When an 18-month-old wants to play with a car, he says, "Car," while pointing to the shelf. By the time he is three years old, the same child says, "I want the red car."

Thinking and language skills are closely related. As a toddler's vocabulary grows, he can begin to talk about the present, past, and future and describe concepts such as over and under, top and bottom. Toddlers ask a lot of questions, often again and again. They are eager to learn and turn to adults for information.

Since they were infants, toddlers have been learning about conversations, and now they can truly participate. For example, they know that it is their turn to talk when the person with whom they are conversing pauses.

Books about real-life experiences and familiar feelings are popular with toddlers. They like predictable books with repetition and rhymes, in part because they like to join in. Sometimes toddlers look at books on their own. They point to pictures and say the words out loud. Older toddlers may remember simple plots and retell stories in their own words.

Toddlers scribble with greater control than they did when they first encountered crayons and paper. With increased small muscle skills, eye-hand coordination, and thinking skills, toddlers begin to explore different techniques, colors, and ways to use writing tools. By about age three, children come to understand that writing and drawing are different. An older toddler might ask an adult to read her writing to her.

The following lists summarize key characteristics and events in the development of young infants, mobile infants, and toddlers that are related to their communication skills.

Development of Infants and Toddlers

Young infants (birth–8 months)

- coo, gurgle, and smile, to themselves at first and then back and forth with others

- listen and respond to sounds and voices around them

- enjoy listening to simple stories, songs, and rhymes

- cry, make other sounds, move their bodies, and use facial expressions to communicate

- understand and respond to their names and very simple, familiar requests

- begin babbling; produce the sounds of their home language

- use their senses to explore books

Mobile infants (8–18 months)

- use gestures to communicate, such as shaking their heads and pointing

- understand and respond to gestures, facial expressions, and changes in vocal tone

- continue babbling to themselves; take turns babbling, talking, and singing with others

- learn to turn pages; may be fascinated with page turning

- begin to understand that objects in pictures represent things in the world

- say a few words that refer to interesting people, objects, and actions

- understand and respond to their own names, a few familiar words, and simple requests

- hold crayons and make marks on paper

Toddlers (18–36 months)

- increase their receptive and expressive vocabularies rapidly

- speak in sentences that gradually increase from two to several words in length

- understand and respond to many words, simple directions, and questions

- talk about the present, and, as language and thinking skills grow, begin to talk about the past and future

- enjoy books with rhymes and predictable words and phrases they can anticipate and repeat

- coordinate eye and hand movements and gain small muscle skills

- tell very simple stories, use language creatively, and begin to express feelings with words

Development: It's All Connected

Infants and toddlers gain communication skills by watching, listening to, and responding to people at home and at their child development programs. They make language and literacy discoveries as they play, explore, and interact with others. Communication skills develop along with cognitive, social/emotional, and physical skills. Here are some examples:

Physical

Infants use the small muscles in their hands and fingers to grasp and hold toys. Soon they will be able to hold crayons and make marks on paper.

Toddlers control their scribbling as their fine motor skills and eye-hand coordination improve.

Cognitive

Infants expand their understanding of language, which corresponds with their thinking about people, objects, and experiences that are not immediately present.

Toddlers learn words and language structures to describe their experiences and observations. They make predictions; ask questions; solve simple problems; invent stories; and talk about what they and others did, saw, and heard.

Self

Infants feel competent when they realize that their sounds and gestures send messages to their families and teachers.

Toddlers gain confidence when they can get someone's attention, take part in conversations, and use words to share their feelings.

Social

Infants learn that it is fun to be with other people, as they talk, laugh, sing, and play with a familiar teacher.

Toddlers who can express their ideas and feelings are more likely to enjoy the company of others. For example, they can say, "Let's play house," or "I'm angry. You broke my tower."

In many states, all newborns are screened for hearing problems before leaving the hospital. Parents and teachers must continue to be aware of signs of possible problems with hearing and speech. If problems are identified, they can be addressed in the first six months of life, a critical period for language development. With early intervention, the child's speech and language development are more likely to be normal. The following development alerts could indicate possible concerns about hearing, speech, or other areas of development related to early language skills.

Some Language and Communication Development Alerts [28]

Note: Because language and cognitive development are so closely related, some of the following alerts also appear in module 5, *Cognitive*.

It may be time to suggest that a family consult their health provider if, by

2 months, a child does not

- notice his hands
- smile at the sound of a favorite adult's voice

2 to 3 months, a child does not visually follow moving objects held near her face

3 months, a child does not

- reach for, grasp, and hold objects
- listen to speech
- smile at people

3 to 4 months, a child does not make sounds by cooing and babbling

4 months, a child vocalizes but does not try to imitate word-like sounds

4 months, a child does not

- bring objects to his mouth
- turn her head to locate the source of a voice or other sound

5 months, a child does not smile spontaneously (i.e., without prompting) in order to begin a social interaction with someone

6 months, a child does not

- laugh or squeal
- notice noisy toys
- respond when someone says, "No"
- reach for objects
- try to locate or move toward the source of a voice or other sound

7 months, a child does not

- try to attract attention by using facial expressions, body movements, cries, or other vocalizations
- follow objects with both eyes at 1-foot and 6-feet ranges

8 months, a child does not show interest in playing peek-a-boo

12 months, a child does not

- say any words, even unclearly
- respond to his or her name
- use gestures such as waving or shaking his head
- point to pictures or things

18 months, a child does not speak at least 15 words

2 years, a child does not

- use one- or two-word sentences to ask questions or make statements
- imitate actions or words
- listen to simple stories, songs, and rhymes
- follow simple instructions

3 years, a child has persistent drooling or very unclear speech or does not

- use words to identify common objects and basic actions and feelings
- use two- to three-words sentences to ask questions or make statements
- understand differences in the meanings of words that sound alike
- follow requests that have two or three steps
- manipulate small objects easily
- engage in pretend play
- copy a circle upon request

---

what's next?

Skill-Building Journal, section **6-5** (*Learning Activity A*), section **6-10** (*Answer Sheets*), and section **6-1** (*Feedback*).

Learning Activities

LEARNING ACTIVITY

B. Creating an Environment That Invites Infants and Toddlers to Enjoy Sounds, Language, Pictures, and Print

In this activity you will learn to

- use the environment to encourage infants and toddlers gradually to learn about listening and speaking

- arrange indoor and outdoor spaces and provide materials that support young children's emerging literacy explorations

The environment can encourage communication and invite infants and toddlers to explore language.

Families introduce children to talking, listening, reading, and writing. Daily read-aloud sessions in a comfortable chair or while sitting outside are opportunities for families and children of all ages to enjoy each other's company while exploring the world of books. A basket of books and writing supplies encourages mobile infants and toddlers to begin making their own literacy discoveries. When families model reading and writing for pleasure and for other purposes, young children realize that these are valuable and useful skills.

You can build on children's positive home experiences and provide opportunities for children who do not have rich language experiences at home, by creating an environment that invites children to explore language and literacy. As they practice and experiment, children build their own understandings about the spoken and written forms of language. You and your colleagues are the most important part of the language-learning environment for several reasons:

- You **respond** to children's communications and **encourage** them to continue expressing themselves. You **talk** with children about their feelings and daily experiences.

- You **have fun** with language by singing and by reciting rhymes and chants.

- You **read aloud** to every child, individually and in very small groups.

- You **model** how language and literacy are a part of daily life at your center.

Try these strategies for using the environment to encourage listening and talking:

Set up the environment so that it is comfortable for children. As discussed in module 3, *Learning Environment*, infants and toddlers are more likely to communicate when they feel safe and secure. A homelike setting helps children feel comfortable in your care and thereby supports their learning.

Arrange the space and schedule so that children can spend time with a teacher individually. Young children tend to get tired and overwhelmed when they spend all of their time in a group. Jerry (11 months) tries new words, "ca" (car) and "dah" (daddy), while he and Ms. Bates play together in a quiet corner. Louisa, Sam, and Mr. Lewis sit on a soft rug, reading a favorite story.

Create a few simple interest areas. As toddlers explore the toys and materials in these areas they can begin learning to play with others and to talk about what they are doing.

Include interesting things for children to see, hear, touch, taste, smell, use, and talk about. Describe the new mobile a parent made from shells collected on vacation; point out the sounds of birds, trucks, or running water; discuss the orange striped fish swimming in the aquarium; put some new funnels at the water table and talk with toddlers as they use them.

Display colorful pictures of familiar people and objects at children's eye level. Talk with infants about what they see in the pictures. Make a comment or ask an open-ended question to engage a toddler in conversation, e.g., "That worm looks like the worm we saw in our garden."

Provide play materials that encourage communication and storytelling. Dolls; dress-up clothes and props (hats, keys, tote bags); household items (pots, pans, dishes); telephones; puppets; and a basket of props in the block area encourage children to pretend and talk to themselves and each other. You can

- model language for pretend play with dolls, puppets, and people, e.g., "I'm so sleepy. Will you please put me to bed?"

- help toddlers pretend to talk on the phone to a friend or family member, e.g., "Is that your dad on the phone, Kayla? Tell him I said hello."

- join in children's pretend play to introduce words and to encourage them to talk, e.g., "I am so-o-o hungry. What do you serve in this restaurant?"

Provide indoor and outdoor settings for children to play house. Cut doors and windows in a large cardboard box, place some household items under a loft or climber, or cover three sides of a table with a sheet. If there is enough room, put two playhouses side by side so the children can pretend to be neighbors.

Use the environment to support reading and writing.

As they are learning to listen and speak, young children are also exploring print. They watch you write and then eagerly make their own marks on paper. Indoors and outdoors, they see how print around them is used to

- provide information, e.g., where the pop beads are kept

- send a message, e.g., a note to a family

- give directions, e.g., how much food to give the fish or a reminder to stop at the corner

- tell a story, e.g., "This is a photograph of the big bus we saw on our walk"

- identify a personal space, e.g., "Peter's Cubby"

Gradually, young children begin to make sense of reading and writing. They think, "That's a picture of a comb like my comb." "Words and pictures are different." "You have to turn pages one at a time."

Here are some additional suggestions about what to include in an environment that supports children's exploration of reading and writing:

Make sets of picture cards. Ask families to share photographs and look in magazines or catalogs for simple pictures of people, animals, and familiar items. Paste each picture on a piece of cardboard; then cover it with clear adhesive paper. Place the finished cards in an open container on a low shelf. Sit and talk with infants about what they see in the pictures. Expect infants to chew on the cards. Make new ones, as needed to replace worn cards and to provide new language prompts.

Make books. You can make "feely" books using different fabrics and textures, and you can write stories about the children's experiences. Titles might include *The Day We Got a New Climber, Wendy's New Puppy* (made with help from her dad), or *Jason Finds the Lost Ball*. Instructions for making simple books follow.

- *Materials:* Use cardboard, paper, clear plastic sleeves or adhesive paper, and bookbinding supplies.

- *Writing and illustrating:* Use a computer, color printer, and/or digital camera to write the text and take and print photographs of the children. Alternatively, print the words by hand and use photographs, magazine pictures, or simple drawings as illustrations. Keep it simple, with only a few words and a single picture per page.

- *Putting it together:* Paste the pages on cardboard; then insert them in clear plastic sleeves or cover them with adhesive paper. Make a cover, then bind the book by punching holes and threading the pages together with a strong lace. Another way to bind the book is by putting the pages in a safe, sturdy binder that will not pinch the children's fingers.

Create a book area. Display books in a quiet corner of the room, out of the way of traffic and noisy activities. Children may look at books there or carry them to other places in the room. When a book is torn, invite toddlers to get the repair kit so they can help you tape the page or cover and learn how to care for books. To make the area attractive and appealing, try these suggestions:

- **Make the area comfortable.** Put a rug and large cushions on the floor. Include an armchair or glider. Use a mattress covered with washable, cheerful fabric or a sheet. A wading pool filled with large cushions also makes a nice place to look at books, alone or with a friend.

- **Display books so that children can see and reach them easily.** Use a shelf that allows books to be displayed with covers in full view. Use clear adhesive paper to preserve the covers of new books, and keep books in good repair. Jim Trelease, an author and expert on reading aloud, suggests hanging inexpensive plastic rain gutters on the wall for displaying books side by side. You will find instructions on his Web site, http://www.trelease-onreading.com/rah_chpt6_p4.html#rain-gutter

- **Provide good lighting.** Locate the book area near a window so natural light is available. If more light is needed, use a ceiling fixture or install lights on the wall, out of children's reach.

- **Make the area attractive.** Display book covers, posters, and photographs of children and adults reading books. Add dolls and stuffed animals for children to read to or cuddle. Spend time there, yourself, so children will know you think books and reading are important.

Put books in other areas. Children will learn about the many different ways books are useful if they find them throughout the room and outdoors. Here are some suggestions:

- Include magazines and catalogs with pretend play props.

- Put books about buildings, farms, trucks, and animals with the blocks.

- Take a basket of books outdoors, particularly books related to outdoor experiences and discoveries.

Offer writing materials. Include writing tools (chunky crayons, washable markers, chalk, paintbrushes, paint, and water) and things to write on (large grocery bags, big pieces of paper, easels, blackboards, and pavement). Offer them indoors and outdoors.

Provide props and activities related to favorite stories. Provide toys and materials that allow toddlers to extend their enjoyment and understanding of books. For example, after reading Sue Williams' *Let's Go Visiting*, put the book and a basket of farm animals like those in the book together on the shelf. After reading several of Eric Carle's books (*The Very Busy Spider*, *The Very Hungry Caterpillar*, *The Very Quiet Cricket*, *The Very Lonely Firefly*), invite children to move like those insects.

Include assorted toys and materials that support the development of the motor skills used to write. Wooden puzzles, beads and laces, interlocking blocks, nesting cups, pegs and pegboards, and sand and water play props are examples of toys and materials that promote development of small muscle skills and eye-hand coordination.

Offer materials that give toddlers a casual introduction to the letters of the alphabet. Provide a few ABC books and items such as alphabet blocks, puzzles, and magnets. It is appropriate to introduce the alphabet to young children, just as you introduce other aspects of language. However, it is not developmentally appropriate to conduct alphabet drills. Each child has a personal schedule for exploring and gradually making sense of print, and you can respond to each child individually as her knowledge of print develops.

Use pictures, signs, labels, and charts to communicate important information. Use pictures and print—in English and children's home languages—to communicate. Label shelves and containers to show where materials belong. Label individual cubbies with children's names and photographs.

what's next?

Skill-Building Journal, section **6-6** (*Learning Activity B*) and section **6-1** (*Feedback*).

LEARNING ACTIVITY

Learning Activities

C. Encouraging the Language Development of Infants and Toddlers

In this activity you will learn to

- pay attention to the verbal and nonverbal communications of infants and toddlers

- respond to infants and toddlers in ways that encourage them to communicate their needs, wants, feelings, and ideas

Language learning is rooted in children's home and family experiences. In the first years of life, with little or no direct instruction, most children come to understand and speak their home language. Although children may learn a second language, the words, tones, and expressions of their home language help them feel secure. Here are a few examples of what children might learn about language from their experiences at home:

- Gina (4 months) cries because she is hungry. While Gina's mother nurses her, she sings a song she learned from her mother. One day Gina might sing it to her baby.

- Barry (17 months) points to a dish on the table. His father says, "That's pollo—chicken." Barry adds a new word to his vocabulary. The next time he sees this food, he'll know two ways to ask for it.

- Kyle (27 months) squeals when he hears his grandpa's booming voice, "Kyle, I'm coming to get you!" Kyle knows his grandpa isn't angry; this is just his way of showing affection.

Children may be learning one language at home and a different language at the program.

There may be children in your care who are learning one language at home and a second language at the program. These children may start talking a little later than those who are only learning one language. When they begin to talk, they are likely to use words from both languages. Some families are afraid that using their home language will get in the way as their child learns a second language. Actually, it is one of the best ways to support language development. Children's understanding of their home language helps them make sense of the second one. The ability to communicate in more than one language benefits a person throughout life. You can support children by learning a few important words, phrases, popular songs, and rhymes in their home languages.

Your practices can also help children feel comfortable and eager to communicate. Infants and toddlers develop communication skills by interacting with adults who talk with them and respond to their coos, smiles, gestures, and words. Children, like most of us, are more likely to want to communicate and learn new language skills if they know someone is paying attention and will respond. Your trusting, responsive relationships with individual children encourage them to listen, experiment with sounds, say single words, and eventually speak in sentences.

Parentese provides babies with essential information about language.

Very young infants prefer and pay attention to the higher pitch of *parentese*, the exaggerated, drawn-out speech that many adults use when talking with babies. In addition to melodic pitch and sing-song rhythm, it is characterized by a slow or deliberate tempo, simplified vocabulary, and repeated questions. Although it may sound silly to an adult ear, it is exactly what infants like and need to hear. Researchers believe that listening to parentese helps children distinguish the distinct sounds of language (see *Learning Activity A*).

Here are some suggestions to support language development:

- Speak slowly and clearly so children can distinguish sounds.

- Emphasize a single, important word to signal important information, e.g., "Omar, there's your **toe**. It's your big **toe**."

- Repeat the same words again and again, particularly while pointing to an object and during conversations, to help children build their vocabularies.

- Face children as you talk, so they can see how you move your mouth to form different sounds.

- Respond to coos, gurgles, babbles, and words, to let children know that their messages are important and to model communication skills. "I'm listening, Andy. Show me which one you want."

For each aspect of language development listed below, the example shows how teachers encourage communication by responding to children.

Crying is a form of communication. Mr. Lewis hears John (4 months) crying loudly. He says, "John, I wonder what you are saying. Did you drop your toy again? Here it is."

Daily routines are opportunities to communicate. Use children's names and a calm tone of voice to talk with children as you dress, feed, and change them. "I'm going to take off your shirt, Timmy. Then we'll put on a clean one." "Would you like another muffin, Mary?"

Games with rhymes and action are great fun. "This little piggy went to market. Where did this little piggy go?" "Pat-a-cake, pat-a-cake."

New words are opportunities to celebrate. "Did you say *truck*? I heard you! Here's the truck."

Serving as a Language Model

Because you are very important to them, infants and toddlers pay close attention to your language, facial expressions, and gestures. They are learning from you, even when you don't mean to be teaching them. Here are some ways you can use your language skills to encourage children to listen and talk.

Name objects, actions, and feelings. Talk about 5-month-old Jesse's *red pants*, the *swirly lines* Erica (18 months) is drawing on her paper, the *giant steps* Lisa (26 months) takes as she crosses the room, and the *frustration* Billy (34 months) feels when his juice spills.

Talk about how things look, feel, smell, taste, and sound. Infants and toddlers use all of their senses to explore. You can provide the words to describe their sensory experiences. "Your blanket feels *soft* and *smooth*." "The pine cone feels *prickly*." "The truck made a *loud* noise when Ricky dropped it."

Use a calm tone of voice. From birth, infants are attuned to the human voice. They get upset when adults yell or speak angrily.

Use interesting words. Children might not be able to say many words yet, but they can learn what they mean. When you bring in a plant to brighten up the room, say it is a *chrysanthemum*, rather than just a *flower*. Ask children if they want to smell the cinnamon before they shake it into the muffin batter. Children do not use these words often, but they enjoy hearing words with rhythmic or unusual sounds.

Use full and complete sentences. When asked where something is, give a complete response. For example, say, "Your blanket is on the floor," rather than simply pointing and saying, "Over there." Using complex sentences provides more information, and it supports children's understanding of language structure.

Help children recognize and name feelings. Ask a weepy infant, "Maria, are you feeling a little *sad*, today?" Tell a smiling, mobile infant, "Jim, you look *happy*." Express your own feelings to a toddler, "Will, I *appreciate* your help."

Play with language. Use rhymes, silly words, and very simple word games. Ask a toddler, "Do you like jumping on the lumpy, bumpy pillow?" Say, "Moo," to a group of toddlers and ask, "Am I a donkey or a cow?"

Introduce rhymes, songs, chants, and fingerplays. When children sing "Head, Shoulders, Knees, and Toes," they have fun and learn the names of body parts. When you repeat favorites, children memorize them and gain a sense of competence because they can join in. These activities also encourage children to begin to become aware of phonemes, the smallest sounds that make up words.

Be quiet sometimes. Like adults, young children ignore constant chatter and treat it as background noise. If you are always talking, you cannot listen.

Engaging Children as Conversational Partners

Talking with adults helps infants and toddlers build their own understandings about language. Starting in infancy, children begin learning about the give-and-take of conversations. When an infant coos, respond in a way that invites the baby to vocalize again. Playing games, such as rolling a ball back and forth, is another way to introduce and reinforce the concept of taking turns when interacting with another person.

You do not need to schedule special conversational times during the day. Opportunities naturally arise during daily routines and activities.

During routines—Ms. Gonzalez points to the image of Jackson (6 months) in the mirror near the changing table and says, "Look, Jackson, that's you." She pauses. Jackson listens, looks, and then gurgles.

When looking at something interesting—Ms. Bates and Emma (16 months) stand at the window watching the snow. Ms. Bates asks, "Emma, do you like watching the snow?" Emma replies, "Snow?" Ms. Bates explains, "That's right, Emma. It's snowing." "Out?" asks Emma. "We'll go out when the snow stops. It's too wet now."

While doing a chore together—Mr. Lewis is clearing the lunch table with Vinh (34 months). He says, "I really enjoyed lunch today. I like macaroni and cheese." Vinh asks, "More cheese?" Mr. Lewis responds, "Are you still hungry, Vinh? Please sit down at the table if you want more macaroni and cheese."

what's next?

Skill-Building Journal, section **6-7** (*Learning Activity C*) and section **6-1** (*Feedback*).

Learning Activities

D. Sharing Books With Infants and Toddlers

In this activity you will learn to

- provide books that are appropriate for the children in your care

- read aloud with infants and toddlers

The more children are read to, the more likely they are to become skilled and enthusiastic readers. Reading researchers have found that reading aloud is one of the best ways to ensure children's later success as readers. Reading aloud helps children build both the skills and motivation to learn to read.

It is never too soon to begin reading aloud. Even the youngest infants in your care will enjoy listening to your voice and the rhythmic sounds of language. Soon they will begin to associate reading with pleasant and secure feelings. If you genuinely enjoy reading, like to tell stories, and appreciate the rhythms and rhymes of poetry, you will encourage children to enjoy them, too.

Encourage family reading times.

Even the busiest families need to find time to share books with their children regularly, and every family needs access to high quality books. Here are some ways you and your program can ensure that children have books at home:

Encourage use of the public library. Ask for multiple copies of brochures that list library hours, special programs, and recommended books for children of different ages. Invite the children's librarian to make a presentation at a family meeting. Urge families to get library cards. Tell families about their children's favorite books and authors so they can look for them at the library.

Create a classroom lending library. Set up a simple system for allowing families to borrow books from the program. Put each book in a separate plastic bag with a few read-aloud suggestions and props for follow-up activities. Include tapes in English (made by teachers and families or purchased) for families who are not comfortable reading aloud and for non-English speakers who want their children to hear the stories read in English. When possible, include tapes in other languages for families who want their children to hear the stories read in those languages.

Link with book programs. There are national and local non-profit groups whose mission includes giving away children's books. Here are a few: Reading is Fundamental (RIF) (www.rif.org), First Book (www.firstbook.org), and Rolling Readers (www.rollingreaders.org).

Seek contributions from local organizations. Many businesses and non-profit groups welcome the opportunity to support reading. Their contributions might pay for a book distribution at your program. Publishers and local booksellers may give you a discount when buying multiple copies of children's books. For example, at enrollment, the program might give families *Read to Your Bunny*, by Rosemary Wells. This charming book encourages families to read with their children so that they will one day read to their families. Another wonderful way to emphasize the importance of books and reading is for your program to give each child a book on her birthday.

Choosing Books for Infants and Toddlers

Select books on the basis of your knowledge about the children in your care.

Use what you know about the children in your care to select books they will enjoy. Your book collection should depict children's cultures, ethnic groups, genders, families, and abilities in positive ways. Offer books in children's home languages and English. Provide a range and variety of books that correspond to children's individual and developmental characteristics. You should have some books to read aloud (e.g., a full-size copy of *Goodnight Moon* by Margaret Wise Brown), some books children can look at on their own (e.g., the board book version of *Goodnight Moon*), and some books that serve both purposes.

Infants explore books with their hands and mouths. Toddlers are a little gentler, but they, too, are still learning how to care for books. Congratulate yourself when you have to replace well-loved books. This means that you have created an atmosphere in which children feel free to explore books.

Change some of the books in your collection regularly to relate to the children's current skills, interests, and activities. The children's librarian at your local library can offer advice. The Association for Library Service to Children, part of the American Library Association (ALA) shares lists of award-winning books and books recommended by a national group of children's librarians (www.ala.org/ala/alsc/alscresources/booklists/booklists.htm). Some general guidelines follow, to help you choose books for infants and toddlers.

Good Books for Infants (Birth–18 Months)

You can read almost anything to very young infants, but they especially enjoy listening to songs and rhymes. For young infants who can focus their eyes, offer board books with simple, bright pictures against a solid background. *White on Black, Black on White* and *What Is That?* by Tana Hoban are board books with high-contrast pictures for this age group.

Provide a variety of book formats.

As infants develop fine motor skills, they can explore books on their own. At about 4–6 months, young infants learn to grasp objects. Board books are a little too heavy for this age group to hold easily. However, they can hold washable cloth and plastic books and explore them by touching, tasting, chewing, and so on. Look for Eric Hill's series of Spot Bath Books and Lucy Cousins' titles, *Flower in the Garden, Hen in the Park*, and *Playtime Maisy*.

When infants are a little older (about 7–9 months), they develop a pincer grasp, the ability to use thumb and index finger together to pick up objects. Then they are most interested in sticking fingers between pages, chewing corners, waving books in the air, and sometimes tossing them on the floor. As their small motor skills grow, they can hold books with both hands and turn pages. Provide sturdy board books with rounded corners and heavy, laminated pages that are easy to turn. The illustrations should have bold colors and present only one or two objects per page. Some board books come in a smaller, chunky format that is just the right size for an infant to hold. Karen Jones has illustrated several chunky board books that this age group enjoys, including *Munch, Munch! Who's There?*; *Tap, Tap! Who's There?*; and *Knock, Knock! Who's There?* Helen Oxenbury's *Big Baby Book*, is just that: an extra-large board book featuring children who use their senses to explore the world.

Nine- to 12-month-old infants continue to explore how books feel and taste, and they want to see what is inside. They begin to recognize pictures of familiar objects in books and understand that they represent real objects. They like books with simple pictures of babies, familiar objects, animals, and everyday experiences. Introduce books with textures to feel, flaps to lift and pull, and holes to poke fingers in, but remember that eager infants might not use them as intended. Board books are the best format for this age group. *Fuzzy Fuzzy Fuzzy!: A Touch, Skritch, and Tickle Book* by Sandra Boynton invites toddlers to respond to words and pictures. *Pat the Bunny* by Dorothy Kurnhardt is a classic touch-and-feel book that comes in various formats for infants and toddlers.

Many 12- to 18-month-old infants are starting to talk. They like simple stories about everyday experiences such as getting ready for bed, and they enjoy books that let them join in with rhyming words and repetitive phrases. *Brown Bear, Brown Bear, What Do You See?* and *Polar Bear, Polar Bear, What Do You Hear?* by Bill Martin Jr. and Eric Carle are available in English and Spanish, and in board and picture book formats.

Do the infants in your care have books with these characteristics?

- **Content:** Books with simple stories about babies, families, animals, and everyday experiences, including wordless picture stories; books that picture familiar objects to name and count

- **Repetitive language:** Books with rhymes, songs, and chants, as well as books with other predictable language patterns

- **Illustrations:** Simple, bright pictures or photographs against a solid background; bold colors; one or two items per page

- **Special features:** Things to touch and feel; flaps to pull or lift

- **Format:** Washable cloth and vinyl books, board books with fold-out pages, and paper and hardback picture books to read aloud

Good Books for Toddlers (18–36 Months)

Books help children understand their experiences.

Toddlers have busy, active lives. Every day they do things for themselves, learn how to play with others, practice talking, discover new things about the world, and make and carry out plans. It can be a confusing time. One minute they seek independence; the next minute they just want to stay close to a trusted adult. They have lots of questions about the ways things work, and they sometimes find the answers in books. Books allow toddlers to use language they already know and to learn new words to name animals, objects, actions, experiences, feelings, and ideas. Books can help them make sense of the world, master concepts, and begin to identify and handle strong feelings.

Toddlers continue to enjoy many of the kinds of books described earlier. In addition, they like picture books with brief, easy-to-follow plots and only a few words on each page. Look for books with illustrations that offer details about the characters and their activities. As you read aloud, a toddler can listen and relate your words to the pictures. Some of the storybooks you read aloud to toddlers can be a few levels above their speaking vocabularies, because their listening vocabularies usually develop more rapidly. This is a good way to introduce new words and concepts and help children expand their listening skills. Janet Morgan Stoeke's picture books about Minerva, a very silly hen, have simple stories that toddlers enjoy.

Books about families and feelings are also popular. In *Owl Babies* by Martin Waddell, three little owls worry that their mother will not return to their nest. When Owl Mother returns, she reassures her babies that she will always come back. This is an ideal book to read aloud with a toddler who is struggling with separation from his family. It could reassure the child that it is all right to feel sad, and it sets the stage for talking about ways to express and cope with strong feelings.

Picture concept books about familiar objects and ideas introduce and reinforce the concepts that toddlers are learning. Look for books about colors, shapes, sizes, time, opposites, numbers, and letters, with large illustrations and a few words. Older toddlers enjoy beginning informational books that match their interests, such as those about trucks, farm animals, trains, and bodies. Toddlers who are learning about body parts will enjoy *Eyes, Nose, Fingers and Toes: A First Book All about You* by Judy Hinley and *Here Are My Hands* by Bill Martin and John Archambault.

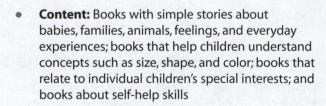

Do the toddlers in your care have books with these characteristics?

- **Content:** Books with simple stories about babies, families, animals, feelings, and everyday experiences; books that help children understand concepts such as size, shape, and color; books that relate to individual children's special interests; and books about self-help skills

- **Repetitive language:** Books with rhymes, songs, and chants, as well as books with other predictable language patterns

- **Illustrations:** Simple, bright pictures or photographs against a solid background; bold colors; one or two items per page; beautiful pictures with details that provide information about the characters and their activities

- **Special features:** Books related to individual experiences; simple storybooks; books with vocabulary at a slightly higher level than the children's speaking vocabularies

- **Format:** Board, paperback, and hardback

Reading Aloud With Infants and Toddlers

Reading aloud with children every day, beginning in infancy, is one of the most effective ways to support language and emerging literacy. Reading aloud helps infants and toddlers

- learn to listen

- associate reading and books with pleasure

- understand language

- use their senses to explore the properties of books

- add new words to their vocabularies

- consider books as valuable and interesting play materials

- link illustrations and stories in books to real-life objects and experiences

- begin to understand a few print concepts such as

    - print is a form of language

    - spoken and written words correspond

    - readers attend particularly to the printed text, not the pictures

Expect young infants to grasp, touch, and taste books as soon as they are able.

When you read aloud with young infants, they listen to your soothing voice and feel safe, secure, and comforted. Most infants enjoy these experiences and come to think of reading as a pleasant activity. Reading aloud lets infants listen to the sounds of language and invites them to coo, gurgle, babble, and say words. For the first few months, infants are a captive audience. They watch and listen as you read. Starting at about six months, many infants are more interested in actively grasping, touching, and tasting books than in listening to you read them. This does not mean you should give up reading aloud. Instead, tailor your read-aloud sessions in response to the child.

Encourage mobile infants to participate while you read aloud with them.

Here are a few suggestions for engaging young children while reading aloud:

Offer a toy to hold and chew while you read. This might engage a child's hands and mouth so she can listen to you.

Read one or two pages at a time. Children build their attention spans little by little.

Share books you can hold easily while a child sits in your lap. This way, you can be close to each other and the child can see the pictures easily.

Let the child turn the pages. Often this is more interesting to the child than listening to your voice.

Seek the child's attention by pointing to and naming things in the pictures. This works particularly well when the book is filled with pictures of familiar things.

Follow the child's lead. Stay on a page as long as he wants to. When he loses interest, put the book away and do something else.

Many mobile infants are fascinated by a new skill: the ability to turn pages. They like to turn the pages in books, magazines, catalogs, or whatever else you provide. When you try to read aloud with them, they may be so consumed by this skill that they will not let you read. That is all right. You are still spending time together, enjoying and exploring books.

When they begin to crawl, infants' interest in books often declines because they want to keep moving their bodies from one place to another. Teachers can continue short read-aloud sessions with board books that match mobile infants' attention spans.

Soon, mobile infants begin to understand language and recognize objects in pictures. They like reading aloud with you and want to join in. They turn the pages and listen while you read or talk about the pictures. At first, mobile infants point to objects and wait for you to name them. It is their way of asking, "What's that?" Soon they respond to your questions and requests, e.g., "Where's the puppy?" and "Show me the hairbrush." Pause in your reading and wait for their answers.

Predictable books with rhymes and repetition are ideal for reading aloud to children who are beginning to talk. As you read them again and again, children become so familiar with these books that they can join at the appropriate moments. They feel very competent when they know what comes next.

When they begin to walk, typically around 9–12 months, infants can get the materials they want to use and bring them to their teacher. They often want to explore books. When an infant holds out a book or plops it in your lap, he is saying, "Read to me." Respond to these requests as quickly as possible, so you can encourage children's interest in books and reading.

Sometimes read-aloud sessions prompt exciting discoveries. Upon seeing a familiar item pictured in a book, a mobile infant might hop down from your lap and run across the room to get it, e.g., "Truck! Truck!" Understanding that pictures represent real things is a major cognitive leap for a child. It is the first step on the long road to understanding that printed words in books are symbols for the words we speak, and vice versa.

Toddlers enjoy individual and small-group read-aloud times.

Toddlers enjoy read-aloud times with a favorite adult. As their attention spans grow, they also enjoy being read to in small groups. They understand more language, and their growing thinking skills allow them to relate characters and events in books to their own lives. It is important to read slowly so toddlers can make sense of the story.

Toddlers like listening to the same books again and again. They gain a sense of security and comfort from familiar things, including books. Multiple read-aloud sessions give them a chance to master the text and join in. When they are ready to explore a new book, they will tell you.

You can read aloud with toddlers at any time of day and in any setting. Let them decide when, where, and what to read. You might suggest reading a book when an active toddler needs some quiet time or when a child needs individual attention.

When you read with small groups of toddlers, let each child decide how long to stay with the group. If a child chooses to leave, you can continue reading with those who are still interested.

Successful read-aloud sessions involve much more than saying words and turning pages. What you do before, during, and after reading aloud helps toddlers understand the meaning of the language and expands their understanding and enjoyment of the story. The following chart offers some suggestions for reading with toddlers one-on-one and in small groups.

Reading Aloud With Toddlers

Before you read aloud

- Choose a book that you enjoy, with large, clear pictures that children can see while sitting next to you or in your lap. Consider reading a book with some new words.

- Get to know the book by reading it and looking closely at the pictures. Think of comments and questions.

- Plan ways to vary your voice (tone, pitch, volume, pauses) to dramatize the story.

- Collect props that can increase children's enjoyment and understanding, such as dress-up clothes, hats, puppets, and flannel board pieces.

- Make sure everyone is comfortable, able to see the pictures, and ready to focus on the story.

During the reading

- Read the title and author and point out details of the cover illustration. Describe what the book is about. Suggest a few things for which to look and listen.

- Vary your voice to fit the characters and the story events.

- Read slowly so the children can process the visual and auditory information.

- Move your finger under the words as you read.

- Stop frequently to

  - repeat interesting words and phrases

  - talk about details of the pictures

  - ask and answer questions

  - make comments and share your reactions.

- Encourage the child (or children) to

  - point to and name things in the pictures

  - help turn the pages

  - join in with sounds, rhymes, and repetitive words and phrases

  - ask and answer questions

  - predict what might happen next

  - link the story to their own lives.

When you are finished

- Read the book again, if asked, immediately or at a later time.

- Display the book within the children's reach.

- Repeat phrases from the book at other times of the day.

- Provide props that are related to the story.

what's next?

Skill-Building Journal, section **6-8** (*Learning Activity D*), section **6-1** (*Feedback*), and section **6-9** (*Reflecting on Your Learning*).

7
Creative

Overview

Creating an Environment That Encourages Exploration and Experimentation

Offering Opportunities for Children to Do Things in Unique Ways

Appreciating Each Child's Way of Being Creative

Your Own Creativity

Learning Activities

A. Using Your Knowledge of Infants and Toddlers to Encourage Creativity

B. Supporting Creativity Through Positive Interactions

C. Encouraging Creative Expression Through Music and Movement

D. Nurturing Creativity Through Art Experiences

7.   Creative

Creative people try new ways of doing things. They combine ideas and materials in different ways for new purposes. They are curious about how things work and why things happen. They are willing to take risks. When their strategies are unsuccessful, they learn from their mistakes and try other approaches.

Infants and toddlers want to learn about the world.

Infants are eager, imaginative, and creative learners. They are curious explorers who use their senses to learn how things look, feel, sound, taste, and smell. They want to know how things work, what will happen next, and how they can affect what happens. As they gain new skills and become more mobile, they find many more things to investigate.

Older infants and toddlers have motor and language skills that support imaginative play. They might sling a bag over one arm and pretend to go to work, figure out how to stack blocks, move and dance to music they like, and use chubby crayons to make marks on paper. They use familiar items in new ways and begin to play with each other.

Arrange the environment and use daily routines and activities to support children's creativity.

Environments that support creativity include toys and materials that are safe and interesting. Teachers can arrange the indoor and outdoor environments so children have the freedom to make messes, explore, and experiment safely. Teachers also encourage creativity by planning daily routines and activities so that children have plenty of time to participate at their own paces.

In infant/toddler programs, there are numerous opportunities to encourage children's creativity throughout the day. Teachers can plan specific activities, such as sponge painting, dancing, and cooking, and they can invite children to think, solve problems, and do things in their own ways.

Respectful, trusting relationships between children and adults are the foundation for nurturing creativity. With responsive care, children feel free to explore and use their imaginations. They know that their teachers will keep them safe and will appreciate their unique ideas and expressions.

You can encourage children's creativity by

- creating an environment that encourages exploration and experimentation

- offering opportunities for children to do things in unique ways

- appreciating each child's way of being creative

Creating an Environment That Encourages Exploration and Experimentation

1. **Create safe, open spaces where infants and toddlers can explore freely.** Rearrange moveable furniture and equipment to accommodate young infants and children who crawl and walk.

2. **Designate areas with a washable floor and surfaces for messy play and meals.** Keep sponges, paper towels, a mini-vacuum, and other cleaning supplies handy so that teachers and children can work together when it is time to clean up.

3. **Offer a variety of open-ended materials.** Provide a box of fabric scraps with varied textures; spoons, plates, and other items for pretend housekeeping; simple props and dress-up clothes for other kinds of pretend play; music and items for making music; and materials for art, sand, and water play.

4. **Invite children to notice and appreciate interesting and beautiful things.** "Malou and Peter, do you see the fluffy clouds? They look so pretty in the blue sky." "Lovette, if you hold the rock under the light, you can see different colors."

5. **Model creativity by solving problems, being resourceful, and trying new ideas.** Make up and sing a getting-ready-to-go-outside song, use recycled items to make a mobile, and move the indoor climber into the hall to make room for dancing.

Musical Spoons and Pots

As you read the following story, pay attention to the strategies
Ms. Bates uses to encourage Jon to explore.

Ms. Bates: That looks high enough, but not too high.

Ms. Bates: Listen! Do you hear the spoons rattle when you touch them?

Jon: Ba, ba, ba.

Ms. Bates: Gently.

Ms. Bates: Jon can make music.

Offering Opportunities for Children to Do Things in Unique Ways

6. **Follow a flexible schedule so children can do things in their own ways and at their own paces.** Change your plans to take advantage of events, such as finding a bird's nest, or to allow children to continue an activity in which they are very engaged.

7. **Offer messy, open-ended activities such as sand and water play, painting, and making and using playdough.** Describe what children are doing as they use the materials. "You flattened the playdough, and now you are poking it."

8. **Include play materials, props, music, books, and other items that reflect the families, cultures, and ethnicities of all children in the group.** "Let's sing one of the lullabies from El Salvador that Luci's mother taught us."

9. **Encourage sensory exploration during routines and activities.** "Touch the skin of the peach. How does it feel? Hold it up to your nose. How does it smell? Let's cut it open to smell the inside of the peach."

10. **Play make-believe games with children.** "What a nice kitty you are! Would you like to drink some milk, little kitty?"

Making Playdough Our Own Way

As you read the following story, pay attention to how Mr. Lewis encouraged each child's involvement in making playdough. Also think about why he said, "There are several ways to stir."

Mr. Lewis: How does the flour feel?

Jessica: Soft.

Adam: Whoosh!

Mr. Lewis: Don't worry. We can clean it up.

Mr. Lewis: There are several ways to stir.

Appreciating Each Child's Way of Being Creative

11. **Respond to and build on children's efforts to communicate.** "I can hear you cooing. You sound like a little bird." "You stretched out your arms. Do you want me to lift you up? Okay, here you go."

12. **Get involved in children's play by following and responding to their cues.** "Yum, yum. Thank you for sharing your yogurt with me."

13. **Describe children's use of creative thinking to solve a problem.** "You couldn't see out the window, so you got a stool to stand on. Now you can see the birds at the feeder."

14. **Respect children's concentration.** "Luci is trying to get the ring on the stacking post. Let's wait to change her diaper."

15. **Share with families examples of their children's creative thinking and learning.** "Adam is getting used to the idea that he will have a new sister soon. He has been spending a lot of time wrapping and rocking our baby dolls."

Singing About Peaches

As you read the following story, think about Ms. Gonzalez's supportive relationship with Peter. Also think about how Ms. Gonzalez lets Peter know that she values his unique approach to feeding himself.

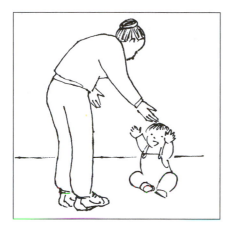

Ms. Gonzalez: It's time for Peter's lunch, lunch, lunch.

Ms. Gonzalez: It's time for Peter to sit, sit, sit.

Ms. Gonzalez: It's time for Peter's peaches, peaches, peaches.

Ms. Gonzalez: You must be very hungry, Peter.

Ms. Gonzalez: Is it my turn yet?

what's next?

Skill-Building Journal, section **7-2** (*Overview*), section **7-10** (*Answer Sheet*), and section **7-1** (*Feedback*).

Your Own Creativity

Teachers of infants and toddlers have many opportunities to be creative.

Creative people are innovative and resourceful. They adapt ideas, plans, and materials to solve problems or make something new. To be creative, you do not have to be able to paint a picture, play an instrument, or write a book. Artists and musicians are creative people, and so are cooks, plumbers, and teachers.

Early childhood teachers are living examples of the saying, "Necessity is the mother of invention." They have to be creative in the way they recycle materials, respond to challenging behavior, and invite family involvement. Adjusting plans in response to children's changing interests and needs is an important part of a teacher's job. Thinking of new ways to help a baby learn to calm himself, making up a special song to sing at the end of the day, and rearranging the room to provide a safe place for infants who are learning to stand are all ways that teachers are creative.

Creative teachers are lifelong learners. They are curious about the world and understand how they

- approach problems and address challenges ("I begin by making a list of possible solutions.")

- make decisions ("Slowly, but thoughtfully.")

- share ideas and listen to other people ("I'm eager to get feedback.")

- respond to stimuli ("Music makes me feel alive.")

Creativity can be very satisfying.

Creative teachers use this self-awareness as they establish environments that support children's creativity and as they interact with children to encourage self-expression.

Creative expression can be very satisfying. Think about the way you feel when you use leftovers to create a delicious meal; turn an old pair of boots into petunia planters; or come up with new ways to involve fathers, as well as mothers, in the program. Those emotions are similar to the pride children feel when they have figured something out for themselves and their pure joy when squishing a lump of playdough. Creative teachers recognize these feelings in themselves and strive to promote them in infants and toddlers.

what's next?

Skill-Building Journal, section **7-3** (*Your Own Creativity*), section **7-1** (*Feedback*), and section **7-4** (*Pre-Training Assessment*).

Learning Activities

LEARNING
ACTIVITY

A. Using Your Knowledge of Infants and Toddlers to Encourage Creativity

In this activity you will learn to

- recognize some typical behaviors of infants and toddlers that are related to creativity

- use what your understand about infants and toddlers to encourage their creativity

Teachers notice and encourage children's explorations.

Three key characteristics of young children are linked to creativity. Young children are **sensitive to stimuli and learn through their senses.** They pay close attention to the sight, sound, taste, smell, and feel of things around them. Young children **lack inhibition and are therefore eager to experiment and to share their ideas.** They do not have an inner voice that says, "Don't try that," or "Stop." In addition, they **can become completely absorbed in an engaging activity** and will stay involved as long as their interest lasts.[29] Think of an infant who is watching a mobile sway back and forth or a one-year-old who is pushing a popper, watching and listening to the beads. It is a teacher's job to support children's creativity by noticing and encouraging such explorations.

Young infants (birth–8 months) are interested in the world around them.

- Sammy (3 months) watches intently as the mobile moves over his crib.

- Jon (6 months) smiles and pats his image in a mirror.

- Luci (8 months) squeals with delight when she makes music on her toy piano.

While you may not usually think about creativity when you think about infants, you build the foundation for creative expression by taking an interest in how they respond to the world. Young infants use all of their senses to gather information about people and things. They listen and respond to voices and other sounds and enjoy simple stories, songs, and rhymes. While nestled in a teacher's arms, a young baby drinks a bottle and watches, listens, and learns. A baby's cries bring a teacher who will solve a problem, such as the discomfort of a wet diaper. When the teacher responds, the trip to the changing table offers more opportunities to explore the world. As infants grow, they learn to kick and use their hands purposefully, for example, to reach for, grasp, and shake a plastic key ring. When they touch a musical toy, it makes sounds. Young infants experience cause and effect and begin to understand that their actions have results. They are eager to repeat their actions in order to bring about a change or desired result. These experiences set the stage for creativity.

Mobile infants (8–18 months) need to move and to explore the world.

- Malou (9 months) bangs two plastic bowls together.

- Peter (12 months) makes crayon marks on paper.

- Zora (16 months) rolls a toy truck across the grass.

Mobile infants are busy movers who are learning that their actions can make things happen. They roll over, creep, crawl, and walk to get from one place to another and to explore more of their world. Mobile infants continue to be sensory learners, and they understand and respond to gestures, facial expressions, changes in vocal tone, and simple language. They use their fine motor skills to hold and handle toys, such as small blocks, cars, and trucks. At this age, infants can hold crayons, clap their hands, bang a drum, and figure out simple puzzle toys such as shape sorters. They are social beings who love to sing, sway to music, and play games such as pat-a-cake and peek-a-boo. Mobile infants are beginning to understand that objects and people exist even when they are out of sight. Teachers encourage creativity by giving mobile infants the freedom to move, explore, and do things for themselves. They also share the pleasure and excitement that infants express as they perform new tasks.

Toddlers (18–36 months) use skills creatively in all areas of development.

- Lovette (20 months) holds a block up to her ear and says, "Hi, Gramma."

- Ricky (28 months) and Adam (30 months) slither across the floor like snakes.

- Jessica (34 months) rolls and pounds a lump of playdough.

Toddlers are often unpredictable. Sometimes they are eager to be independent and to do things for themselves. At other times, particularly when they are tired or stressed, toddlers' behavior becomes more baby-like. Although it can certainly be frustrating, teachers need to understand and accept this aspect of toddlerhood. Responding to toddlers' needs for both independence and assistance is key to supporting their curiosity, creativity, and unique forms of self-expression.

Toddlers love to move their bodies in new ways. They can push, pull, throw, catch, kick, and jump. They now have the fine motor skills needed to turn pages; use scissors; open containers; pour; and manipulate crayons, markers, and paint brushes. They discover that playdough is something to poke, pound, roll, and squeeze. As toddlers become more able to coordinate eye and hand movements, they enjoy threading beads on laces and pasting scraps on paper.

Toddlers' language skills also expand rapidly. They enjoy rhymes, songs, fingerplays, and simple stories with predictable language. They also love to talk with teachers and other children. Toddlers enjoy simple forms of dramatic play, using realistic props related to familiar activities such as cooking, cleaning, and caring for babies.

Teachers can encourage creativity during every routine and activity. Throughout the day, there are many opportunities for teachers to talk and respond to children and opportunities for children to make choices, solve problems, and express themselves.

what's next?

Skill-Building Journal, section **7-5** (*Learning Activity A*) and section **7-1** (*Feedback*).

Learning Activities

B. Supporting Creativity Through Positive Interactions

In this activity you will learn to

- interact with infants and toddlers throughout the day in ways that encourage creativity

- establish an atmosphere that supports creativity

Positive relationships lead to security and creativity.

The positive relationships between teachers and the infants and toddlers in their care build the foundation for children to express themselves creatively. When young infants know their needs will be met promptly and consistently, they learn that the world is a safe, predictable place. This sense of security allows children to turn their attention to exploring the world. Teachers encourage creativity by responding to children's needs, talking with children, and taking delight in their independent discoveries. Mobile infants and toddlers, in particular, need many opportunities to experiment and learn firsthand from their experiences. Their creative explorations help them to understand concepts such as hard and soft, in and out, up and down, and big and little.

Supportive environments allow safe exploration.

Infants and toddlers experience the challenge and joy of discovery when indoor and outdoor play areas are arranged to support active, safe exploration and when play materials are interesting and varied. In such an environment, children can move freely and teachers can focus on interactions rather than on rescuing children from unsafe situations. Children can observe and learn from their actions, and they can actively investigate new, fascinating, and beautiful things.

Interactions That Encourage Creativity

Responsive caregiving provides a secure base for exploration.

Infants communicate their needs and feelings long before they can talk. They have different cries for different purposes, wave their arms and kick their legs when excited, and smile and coo to say, "I like being with you." Responding to infants' movements, cries, gestures, and babbling is critical in setting the stage for creative thinking. Your response sends an important message to a child: "You are a valued and important person. What you do matters to me. You can explore." Over time, these messages lead to the feelings of security and trust that are the foundation for creativity.

Every infant has unique and multiple ways to express needs and feelings. Here are some examples of teachers responding to infants' communications.

- Jean's (5 months) actions speak louder than words. She is awake and staring intently at the mobile over her crib. Mr. Lewis sees Jean's concentration and decides to wait before changing her diaper. In a few minutes, Jean begins to whimper and kick her feet. Mr. Lewis goes to her and says, "I think you are finished watching the mobile. Let's change your diaper."

- Peter (10 months) expresses his needs nonverbally. He lies down in the book corner with his thumb in his mouth. Then he crawls to the crib area, where he lies down again and sucks his thumb. Ms. Bates kneels, looks in his eyes, and says, "Peter, it's earlier than your usual nap time, but you are saying that you are tired. Let me put you in your crib."

- Jorge (16 months) combines babbling with actions, to make a request. He hands the toy radio to Ms. Gonzalez. She asks, "What do you want, Jorge?" He sways back and forth. She responds, "You want me to wind up the radio so you can dance. Let's do it together." Ms. Gonzalez places Jorge's hand on the radio dial and then puts her hand on top of his. They wind the radio together, and music starts playing. Jorge says, "Ah, ah, ah," as he dances around.

- How do the infants in your care communicate with you and your colleagues?

- How do you know what they are telling you? How do you respond?

Toddlers often want to be independent.

Toddlers often want to do things for themselves, but sometimes they want and need to be helped. A child who refuses to let you help her eat one day might climb into your lap and ask to be fed the next day. While toddlers are eager to try things on their own, they are not completely confident in their abilities. For this reason, toddlers are likely to come back to you to make sure that help is available. It helps to talk with toddlers about their needs. For example, you might say, "It's okay to need help. I will be here if you want my help." "Should I help you get your zipper started? Then you can zip your coat by yourself." It also helps to teach toddlers to do things before they get too frustrated to learn. "Put one hand on the pump, and the other one underneath it. Now push hard to make the soap come out. You did it! Now rub the soap all over your hands and between your fingers."

Responding to toddlers' needs for both independence and assistance helps them try different ways to solve problems. Here are some examples of how you can support toddlers' independence and creativity:

Notice and comment on toddlers' efforts to be independent. "Allison, you put your sock on, all by yourself!" "It's okay if some juice spills, Craig. You are learning how to pour."

Help toddlers focus on cause and effect relationships. "Jeremy, you pushed the truck with both hands. It rolled across the table." "Anita, you blew bubbles with your wand. They are floating in the air."

Talk with toddlers throughout the day to help them build language skills. "Belinda, your mom says you slept in your new bed. What was it like?" "Let's sing while we wash our hands. 'Así es como nos lavamos las manos, lavamos las manos, lavamos las manos.'" "Look outside! The sun dried up all of the puddles. Now we can go outside."

THINK

- How do you provide opportunities for toddlers to explore cause and effect relationships?

- How do you and your colleagues offer a language-rich environment?

Encouraging Creativity Throughout the Day

Infants and toddlers are naturally curious. They make discoveries constantly as they investigate the world. Each discovery helps them feel capable of trying new things. You can encourage this natural process by giving children a variety of opportunities to learn from ordinary experiences. Here are some suggestions:

Provide materials to make discoveries. Place new toys or interesting objects on the floor. Without pointing to them or saying anything, watch children's reactions as they explore the items on their own.

Promote sensory exploration. As you prepare snack with the children, ask questions and make comments, such as, "How does that banana taste?" or "The milk feels very cold!"

Allow plenty of time and support for children to help with everyday tasks. A child can learn a lot from squeezing a sponge and wiping up water, again and again.

Talk and sing with children. At diaper-changing time, talk about what you are doing. Help children become more aware of their bodies by playing "Where Are Sammy's Toes?" or "Here Is Sammy's Chin, Chin, Chin" and substituting the child's own name.

Prompt children's creative thinking. After sharing a simple picture book, ask open-ended questions that encourage imagination. "Why is the little boy in the picture crying?" "Where do you think the duck is going?"

Providing Opportunities to Make Choices

Offer children safe and meaningful choices.

Creativity involves making choices about what to do, what materials to use, and how to proceed. Making decisions allows children to feel important and helps them see themselves as individuals, separate from their families and teachers. When offering choices, be sure that the children can handle the options safely and successfully.

Let children decide with which toys to play. Hold two rattles within a baby's reach and let her choose the one she prefers. Arrange toys on low, open shelves so mobile infants and toddlers can choose the ones they want without asking a teacher for help. Offer a variety of pretend play props, art supplies, blocks, and other materials so children can decide what they want to use.

Let children decide how to play with a toy or material. Open-ended play materials, such as blocks or nesting bowls, have multiple uses and appeal to children of different ages and stages of development. For example, one child might wear a bowl on his head, while another child might use it as a container for filling and dumping large beads.

Offer a choice of snacks. When possible, offer two nutritious and appropriate snacks. "Would you like a graham cracker or a wheat cracker?" "Do you want water or juice?"

Allow children to discover approaches to new tasks. Infants and toddlers can figure out how to do many things for themselves without adult intervention. For example, different children have different approaches to learning to use a spoon. Some beginners hold the spoon in one hand, while picking up and eating food with the other. Others pick up food with their fingers and then carefully place it on the spoon. Some children scoop up food with the spoon and then use their fingers to eat it. Teachers can observe many examples of creative thinking as children try their own ways of doing something new.

- Do the children in your care have opportunities to make choices?

- How can you and your colleagues provide additional opportunities for children to make decisions?

When offering choices to infants and toddlers, it is important to remember that very young children depend upon consistency and develop trust by knowing that their needs will be met. Toddlers, in particular, want routines to remain the same and like to know what will happen next. For this reason, choices that involve changing daily routines and transitions should be handled carefully.

what's next?

Skill-Building Journal, section **7-6** (*Learning Activity B*) and section **7-1** (*Feedback*).

Learning Activities

LEARNING ACTIVITY

C. Encouraging Creative Expression Through Music and Movement

In this activity you will learn to

- recognize how music and movement foster infants' and toddlers' creativity

- encourage infants and toddlers to listen, sing, move, and make music

Children easily connect music with body movements.

Even before birth, babies are aware of sounds and rhythms. They continue to respond to sounds in their first weeks and months of life, and they recognize family voices. Infants smile when adults sing to them. They begin to move their arms and legs when they hear music, and they respond to toys that make noise.

Infants notice many sounds, such as wind chimes, a song on the radio, the whistling kettle, and singing birds. Crying babies are often soothed by music: a lullaby or the repetitive, rhythmic words of a teacher or parent, e.g., "Jeremy, Jeremy, I love you. Where's your smile? There it is!"

Listening and motor skills support creative expression.

Children easily connect music with body movement. When infants listen to a song, they may turn their heads in the direction of the music, smile or laugh, or sway from side to side. As their coordination increases, mobile infants and toddlers begin moving deliberately to music. They sway, dance, bounce up and down, clap their hands, and stamp their feet.

Music and movement contribute to the development of listening and motor skills. As they develop new skills, infants and toddlers have new ways of expressing themselves.

- Young infants become aware of what their bodies can do and begin to coo and babble to themselves and to others.

- Mobile infants imitate simple action rhymes and fingerplays, which support the development of eye-hand coordination and fine motor skills.

- Toddlers can participate in a wide range of music and movement activities. They can sing, chant, hum, and make other sounds in response to music.

Teachers can offer spontaneous and planned music and movement activities that encourage listening, singing, fingerplay, dancing, and other ways of moving and making music.

Listening to Sounds and Music

Help infants and toddlers focus on the sounds around them.

Infants and toddlers develop listening skills when you call their attention to sounds, respond to the sounds they make, and play a variety of music.

Your classroom and outdoor areas are filled with sounds. Some are in the background, such as the hum of a refrigerator or a bird singing in her nest. Other sounds—chimes, rattles, or jingles—are affected by the children as they handle toys. You can make "sound makers" by filling small containers with items such as buttons, beads, or acorns. Fill a plastic yogurt container with the items; then replace and secure the top with tape or glue. Be sure to check them frequently to make sure the children cannot open them.

Young children tend to be fascinated by animals and animal sounds. When reading aloud with infants and toddlers, you can introduce animal sounds. For example, you might say, "That's a pig. The pig says, 'Oink.' Here's a cow. The cow says, 'Moo.'" You might then turn the page, point to the picture, and ask, "What does the cat say?" Many older mobile infants (15–18 months) can answer that question by saying, "Meow!" This age group enjoys songs with animal sounds, such as "Old MacDonald." They sing along—as best as they are able—and feel very competent.

Introduce children to a wide variety of musical styles.

In addition to music written for children, teachers can introduce infants and toddlers to different musical styles, including classical, jazz, marches, musical plays, instrumentals, and traditional music from a variety of cultures. Each type of music may have a different effect on children's moods. Classical music or quiet instrumentals can be relaxing. Marches and jazz prompt swaying and dancing. Many public libraries have a wide selection of CDs and tapes that children will enjoy. Ask families what kinds of music their children like to listen to at home and try to include these preferences when playing music in your room.

Play music for different reasons, throughout the day.

You can play music at different times of the day, as a listening activity, to signal a transition to a new activity, or while other activities are taking place. Most infants and toddlers do not have the attention span or ability to sit still to listen to music for very long. You might invite them to listen for a few minutes or play music while children are doing something else. Sometimes a child might stop playing to listen to a favorite song or an appealing melody.

Play music selectively, however. If it is playing all the time, it will become background noise rather than something to listen to and enjoy.

Singing and Doing Fingerplays

Young children listen to and sing along with their favorite songs again and again. They are not concerned with the quality of their voices or their teacher's ability to carry a tune.

Young infants can be very vocal. They try different ways to make sounds with their mouths, just as they explore everything else. When adults respond to their coos, gurgles, and squeals, infants try to repeat these sounds and to imitate adult sounds. Teachers can also make up short songs to sing while feeding a baby or changing a diaper.

Children enjoy listening to their teachers and family members sing.

Infants and toddlers can be an enthusiastic and engaged audience for teachers who like to sing—even teachers who cannot carry a tune. They move, clap their hands, and smile, especially if they hear their own names in a song. Individualize a familiar song by revising it to include a child's name. Thus, "Twinkle, Twinkle, Little Star," might become "Luci, Luci, Luci, Dear, how I like to have you near." "Where Is Thumbkin?" can be revised as "Ricky, Adam, Ricky, Adam, like to play, like to play…," and so on.

Children's attempts to sing can be enjoyable for everyone. First songs might be a sound repeated over and over, such as "b-b-b-b" or "da-da-da-da-da." Gradually, children half-babble, half-talk their way through familiar songs such as "Happy Birthday." They sing, "Happy, happy, happy, b-b-b-b-b-b-b."

Think about writing down the words to the songs that the children enjoy and posting them in convenient places, such as over the changing table or on a cabinet door. That will remind you to sing and provide the words to less familiar songs. Share these songs with families, and ask families to share the songs they sing at home with you.

Infants and toddlers enjoy watching fingerplays.

Some popular children's songs can be accompanied by fingerplays. You might have learned classic fingerplays, such as "Itsy-Bitsy Spider" and "Two Little Blackbirds," when you were young. Infants and toddlers enjoy watching adults do fingerplays. When they are ready, they gradually try to imitate the movements. Although children enjoy watching the combination of song and movement, it may be a while before they have the language skills and coordination to sing and move their fingers at the same time. When doing fingerplays, place a child in your lap or sit with several children on the floor. Have the children face you so that they can watch your hands and face. Children can participate at whatever level is comfortable, from smiling and laughing to singing and doing a few movements.

Moving and Dancing

When young children hear music, they respond by moving their bodies. At first they might wave their arms and kick their legs. Soon they sway back and forth. As their motor skills grow, they become creative movers and dancers, eager to move to rhythms. Here are some ways you can support children's moving to music.

Dance with a baby in your arms. Hold a very young infant, support his or her head, and dance with the baby as your partner.

Move a baby's arms and legs. Gently hold and clap a baby's hands together. Move her legs as though pedaling a bicycle.

Hold hands and dance together. Children who stand and walk can hold your hands and move to the music. You might bob up and down in place, or you might sweep the child off his feet and dance with him in your arms.

Encourage experimentation. When mobile infants and toddlers are steady on their feet and their balance improves, they can become very creative movers and dancers. They enjoy dancing alone, with another child, and with a teacher. Encourage children to move creatively by asking questions and making suggestions as you move with them:

> *What can your feet do? Can you take a giant step? A tiny step?*
>
> *Let's wiggle our fingers.*
>
> *How high can your hands reach?*
>
> *How does a snake move? How does a fish swim?*
>
> *Can you clap very softly? Very loudly?*

You can introduce older toddlers to musical games such as "Bluebird, Bluebird" and "Ring Around the Rosie." Review the words and actions; then adapt the games, if necessary, to make them appropriate for toddlers.

Making Music

Older toddlers can learn to play musical games.

Infants and toddlers use their bodies as their first rhythm instruments. By clapping hands and stamping feet, children can make their own sounds and rhythms without recorded music. Teachers can start the music-making by clapping out a tune and inviting the children to join in, "Clap; clap, clap; clap; clap; clap, clap, clap."

Mobile infants and toddlers enjoy using other simple rhythm instruments. When you first introduce them, give each child the same kind of instrument. When you bring out others, provide duplicates to avoid conflicts over sharing. Here are some simple rhythm instruments that can be purchased or made by families and teachers.

Simple Rhythm Instruments

Bells

- Handbells are fun for children who can grasp and shake them.

- Look for sleigh bells that are securely attached to a handle.

Drums and drumsticks

- Make a drum from a cylindrical container such as an oatmeal box, using tape to secure the top and cover any rough edges.

- Drums can be played with hands, spoons, or dowels of different lengths and diameters.

- Children who are able sit up can play a drum that is large enough to fit between their legs.

- Pots and pans with wooden spoons are another way to provide drums.

Maracas

- Several companies make small maracas that fit in toddlers' hands.

Tambourines

- These are available in different sizes.

Rattles and shakers

- A wide variety of rattles and shakers is available for this age group.

- If you make your own, secure them tightly and inspect them regularly so that children cannot reach the small pieces inside.

Rhythm sticks

- Cut dowels in 12"–15" lengths. Sand the ends to make them smooth.

Sand blocks

- Start with smooth wooden blocks. Glue sandpaper to one side, with the rough side up. Children make and hear interesting sounds when they rub the sandpaper sides together.

Xylophones

- Look for instruments designed for this age group with a few notes and a wooden stick with a knob on the end. Some are also pull toys.

Allow plenty of time for children to explore the instruments. They will be excited to learn that different sounds can be produced by shaking and tapping them in different ways. Infants and toddlers are not ready to perform with the instruments. For example, it is too difficult for them to march and play instruments at the same time. Nevertheless, you can make music and movement a daily experience for the children in your care.

what's next?

Skill-Building Journal, section **7-7** (*Learning Activity C*), and section **7-1** (*Feedback*).

Learning Activities

LEARNING
ACTIVITY

D. Nurturing Creativity Through Art Experiences

In this activity you will learn to

- provide a variety of art materials that encourage children's exploration

- plan activities that allow children to use art materials in interesting ways

Infants and toddlers are interested in finding out what art materials are like and, as they get older, what they can do with them. They focus on the process of investigating art materials rather than on the products, or creations, they might make with them. Squeezing a lump of playdough and tearing paper are very satisfying experiences.

The world is filled with interesting and beautiful things for infants and toddlers to examine.

A first step on the road to artistic expression is to notice and value the world's beauty. For infants, the world is a gallery filled with things to see and touch. When babies rub small squares of corduroy and terry cloth with their fingers, they learn about textures. Their teacher can direct their attention and encourage language skills by introducing new words like *soft* and *rough*.

Infants and toddlers can gain an appreciation for beauty in the natural and human-made worlds. Teachers can point out a ladybug and talk about the black spots on its red body. She can place a baby on a blanket outdoors so he can watch a colorful windsock waving to and fro.

Teachers introduce art processes to infants by encouraging them to explore the textures, shapes, sights, and colors all around them and by talking with infants about their discoveries. Have you ever seen a baby stroking the fringe on a blanket or delighted by a dancing rainbow made by a prism hanging in the window? Many infant toys are designed to provide visual and tactile experiences. You might also try these suggestions to support creativity.

Provide beautiful things to look at and to touch.

- Hang a patchwork quilt or piece of patterned fabric on the wall at infants' eye level. Attach each item securely so infants can touch it without pulling it down.

- Float bubbles in the air, indoors and outdoors, and lift babies so they can see and touch them.

- Post photos of the babies' families—the most important pictures of all—where the children can examine them during the day.

- Make mobiles to hang over cribs, changing tables, and throughout the room. Choose interesting and colorful things to include in the mobile.

Introduce a variety of textures.

- Offer cardboard, cloth, and plastic books that infants can pat, chew, and wave. Touch-and-feel books are fun for this age group, too. When babies are ready to respond, sit and read with them and talk about the pictures. "Here's a bunny. He feels soft."

- Put scraps of fabric to good use. Cut your collection into 5" x 7" pieces. Include a wide variety of shapes, colors, and textures. Store the scraps in an open basket. Place the collection in front of a seated infant or allow an older infant to find it for herself.

- Stitch scraps of different kinds of ribbon to the edges of a small piece of fabric. Babies will enjoy feeling all of the different textures.

- Collect carpet samples and large pieces of thick fabric, such as heavyweight fleece. Scatter them where infants can crawl to or over them safely.

Introduce a few simple activities.

- Give infants paper to tear: magazines, junk mail, and scraps. Offer these items to seated babies.

- Have older infants kneel or stand near a large piece of paper that is taped to a low table. Give each child a large nontoxic crayon so she can discover what she can do with it.

- Place infants on large towels (on the floor) or on grass near a shallow plastic tub. Fill the tubs with about 2 inches of water. Let the children splash and play. Another time, also offer a few simple props such as cups and sponges.

- Offer indoor and outdoor sand play for older infants who are about 15–18 months old and who are more interested in playing with sand than in tasting it. Teachers can create miniature sand boxes in individual trays or tubs. When children seem ready to use more than their hands to explore, offer a few simple props, such as sprayers to wet the sand; small cars and trucks; pails, shovels, and small rakes; small containers to fill and dump; ice cube trays; and muffin tins.

Art materials present a wide range of exciting and challenging creative experiences for toddlers. Art experiences for toddlers are opportunities to explore cause and effect, increase fine motor skills and coordination, make choices, feel competent, build social skills, and increase language skills. While it is important to supervise toddler art activities, this does not mean that toddlers will not be able to do things on their own. Offer activities that allow toddlers to make many decisions about what and how to use art materials.

The key to providing successful art experiences is to remember what toddlers are like.

As a teacher who works with toddlers, you know the characteristics of children this age, and you can anticipate what might happen during an activity. Keep both developmental and individual characteristics in mind as you prepare to offer an activity and while you implement it. Here are some suggestions.[30]

Have everything ready. Toddlers can be very eager to get started and will be frustrated if they have to wait for you to set up or to get things that you forgot. Make sure you have enough tools and materials so that each child has his or her own. Remember to set up an area where children can store their creations safely, in case they want to save them or so you can collect them for the child's portfolio. For example, toddlers can put their pasted papers on a low shelf to dry flat or hang their paintings on a clothesline.

Work with children individually or in small groups. Divide the class so one teacher can supervise the art experience while another plays with the other children. Be sure that the children who are participating have the skills needed for the particular activity. If a child has trouble with the activity or if you have to do it for him, it is too difficult. Redirect the child to a more successful activity. If the whole group is getting frustrated, change the activity so it matches their skills, needs, and interests.

Provide a way to keep clothes dry and clean. Toddlers explore art materials enthusiastically, so they often get wet or dirty. Plastic smocks provide the best protection for toddlers' clothing. Some programs encourage families to provide additional clothes for art activities, such as a large t-shirt, pull-on pants, and old shoes that still fit.

Involve families in recycling items for art experiences. Toddlers are eager to use all kinds of materials, both purchased and recycled. Give families a list of what the children can use. Visit a reusable resource center to find interesting items.

Allow plenty of time for exploration. Children need time to become familiar with materials and more time to continue to explore them. Some children will spend so much time exploring in their own ways that they won't have time to do what you planned. This is to be expected, and their self-directed explorations are valuable learning experiences.

Expect spills and messes. Toddlers are concerned with their explorations. They are not focused on keeping things clean and dry. Before you get started, cover the counter, table, or floor with newspaper, butcher paper, or a vinyl tablecloth or shower curtain. This makes cleaning easier.

Encourage independence. Toddlers like to do things for themselves. Support their self-help skills by providing supplies to clean their hands during art experiences. Place wet sponges, washcloths, or paper towels near the children. You might also provide a bucket of warm, soapy water and paper towels for washing and drying hands during the project. Children will also need to wash their hands thoroughly when they are finished with the art experience.

Repeat activities over and over. Toddlers need many opportunities to explore materials. Each time they take part in an art activity, they have a different experience and learn different things. Offer the same activity again and again, until the children lose interest.

Keep safety in mind. Toddlers are sensory learners who put things in their mouths and may accidentally swallow them. Use a choke tube to test the sizes of materials provided for art activities. Also remember that toddlers act first and think about cause and effect later. They must be supervised at all times, including when working with art materials.

Basic Art Experiences for Mobile Infants and Toddlers

Five major categories of art experiences are appropriate for some mobile infants and for toddlers: painting, finger painting, drawing, tearing and pasting, and using dough. Children can participate while sitting or standing at a low table. Some children like to sit on the floor to work. The next few pages summarize a few basic art experiences for mobile infants and toddlers, including materials, tools, and notes for each category. You can find additional ideas and recipes for making art materials in books and on the Internet.

Painting

Materials	Tools
• Large pieces of paper (newsprint, wallpaper samples, paper bags)	• Paintbrushes (flat bristles, short handles [5"–6"])
• Recycled items such as egg cartons and boxes	• Sponges cut in different shapes
• Liquid tempera paint (vibrant colors; already mixed)	• Small paint rollers
	• Straws
	• Easel for older toddlers

Notes

Expect children to paint their hands and fingers.

If necessary, cut down and sand the handles of longer brushes.

Look for interesting painting tools at hardware stores.

Watercolor sets are not a satisfying medium for this age group.

Introduce variations, such as applying paint to a sponge or other object and then using it to stamp paper.

Experiment with other items that can be dipped in paint and dripped or placed on paper.

Finger painting

Materials

- Finger paint
- Paper (glossy paper for older, experienced finger painters)

Tools

- Large combs (plastic or cardboard)
- Shallow trays or cookie sheets (alternatives to a plastic- or vinyl-covered tabletop)

Notes

Demonstrate techniques for first-time painters. Show them how to use their hands and fingers and how to make various lines.

Make sure that children have plenty of room to experiment and make broad movements.

Begin with two or three tablespoons of one color. Offer more colors if children seem interested. Expect that some toddlers will not want to get their hands messy. Offer such children a small dot of paint. If they are still reluctant to paint with their fingers, try again in a few weeks.

Recipe 1:

Combine 1 C liquid starch with 6 C water, 1/2 C soap flakes, and a few drops of food coloring.

Recipe 2:

Mix 3 T sugar with 1/2 C cornstarch in a pan; add 2 C cold water. Cover and cook over low heat until thickened. Cool; then add food coloring.

Drawing

Materials

- Large sheets of paper (newsprint, construction paper, cardboard)
- Cardboard boxes

Tools

- High-quality crayons
- Chalk and chalkboard
- Markers (non-toxic, wide, washable)
- Clipboards

Notes

It is important to provide crayons that color evenly and steadily.

Expect children to peel the wrappers off crayons. This allows them to use the sides of the crayons as well as the tips.

Attach a large piece of paper to the wall, tie strings around crayons, and attach the strings near the paper. Invite children to draw throughout the day.

Have children draw with chalk on a chalkboard or outdoors on the playground.

Tearing and Pasting

Materials	Tools
• Paper scraps, including magazines, catalogs, junk mail, or old calendars • Paper (large pieces) • Paste or gluesticks	• Brushes or tongue depressors

Notes

Tearing is a fun activity for this age group.

Older toddlers might be ready for pasting. You will need to show them how to put non-toxic paste on the back of a scrap and then place it on paper.

Redirect children who might eat paste.

Dough

Materials	Tools
• Playdough	• Wooden spoons and mallets • Small rolling pins or thick dowels

Notes

Involve children in making the playdough. Commercial playdough can be harmful if swallowed and can be difficult to remove from carpets.

Give each child a lump of dough because they are not developmentally ready to share.

Expect children to smell, taste, pat, and poke the dough during their first encounters with it.

Show older toddlers how to roll snakes and balls.

Recipe:

Combine 2 C flour, 1 C salt, 2 T oil, 1 C water, and a few drops of food coloring. For smoother dough, add 1 T cream of tartar. Heat in a pan, stirring constantly, until the dough pulls away from the sides and forms a lump. Knead the dough. Store in plastic bags or airtight containers in the refrigerator.

what's next?

Skill-Building Journal, section **7-8** (*Learning Activity D*), section **7-1** (*Feedback*), and section **7-9** (*Reflecting on Your Learning*).

8

Self

Overview

Helping Children Learn About Themselves and Others

Providing Experiences That Allow Children to Be Successful

Building Supportive Relationships With Individual Children

Your Own Sense of Self

Learning Activities

A. Using Your Knowledge of Infants and Toddlers to Foster a Sense of Self

B. Offering a Program That Promotes Success

C. Helping Children and Families Cope With Separation

D. Supporting Toddlers During Toilet Learning

8. Self

From birth, children begin to learn about themselves. They learn who they are, how they are like other people, and how they are different. A sense of self includes recognizing physical traits and much more. When family and teachers smile and laugh with children, marvel at their growing skills, and celebrate their very being, children learn to see themselves as persons of value.

Establishing trust supports children's curiosity and exploration.

Infants are totally dependent on family members and teachers to meet their basic needs for food, warmth, comfort, and love. When these important people provide food, make them comfortable, relieve their pain, hold them, and talk to them in loving ways, they learn that the world is a place they can trust. A sense of trust fuels an infant's curiosity, leading her to explore the world and her place in it.

Toddlers are becoming more and more independent.

Toddlers continue to rely on you to make them feel secure. They need you to understand who they are at different stages, respond to their feelings, and encourage them to move and explore. By nurturing their trust, you encourage them to accept new challenges and become increasingly autonomous (able to do things on their own). When you comment on toddlers' efforts and accomplishments, you help them feel good about who they are and what they can do.

Your supportive interactions help infants and toddlers learn about themselves. By demonstrating respect for individuals, you convey the message that each person is valued. Young children need opportunities to succeed and to experience the deep satisfaction that comes from mastering a new skill. Meaningful success leads to feeling competent and capable. When you offer help in solving a problem, listen and respond to feelings, or comment on a new painting technique, you are building a supportive relationship and fostering a child's developing sense of self.

You can promote children's sense of self by

- helping children learn about themselves and others

- providing experiences that allow children to be successful

- building supportive relationships with individual children

Helping Children Learn About Themselves and Others

1. **Include family photos and familiar items that help children feel connected to home while they are at the program.** Hang laminated photos of children's families on the wall within children's reach and include household items and decorations that make the room look and feel like a home.

2. **Include books, decorations, music, and other items that reflect the cultures of all of the children and teachers.** Ask families to share recipes, books, pictures, photographs, music, and other items the children will enjoy.

3. **Provide multiples of popular play materials so children do not have to share or take turns before they are ready.** "Ricky, you and Adam may each have your own lump of playdough."

4. **Arrange the furniture, materials, and equipment so mobile infants and toddlers can do things on their own when they are ready.** Place self-help items such as tissues and paper towels on low shelves where children can reach them.

5. **Learn and use a few words, songs, and rhymes in the home languages of children whose home language is not English.** To the tune of "Frère Jacques," you might sing, "Buenos días, buenos días. ¿Cómo estás? ¿Cómo estás?"

Two Firefighters

As you read the following story, think about why Mr. Lewis told Lovette that there was another hat on the shelf. Also think about how Mr. Lewis helped Lovette and Adam learn about themselves.

Lovette: My hat?

Mr. Lewis: There's another firefighter's hat on the shelf.

Lovette: Me hat, too.

Mr. Lewis: Two firefighters. Lovette and Adam.

Adam: We saw the fire truck.

Mr. Lewis: That's right. We saw the trucks at the fire station.

Providing Experiences That Allow Children to Be Successful

6. **Provide a range of activities and materials that can be enjoyed by children with varied skills, abilities, and interests.** Sit an infant in your lap while you both roll a ball to a toddler. An 18-month-old can grasp a crayon and make marks on paper while several toddlers scribble.

7. **Acknowledge children's efforts as well as their accomplishments.** "Wow, you almost got your thumb in your mouth. You are trying very hard."

8. **Invite children to participate in daily routines to the extent that their abilities and interests allow, even if they take a long time.** "Thank you for holding the fresh diaper. Now that you're clean, we can put it on."

9. **Accept mistakes as a natural part of learning.** "Oh, the water splashed on the floor. Let's get a sponge and clean it up."

10. **Repeat activities so children can master skills and experience success.** "You liked crawling through the box. Do you want to do it again?"

Zora Can Do It!

*As you read the following story, think about why Ms. Gonzalez watched Zora
from a slight distance and why she decided to offer Zora some help.*

 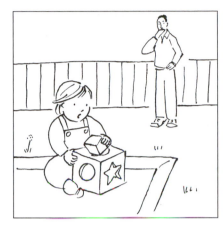 

Ms. Gonzalez: Try another
hole, Zora. You can do it.

Zora: Zora do!

Building Supportive Relationships With Individual Children

11. **Observe each child regularly to learn about individual needs, skills, abilities, interests, culture, and family experiences.** "Sammy pulls on his ear when he's tired and ready for a nap."

12. **Offer verbal and gentle nonverbal contact to show you care about a child's well-being.** Give plenty of hugs, smiles, and gentle touches to tell infants and toddlers that you value them.

13. **Identify and respond to children's needs and emotions with respect and empathy.** "You want to pump the toothpaste by yourself, but it keeps falling off your brush. Hold your toothbrush right under the nozzle and try again."

14. **Help children cope with their feelings about separating from and reuniting with their family members.** "It's hard to say goodbye to Daddy. We'll take good care of you. Daddy will come back to get you after snack."

15. **Spend individual time playing, laughing, and talking with each child, every day.** "Jessica, tell me about your pizza. I see that it has lots of veggies on top."

Luci Loves Yogurt

As you read the following story, think about how and why Ms. Bates used a feeding experience to build a positive relationship with Luci. Also pay attention to how she encouraged Luci's sense of self.

Ms. Bates: I hear you cooing. Your mommy told me you love yogurt.

Ms. Bates: You want to help. Would you like your own spoon?

Ms. Bates: First a spoon from me, and then one from Luci.

Ms. Bates: Your mommy was right. Luci loves yogurt!

what's next?

Skill-Building Journal, section **8-2** (*Overview*), section **8-10** (*Answer Sheets*), and section **8-1** (*Feedback*).

Your Own Sense of Self

People with positive self-esteem value their abilities and accomplishments.

How an individual feels about his or her personal characteristics is one part of a sense of self, which is also called self-esteem. People with a positive sense of self are comfortable with who they are, what they can do, and what they have accomplished. They have achieved meaningful goals and set new ones. Overall, they have a realistic appreciation of their abilities and contributions and feel valued by others.

Teachers' sense of self, or self-esteem, affects their understanding of children.

Do you describe yourself by your physical appearance or other personal attributes? Perhaps you say, "I am lots of fun, a nurturing teacher, a thoughtful colleague." Your sense of self reflects your experiences. Your culture, home life, school experiences, successes, and failures contribute to your sense of self. They also affect your understanding of child development and of individual children. Do you sometimes make assumptions about children whose characteristics and experiences differ from yours? Do those assumptions turn out to be true or false?

Think about your likes, dislikes, learning style, opinions, and feelings. What are your individual characteristics and abilities? How are you the same as and different from other people in your family, at work, in the community, in the country, in the world? The more you know about yourself, the more you can help infants and toddlers understand and appreciate themselves, their families, and their peers.

Our experiences shape our views and interactions.

As you think about your childhood experiences and what was important in your home and community, consider how your values have changed over time. Your experiences (or lack of experiences) with people of diverse backgrounds may have helped to shape your views and interactions with people today. With self-awareness, you can make a conscious decision to keep the beliefs and behaviors that match your current experiences and change those that do not.

With greater personal awareness, you will be able to help infants and toddlers accept and appreciate their individual characteristics. You can help them identify with and feel positive about their own family, culture, ethnicity, and home language. With your support, they will learn that there is a place for everyone in the group and that people are alike and different in many ways. How you interact and respond to children conveys your respect and acceptance of them. Respect and acceptance are what most children and adults ultimately want from others.

what's next?

Skill-Building Journal, section **8-3** (*Your Own Sense of Self*), section **8-1** (*Feedback*), and section **8-4** (*Pre-Training Assessment*).

Learning Activities

LEARNING ACTIVITY

A. Using Your Knowledge of Infants and Toddlers to Foster a Sense of Self

In this activity you will learn to

- recognize some typical characteristics of infants and toddlers

- use what you know about infants and toddlers to help them build a sense of self

Young infants (birth–8 months) begin developing a sense of self.

- Sammy (3 months) has just started putting his hands in his mouth.

- Jon (6 months) gently pats the sides of his bottle during feedings.

- Luci (8 months) plays peek-a-boo with Ms. Gonzalez.

Like other kinds of development and learning, building a sense of self starts early in life and continues into our adult years. When adults respond to babies' coos and smiles, infants learn that they are important people. Later adults talk with babies about what they look like and what they can do. "Your eyes are brown." "You have strong legs." "You smiled for Grammie." Such comments help a child understand who she is and that other people value her.

Mobile infants (8–18 months) need the right amount of support.

- Malou (9 months) looks toward the door when she hears her daddy call her name.

- Peter (12 months) examines the photos in the book Ms. Gonzalez made about him.

- Zora (16 months) squeezes toothpaste on her brush.

As young infants' physical skills grow, they learn to move their bodies and creep, crawl, and walk around the indoor and outdoor space. With a new perspective on the world, their interests and abilities expand. Teachers need to watch closely so they can offer the right amount of support: enough to help a child progress, but not so much as to take away the thrill of learning to do something for herself.

Toddlers (18–36 months) struggle to deal with strong feelings.

- Lovette (20 months) looks in the mirror, points, and says, "Vette."

- Ricky (28 months) asks Mr. Lewis to help when Adam (30 months) skins his knee.

- Jessica (34 months) lifts a block to her ear and pretends to phone her mom.

Young children's self-awareness becomes obvious in the toddler years. Their growing language skills provide the evidence: "My shoe," "Mine," and "Me do it." Two year olds begin to pay attention to physical characteristics such as eye and hair color. They learn how to name some of their feelings, but they often have difficulty coping with anger and frustration.

Establishing trust and autonomy are extremely important for infants and toddlers.

Social/emotional development is closely linked with gaining a sense of self. At every stage of life, children (and adults) must deal with age-specific challenges before they move on to the next stage. If these challenges are handled successfully, children's social/emotional development is enhanced. Psychologist Erik Erikson outlined eight stages of social/emotional development from infancy to old age.[31] The first stage, trust, begins during infancy. The second, autonomy, usually begins during the toddler years. Teachers and families play key roles in supporting the development of trust and autonomy.

A teacher's attention helps infants trust themselves and others.

The most important way to help infants build a sense of trust is to meet their basic needs promptly, consistently, and with care. Infants need to be fed when hungry; changed when wet, soiled, and uncomfortable; and held and loved when they cry and at many other times, too. In addition, infants need safe and interesting things to explore and adults who will talk, play, and read books with them. They thrive in supportive relationships with adults who celebrate their efforts and accomplishments and encourage them to take on new challenges. Your attention helps infants learn to trust themselves, other people, and the world around them. Feelings of trust continue to grow and support development and learning throughout childhood and into the adult years. A sense of trust supports the development of autonomy, which usually begins during the toddler years.

Autonomy concerns being independent, doing things for oneself, making decisions, and exploring the world. Toddlers spend much of their time testing limits and asserting themselves. They see things from their own point of view. If they want something, they think that no one else could want it more. The *M* words—*me*, *mine*, and *my*—are heard often in toddler rooms.

Toddlers want to be grown-up and to stay young.

Toddlers have conflicting feelings, however. They want to do grown-up things but don't always want to leave behind things they did when younger. Drinking from a cup seems wonderful until a toddler realizes that it takes the place of nursing or using a bottle. Wearing underpants and learning to use the toilet are a lot more challenging than wearing diapers.

Your knowledge of typical toddler behaviors will help you understand how to respond to them. Toddlers aren't misbehaving; they are struggling to establish and feel good about being independent. When you respond to toddlers in a calm and patient manner, you help them build a sense of self.

Development of Infants and Toddlers

Young infants (birth–8 months)

- form strong attachments to family members and teachers
- smile and coo on their own initiative and in response to others
- turn their heads and look away when not interested in an activity or toy
- discover and learn to control the movement of their hands and other body parts
- like to be held, cuddled, and amused by simple games and toys

Mobile infants (8–18 months)

- respond differently to different people they know and may exhibit stranger anxiety
- watch people, objects, and activities in their environment
- become attached to favorite items such as stuffed animals or blankets
- move from one place to another by creeping, crawling, or walking
- understand many more words than they can say

Toddlers (18–36 months)

- like doing things for themselves most of the time
- learn to use the toilet on their own
- begin to notice individual characteristics such as gender and skin color
- say no when adults ask them to do something
- use words such as my and mine frequently

Development: It's All Connected

In addition to social and emotional skills, building a sense of self relies on physical, cognitive, and communication skills. Here are a few examples:

Physical
Infants study their hands and soon understand that their hands are part of their bodies. They hold and grasp objects and explore more and more new things.

Mobile infants move their bodies from one place to another. They explore and begin to make sense of the world and their place in it.

Toddlers feel a sense of pride in learning to run, climb, and jump. Activities such as scribbling let them see that their actions have an effect. Physical skills also enable toddlers to do things for themselves, for example, to get a step stool to use at the sink or to put shoes on and take them off.

Cognitive
Infants play simple games, such as peek-a-boo, with the important people in their lives: family members and teachers. They recognize the voices and faces of the adults who care for them.

Mobile infants may be afraid of unfamiliar people and may be anxious when separated from their families. They eventually realize that their families will return at the end of the day.

Toddlers become more aware of other children and begin to notice individual characteristics, such as hair and eye color.

Communication
Infants express their needs and feelings through cries, coos, gurgles, smiles, and babbling.

Mobile infants point and make sounds to tell others what they want. They understand more than they can say.

Toddlers often say *no* to express themselves as individuals. They label things and themselves using the M words: *me*, *my*, and *mine*.

what's next?

Skill-Building Journal, section **8-5** (*Learning Activity A*) and section **8-1** (*Feedback*).

LEARNING ACTIVITY

Learning Activities

B. Offering a Program That Promotes Success

In this activity you will learn to

- plan a program that encourages individual children to experience success

- offer new challenges to encourage growth and learning

In their first months of life, infants depend on you to meet their needs. They can do very little for themselves. As they get older, they come to understand that they are separate individuals, and they begin to gain skills that they can use to meet their own needs. Young infants might pat a bottle, reach for a rattle, or smile to get you to smile back at them. By the time they are toddlers, children are eager to use and master new skills, and they begin to see themselves as competent and capable individuals.

Frequent observations provide information about children's skills and needs.

You and your colleagues probably spend much of the day doing things for children that they cannot do for themselves. It is your job to keep children safe and to notice and meet their needs. It is also your job, however, to recognize when children are ready to help themselves and to provide opportunities for them to be successful and feel competent. For example, you might place a rattle in a four-month-old's hand because you know what he can do (shake the rattle) and what he cannot do (pick up the rattle on his own). Your frequent observations provided this information, and they will let you know when he is able to pick up rattles and other objects without your help. Similarly, when watching an older infant playing with a shape-sorting box, you wait before stepping in to help because you think she has the skills to put the shape blocks into the right holes on her own. Young children learn to feel good about themselves when they can practice skills they already have and when they can learn new skills in a safe and accepting atmosphere.

Many of the practices suggested in other modules allow infants and toddlers to be successful, whether kicking a mobile or taking off their socks. Here is a summary of ways for your program to promote success through the environment, routines, activities, and interactions.

Children can experience success in a safe and challenging environment.

The Environment

How can the environment contribute to children's success? First, the furniture and equipment must be the right size, sturdy, and safe. Children need to reach the things they need, such as toys, books, tissues, so they can make decisions and learn to do things for themselves. If you don't have wedges or seats where infants can sit, they will have to lie flat on their backs and they will not be able to see much of what is going on. If the climber is too large, you will have to help them climb, and toddlers won't be able to enjoy the feeling, "I did it on my own." It's much more fun—and meaningful—for a child to climb to the top by himself than to do so while holding your hand. By providing a safe but challenging environment, you allow children to explore, make discoveries, and feel competent.

Play materials should be in good repair and match the interests and skill levels of the group. Open-ended materials, such as blocks or a basket of plastic lids, can be used in different ways, depending on children's ideas and abilities. A young infant grasps and waves a lid; a mobile infant holds two at a time and claps them together; a toddler dumps the lids on the floor, puts them back in the basket, and then dumps them out again. Each child experiences success by using a very simple object that you provided.

The children in your care learn new skills and develop new interests all of the time. The environment and play materials you create must be reviewed often in terms of each child's growing abilities and changing interests. Conversations with families and your ongoing observation notes can provide the information you need to make sure the environment is safe and challenging for all of the children.

- How does your environment provide safe challenges?

- How frequently do you assess your environment to make sure it is still appropriate for the children in your group?

Routines

Much of the day in an infant/toddler room is spent carrying out routines. All of the children—even young infants—can play a role during routines such as diapering, toileting, feeding, and dressing. For example, when diapering a young infant, have her hold the clean diaper. When a toddler needs a diaper change, have him climb up the steps to the changing table. Both children will feel good about using their self-help skills.

There is no need to hurry during routines.

Toddlers, in particular, like to do things on their own. It might be faster or easier for you to wipe the table or put the books back on the shelf, but involving toddlers provides opportunities for them to be successful. There is no need to rush through routines. They are opportunities for children to learn and to feel good about their efforts and accomplishments.

THINK

- How can you involve a mobile infant in feeding herself?

- How can you involve a toddler in making snack?

Activities

Infants and toddlers spend much of the day engaged in routines and playing with toys and with you. Mobile infants and toddlers also enjoy simple activities such as taking a nature walk in the playground, reading aloud, singing, cooking pizzas, and scribbling with jumbo crayons. They are interested in the process involved in these activities, rather than the products. You can plan some activities in advance and provide special materials that are not always available in the classroom. Other activities happen spontaneously because the materials are available and children are interested in using them.

Offer activities that match a range of abilities and interests.

When you carry out an activity with mobile infants and toddlers, it is important to consider the range of abilities and variety of interests of the group. Make sure your plans allow multiple levels of success. It is also important to repeat activities. Repetition allows children to practice and master their skills and gain new ones.

For example, when choosing or making up a song, keep it simple and include a chorus. The singers can make sounds, join in with the chorus, and repeat the words. Everyone will have fun and feel competent. Sing it every day until you or the children are ready to try a new one.

When you take the children for a walk in the neighborhood, make sure your plans allow children to ride in wagons or buggies if they get tired, and use a rope line or other strategy to help toddlers stay with you. One day you might walk by the pet store and watch the birds in the window. Another time you might go in a different direction to see the "big kids'" school.

The one thing you can depend on when planning activities for infants and toddlers is that things seldom go as planned. You need to be both willing and able to revise your plans if something else interests the children. By doing so, you will be honoring the children's ideas and showing respect for them as individuals.

- What kinds of activities do the children in your group enjoy?

- How do you respond to children's interests through activities?

Teacher Interactions

Children remember our language for a long time.

Infants and toddlers learn a lot about themselves through their interactions with the important adults in their lives. Teachers and family members are like mirrors, reflecting back to children images of their individual characteristics, abilities, and importance. Our nonverbal communications—smiles, hugs, and nods in a child's direction—convey supportive messages: "I care about you. You are a valued person." Our language is extremely important and stays with children long after words are uttered. When language is caring, it helps a child feel valued and respected. Here are some examples of caring language:

You are the first one here this morning. You and I can spend some time singing together. (This says, I enjoy our one-on-one times together.)

Robin, I see you got out some paper. Are you looking forward to finger painting again today? (This suggests, I pay attention to you and notice what you do here.)

I have to lift you down from the shelves. The shelves are for toys, not for climbing. Let's go to the climber. (This explains, I know what you like to do, and I will help you do it safely.)

I'm wrapping you up in your blanket. Swaddling helps you stay calm so you can fall asleep. (This says, I know what you need, and I am helping to meet that need.)

- What might you say to a child at the end of the day?

- What can you say to a child who must wait for your attention?

A Word About Praise

Many of us grew up hearing general words of praise, such as "Good job," and we may still hear phrases like "Great idea." Most likely you don't place much value in such vague statements. It is more meaningful and useful when someone comments specifically on your efforts and accomplishments, e.g., "I see that you spent a long time researching new ways to communicate with families."

Comment on what children do, rather than pass judgment.

When children work hard and apply new skills, they need to know that you noticed their effort and believe their work is important. When you get the urge to say, "Good job," try to stop yourself. Instead, comment on what you witnessed, without passing judgment. Describe the child's actions: "I saw you put the beads in the basket." Then explain why this is appreciated. "Now they can go back on the shelf, and we'll know where to find them."

- Do you catch yourself saying, "Good job," throughout the day? What can you say instead?

- What else can you and your colleagues do to offer support for children's efforts and accomplishments?

One of the hardest things to know is when to offer help to a child and when to gradually withdraw help so the child can manage independently. Too much or too little support can rob a child of the opportunity to feel successful, competent, and proud. Observe children closely to learn who needs help, who needs a few words of encouragement, and who simply needs a wave or a smile when practicing a new skill. If you step in only when necessary, you help infants and toddlers acquire new skills in a way that builds their sense of competence.

what's next?

Skill-Building Journal, section **8-6** (*Learning Activity B*) and section **8-1** (*Feedback*).

Learning Activities

C. Helping Children and Families Cope With Separation

In this activity you will learn to

- understand why and when infants and toddlers have difficulty handling separation

- help children and families cope with strong feelings about being apart

At the start of every day in a child development center, teachers greet children and families. They help children get settled while also exchanging important information with families. A parent might say, "Mary had great fun playing with her measuring cups in the bathtub last night." This knowledge gives you an idea of what Mary might enjoy doing at the program. The morning routine also involves families and children in saying goodbye as they separate for the day. These morning partings can evoke strong feelings in children, families, and teachers. It can be tempting to encourage them to say goodbye as quickly as possible, but that is not what children and families need from you.

Trusting relationships help children feel confident and capable.

Children need your help to manage their strong feelings about separation and its counterpart, reunion. They learn that it is okay to miss their family members and that you are there to help them learn ways to cope. Through your trusting relationships with individual children and through specific games and strategies, you can help children feel more confident and capable.

The ways in which infants and toddlers experience separation are closely tied to their stages of development. During their first few months of life, most babies adjust well to new situations and caregivers if their needs are met promptly and consistently. At about 4–5 months, infants begin to understand that they are separate beings, distinct from other people. They prefer being with familiar caregivers, but they usually respond well to other people, too.

At about eight months, babies realize that there are special people in their lives.

As early as six months, but more typically at about eight months, infants begin to show that they do not like being around new people. They prefer to be with you or someone else whom they know well, and they may get quite upset in the presence of strangers. The onset of this stage indicates that the baby now knows that the special people in his life—family members and teachers—are different from everyone else.

Separation anxiety typically lasts about four months.

Infants at this stage are beginning to develop an understanding of an important concept: object permanence. They are learning that people and things continue to exist even when they cannot see them, such as the toy that fell behind a chair. They also realize that there is only one of each beloved person. When mom or dad or grandma goes away, the baby is not sure if or when the well-loved person will return. Children at this stage have a hard time saying goodbye. They miss the absent person and find it very hard to wait for his return. This period of separation anxiety typically passes in about four months, around the time when infants become mobile.

Children who crawl and walk are joyful explorers who appear to be in love with the world around them. Duane, who just weeks ago cried when his father left him each day, is so busy crawling through a tunnel that he hardly says goodbye. His father says, "He doesn't seem to care if I am here or not." Duane does care, however. He is not only aware of his father's presence, he is energized by having his father nearby.

Separation anxiety can recur during toddlerhood.

At around 18 months, toddlers such as Duane may experience another bout of separation anxiety. Although their new skills allow them to be more independent, they may be afraid of being on their own. By the time they turn two, toddlers are old enough to know how important their families are. Their strong feelings can cause children to be fearful and anxious when their parents are away. Some children express these feelings by withdrawing silently; others might express their feelings by kicking or screaming. As their language skills grow, older toddlers become more able to name their strong feelings and express them in words.

To help children cope with separation, it is important to acknowledge the strong feelings of family members as well. Some may feel guilty about leaving their child while they attend school or go to work. Others may worry about what their child is doing in their absence or feel sad that they are not with them. Think about how you feel when you have to say goodbye to someone you love. Families have these feelings, too, and young children sense when their family members are anxious or worried about separation.

Separation can cause everyone to have strong emotions.

It is likely that you also have strong emotions about separation. It is important to examine these feelings. What are your views about families' enrolling their infants and toddlers in the program? Do you agree with their decision to place their children in your care? How do your feelings influence the way you support families and children during separations?

When planning ways to help children cope with separation, begin by thinking about what you can do to involve and support families. Here are some strategies.

Establish and maintain a strong partnership with each family. Get to know each other and figure out the best ways to communicate. Encourage families to spend time in the classroom so they can see firsthand what goes on. When families understand and value what you and the children do each day, they will communicate positive feelings to their children. Children are more able to handle separations when their families have confidence in you and your program.

Create a welcoming environment. Have an open-door policy that encourages families to come to the program at any time. Offer tea and coffee in a family area, to take with them or to drink during visits. Provide comfortable seating.

Show what goes on during the day. Make and post photo panels that depict routines and activities from start to finish. Make videos to lend to families. Create photo albums and ask families to help you keep them up to date.

Help families establish goodbye rituals. Many families already have special ways to say goodbye. When she leaves, an aunt might say, "Here's a hug. When Mommy comes to pick you up, pass it on to her." If they do not have a ritual, you can help them establish a special way to say goodbye. You might encourage a child, "Blow a kiss to Grandma. Say, 'See you after my nap.'" In one program, a "waving window" near the entrance evolved into the place where children and families say goodbye.[32]

Encourage families to bring their child's comforting item from home. Most children have something special that helps them feel connected to home. It might be a special blanket, a stuffed animal, or an outgrown shirt.

Explain the importance of saying goodbye. Families may think it is best to sneak out while their child is crying. Help them understand how it would feel if the most important person in their life disappeared with no warning. Saying goodbye gives children the security of knowing their families will always let them know what is happening.

Your program's practices can help children learn to trust. Your environment, routines, play materials, and interactions with children can help children build a sense of trust, feel secure, and manage their feelings about separation. Here are some suggestions to try in your classroom:

Maintain a homelike environment. Children tend to feel secure when the classroom has familiar items and furnishings. Soft lighting, carpets, curtains, and comfortable chairs help create a welcoming setting.

Include family photos in the room. You can take photos, yourself, or ask families to provide them. They can even include family pets. In addition to seeing large photos on the wall at their eye level, children will also be comforted by photos small enough to hold or to put in a pocket.

Engage children in daily routines. Children can do things at the program that they typically do with their families. Preparing food, picking up toys, and mailing a letter can help children build a bridge between home and child care.

Play games and read books that help children gain a sense of mastery over separation. Games like "Where's Jeremy?" and peek-a-boo help children understand that things—including people—continue to exist even when they are not visible. Children can use props such as hats and coats, briefcases and tote bags, and other familiar items to pretend to leave and come back. Ask the librarian to recommend books about departures and reunions.

Acknowledge children's feelings. Younger children need you to name their feelings for them. "You are crying because you are sad. You miss your daddy." A good listener can also help older children cope. "You feel sad when Mom leaves because you love her. She will come back. Would you like to look at her photo?"

Talk with children about their family members during the day. Comments and questions can help children feel connected to their absent families. For example, you might make comments and ask, "Your daddy told me you can get up on your knees," and "Is this pizza like the one you made with your grandpa?" Toy telephones are useful for pretending to call an absent family member.

Children might express their strong feelings at the end of the day.

As noted earlier, each day's separation ends with a reunion. Some days babies smile and wiggle in delight when they see their families. On other days they are cranky or indifferent. Toddlers might run gleefully into their parents' arms, or the sight of the beloved family members might bring on tears or tantrums. It may seem as though the children are not glad to see their families, but that is not usually so. Often children have worked hard all day to cope with their feelings about missing their families. They have saved their deep feelings for their families, the people they trust the most. You can help by explaining the situation to their families and by sharing the wonderful things their children have been doing all day. Help the children and their families make the transition to home.

Separation is not a problem to be solved or a goal to be achieved. Rather, it is a lifelong process that children and adults will encounter repeatedly. By supporting children with their early separations, you can help them become competent individuals who can handle the comings and goings of loved ones throughout their lives.

what's next?

Skill-Building Journal, section **8-7** (*Learning Activity C*) and section **8-1** (*Feedback*).

Learning Activities

LEARNING ACTIVITY

D. Supporting Toddlers During Toilet Learning

In this activity you will learn to

- recognize the signs that a toddler is ready for toilet learning

- work with families to support toddlers during toilet learning

For successful toilet learning, adults need to follow the child's lead.

Toilet learning begins with changing infants' diapers. When you talk about what you are doing, maintain a positive tone, and avoid using words like yucky or stinky, you communicate to infants that there is no task more pleasing than changing their diapers. How is this related to toilet learning? When diapering is a pleasant experience, children begin learning to accept and value their bodies. When they are interested and able to begin toilet learning, they will already be aware of and accepting of their bodily functions.

Successful toddler teachers know that toilet learning—like many kinds of learning—must follow the child's lead. They accept that the learning process will probably include delays and setbacks. They respond matter-of-factly to toilet learning accidents—just as they would in any other learning situation—by allowing the child to be as independent as possible while getting washed and dried and putting on clean clothes. Such teachers understand and enjoy toddlers' unique characteristics.

Typical characteristics of toddlers affect toilet learning readiness and success.

Toddlers' **interest in cause and effect** helps them understand what causes wet and messy diapers. They learn to sense the difference between wet and dry diapers and know when their diapers are soiled. You can help them understand the cause of their discomfort by observing, "I see you tugging on your diaper. Is it wet?"

Toddlers have a growing **awareness of standards** for behavior and cleanliness set by their family and community. They want to be clean and orderly like older children and adults and delight in pointing out mistakes, such as spilling a drink. Some toddlers show concern about dirt and messes, and that concern can foster an interest in toilet learning. You can encourage their interest by commenting, "You like to feel clean and dry."

Toddlers are **curious explorers** who want to know how things work, including their bodies. They may want to splash the toilet water or flush and watch the water drain away. Some toddlers want to watch other people using the toilet and may ask questions about how bodies and toilets work. You might read aloud books that help answer toddlers' questions. "Remember *Everyone Poops*? The pictures showed what happens after the toilet is flushed. Let's read it again."

Toddlers are beginning to **think of themselves as individuals.** A toddler might go to a corner or other sheltered place when wetting or soiling his diapers. When learning to use the toilet, a toddler might want some privacy. You can respect a toddler's sense of privacy by offering, "I'll stand in front of you until you are done."

Toddlers' can use their **rapidly expanding communication skills** to tell you when their diapers are wet or soiled, and they can use specific words to announce when they are urinating or defecating. They can understand and follow simple directions, e.g., "Hannah, remember to wipe from the front to the back."

Toddlers can be **fearful** and may resist toilet learning because they are afraid of losing part of themselves when urine and feces are flushed down the toilet. They may also fear falling into the toilet and being flushed away. "You seem worried about sitting on the potty."

Ready, Willing, and Able to Start Toilet Learning

Toddlers who are ready to start toilet learning

- are usually between 18–24 months old, although they could be as old as 30 months

- show signs when they are pushing (look focused and crinkle their foreheads)

- go to a specific place in the room to urinate or defecate in their diapers

Toddlers who are willing to start toilet learning

- say that they want to learn to use the toilet instead of wearing diapers

- ask to wear "real" underwear

- show an interest in imitating older children and adults

Toddlers who are able to start toilet learning

- stay dry for 2–3 hours at a time

- are aware of internal body signals and know what they mean

- pay attention to physical signals even when involved in another activity

- can walk to the bathroom or potty, pull down their pants, stoop and sit, wipe their bottoms, and pull up their pants

---

When to Begin Toilet Learning

The decision to begin toilet learning is a joint one that must involve the family, the teachers, and, perhaps most importantly, the child. The family and the teachers might have seen signs that the child is ready to learn how to use the toilet. The child's interest and cooperation, however, are the keys to successful teaching and learning.

Signs that a child is ready for toilet learning can appear at home and at the center.

As described in the box "Ready, Willing, and Able to Start Toilet Learning," a number of signs indicate that a child might be ready to begin toilet learning. Typically, between 18–24 months of age, toddlers are physically able to stay dry for 2–3 hours at a time. For some children, an extra six months or so are needed before they stay dry for several hours. In addition, a toddler who is ready for toilet learning is aware of internal physical signals that he needs to urinate or defecate. He also wants to be like older children and adults. He can pull his pants down, sit on the toilet, and pull his pants back up. He may announce his interest, "Jay wear big boy pants?" Teachers might notice signs at the center, and his family may have observed them at home. One or both will raise the question, "Do you think Jay is ready to learn to use the toilet?"

Families and teachers work together to implement a toilet learning approach.

After a number of readiness signs have been observed, it is time to discuss and agree on an approach to use at home and at the program. Here are some of the points one teacher addressed as she and a family planned ways to help two-year-old Jay achieve this important goal.

Active learning

We like the term toilet learning, *rather than* toilet training, *because Jay is an active learner. We won't control or train him. We will help him make the transition from diapers to using the toilet.*

Self-help skills

Jay will be more independent if he can pull his pants up and down without our help. Pants with elastic, rather than zippers, work well. Most toddlers have a hard time getting overalls off and on. This used to be a major cause of accidents in our room.

Accidents

We know that accidents are part of toilet learning. When they happen, we are calm and patient. We might make a matter-of-fact comment, "Jay, it looks like your pants are wet." Then we will help Jay clean himself and change into the fresh clothes you have provided. To acknowledge Jay's efforts I might say, "I know it is hard to learn something new." I might explain what I think happened, "You were having fun playing with Kip. You didn't notice you had to pee until it was too late to get to the potty."

Communication

During this toilet learning period we need to talk with or e-mail each other every day. As partners, we need to keep in touch about Jay's progress and successes and to figure out the times of day when he is most likely to use the toilet.

Gentle reminders

During the day we will pay attention and look for signs that Jay needs to use the potty. We will suggest that he use the toilet, acknowledge his effort by telling him what we see (for example, "Jay, it looks like you are pushing."), and help with his clothes, if necessary.

Home and program connections

When talking with Jay, we will use "potty" and the other words you use at home for toileting. We'll also read Fred Rogers' Going to the Potty with Jay, just as you do at home. We don't have potty chairs here, but we do have low toilets designed for toddlers. He can keep his feet on the floor and won't feel as though he is falling in.

Rewards

One way we know that Jay is ready for toilet learning is because he told us. He wants to succeed, and when he does he will feel proud of himself for mastering a new skill.

Handling Accidents and Setbacks

Accidents and setbacks are a normal part of toilet learning. If it seems as though they are happening more and more often, you need to consider the possible reasons. Here are some examples of why toddlers can have problems with toilet learning and how a teacher might respond.

- Sam's mother has him wear **pull-up diapers**. Sam (20 months) seems confused. The pull-up diapers feel like regular diapers, so he continues to wet and soil them. Sam's teacher asks the family to try using cotton underpants, to see if that might help Sam have greater success with toilet learning.

- Katy's parents recently separated. Katy (24 months) spends time with each parent, but she is having trouble getting used to her **family's new arrangement**. She has started having a lot of accidents at the center. It seems as though the stress of the separation is causing Katy's toilet learning setback. Katy's teacher suggests to her family that they ask Katy if she wants to use diapers again for a while.

- Brett (33 months) sits on the toilet for a long time when trying to have a bowel movement. Brett's teacher thinks that he **might be constipated**. She encourages his family to offer Brett more high-fiber foods, such as fresh fruits and whole grain bread, and she offers fiber-rich snacks at the program.

- Gina (34 months) had been using the toilet successfully for six months. After **moving to a new classroom**, she started having accidents two or three times a week. She went from being the oldest in her group to being the youngest. Gina's new teacher suggests to the director that Gina return to her former group. She also asks that the program review the way they decide which classroom is most appropriate for individual children.

As a teacher of toddlers, you will be helping children learn to use the toilet throughout the year. Some children have a relatively easy time with toilet learning; others have a harder time. It is your job to respect each child and family, to make sure that every child has a successful experience in learning to use the toilet.

Books for Toddlers About Learning to Use the Toilet

Everyone Poops by Taro Gomi

Going to the Potty by Fred Rogers

KoKo Bear's New Potty by Vicki Lansky

No More Diapers by J.G. Brooks

Once Upon a Potty—Girl by Alona Frankel

Once Upon a Potty—Boy by Alona Frankel

The Potty Book for Boys by Alyssa Satin Capucilli

The Potty Book for Girls by Alyssa Satin Capucilli

Time to Pee! by Mo Willems

---

what's next?

Skill-Building Journal, section **8-8** (*Learning Activity D*), section **8-1** (*Feedback*), and section **8-9** (*Reflecting on Your Learning*).

9
Social

Overview

Creating an Environment That Helps Children Develop Social Skills

Providing Opportunities for Children to Enjoy and Appreciate Other People

Helping Children Get Along With Each Other

Your Own Social Development

Learning Activities

A. Using Your Knowledge of Infants and Toddlers to Promote Social Development

B. Creating an Environment That Supports Social Development

C. Helping Infants and Toddlers Learn to Care About Others

D. Supporting Children's Play

9. Social

Most children enjoy being with people.

Social development involves learning to relate to adults and other children in positive and caring ways. Social skills are evident as infants respond to the familiar voice or touch of a parent or teacher, as toddlers learn to play alongside and with each other, and as preschoolers play cooperatively with friends. An important goal is to help children begin to care about and appreciate other people. Although living in a group setting like child care can sometimes be challenging, children's social development is nurtured by caring adults. With responsive care, children learn to relate positively to others and to enjoy being around other people.

Social skills are critical to success in school and life.

The social skills children gain as infants and toddlers are a foundation for their success in school. When asked to identify the characteristics of children who are ready for school, kindergarten teachers put social skills, such as taking turns, following directions, sharing, and getting along with others, at the top of their list. You and your colleagues can help infants and toddlers begin to learn these skills.

Children learn social behaviors through their relationships with caring adults.

Your secure relationships with individual children help them learn acceptable social behavior. Your interactions with children help them recognize, name, and understand their feelings and teach them to express themselves in acceptable ways. The development of a social being takes a long time, but it is worth the effort. Children who can establish and maintain friendships and who have positive relationships with others tend to be confident and eager to learn.

Children's social development is strengthened through secure relationships with their families and teachers. As a teacher, you let children know that they are loved and accepted, and you meet their needs as consistently and promptly as possible. This helps children feel secure, which in turn allows them to appreciate, respect, and get along with other children and adults.

You can promote social development by

- creating an environment that helps children develop social skills

- providing opportunities for children to enjoy and appreciate other people

- helping children get along with each other

Creating an Environment That Helps Children Develop Social Skills

1. **Provide play materials that can be used by more than one child at a time.** "Heather, if you sit on the other side of the rocking boat, you and Corinna can have fun together."

2. **Encourage children to be helpful.** "Reggie, you handed Sandy his rattle. That was very helpful."

3. **Include simple, homelike props that encourage beginning forms of pretend play.** Provide sturdy plastic utensils, bowls, pots, pans, dolls, stuffed animals, and other items found in the children's homes.

4. **Provide duplicates of popular items so children can play without having to share.** "Teresa, here is a pot for you to bang. Marc, there's one for you, too."

5. **Respond to children's communications.** "Hi, Carla. Are you smiling at me? I can see your new tooth! Are you ready to get up?"

Ricky Finds Lovette's Sneaker

As you read the following story, pay attention to the way Mr. Lewis used a daily routine to help the children develop social skills. Also think about what social skills the children practiced as they got ready to go outside.

Mr. Lewis: Lovette, where's your other shoe?

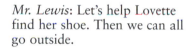

Lovette: Shoe?

Mr. Lewis: Let's help Lovette find her shoe. Then we can all go outside.

Ricky: Here it is!

Mr. Lewis: Who will help carry this big bag of balls?

Mr. Lewis: Carrying a big bag is easier when we help each other.

Providing Opportunities for Children to Enjoy and Appreciate Other People

6. **Plan daily jobs so one or two children can work together with a teacher.** "Sean, you may use the broom, and I'll hold the dustpan."

7. **Use routines as opportunities to interact with individual children.** "Yolanda, do you want some help with your mittens? Your granny told me she knit them for you. They look nice and warm."

8. **Play with children to model social and pretending skills.** Roll a ball back and forth, play peek-a-boo, and respond to children who are imitating and pretending by participating in their play.

9. **Involve children in simple activities that involve cooperation.** "If you hold the bowl for Lottie while she stirs the cinnamon into the applesauce, it won't tip. Then she can hold it for you."

10. **Help children value the contributions of others.** "Steven helped you to put all those blocks away. That made the job much easier."

Sammy Wants Some Company

As you read the following story, pay attention to how Ms. Bates figured out what Sammy wanted.
Also think about how she helped Sammy learn about enjoying another's company.

Ms. Bates: What's the matter, Sammy?

Ms. Bates: Your diaper is clean and dry. I wonder what's wrong.

Ms. Bates: You've had plenty of sleep, and you ate most of your lunch.

Ms. Bates: Now I know what you wanted: some company.

Helping Children Get Along With Each Other

11. **Pay attention to children's expressions of feelings and respond appropriately to show them how to get along with others.** "You want to stay outside and play in the sand box. I will wait for you to fill the bucket one more time."

12. **Introduce spoken language children can use to express what they want and how they feel.** "Tell her, 'No. Please let go,' when she grabs the truck you are playing with."

13. **Model ways to express feelings by sharing your own.** "This is a photograph of me with my family's new kitten. My smile shows how happy I am."

14. **Explain how another child might be feeling.** "Jan is getting a new tooth, so her gums hurt. That's why she's not very happy today."

15. **Help children learn how to treat others well.** "When you push Marc, it bothers him. He doesn't know you want to play with him. Why don't you sit near him? Then you can both play in the sand."

Peter and Malou Read Together

As you read the following story, pay attention to how Ms. Gonzalez included both Peter and Malou in an activity. Also think about what Ms. Gonzalez taught the children about relationships with other people.

Ms. Gonzalez: That's a cup, Peter. Do you drink milk from a cup?

Ms. Gonzalez: There's a wagon, like our wagon. This one is blue, but ours is red.

Ms. Gonzalez: Hi, Malou. Do you want to sit and read, too?

Ms. Gonzalez: Malou wants to join us. My lap has room for two children.

Ms. Gonzalez: Look, there's a banana. We had bananas for snack.

what's next?

Skill-Building Journal, section **9-2** (*Overview*), section **9-10** (*Answer Sheets*), and section **9-1** (*Feedback*).

Your Own Social Development

Adults use social skills every day.

When you yield to another car in traffic, share your lunch with a colleague who forgot hers, or wait for your turn to speak at a staff meeting, you are using social skills. Adults who cooperate, compromise, share, take turns, negotiate, empathize, and so on get along well with others in their families, workplaces, and communities.

Social skills help us interact with new people and get used to new situations.

Sometimes adults need to adapt to a new group of people. Perhaps you just joined a reading group or started attending an exercise class. You use social skills to get to know the other members and to adjust to the group's accepted ways of doing things. "We always start our meeting by catching up with each other's lives. Then we discuss the book."

Some adults find it very hard to adjust to new situations. This difficulty may be due to their temperaments or personalities. It's possible, though, that during childhood they did not have many opportunities to get to know new people.

Everyone benefits when teachers model positive social behavior.

Young children learn how society expects them to behave by watching adults interact with each other as well as with children. When children see the important adults in their lives working cooperatively, sharing feelings and ideas, having friendly conversations, and enjoying each other's company, they learn important lessons. Sometimes teachers are so busy that they forget to say *please* or *thank you* and don't take time to enjoy the company of their colleagues. However, when teachers feel positive about their jobs and the people they work with, children can gain a more complete picture of what it is like to be an adult. They see adults working out problems, sharing happy experiences, and cooperating with each other.

what's next?

Skill-Building Journal, section **9-3** (*Your Own Social Development*), section **9-1** (*Feedback*), and section **9-4** (*Pre-Training Assessment*).

Learning Activities

LEARNING ACTIVITY

A. Using Your Knowledge of Infants and Toddlers to Promote Social Development

In this activity you will learn to

- recognize some typical social behaviors of infants and toddlers

- use what you know about infants and toddlers to support social development

Social development begins at birth. Children's early experiences with their families and teachers are the foundation for building positive relationships throughout their lives.

Young infants (birth–8 months) rely on the loving, consistent care provided by their families and teachers.

- Sammy (3 months) looks toward the door and smiles when he hears his mother's voice.

- Jon (6 months) bangs a pie pan on the floor, looks at Ms. Gonzalez, and says, "Bu-u-u-u-uh. Bu-u-u-u-uh."

- Luci (8 months) squeals with delight while playing peek-a-boo with Mr. Lewis.

Newborn babies are entirely dependent on their families and teachers. They rely on adults to meet their basic needs—to comfort, diaper, and feed them. They also count on adults to introduce them to the joy of human relationships by talking and playing with them.

During the first few months of life, young infants learn to enjoy being with other people. Babies show a preference for human faces and voices, particularly those of primary caregivers such as family members and teachers. Their social interactions include turning their heads when someone speaks, focusing steadily on faces and objects, and making noises in response to the sounds and words around them. They respond to the loving and consistent care provided by family members and teachers by smiling, laughing, and kicking. When they are hungry, bored, or uncomfortable, they ask for attention, usually by crying.

Most babies are fascinated by other people. They will put their fingers in your mouth, touch your hair, and pull on your earrings or glasses. This exploration helps them understand that they are separate persons.

Responsive caregiving leads to trust, which is the foundation for social development.

Infants' positive experiences with their families and teachers help them build strong and secure attachments. Attachment is an ongoing, mutual relationship between infants and their primary caregivers. Attachment develops gradually during the first year of life when infants receive consistent, dependable, and responsive care from loving adults. This kind of care teaches infants to trust other people and themselves. This trust is the foundation for social development. Research conducted over time showed that securely attached children are more likely in later years to

- be better problem solvers

- form friendships and be peer leaders

- be more empathetic and less aggressive

- engage their world with confidence

- have higher self-esteem

- be better at resolving conflict

- be more self-reliant and adaptable[33]

Secure early attachments are important to infants' healthy growth and development.

Mobile infants (8–18 months) learn social skills through their relationships with teachers.

- Malou (9 months) holds onto Ms. Bates's hands, takes two steps, and smiles broadly.

- Peter (12 months) and Ms. Gonzalez use a big sponge to wipe the table together.

- Zora (16 months) picks up Sammy's blanket and hands it to Mr. Lewis.

Mobile infants are eager explorers who crawl and then walk where they want to go. They enjoy watching other children and often imitate what they see others do. They love the important people in their lives—including you and their family members—and may crawl after you and clutch your leg or climb into your lap.

It is very important to play, talk, and just enjoy being with mobile infants. Your responsive and positive interactions teach children that it is interesting, fun, and rewarding to be with other people. Mobile infants are gaining so many new skills that there are numerous ways to show them that it is fun to play games and respond to other people. You can play peek-a-boo over and over again; roll a ball back and forth; and read books, inviting children to point to pictures and to identify their body parts. You can also begin to teach children to help and comfort others. Many mobile infants are eager to help with tasks and, as they get older, help each other.

Toddlers (18–36 months) also depend upon secure relationships with caring adults.

- Lovette (20 months) looks at her frowning image in the mirror and says, "Sad."

- Ricky (28 months) hands a toy to a crying friend and asks, "Feel better?"

- Jessica (34 months) rocks her doll while Katy feeds her doll a bottle.

Toddlers work hard to learn about themselves. When they run, climb, jump, test limits, and shout, "No! Me do," and "Mine," they are trying to define who they are, what they can do, and how they are both alike and different from others. Much of this learning takes place through trial and error and depends upon their relationships with caring adults. A toddler learns about patience and cooperation when you wait for him to go around the track one more time before you go inside. She learns to feel good about herself and her abilities when you notice and respond to what she has done. For example, you might acknowledge, "You gave half of your cookie to your friend. You knew that Kim wanted some, so you shared your cookie. Look how happy you made her feel!" Toddlers also learn to have fun with other people when you sing, dance, and play with them.

As discussed in earlier modules, toddlers have strong and conflicting feelings. They are often eager to do things on their own, but they sometimes want assistance. They go back and forth between feeling capable and independent and wanting to return to a time when teachers and families took care of all their needs. These conflicting feelings can be confusing to a toddler, and they can be confusing to a teacher of toddlers.

Toddlers need your help to learn how to express strong feelings.

Having strong feelings does not mean that toddlers know what the feelings are, where they come from, or how to express them. Toddlers need your help to identify and name emotions like fear and anger. They need your help to learn spoken language that allows them to express strong feelings. They also need your help to learn to cope with feelings without resorting to aggression toward people or things. Being able to express feelings appropriately is an important skill for developing healthy social relationships throughout life.

Toddlers are very curious about each other. They observe carefully to figure out relationships. For example, they can figure out that the tall man with a moustache is Jackie's dad and the short lady with the red tote bag is Ana's mom. They are keenly aware of what belongs to them and what belongs to others.

Toddlers' ability to do things with each other grows rapidly. This is especially so for toddlers who have secure attachments with their primary caregivers and who have many opportunities to interact with other children in supportive environments. They may need a teacher's help to begin playing, to continue, and to handle disagreements. It is important to observe closely to learn what toddlers need. Often they just need time to figure out what to do. Toddlers can be very sensitive to each other and capable of working things out without adult assistance.

Development of Infants and Toddlers

Young infants (birth–8 months)

- enjoy being held and cuddled

- recognize and smile at the sight of familiar faces and things

- pay attention to the actions and sounds of children and adults

- smile, coo, and babble with familiar people

- ask for attention by crying, laughing, and smiling and through other vocalizations and actions

Mobile infants (8–18 months)

- look to adults for encouragement, support, and approval

- like to be near favorite adults and included in daily routines

- follow simple requests and understand more language than they can express

- are increasingly aware of their possessions

- may experience and express a fear of strangers

Toddlers (18–36 months)

- have strong feelings and may use physical actions—instead of speech—to express anger and frustration

- begin to learn about taking turns and waiting but should not be expected to share without great difficulty

- interact with other children for longer periods and exchange roles in the action when they play together

- engage in simple forms of pretend play

- begin to use caring behaviors to help and comfort others

Development: It's All Connected

The social development of infants and toddlers is closely connected with other aspects of their development. Here are a few examples:

Physical

Infants learn that it is fun to be with other people while being bounced on a knee and when someone offers them a rattle or other toy to grasp.

Mobile infants learn to appreciate the help of others when a teacher or family member holds their hand while they try to walk.

Toddlers use their fine and gross motor skills to carry out many different routines and activities—side by side or together, with individual children or in small groups.

Cognitive

Young infants begin to make sense of the world by watching and imitating others and by playing games such as pat-a-cake and peek-a-boo with teachers and family members.

Mobile infants also enjoy games in which they copy a teacher's actions, such as putting a block in a bucket just as the teacher did. They watch and imitate the actions of other children and adults.

Toddlers learn concepts such as in and out, up and down, empty and full, while playing and learning with other children.

Communication

Young infants coo, gurgle, and babble with others—especially their teachers and family members. They learn that they can get the responses they want by using their face, body, distinct cries, and other vocalizations.

Mobile infants wave bye-bye to family members and say the names of important people such as "Gamma" or "Dada." They make and repeat sounds and gestures as they interact with other people and learn about the give-and-take of conversations and other social interactions.

Toddlers begin to use spoken language to tell others how they feel and what they want or need. Their developing language skills help them play and get along with others.

Emotional

Young infants feel safe and secure because of their supportive relationships with teachers and family members. Feeling safe and secure is the foundation for learning to get along with others.

Mobile infants learn about themselves and others as they play and do things with their teachers. They can have strong feelings and act out because they are upset, frustrated, or scared. They trust that their special adults will help them manage their feelings.

Toddlers like to do things on their own and become more comfortable in a variety of environments. They begin to interpret and identify how others are feeling and begin to show empathy.

Some Social Development Alerts [34]

It may be time to suggest that a family consult their health provider if, by

3 months, a child does not

- smile at the sound of a primary caregiver's voice

- pay attention to new face, or if he seems very frightened by new faces or places

5 months, a child does not smile spontaneously

6 months, a child does not laugh or squeal

7 months, a child

- refuses to cuddle

- shows no affection for primary caregivers

- does not seem to enjoy the company of others

- does not try to attract attention by actions

8 months, shows no interest in playing peek-a-boo

12 months, a child does not imitate actions or words

2 years, a child does not follow simple instructions

3 years, a child

- does not engage in pretend play

- shows little interest in other children

- has extreme difficulty separating from family

---

what's next?

Skill-Building Journal, section **9-5** (*Learning Activity A*) and section **9-1** (*Feedback*).

Learning Activities

LEARNING ACTIVITY

B. Creating an Environment That Supports Social Development

In this activity you will learn to

- identify the features of your environment that promote social development

- make changes in the environment to support children's social development

Teachers help children learn to trust themselves and others.

The Crucial Role of Teachers

Several of the modules in this training program discuss the role of teachers as the most important part of an infant/toddler environment. That message is worth repeating: You and your colleagues who care for young children are indeed the most important part of the environment. Your supportive, responsive interactions with individual children help them feel valued and loved. Your interactions help children build a sense of trust that fuels their exploration and learning. Trust supports children's self-confidence and allows them to reach out and get to know others. Much of what you and your colleagues do helps infants and toddlers build social skills. Here are a few examples:

- Playing peek-a-boo shows a baby that it is fun to play with someone else. "Where did Jeremy go? Oh, I see him. He's under his blanket."

- Smiling, babbling, and talking with a baby while changing her diaper teaches her about taking turns. "Bah, bah, bah? How about boh, boh, boh?"

- Rubbing a toddler's back shows him that you care about his well-being and want to help him fall asleep. "I know it's hard for you to settle down after a busy morning. I will help you relax."

- Offering assistance to a mother at the end of the day models helping and empathy. "Sadie's bag is all packed and ready to go. Let me help you get it on your shoulder. I see that Sadie wants to hold your hand."

Addressing Different Needs

The children who are cared for in your room have different individual and developmental needs and abilities. As you think about room arrangement, remember that some areas must stay the same, to provide the predictable setting on which children rely. Depending on the available furniture and equipment, you might be able to change other areas to meet children's changing needs. Programs can build flexible units using wood, foam, carpeting, and washable fabrics. Alternatively, similar units can be purchased from early childhood suppliers.

An environment for infants includes small, protected places.

Young infants spend much of their days with their primary caregivers, so the environment should provide cozy places where a teacher can cuddle, sing, talk, and read with a baby or where a teacher can help two babies get to know each other. A glider or other comfortable chair is one such setting. You might use covered foam units to create nests, or you might pile cushions in a corner. A thick quilt or blanket spread on the floor or on the grass can also create a cozy area.

Young infants are very interested in each other and in other children. They need safe places to be with one another and to watch the activities and interactions of mobile infants and toddlers. These places allow young infants to watch and listen without getting in the way of children who crawl and walk. You might sit with a baby and talk about what the other children are doing. "Toby picked up the colander. He put it on his head. Doesn't he look silly?" Some programs build safe areas for watching by covering wood with carpet or vinyl-covered foam. Others purchase equipment that can be arranged and rearranged as needed.

Children and adults need some quiet places.

Living all day in a group setting can be stressful for children and adults. An environment for infants and toddlers needs places where they can be alone for a while, such as a table with one chair, a cardboard box lined with quilts and cushions, or a padded mat in a corner. Like young infants, mobile infants and toddlers need places where they can watch what is going on around them without being actively involved. A platform or window seat can allow children to take a break and stay aware of what is happening in the room. The room also needs small places where two or three children can play. A refrigerator carton with cut-out windows and front and back doors gives two children a setting to play side by side or together.

Toddlers need plenty of space to move and play.

A comfortable room for toddlers includes plenty of space for them to move their bodies as well as places for quieter play and activities. You can offer them choices by defining protected areas where a few children can play beside or with each other. A sand or water table where several children can play at the same time encourages interaction. You can also set up several individual sand or water trays with simple props for children who want to play alone. Toddlers like to imitate and pretend, especially when you offer them simple props such as hats, bags, plates, pans, and wooden spoons. You can enhance their play by asking questions such as, "What are you cooking?" or "What's in your bag?" You can offer subtle suggestions by making simple comments such as, "That smells so good! I'm getting hungry!" or "Your bag looks very full. Are you taking it somewhere?"

Including Familiar Objects From Home

Many adults feel most comfortable in settings that look and feel like home. Infants and toddlers also need the security that comes from having things from home in their room at the program.

Family photographs help children feel connected during the day.

One way to create a secure setting is to include photographs of children and their families. The photos remind children of their families and help them feel connected during the day. You can take, or ask for, new photos every few months. With today's technology—digital cameras, laser printers, and scanners—there are many ways to take and display photos. Here are some ways to include family photos in your room:

Provide individual photo albums. Infants and toddlers can look at their family albums on their own and with teachers. Families can help by providing the photos or by making the albums.

Use photo fabric. Copy photos on special transfer paper and then iron them onto fabric. Use the fabric to make quilts, curtains, wall hangings, or whatever else you can think of.

Hang wall photos. Use a scanner, computer, and printer to enlarge photos. Laminate the photos and hang them at children's eye level.

Offer pocket-size photos. Protect small photos by laminating or enclosing them in plastic sleeves. Make them available to children so they can handle them whenever they want. Children might want to pretend to converse with the people in the pictures.

Create a homelike setting with familiar play materials and decorations.

You can also achieve a homelike setting by including familiar household items as play materials, such as pots and pans, baskets, and small brooms. In addition, you can decorate the room with curtains, cushions, baskets, textile wall hangings, plants, and flowers. Check your licensing requirements to find out what is approved for use in your area. You may have to place some things within sight but out of reach because they are not safe for children to handle. They will still be visible to help create a comfortable caregiving setting.

what's next?

Skill-Building Journal, section **9-6** (*Learning Activity B*) and section **9-1** (*Feedback*).

C. Helping Infants and Toddlers Learn to Care About Others

In this activity you will learn to

- recognize the signs that children are learning to care about others

- help children develop and use caring behaviors

From the time that children are very young, adults can help them begin to care about others and to appreciate relationships. In the United States, a high value is placed on independence, and children are generally expected to learn to do things on their own. The concept of interdependence is equally important and highly valued by many cultures. This is the understanding that we are all connected to each other and need to live cooperatively.

Caring for others eventually means learning to take turns and to help others, as well as higher-level social skills such as feeling empathy and being generous. Empathy is the ability to recognize and identify with another person's feelings, thoughts, and experiences. Children need to be aware of their own emotions before they can empathize with and respond to someone else's happiness, sadness, or pain. Generosity is the ability to give to others. While a baby might playfully offer you a bite of her cracker and then take it back, she is not likely to be truly generous until she has learned to take turns and share. She will need several years to master these skills.

Your positive interactions with children help them learn about caring.

The attachment relationships that infants and toddlers build in the first year of life are the foundation for learning to care about others. When you respond to children in caring and reliable ways, they learn that their needs will be met and that they can depend on you. When you take an interest in what infants and toddlers do, express joy at each accomplishment, and play with them, they learn that it is good to be with other people. Throughout the day, as you make up a rhyme while changing a diaper, help put on socks and jackets, give hugs, and sing silly songs, you help children experience and learn to show positive feelings toward others.

- What caring behaviors are used by the infants and toddlers in your care?

- How do you acknowledge children who are kind, thoughtful, and pay attention to the needs of others?

Very young infants respond to human voices and faces, and they often cry when they hear another baby crying. They also react to changes in adult voices, for example, by frowning if a voice is loud or angry. They soon learn to identify and respond positively to their primary caregivers, forming the secure attachments that are the foundation for caring and prosocial behaviors.

Like young infants, mobile infants enjoy being around other children, although they may struggle over sharing favorite play items. They also begin to understand that others have feelings. A teacher might invite a child to help soothe a baby. "Lovette, you look worried about Sammy. I'll pick him up, and we'll see what he needs." With the help of a teacher, one-year-olds can begin to learn about sharing if there is enough to share. For example, they can help themselves to a few apple slices from a bowl and then pass it to another child.

Toddlers feel proud when they do meaningful work.

Two-year-olds are beginning to interpret and identify how others are feeling. They are also becoming more independent and are pleased with their abilities. They like to help and take great pride in doing meaningful work. As they interact with people over time, they continue to develop and use social skills.

The most direct way for infants and toddlers to begin learning caring behaviors is by watching the adults who care for them. During a typical day, you model caring behavior again and again. You help a mobile infant store his stuffed bunny in his cubby where it will be safe. You might say to a toddler, "I know you want to climb the ladder, but only one child may climb at a time. I will wait with you until Russell reaches the top." You offer an extra pair of mittens to a child who lost hers at the park. Your dependable, responsive interactions help all of the children feel secure. Because children learn by watching and then imitating adults, your modeling teaches them how to notice and respond to the needs of others.

- What caring behaviors were valued in your own family and community as you grew up?

- What caring behaviors are valued by the cultures of the children in your group?

Here are some ways teachers can help infants and toddlers begin to learn caring behavior.

Encourage and acknowledge cooperation. Thank a baby for cooperating during diapering. Involve mobile infants as partners in getting dressed. When Ricky holds out his right arm, put on the right sleeve first. Ask a child who can peel a banana to help a child who is having trouble peeling his fruit.

Use each child's name often. Call children by their names when you talk with them and when you refer to them while talking with another child. Listen to the way the family pronounces the name and practice saying it until you can say it as they do. Insert children's names in appropriate places as you sing, or make up songs about the children in your room. Label cubbies with the children's names and photographs.

Suggest ways for two or three children to cooperate as they work and play together. Cooperative activities could include hanging a new piece of paper on the drawing wall, folding a blanket, carrying a basket of balls outdoors, or using a rocking boat.

Write, read, and discuss stories about caring behaviors. Write books in which the main characters are the children in your room and the story is about something they did together. For example, your book might be titled, *Jeremy Let Amanda Play With the Truck* or *Lois and Troy Cleaned Up the Blocks*. Illustrate the story with photographs.

Share your excitement and pleasure in children's efforts and accomplishments. Watch and respond as Sarah pulls herself up to standing and while Travis puts together a new puzzle.

Plan routines and activities so children can work and play together some of the time. Have several sponges so several children can wipe the table; put out some rhythm instruments (multiples of each kind) and invite the children to make music together; plant a garden that will need to be watered by several children at a time.

It takes a long time to learn caring behaviors.

Caring behaviors are not learned quickly. The children will continue to learn how to cooperate, take turns, share, and negotiate during their preschool and elementary school years. It is very natural for young children to put their own needs first. When their needs are met—"I have a muffin"—they gradually learn to think about the needs of others—"Mindy needs a muffin." To reach this point, they will need lots of help from their families and from you and your colleagues.

what's next?

Skill-Building Journal, section **9-7** (*Learning Activity C*) and section **9-1** (*Feedback*).

Learning Activities

D. Supporting Children's Play

In this activity you will learn to

- observe how infants and toddlers learn and develop through play

- guide children's play in ways that support social development

Young children learn best by playing. Through their play, children develop physical, cognitive, language, self-help, and social/emotional skills. For example, when a baby grasps and touches a fabric ball, she is building small muscle skills and using her senses to notice and explore different textures: smooth, fuzzy, and rough. If an older child or an adult is playing with her, she might also hear language, "The red part feels soft. The shiny piece is smooth." Through play, infants and toddlers explore the ways that objects can be used and grouped, develop a beginning understanding of cause and effect, and start to develop and use problem-solving strategies.

Play enables children to establish relationships with others.

Play also enables infants and toddlers to continue the extremely important task of establishing relationships with others. Learning to play well with others, make friends, and sustain friendships is difficult. Secure relationships with family members and teachers enable children to engage with others, especially when adults deliberately create opportunities for children to interact with each other. Children develop strong social skills by having opportunities to play with peers who are familiar and who like to do the same things. Family members and teachers also support social development by encouraging children's observational skills and coaching children's social attitudes and behavior. Temperament, cultural issues, and developmental disabilities influence play as well.[35]

Engaging Infants Through Play

Almost everything infants do while they are awake can be called play. They are excited when they discover their fingers and toes, and they frequently interact with their primary caregivers and with other children. You teach young infants about play each time you shake a rattle, twirl a mobile, or bounce a stuffed puppy near them, saying, "Here's Mr. Ruff. He says, 'Ruff, ruff, ruff.'" Infants use their senses to learn about people and things. Infant play includes activities such as rolling balls, dropping rattles, and picking up and mouthing everything within reach.

Infants and toddlers pass through several stages of social engagement.[36] As early as two months of age, babies are very interested in each other. They get excited when they see other infants, and they stare at each other with great interest when they have opportunities to do so. By about six months, young infants try to get and return the attention of other babies by smiling and babbling. Mobile infants imitate and touch each other, and they handle objects together.[37]

Older mobile infants and young toddlers play for longer periods, and their play becomes more complex. They imitate each other more and continue to develop the ability to take turns. Between 13–24 months, children begin to exchange roles in action games, such as taking turns being the chaser and being chased when they play tag. When they have the opportunity to play with familiar peers, children tend to engage in the same kinds of play with particular children. Even at this young age, children seem to understand when another person wants to play and what the person wants to do. Children's developing language skills also help them establish these early play routines.[38]

During their first year, infants also begin to understand the purposes and functions of various objects. They learn how objects work by handling them and by watching others use them. They notice the particular characteristics of objects: how they feel, sound, look, taste, and smell; which ones fit inside others; which they can bang together to make a noise; and which roll. For example, they know that spoons are used for eating and cups for drinking. This knowledge is a necessary first step for more complex play, such as pretending to fill a cup with juice and then handing it to a teacher.

Here are some suggestions for engaging infants in play.

Use routines, such as diapering and getting dressed, as play times. Engage infants by asking, "Where's your nose?...ear? …leg?...toe?...head?" You might have to show young infants the body part in question and explain, "Here it is. Here's your nose." Older infants will be able to respond on their own and may be learning to say some words.

Observe infants and interpret their cues about play preferences. If a 5-month-old is tugging his ear and you know that, for him, ear tugging is a sign that he is getting tired, sing quiet songs together rather than play an active game. On the other hand, if the child seems full of energy, play a game that lets him move his body.

Be spontaneous. Hold hands and dance with a one-year-old. Move an infant to a blanket on the grass so she can try to catch the bubbles you blow for her. Respond to a kicking baby by exercising her legs as if she were pedaling a bike.

Enjoy special play activities with one or more infants. Special activities might be spontaneous or planned. Introduce simple games, such as crawling in and out of a box. Next time the baby sees a large box, she might play the game on her own. Hold hands with two mobile infants and play "Ring Around the Rosie." Soon you might see one of them twirling himself around.

Talk and play with words and other sounds. Talk with infants about what you and they are doing. When other children are also playing, describe their actions as well. Repeat a baby's babble and introduce new vocal sounds. Most babies find this kind of play hilarious.

Respect each infant's style. Some infants approach activities with hesitation; others get involved quickly. Adapt your interactions accordingly. You might need to invite one child to play and provide suggestions, "Would you like me to roll the ball to you? Okay, here it comes. You caught it! Now roll it back to me." You might know that another child is ready to play, so you might say, "Here comes the ball! Roll it back to me."

Supporting the Play of Toddlers

As children get older (25–36 months), their play becomes more shared, and social pretend play begins. They are more likely to assume pretend roles that go together, such as parent and baby. One toddler might pull another in a wagon, or they might put on firefighter hats and pretend to put out a fire together. Finally, older toddlers become aware of group membership. They use language to communicate their wishes, their simple play routines become more complex, and their play involves more fantasy.[39] Toddlers also begin to use objects to represent other items. For example, a mixing bowl might become a hat, or a block might be used as a telephone.

Social play is difficult, however, so the way adults structure play environments for toddlers affects how often, how long, and how well children play together. Toddlers seem to find it easier to play with the children they play with often, so it is important for teachers to pay attention to which children seem to enjoy playing together.[40]

Conflict and aggression are not unusual when toddlers play, and a certain amount of conflict even promotes children's development. When play is disrupted by conflict, children are challenged to figure out what is wrong and what they need to do to continuing playing. Researchers who have observed what children do during conflicts find that children often stop playing together if adults intervene too quickly.[41]

However, recognizing that conflict and aggression increase as children begin to try to play together does not mean that highly aggressive interactions are good for the children involved. Social development is supported when teachers help children understand which behaviors are unacceptable, by using consistent discipline that acknowledges children's feelings and relies on reasoning and explanations rather than punishment.[42] Module 10, *Guidance*, explores this aspect of the teacher's role in greater detail.

Observe carefully to figure out what messages toddlers are giving you.

Teachers support toddler's play by maintaining secure relationships with the children in their care. They structure opportunities for children to play with each other and with adults, monitor and coach children's play behavior, and provide interesting play props. To do this, teachers must notice what children need. The following examples of children's messages to teachers are presented from the children's point of view.

"We learn a lot from playing with you." Toddlers practice many of the social skills they will use in cooperative play by playing games with you. For example, you can play simple lotto, card, or board games that involve taking turns. (Adapt the rules so there are no winners or losers). You might also sit beside a toddler and model how to share the bucket of beads while threading them on laces.

"We can choose our own friends." Teachers might be tempted to pair toddlers, but toddlers are very capable of finding their own friends. You can help by following a flexible schedule and by providing an open-ended environment and activities in which friendships are likely to flourish.

"We need opportunities to play on our own, without your help." The toddlers in your care need constant supervision, but this can be provided by staying nearby, observing what they do, and stepping in only when needed. Be aware that many toddlers prefer to have adult playmates because adults are easier to play with; adults know how to cooperate and have good ideas about what to do. However, learning to begin and continue playing with peers involves skills that are very important for toddlers to acquire.

"We are still learning about sharing." Sharing is a realistic expectation for preschoolers, but toddlers are still learning to take turns. First they need to develop a sense of ownership. Provide multiples of favorite toys and plenty of items such as markers and playdough tools. Model turn taking as you interact with children, colleagues, and families. Point out the benefits of sharing materials when you have an opportunity, e.g., "There are plenty of large beads for both of you. You can each make a necklace and have fun sharing the beads."

"We learn more if we try to work things out without your help." Wait, watch, and think about what you see and hear before intervening. When Katie (22 months) pulls Lina's (23 months) hair, it might be because she is curious about Lina's curls. Katie might not mean to hurt Lina, and Lina's "Ouch!" might be enough to remind Katie that hair pulling hurts. Be ready to jump in, however, to keep all children safe.

"We learn a lot from watching other children play." It is not necessary for every child to be active at all times; sometimes children want to watch what is going on. For example, a child might want to watch Carl putting pegs in the pegboard or Rhonda and Lacy donning hats and looking at themselves in the mirror. Watching provides information the child can use to enjoy the activity by himself or to get involved in group play.

Encouraging Pretend Play

Although children begin to imitate and even pretend as infants, they become more capable of imaginative, pretend play in the toddler years. Toddlers' play is often focused on familiar family activities such as eating, cooking, cleaning, and caring for babies. You might have seen a toddler patting a doll while saying, "Sleep, Baby." Perhaps you have seen several toddlers sling tote bags on their shoulders and pretend to go to work. They are copying and trying to understand their own experiences.

You can support toddlers' pretend play by providing time, space, dress-up items, and other open-ended props. Toddlers' imaginative play takes time: time to choose props, time to plan, time to put on hats or other clothes, time to be a cook or a daddy or a firefighter. A flexible daily schedule can provide sufficient time. Pretend play can take place anywhere: indoors, outdoors, in the sandbox, in the block area, on top of or under a loft. It is more likely to happen if you provide a specific setting such as a house corner.

Simple, familiar props inspire toddlers to engage in pretend play.

Teachers encourage imaginative play by offering a variety of open-ended props and dress-up items. Familiar items, such as pots and pans and a few dishes, can prompt a pretend party or picnic. A yard of colorful fabric can become a cape, a tablecloth, or a baby blanket. Cardboard cartons can be boats, trains, or beds. Telephones—toys or perhaps the mouthpieces of old phones—are particular favorites of this age group, so it is important to have plenty on hand. Toddlers can use the phones to call each other, "Hello." "Bye." "Hello." They can also use the phones to pretend to call family members, the doctor, or the volunteer who reads to them once a week.

As the most important part of the environment, you and your colleagues can encourage pretend play by talking and playing with toddlers. For example, to suggest a play theme at the water table, you might pick up a plastic container and say, "Toot, toot. Here comes my boat." Once the children start to play, step back. Too much adult involvement can inhibit children's play. If the children are going to have fun and learn, they must direct it themselves. You might also serve as a commentator for children's play, describing what they are doing. "Jack is at the stove, stirring the pot. M-m-m. It smells like chili. Jack stirs some more. Lacy puts two bowls on the table. The chili is ready. Jack pours chili into each bowl."

Toddlers often express strong feelings through their pretend play.

Pretend play is also a useful way for children to express and manage their feelings. For example, when a toddler is missing his family, you can pretend to call one of his parents on the telephone. "Hello, is this Rudy's mommy? He'd like to talk to you." Then hand the phone to the toddler and encourage him to pretend to talk to his mother. If he doesn't know what to say, you can suggest that he tell her what he has been doing. "Tell her about playing in the sandbox with Jake this morning."

Play helps young children learn to take turns, share favorite things, make friends, express their thoughts and emotions, and try out grown-up roles. It is a very important part of every day in an infant/toddler program.

what's next?

Skill-Building Journal, section **9-8** (*Learning Activity D*), section **9-1** (*Feedback*), and section **9-9** (*Reflecting on Your Learning*).

10
Guidance

Overview

Providing an Environment That Supports the Development of Self-Control

Helping Children Understand and Manage Their Feelings

Using Positive Guidance to Help Children Gain Self-Control

Your Own Self-Discipline

Learning Activities

A. Using Your Knowledge of Infants and Toddlers to Guide Their Behavior

B. Understanding and Responding to Children's Temperaments

C. Using a Positive Guidance Approach

D. Preventing and Responding to Problem Behavior

10.   Guidance

Positive relationships are essential in guiding children toward self-control.

To guide children toward understanding their feelings and controlling their behavior, adults need to build positive relationships with every child. Children who develop strong attachments to their caregivers want to please them and often imitate what they do and say. This is why modeling positive behavior is such a good way to teach children what behavior is expected. When adults try to understand how a child is feeling, explain those feelings to children, and show respect for every child, they help children to understand and manage their feelings.

Infants and toddlers are just beginning to learn to control their actions.

Self-control, the ability to manage feelings and control actions, is something that infants and toddlers are only beginning to develop. However, everything that happens to children during their first three years of life lays the foundation for developing these abilities. Guiding children's behavior begins with the responsive and loving care that adults provide for children from the time they are born.

Adults should not expect very young infants to show self-control. They cry to express discomfort, such as when they are hungry, tired, in pain, or in need of a clean diaper. Soon their needs become more regulated and predictable. They are hungry every three or four hours, rather than seemingly all of the time. When an infant's needs are met promptly and lovingly, she begins to recognize her body's signals and wait for a need to be met. For example, when hungry, she can tolerate discomfort for a short while if she sees you preparing her cereal or bottle and knows that food is coming. Being able to wait to have a need met is the beginning of self-control.

It is important to understand the reasons for a child's behavior.

Children act the way they do for a reason. Knowing typical child development will often help you understand the behavior of individual children. Toddlers, for example, typically test limits and like the power of saying *no* even to something they want to do. Sometimes children act inappropriately when they are unhappy or confused. When you want to discourage a particular behavior, it is important to find out what might be causing it so that you can respond in a positive way. You can help children increase their self-control by carefully organizing the environment and using a number of positive approaches.

Guiding children's behavior involves

- providing an environment that supports the development of self-control

- helping children understand and manage their feelings

- using positive guidance to help children gain self-control

Providing an Environment That Supports the Development of Self-Control

1. **Provide safe, well-organized spaces that let children make choices and use materials.** Provide young infants with a safe haven, and make sure that mobile infants and toddlers have plenty of space to move and explore.

2. **Follow a flexible schedule so teachers can respond promptly to children's needs.** "Danny's mom said he was awake a lot last night. He'll be ready for an early nap this morning."

3. **Plan daily routines and activities to minimize waiting time.** "Will you help me hold the bowl while Sara stirs the batter? Then you and Sara may switch places."

4. **Create visible, cozy areas where a child, or a child and a teacher, can spend time alone.** "When Marcus needs a break, he gets his blanket from his cubby and sits under the loft for a while."

5. **Prepare children for changes and transitions.** "I had fun singing with you. Now I'm going to put you on your blanket for some tummy time."

Jon Falls Asleep At Last

As you read the following story, pay attention to the way Ms. Bates and Ms. Gonzalez supported each other. Also think about how they helped Jon.

Ms. Bates: Your diaper is clean, and your tummy is full. I hope you feel better now.

Ms. Gonzalez: Oh, dear. Jon is crying again.

Ms. Bates: I wonder what could be wrong.

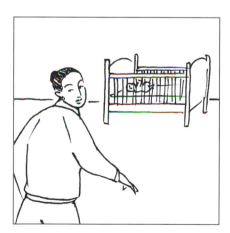

Ms. Gonzalez: I'll take a turn with Jon.

Ms. Gonzalez: I know you want to feel better. Maybe this will help.

Ms. Bates: Thanks for your help. I know Jon thanks you, too.

Helping Children Understand and Manage Their Feelings

6. **Teach children words to name their feelings.** "Ricky, I think you felt angry when Adam grabbed your shovel. Tell Adam, "No. That's my shovel.""

7. **Model appropriate ways to identify and express feelings.** "Jessica, your loud voice is making me feel upset. Please use your quiet, inside voice."

8. **Read books, tell stories, and talk about feelings.** "Do you see Cara's smile? She feels happy when her grandpa visits our classroom."

9. **Accept and respond to the feelings expressed through crying, words, other vocal sounds, and gestures.** "That is the way Sam cries when he is hungry. I'm glad that his bottle is ready."

10. **Offer materials and activities that may calm and soothe children who are upset.** "Would you like to play with the sand tray? We have some new farm animals that you may use."

Zora Uses Words

As you read the following story, think about how Zora felt when Lovette took her orange slice.
Also pay attention to how Mr. Lewis helped Zora express her feelings in an acceptable way.

Zora: No!

Mr. Lewis: Zora, I won't let you hit Lovette.

Mr. Lewis: You don't want Lovette to take your orange. Use words to tell her that. Say, "Lovette, don't take my orange."

Zora: Mine.

Using Positive Guidance to Help Children Gain Self-Control

11. **Get to know and understand each child's temperament.** Some children respond better to a firm tone; others respond to a more gentle tone.

12. **Use simple, positive statements that tell children what to do, rather than only what not to do.** "Use the crayons on the paper, Jerry, not on the table."

13. **Redirect children from unwanted to acceptable behavior.** "You may use the step stool to see out the window. It's not safe to stand on a chair."

14. **Anticipate problem behaviors and take steps to prevent them.** "Ruby often gets tired on our walks. Let's save a space in the wagon so she can ride on the way back if she wants to."

15. **Look for the reasons behind a child's problem behavior.** Work with the family to learn what happens before and after an unwanted behavior (such as biting or hitting) and to plan strategies to help the child cope with strong feelings.

Adam Throws Safely

As you read the following story, think about what Ms. Bates knew about Adam. Also consider how Ms. Bates guided Adam's behavior.

Ms. Bates: Adam, you are learning to throw well. If you hit people, though, they might be hurt or angry.

Ms. Bates: You may practice throwing safely on the grass, or you may do something else.

what's next?

Skill-Building Journal, section **10-2** (*Overview*), section **10-10** (*Answer Sheets*), and section **10-1** (*Feedback*).

Your Own Self-Discipline

Self-discipline makes some behavior automatic.

Much adult behavior is automatic. When you put money in a parking meter, come to work on time, or thank a store clerk, you are probably acting without thinking about what you are doing. You have learned and accepted certain rules of behavior, and because you have self-discipline, you don't need to be reminded of them.

Self-discipline guides your behavior at work.

- You let the center director know when you're sick so a substitute can be called.

- You ask a colleague for her help rather than complaining about a problem.

- You volunteer to help plan a weekend field trip for families.

Self-discipline also guides your behavior at home.

- You water the plants because you know they'll die if you do not.

- You clean the coffee pot so it will be ready to use in the morning.

- You resist eating cake because you are watching your weight.

Few people use self-discipline all of the time and in every situation. Sometimes we experience very strong feelings that make us feel out of control, and sometimes we lose control. Fortunately, most of us have learned ways to regain control. We use different strategies to calm ourselves. For example, if we are very angry, we might count to ten before responding, breathe deeply, or take a walk. Once we have calmed down, we are better able to make clear statements about our feelings instead of lashing out, accusing someone, and making that person defensive.

Being in control of your own behavior frequently enhances self-esteem. Having positive feelings about your abilities will make you a more effective and skilled teacher. Your self-discipline is a good model for the children. They will learn a lot from being cared for by a responsible and competent person.

what's next?

Skill-Building Journal, section **10-3** (*Your Own Self-Discipline*), section **10-1** (*Feedback*), and section **10-4** (*Pre-Training Assessment*).

Learning Activities

LEARNING ACTIVITY

A. Using Your Knowledge of Infants and Toddlers to Guide Their Behavior

In this activity you will learn to

- recognize some typical behavior of infants and toddlers

- offer a program that prevents or minimizes unwanted behaviors

Knowing what to expect of infants and toddlers and what they need from you at each stage of development is very important to helping children understand their feelings and manage their behavior. Guiding children's behavior also depends on up-to-date information about each child's abilities, interests, and needs. You can use this information to evaluate and, if necessary, adapt your environment, interactions, routines, or activities to meet the needs of individual children and the group. As part of a well-planned program that meets children's needs, your supportive relationships will go a long way toward preventing or minimizing problem behaviors.

Young infants (birth–8 months) depend upon supportive relationships with adults.

- Sammy (3 months) is having trouble falling asleep. Ms. Gonzalez sees that his blanket has come undone, so she swaddles him again.

- Jon (6 months) reaches out to touch and hold everything within sight. Ms. Bates makes sure that only safe things are within Jon's reach.

- Luci (8 months) tugs and tugs at her socks until she gets them off. Mr. Lewis smiles and asks Luci to hold one sock while he puts the other on again so they can go outside.

Young infants insist on what they need, when they need it. They do not cry to annoy their families and teachers or because they are "bad." They cry to express frustration and discomfort, e.g., "I'm hungry, please feed me," or "My diaper is soggy, please change me," or "The music stopped. Please turn it on again." Infants tend to cry less frequently when their needs are met promptly and consistently. They learn that a loving person will soon respond and help them feel better.

Starting at about four months, infants begin to have some control over their actions. They discover their hands and learn to suck on a fist or thumb purposely, instead of accidentally. They are fascinated with what they can do with their hands and fingers and with their legs and feet. They grasp, pull, squeeze, poke, and kick objects (and people) within their reach. Sometimes it is necessary for teachers to step in so infants do not get hurt or hurt others. For example, it is time to remove the crib mobile when the baby is able to reach it. Of course, you also step in when you see one curious infant about to accidentally poke another child in the eye.

Mobile infants (8–18 months) are busy—moving, exploring, and learning.

- Malou (9 months) pulls herself up to standing in her crib and coos. Ms. Gonzalez claps her hands to share Malou's delight.

- Peter (12 months) drops his spoon off the table again. Ms.Bates picks up the spoon and moves it to the side. She offers him a toy, saying, "You may drop this toy on the floor."

- Zora (16 months) puts one leg on the table and looks at Mr. Lewis. He responds with a frown, and Zora gets down.

For mobile infants, the world is an enormous place with an endless array of things to see and do. With expanding skills in all domains, they can move and accomplish more and more. For example, mobile infants can transfer toys from one hand to another and hold a block or piece of food between thumb and forefinger, using what is called a pincer grasp. At first, dropping and throwing are the only way mobile infants can put things down, because they have not developed much small muscle control. Their teachers understand this and know that mobile infants are practicing their new skills when dropping and throwing become favorite activities.

As their language skills develop, mobile infants understand simple requests made through words and gestures, e.g., "Please put the rattle in my hand." They enjoy spending time with grownups and are verifying their understanding of language, so they are usually willing to comply with these requests. They also learn their names and point to body parts when asked. As they get older, mobile infants begin to say a few words, including *me, mine,* and *I.* Creeping and crawling soon give way to standing and walking, so their teachers need to maintain indoor and outdoor environments that are free of hazards.

Between 10–12 months of age, infants begin to realize that adults do not want them to do some of the things they do. Your patient but firm language can be a powerful positive guidance strategy for keeping older mobile infants safe. They recognize when your tone of voice means *stop* and *no,* even if you do not say those particular words. This allows you to save those strong words for when they are needed immediately to keep children safe.

Toddlers (18–36 months) frequently act on impulse, but they can also become completely absorbed in activities that interest them.

- Lovette (20 months) yells, "No, no, no!" when told that it is time to go indoors. Ms. Bates bends down to explain to her that it is time for lunch.

- Ricky (28 months) and Adam (30 months) laugh and chase each other around the playground. Mr. Lewis watches from a distance.

- Jessica (34 months) works on a puzzle until it's finished, even though it takes a long time. Ms. Gonzalez records this example of her growing attention skills in Jessica's portfolio.

Toddlers have the skills to do many things for themselves. A toddler might choose what dress-up clothes to wear, what book to read, or which piece of fruit to put on his plate. A strong desire for independence often leads toddlers to act impulsively. They do not fully understand that their actions have consequences.

Toddlers are learning to talk, and they understand even more spoken language than they can produce. They need adult assistance, however, in learning how to use spoken language to express their strong feelings. Toddlers are likely to express their emotions through actions rather than words, for example, by grabbing a desired toy instead of asking for it. They may feel frustrated when things do not go as intended and proud after accomplishing a challenging task.

Although toddlers can learn which behaviors are acceptable and which are not, they are not always able to stop themselves from doing what they have been told is not allowed. Toddlers find it easier to behave when teachers set clear and consistent limits. It may seem contradictory, but setting clear limits for toddlers gives them the freedom to be active, curious explorers. Toddlers often forget the limits, so you will have to offer frequent positive reminders of which behaviors are acceptable and which are not.

While building a sense of self, toddlers can be quite focused on belongings, both their actual possessions and things they think of as their own. Toddlers are still developing a sense of ownership, so it is hard for them to share and take turns. Many problems can be prevented by providing multiples of favorite items and continuing to offer activities until everyone who wants to participate has had a turn.

Toddlers sometimes lose control completely and have tantrums. A tantrum is scary for the toddler experiencing it and for the other children and adults in the room. It is your job to help the child regain control and to show the others that you will always keep everyone safe. Sometimes just holding a child is enough to calm him. At other times you need to sit nearby and wait until the child is calm enough to respond to your presence. *Learning Activity D* includes more information about ways to help children cope with tantrums.

Development of Infants and Toddlers

Young infants (birth–8 months)

- cry to express physical discomfort, boredom, or stress

- respond to faces and voices

- reach out and grab things that might not be safe

- learn to wait for a short time and to comfort themselves if their needs have been met consistently

- use their growing skills to make things happen

Mobile infants (8–18 months)

- experience and express a wide range of feelings

- are interested in other children

- know how their families and teachers feel about them

- watch and learn from the important adults in their lives

- learn to move their bodies in new ways

Toddlers (18–36 months)

- admire and want to please adults

- want to make decisions for themselves

- test limits often and say *no*

- experience a range of emotions

- are sometimes overwhelmed by intense feelings and may behave in ways that hurt other children or adults

what's next?

Skill-Building Journal, section **10-5** (*Learning Activity A*) and section **10-1** (*Feedback*).

LEARNING
ACTIVITY

Learning Activities

B. Understanding and Responding to Children's Temperaments [43]

In this activity you will learn to

- identify how temperament affects the behavior of infants and toddlers

- consider the role of temperament in responding to the behavior of individual children

Individual temperament affects us throughout life.

As you learned in previous modules in this training program, many factors affect children's development. Most children pass through the same stages of development, in the same order but on individual timelines. Development is often uneven; a child may be more advanced than her peers in one area and less advanced in another. Culture, family, and community have a great influence on a child's learning and skill development.

In addition to these factors, we all are born with characteristics that shape our personal style, or temperament. Temperament affects how we respond to people, experiences, and environments throughout life. For infants and toddlers, temperament plays a part in how individual children respond to feeding and mealtimes, diapering and toileting, going to sleep, being with other people, and playing alone and with others.

The following section describes several aspects of temperament that affect the behavior of infants and toddlers. Children vary in how they get to know and respond to the world, and how they handle frustration and cope with change. Getting to know each child's usual style and being aware of your own temperament can help you decide the best way to encourage positive behavior.

Observe how each child responds to people, events, and experiences.

A person's intensity has to do with the way he responds to the world. Some children seldom cry, are able to fall asleep with relative ease, and can sleep through anything. They might be so quiet and easygoing that they need your encouragement to communicate their interests and needs. You can play games together and invite them to move and explore. Watch them at play so that you can understand their skills and interests, and then join their play to extend it and to engage them socially.

There are also children who squeal with delight when happy, cry inconsolably when upset, and lash out when angry or frustrated. Some children are extremely sensitive to light, sound, texture, and temperature. If things are not just the way they like them to be, they have difficulty falling sleep and are easily startled. They need you to be patient, to remove some of the causes of overstimulation, and to help them learn to calm themselves. Keep play times fun but not overly exciting. When children do lash out, you can accept and name their strong feelings for them and describe what they did to express their emotions. "You feel sad because your friend left early today. You threw the pillow on the floor to tell me how much you miss her." A hug or rocking and reading together might help the child regain control of his emotions.

Observe how each child explores and learns about the world.

A person's activity level has to do with the way she gets to know and take part in the world. Children who have a low activity level tend to explore and learn by watching, listening, and using their hands and fingers. They can stick with a task or work on a problem for a long time. They might need you to step in to make sure they get enough exercise to stay fit and healthy. You could bounce a baby on your knee, take turns chasing a ball with a child who crawls, or dance to music with a toddler.

Highly active children move all of the time and touch everything within reach. They creep, crawl, run, climb, and jump with a purpose: to get to the next place and explore what is there. You can respond to their need to move by inviting mobile infants and toddlers to help with classroom chores and to be active participants during routines. Active children do not need to be discouraged from moving. In fact they need the opposite: more opportunities to move.

Observe how each child handles frustration.

Persistence refers to the way a person handles frustration. A child with a low capacity for persistence can be easily frustrated when a task is challenging. He might cry to ask for help or drop what he is doing and move on to another activity. You can help children learn to cope with frustration by acknowledging their feelings and modeling ways to deal with them. You might use humor to defuse the situation, e.g., "That silly noodle keeps jumping out of your spoon." You can also offer help, e.g., "That is a hard job. Let's do it together."

An extremely persistent child might try the same approach again and again, even when it does not work. For example, when Hannah (20 months) wants to climb on the table, she tries and tries, even though her teacher keeps stopping her. Hannah's teacher can guide her to a safe climbing place that provides the same challenge, such as a pile of cushions.

Observe how each child reacts to new people and situations.

A person's ability to cope with change affects her response to new people, routines, and environments. Change is a part of everyone's life, but it particularly affects infants and toddlers because they have little control over their daily lives. Some children adapt to change very easily and need little or no support from adults. For example, Kim (20 months) is curious about newcomers to the classroom and has no trouble getting used to napping on a cot instead of in a crib. Teachers need to be sure that they also pay attention to children such as Kim. It can be easy to overlook a child who handles change with great ease.

Other children have adverse reactions to change. They need understanding, responsive teachers to help them get used to new people and new ways of doing things. For example, Michael (22 months) clutches his teacher's leg when a new maintenance person comes to fix a drippy faucet. She repeats what she told him the day before, "That's Ms. Perry with her toolbox. She's going to take the faucet apart to find out why it is dripping. Would you like to watch her work?"

Children who are upset by change often find it hard to handle transitions, such as getting ready to go outdoors or reuniting with families at the end of the day. You can acknowledge their strong feelings, offer extra support, and give notice that a change is coming. "You like patting the bunny very much, so you don't want to stop. It's almost lunch time. You may pat him once more. Then it will be time to put him back in his cage."

Appreciating children's temperaments allows teachers to choose appropriate guidance strategies.

The aspects of temperament described above are neither good nor bad traits. They simply describe the different ways children (and adults) respond to people and experiences. When families and teachers understand a child's temperament, they can respond in ways that acknowledge the child's unique characteristics while successfully guiding the child's behavior.

what's next?

Skill-Building Journal, section **10-6** (*Learning Activity B*) and section **10-1** (*Feedback*).

Learning Activities

LEARNING ACTIVITY

C. Using a Positive Guidance Approach

In this activity you will learn to

- use a variety of positive guidance strategies

- tailor positive guidance to match individual skills, needs, and characteristics

Positive guidance depends upon responsive relationships with individual children.

A positive guidance approach relies on your responsive and nurturing relationships with individual children. You can learn a lot about individual children and what they need from you by paying attention to their verbal and nonverbal communications. This simple practice lets children know that you care about them and accept their feelings, and it begins to guide them toward self-control. You can listen to a baby's cries and watch for physical cues that tell you what she needs, e.g., perhaps she needs you to pull down the shade so the sun does not shine in her eyes. Mobile infants and toddlers use body language and spoken language to share their feelings. Watch, listen, and think so that you can accept the child's feelings and acknowledge them verbally. For example, you might say, "You are frustrated because your ball rolled behind the bush. Should I help you find it?" "You are looking at daddy's picture. You feel sad because you miss him. He will come back for you."

In addition to accepting and responding to children's feelings, a positive guidance approach teaches infants and toddlers which behaviors are acceptable. It introduces self-control, which involves skills that children will be building for many years.

Guiding the Behavior of Young Infants (Birth–8 Months)

Young infants sometimes do things that you do not want them to do, but they do not misbehave. They cry because they need something, not because they want to have their own way. Here are some positive guidance approaches for young infants:

Anticipate and move infants away from potential hazards. When an infant starts rolling over, make sure that there are no objects in his way or places from which he can fall.

Remove objects that children should not handle. Close cabinet and closet doors. Store your delicate earrings and necklace in your purse on a high shelf.

Separate children whose explorations of each other might cause harm. Sit between two babies and model ways to get to know someone without pulling hair or poking eyes.

Play games that introduce turn taking. Games like peek-a-boo, rolling a ball back and forth, and "Where Did the Puppy Go?" help young babies learn that they can have an effect on other people and things. That is a first step in eventually learning self-control.

Use simple, positive, caring words. Use a natural tone of voice, look into the baby's eyes, touch an arm or shoulder, and give the baby your full attention. "Here's a rattle for you, Jack. Sara may shake one, and you may shake another."

Guiding the Behavior of Mobile Infants (8–18 Months)

Mobile infants explore and learn by moving and doing. Their experiments teach them about cause and effect and many other concepts. Some explorations have unwanted results. An infant might accidentally harm people or things or end up in an unsafe situation.

As infants begin to understand that their actions affect other people, your guidance can encourage positive behavior and discourage unsafe or unwanted behavior. You can continue to use the strategies for younger infants described above, along with the following suggestions:

Use facial expressions, body language, tone of voice, and "I" statements to communicate. Babies do not understand long strings of words, but they understand and respond to other ways of communicating, such as a smile, your outstretched hands, and a few words. For example, when you move a child to crawl on the soft grass rather than the hard sidewalk, you might say calmly, "I want you to be safe, so I'm moving you. Here you go."

Watch before stepping in to prevent a conflict. Infants can often work things out themselves. When Jack takes a toy from Sara, wait to see if Sara minds. She might simply pick up something else to play with.

Use *no* sparingly. Save this word for when it is needed immediately to prevent a child from harming himself or other people.

Offer two acceptable choices. Mobile infants can choose which book they want to read, whether to crawl or be carried to the changing area, or whether they want to hold a teacher's hand or ride in the buggy. Giving children the opportunity to make decisions helps them feel powerful and allows them to experience a sense of control.

Describe for children what they are doing and what they might be feeling. This lets a child know that you value them and accept their feelings. "You are watching Tory crawl through the box. You want to crawl through the box, too, but you feel a little scared. Would you like me to watch you?"

Guiding the Behavior of Toddlers (18–36 Months)

Toddlers can sometimes try the patience of even the most calm and collected teacher. One minute they demand to do things on their own; the next minute they want you to do things for them. Toddlers need clear, realistic limits that communicate which behaviors are acceptable and which are not. Limits are a teaching tool: They tell toddlers what they may do. As for children at any age, limits for toddlers should correspond with the developmental and individual characteristics of the children. Limits give toddlers the freedom to explore and experiment, and they help toddlers begin to gain self-control. You can involve older toddlers in developing a few simple rules and in setting limits, such as when you get a new piece of equipment or before going on a walk in the neighborhood. When toddlers help set the limits, they are more likely to understand and remember them.

Toddlers are able follow limits, but it is important to remember that they might not always do so. Positive reminders can help, e.g., "Walk inside, please." You might also add the reason for the limit, "If you run, you might get hurt."

With your help, toddlers can also construct a better understanding of how their behavior is related to other actions or events. For instance, if a toddler does not want to stop playing and get ready for lunch, you might explain, "When you finish cleaning up, you may wash your hands. Then we will have lunch." Sometimes you calmly explain why something the child did had an effect on another child. "You pushed Paul, so he fell. That's why he doesn't want to play with you."

To guide toddlers' behavior, you can continue using the strategies described above, along with the following suggestions:

Make a positive suggestion. A toddler is more likely to go along with a suggestion or an invitation to do something ("Let's hang up our coats.") than with a direct order ("Hang up your coat.").

Anticipate potential problems. Use what you know about children to predict how they might behave in given situations. For example, if you know that a child is easily frustrated and acts out when the schedule is changed, let her know about the change in advance. You will also want to watch her so you can step in to stop unwanted behaviors.

Provide opportunities to say *no*. Toddlers enjoy saying *no* because it is such a powerful word. You can ask silly questions that let them say *no* and feel a sense of control. "Do rabbits wear boots?" "May I wear my pajamas to work?" "Will it snow on this hot, hot day?"

Support toddlers' need to be independent. Plan routines so that toddlers are able to participate, and place supplies within their reach so they can help with tasks. For example, toddlers can help to set, clear, and wipe the table; hold a clean diaper while you remove the wet one; and clean up water that spilled by the water table.

Maintain appropriate expectations for behavior. Always remember that toddlers are just beginning to learn self-control. Provide duplicates of favorite toys so they will not have to share and offer activities several times so everyone who wants to participate may have a turn. Store unsafe materials in locked cabinets and make sure that the playground gate is fastened securely.

Choose positive guidance strategies that fit the child and the situation.

You can use a wide variety of positive guidance techniques to prevent, minimize, or respond to unwanted behaviors. No single approach works for every child, at every age, and in every situation. Try to think before responding. The answers to the following questions will help you choose an appropriate next step.

Choosing an Appropriate Response

What happened? DeeDee dumped her cereal on the floor again.

What behavior is typical for a child of this age? DeeDee is 18 months old. Pushing a bowl off the table and onto the floor is more typical of a younger child.

How might this child's temperament, skills, needs, and other individual characteristics affect behavior? DeeDee is sometimes a finicky eater and gets frustrated by changes at home and at the center.

What was going on in the environment? DeeDee has not had this kind of cereal before. Her teacher just returned from a week's vacation, and breakfast was late this morning.

What are the possible reasons for the behavior? DeeDee liked her old cereal. She does not like the new kind. She is upset because her teacher was gone for a week. She has difficulty coping with the new breakfast routine.

These questions are a lot to think about. However, with practice, thinking before responding with an appropriate positive guidance strategy will become automatic.

Team with families to use positive guidance at home and at the center.

Teachers and families need to talk about the positive guidance strategies they think are most effective. Many of the approaches you use at the center can be used at home as well. You can help families understand what behaviors to expect at different stages of development. They can help you learn which behaviors are valued by their culture and which are not. Together you can share information about a child's individual characteristics and discuss how they affect the child's feelings and actions. A consistent approach at home and at the center will guide a child toward self-control. Building partnerships with families is discussed in greater detail in module 11, *Families*.

what's next?

Skill-Building Journal, section **10-7** (*Learning Activity C*) and section **10-1** (*Feedback*).

Learning Activities

LEARNING ACTIVITY

D. Preventing and Responding to Problem Behavior

In this activity you will learn to

- discover the reasons for a child's problem behavior

- partner with families to develop a plan for responding to ongoing problem behavior

---

Some child behaviors that bother adults are signs of normal development.

Some child behaviors that trouble teachers and families are actually signs of normal development. Many behaviors give way to new ones when children move to the next stage of development. Here are some examples:

> *A 5-month-old often rolls from his back to his tummy and then cries until his teacher helps him turn back over. When he learns to roll both ways on his own, he stops crying when he wants to roll onto his back.*

> *An 18-month-old responds to most requests with a loud no. She is proud of having learned this new word and eager to assert herself. Her teacher asks a playful question, "Do your shoes fit on your hands?" that lets the child respond, "No!"*

> *A 2 1/2-year-old refuses to eat foods that are touching or mixed together. He says that they are yucky. His center provides plates with separate sections for children who want foods to be kept apart.*

Some behavior causes problems for children and for adults.

The fact that some problem behaviors are typical of mobile infants and toddlers does not mean that self-control develops automatically and without the support of teachers and families. Children need consistent guidance to understand that temper tantrums and highly aggressive interactions such as hitting and biting are unacceptable. A positive guidance approach that builds upon your responsive relationships with infants and toddlers can help most children learn to express their feelings without harming themselves or others. If more serious problem behaviors are common in your classroom, you will need to examine the program to make sure that the environment, materials, interactions, and experiences are meeting the needs of the children in your care.

There are a number of possible causes for problem behaviors.

Here are some reasons why children might behave in unwanted ways: [44]

"I don't feel well." Health problems and conditions such as illness, allergies, disabilities, lack of sleep, poor nutrition, or hunger can contribute to children's problem behaviors. If you think a child's problem behavior is the result of a physical condition, discuss examples of the child's behavior with the family and request that the child be evaluated by a physician.

"I need your attention." Young children need to feel important and valued. When they do not receive enough positive attention, children may seek negative attention. They learn that, when they use certain behaviors, adults notice and spend time with them. Unfortunately, once children are successful in getting attention by misbehaving, they are likely to continue until someone teaches them to ask for attention in appropriate ways.

"I want to be in charge." Mobile infants and toddlers want to be independent. Perhaps between home and center there are too many rules and too few opportunities to make choices and do things for themselves. When children may make choices about what to do, which materials to use, and with whom to play, they have a sense of control over their lives and begin to develop self-control.

"I'm scared." Very young children have strong feelings, limited language skills, and very little ability to control their impulses. A child who is overly aggressive might be a fearful child who acts as if he is powerful in an attempt to overcome his fears. To help this child, try to identify his fears and what might be causing them. Reassure him that you and his family will work together to keep him safe. Talk about what is real and what is not, and provide information that might help the child resolve his fears.

"I am getting ready to reach a major milestone." Dr. T. Berry Brazelton has defined several typical, major "touchpoints" in a child's development. At these stages, the child may get upset easily, act out, or go back to behaviors used when younger. For example, a 9-month-old might suddenly refuse to eat foods she once loved or a once-happy and easygoing 1-year-old might begin to protest every adult request. Such changes are typical and predictable. They will pass as the child masters the new skills that he or she is working on. [45]

Teachers who are keen observers of children can learn to identify the signs that a child is about to lose control. When they see these signs, they can step in to guide the child to an activity that reduces the stress and frustration that often results in problem behavior. Activities such as pounding playdough, kicking balls, or listening to music through headphones can help children relax.

Understanding and responding to unwanted behavior involves several steps.

The following steps can help you understand a child's problem behavior; collect information about when the behavior occurs; and take steps, over time, to help the child learn appropriate ways to behave.

Define the behavior. Begin by clearly defining the behavior in terms that will be easily understood by the adults who are involved with the child. Use objective, descriptive terms that do not label or judge the child.

Collect information. Next, collect information about when the behavior occurs. Observe the child at different times of the day and while engaged in different routines and activities. Ask families to share information about the child's home activities.

Review and analyze the information. Review your observation notes and the other information you collected. Try to identify possible causes for the behavior. A situation at home might be causing the child to feel upset or frustrated. Perhaps the classroom environment—the schedule, routines, or play materials—does not meet the child's needs. Perhaps the behavior is caused by one or more of the reasons described earlier.

Work with the child's family. Families can be valuable partners in dealing with problem behaviors. They know what is going on at home and can offer insights about possible causes. Families can support the child at home as you offer support at the program to help the child stop unwanted behavior.

Find a time to discuss the situation without interruption. Reassure the family that unwanted behaviors are sometimes typical of young children, but explain your concern that the child's behavior is interfering with her full participation in the program. Also explain that other children and adults are being affected. Make sure the family understands that you are not assigning blame, that you are looking for ways to support their child. Many times, just as soon as you decide to involve the family, the behavior will pass as the child gains new skills for expressing feelings and getting along with others.

Develop and implement a plan. Together, you and the family can develop a written plan for responding consistently to the behavior and for teaching the child better ways to communicate strong feelings. It is very important to continue letting the child know that he is loved and cared for, even though his behavior must change.

Assess progress. Watch to see how well your plan is working. Continue to observe, to see if the child's behavior is changing. Maintain regular communication with the family so you can evaluate how well the plan is working and make adjustments if needed. Change takes time, and it takes some children longer than others to learn new ways to express their feelings and needs.

The following discussion of common problem behaviors includes suggestions to help children stop unwanted behaviors.

Temper tantrums are some children's way of expressing strong emotions.

Temper tantrums are a child's way of expressing frustration and involve total loss of control. As noted above, they can be very frightening for the child having the tantrum and for the other children and adults in the group. Your calm response will help the child and show everyone that you will keep them safe.

Temper tantrums often occur when children are tired, hungry, lonely, bored, or have other feelings that they cannot express verbally. Some tantrums are triggered by seemingly minor events, such as not being able to reach the blanket in a cubby, but the reason a child reacts so strongly is more complicated. Perhaps she is thinking, "I don't understand why my grandma left me here. Where did she go? When will she come back?" Perhaps the child does not know a better way to express, "I am hungry and tired, and I want the red truck. Janna took it from me, and I don't know how to get it back." He might not know how to tell you, "You gave me a glass of milk, but I want juice like my dad gives me at his house."

Sometimes showing a child how to express his feelings verbally can defuse a tantrum. You may need to state the feelings over and over and in different ways, until the child is calm enough to listen to you and realize that you understand. "You are angry because you want to play with the red truck. You like the red truck. You want to play with the red truck. You don't know how to get the red truck back. You are mad at Janna and the truck and everything else." Hearing that you understand his feelings can calm a child and help him regain control.

During a tantrum, a teacher may need to protect the child as well as other people and things. Stay calm while you firmly hold the child's arms and legs until the tantrum subsides. The child will recover more quickly if the tantrum caused no harm to people or objects. Once calm is restored, you can acknowledge the child's feelings, "You had a hard time. You were very upset." Talk about what happened and let the child know that you will listen to and accept her feelings. On another day, you might read a story about emotions to older toddlers, such as *When Sophie Gets Angry—Really, Really Angry* by Molly Bang or *The Chocolate-Covered-Cookie Tantrum* by Deborah Blumenthal. Stories help toddlers begin to understand feelings, why they change, and how to express them.

Physical aggression is also an expression of strong feelings.

Physical aggression is another way that some children express strong feelings. At times, mobile infants and toddlers express frustration, anger, and other feelings through hitting, scratching, kicking, and other forms of aggression. They do not yet understand that it is possible to feel a negative emotion, such as anger, without acting on it by hitting, tearing up a picture, kicking, and so on.

It is important to respond immediately to physical aggression. Stay calm as you position yourself at the child's level. Clearly and calmly, describe what happened and your response. For example, suppose a teacher sees and hears Laurie and Andi (both 2-year-olds) fighting over a toy. Laurie kicks Andi in the leg. The teacher would step in and say, "You kicked Andi. It hurt her leg, so she is crying. I cannot let you hurt people, and I won't let them hurt you. You need to use words to say what you want. You can say, 'I want the toy, too.'" She could then invite Laurie to help comfort Andi so she can understand the connection between her actions and Andi's pain. "Let's get the ice pack from the freezer so Andi can put it on her leg." Then the teacher would help both children find something else to do.

When a child is physically aggressive and loses control, you may need to hold her until she calms down. Ask a colleague to respond to the hurt child if someone was injured before you could intervene. Children feel scared when they lose control, and your firm arms can help a child feel safe because you have taken charge. It may take a few minutes, but the child will quiet down. Then you can try to talk about what happened. With a younger, less verbal child who cannot articulate his feelings, you can describe what you saw and what you think the child was feeling. An older toddler might be able to talk about her feelings. "Can you tell me what made you so angry? I know that you were upset." Help her understand that you are willing to listen to her feelings.

It is best to let a child recover from an outburst before discussing alternative ways to handle anger and frustration. You can do this during a quiet, one-to-one conversation later in the day or even the following day. "Yesterday, you kicked Andi. You were very upset because she had the toy you wanted to use. Next time you are upset about a toy, remember to say, 'I want a toy, too.'" This discussion can include a rehearsal so that, next time the child begins to get upset, she will have an alternative to being physically aggressive. Encourage the child, "Saying what you want is a good plan. You can also ask me to help."

Biting is arguably the most emotionally charged problem behavior. Adults tend to have very strong reactions to biting, and they may overreact instead of trying to solve the underlying problem. The family of a child who has been bitten is likely to be horrified and fear for their child's safety. The family of the child who did the biting may be embarrassed, ashamed, defensive, and unsure of how to respond.

Biting is not always an act of aggression.

Biting is not always an act of aggression. There are a number of reasons why infants and toddlers bite. It is important to consider these reasons when deciding on a positive guidance response.

For young infants, the mouth is one of the most developed body parts. They often bite as a way to use their senses to learn more about the world. They also bite to experiment with cause and effect or to relieve the pain of teething. Sometimes when infants get excited they bite to express their delight. In these cases, a firm *no* will help to stop the biting and prevent further injury to the victim. In addition, it helps to give the child something that is appropriate to bite, such as a teething ring; a frozen bagel slice; a piece of watermelon rind; or another hard, safe item.

Mobile infants and toddlers bite as a way to learn about the world and to experiment to see what happens next. Often when a child bites a playmate, he has not made the connection between his biting and the other child's pain. Sometimes biting is a form of aggression used by young children to get what they want. They lack the ability to control impulses, so they sometimes express desires by biting other children. Children also bite to seek attention, to protect themselves, or because they are imitating others.

Whether biting is a one-time occurrence or a phase a child is passing through, you must respond immediately. As with any other problem behavior, you should remain calm and consider the needs of the children involved. If the child who did the biting is still out of control, help the child move away from the setting until the outburst is over. Comfort the child who was bitten and apply ice or provide other first aid as needed. When an older toddler bites a child, you can invite him or her to help the victim feel better. "Rita's arm is sore where you bit it. We can both hold her until she feels better."

Once the victim has been consoled, it is time to address the child who bit him or her. Clearly state what happened and why biting is not allowed. Later you and the child can talk about and practice appropriate ways to express feelings.

In addition, you will need to talk with the child's family to investigate the probable cause for biting. You can explain what happened and how you responded. Encourage them to help the child learn to use speech to tell others what he or she wants. Some children have great difficult controlling their urge to bite. It may help to give them something they are allowed to bite (for example, a clean washcloth) until they learn to control their behavior.

what's next?

Skill-Building Journal, section **10-8** (*Learning Activity D*), section **10-1** (*Feedback*), and section **10-9** (*Reflecting on Your Learning*).

11

Families

Overview

Developing a Caregiving Partnership With Each Family

Offering a Variety of Ways for Families to Be Involved in the Program

Providing Support to Families

Your Own Views About Families

Learning Activities

A. Building Partnerships With Families

B. Resolving Differences

C. Offering Ways for Families to Be Involved

D. Planning and Holding Conferences With Families

E. Providing Support to Families

11.   Families

Families are the most important people in children's lives. They are children's first teachers. Families are therefore your partners in nurturing young children's development and learning.

Positive relationships with families are the basis for caregiving partnerships.

Effective infant/toddler programs build positive relationships with families. Some families are eager to be involved, but others might seem reluctant or have responsibilities that prevent active participation. Family members may not speak English well. In some cultures, family involvement is seen as interference. You must address these concerns and value all families as caregiving partners.

Everyone benefits from a partnership.

Parents and teachers have much to learn from one another. Families know about their children: their personalities, how they respond to new experiences, what they like to do, and what new skills they are developing. Teachers know about child development and learning. Your perspective is based on your experiences caring for many children of the same age. When families and teachers exchange information regularly, they create bridges between children's homes and the program.

Learning about each family supports effective communication and caregiving.

Every family is unique. Their beliefs about how to care for and support children are part of their culture. By observing, listening, and asking questions, you can begin to understand each child's cultural background. This will help you meet children's needs and communicate more effectively with families.

Infant/toddler programs can help families understand and support their children's development. In addition, teachers are likely to be the first people to see signs that family members are stressed and having difficulty with the challenges of rearing an infant or toddler. Sometimes teachers are also among the first to recognize an individual child's special needs. You and families can often work together to figure out possible remedies. At other times, your role is to help families find the assistance they need.

You can build partnerships with families by

- developing a caregiving partnership with each family

- offering a variety of ways for families to be involved in the program

- providing support to families

Developing a Caregiving Partnership With Each Family

1. **Exchange positive and current information about each child's routines and activities every day.** "Luci has been a little fussy this afternoon. She may be getting a second tooth."

2. **Invite and respond to families' questions and concerns.** "Lately it's been hard for Sara to say goodbye to you. If you have some time this afternoon, we can talk about why this happens with many toddlers her age and figure out how to support her."

3. **Get to know a little about each family.** Learn about their culture, language, interests, and wishes for their child so you can respond appropriately.

4. **Use information provided by families to meet individual needs.** "Richie likes it when you sing quietly to him for a few minutes after you lay him in his crib for a nap."

5. **Plan jointly with families to offer children consistency and security at home and at the program.** "William loves his stuffed bear. Please send it each morning, and we'll be sure it goes home with him at the end of the day."

Luci Pulls Herself Up

As you read the following story, pay attention to the signs that Ms. Gonzalez and Luci's father have a strong partnership. Also think about how Luci benefits from their partnership.

Ms. Gonzalez: Good morning, Luci. I'm happy to see you and your dad.

Luci's father: Luci pulled herself up like this last night.

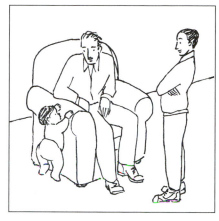

Ms. Gonzalez: Wow! She must feel very proud!

Luci's father: We're all proud!

Ms. Gonzalez: Soon she'll be moving all over. We'll have to Luci-proof this room.

Luci's father: You're right about that. We're going to Luci-proof our home tonight.

Offering a Variety of Ways for Families to Be Involved in the Program

6. **Encourage families to visit the program at any time.** Provide a comfortable place for family members to sit in or near the room, and invite them to stay whenever they wish.

7. **Invite families to share their talents, interests, home languages, and aspects of their cultures.** Learn about each family so you can identify ways they might enjoy contributing to the program.

8. **Offer a variety of family-involvement opportunities to accommodate individual schedules, interests, and skills.** Family members might keep the program Web site updated, sew doll blankets, make lullaby tapes, or volunteer in the classroom.

9. **Hold meetings and events at times that are convenient for most families.** "We know that working parents are very busy, so we're planning a dinner meeting and will provide child care."

10. **Offer workshops and resources on topics of interest to families.** "We're having a workshop on toilet learning. It seems to be a topic that lots of parents are eager to discuss."

Sammy's Mother Updates the Newsletter

As you read the following story, pay attention to the way Ms. Bates helps Sammy's mother handle her feelings about leaving him. Also notice how Ms. Bates helps Sammy's mother participate in his life at the program.

Sammy's mother: It's hard to leave Sammy while I go to work. I miss him and want to be a part of his life at the center.

Ms. Bates: We take lots of photographs of the children. Could you help us share them with their families?

Sammy's mother: I'll help you scan some photos for the newsletter. Then everyone can see what the children do here.

Lovette's mother: The photos in this month's newsletter are wonderful!

Ms. Bates: Sammy's mom will be glad you like them. She helped us update the newsletter.

Providing Support to Families

11. **Maintain confidentiality about children and families.** "Thank you for sharing this information. With your permission, I'll tell the director. We will keep the information private."

12. **Recognize when families are under stress and offer additional support.** "Having a new baby and a toddler is a lot of work. Let's talk about some ways to make life a little easier for you and the rest of your family."

13. **Encourage families to relax and enjoy their children.** "Rina's eyes get wide and sparkly when she sees you at the end of the day."

14. **Help families recognize what their children learn through daily routines and activities.** Take photographs of children engaged in daily routines and activities to display on a bulletin board. Under each photo, write a description of what the children may be learning. Change the photos and captions monthly.

15. **Share information about child development and typical behaviors of infants and toddlers.** Collect up-to-date, easy-to-read articles about how infants and toddlers grow and develop. Share these articles with families as topics arise when you observe or discuss their children together.

16. **Use familiar terms, instead of professional jargon, when communicating with families.** "Playing with the shape-sorting box helps Sammy become aware of different shapes."

17. **Notify a supervisor when a family seems to need professional help.** Give factual information to a supervisor if any behavior, conversation, or injury to a child raises concerns.

Mr. Lewis Reaches Out to Zora's Mother

As you read the following story, pay attention to the way Mr. Lewis offers support to Zora's mother, Ms. Trent. Also think about why he will talk to the other teachers before calling her.

Ms. Trent: Zora has been fussing a lot more often at home lately. She seems very tired.

Mr. Lewis: Zora has been fussing a lot here, too. Let's plan a time to talk.

Ms. Trent: That would be great. Can we talk by phone?

Mr. Lewis: Sure. How about tomorrow evening at 7:30?

Ms. Trent: Great. I'll be ready for your call.

Mr. Lewis: I'll review our observation notes and ask Ms. Gonzalez and Ms. Bates for their ideas before I call.

what's next?

Skill-Building Journal, section **11-2** (*Overview*), section **11-11** (*Answer Sheet*), and section **11-1** (*Feedback*).

Your Own Views About Families

There are many different kinds of families.

What does the word *family* mean to you? Do you think of a mother and father and one or more children living together? Do you think of different kinds of family relationships? Our experiences influence our views about families and how children should be reared.

The traditional view of a family as a mother and father with several children does not always apply today. Few families in the United States typify the traditional model of a mother who works in the home, a father who works outside the home, and their two children. Children may be growing up with a single mother or father or in step-families. They may live with several relatives—their mother, a grandmother, an aunt and her children—or they may live with a grandparent who has legal custody. A family might include children, a parent, and his or her partner of the same or different gender.

Parenting can be a challenging job.

Many of today's families are affected by multiple sources of stress that can make parenting a very difficult job. Not only are parents of infants often confused by a child's behavior and unsure of what to do, but they are also very, very tired. Lack of sleep makes it easy for even the most advantaged parents to lose perspective and to despair about ever being able to manage their new role. Some families are also struggling to provide for their children's basic needs. They may live in substandard housing, use unreliable transportation to get to their jobs, and lack health insurance. These factors, sometimes accompanied by violence, drug and alcohol abuse, and other sources of stress, can leave families with little energy to meet the needs of their children.

It is easy to blame families for their children's problems, especially when families do not behave toward their children as you think they should. If you have difficulty accepting the values and lifestyles of some children and families in your program, examine the source of your negative reactions. Do you expect children's families to conform to your personal values? Are you willing to learn about different cultural practices and parenting styles? It may help to remember that most families want the best for their children and try hard to be supportive. They, too, are guided by their own experiences growing up in a family.

Before you begin the learning activities in this module, spend a few minutes thinking about how your own views and experiences affect the way you work with families.

what's next?

Skill-Building Journal, section **11-3** (*Your Own Views About Families*), section **11-1** (*Feedback*), and section **11-4** (*Pre-Training Assessment*).

Learning Activities

LEARNING
ACTIVITY

A. Building Partnerships With Families

In this activity you will learn to

- work with families to share information about each child

- develop and maintain a partnership with each family

High-quality early childhood programs depend on strong partnerships between teachers and families. Successful partnerships are based on mutual respect, trust, and the understanding that a child's development is enhanced when all the adults who care for the child work together.

The Benefits of Partnerships

Strong partnerships benefit everyone involved. As families learn more about their infants and toddlers and about the program, they strengthen their parenting skills and are assured that their children are safe and nurtured. When families help teachers learn about each child's needs, personal style, everyday routines at home, special family experiences, and likes and dislikes, teachers are more able to respond to children as individuals. Children feel secure when their families and teachers work together.

Families and teachers share a common concern for children's well-being.

Developing partnerships can be challenging and time-consuming. Sometimes a child's teacher and family have different views about childrearing in general. They may even have different ideas about what is best for a particular child. A family and teacher might not always understand each other's point of view and may disagree about how to solve a problem. What they almost always have in common, though, is genuine concern for the child's well being.

Families know a lot about their children.

Although both the teacher and the family know a great deal about a particular child, their knowledge and information needs to be combined to create a total picture. Families typically have information about the following areas of a child's life:

- **Health and growth history.** "After Ben's checkup by the pediatrician, I'll let you know how the treatment is progressing to help him stop turning his toes in when he walks. I'll be able to tell you whether we need to change our strategy."

- **Relationships with other family members.** "Carla really enjoys being with her brother. In the morning I feed her at the table with him, and he talks with her as much as with me. She coos and smiles with him as they eat."

- **Ways the child likes to be held or comforted.** "When Yancey is tired, he likes to have his back rubbed. It helps him settle down."

- **Foods the child enjoys.** "Tom started eating carrots today. He really enjoyed them."

- **Foods the child must not eat.** "Donna is allergic to all kinds of berries."

- **How the child reacts to changes in routines.** "Sonia gets very upset if I ask her to get dressed before breakfast. She likes to eat before putting her clothes on."

- **The child's favorite activities at home.** "Timmy always wants to stay in the water and play with his toys. He loves bath time."

- **The child's fears.** "Travis is afraid of loud noises. He cries and wants to be held."

- **The family's lifestyle.** "We like to get outdoors as much as possible. Peter likes to ride in the backpack when we hike in the mountains."

- **How the child used to be, as well as how the child is now.** "When he was 18 months old, Nick never sat still except to eat. Now that he's two, he'll sit down to look at a picture book alone, several times a day."

- **Experiences outside of the program, such as what happened last night, over the weekend, or on vacation.** "We all went to the beach for our vacation. Stacy collected buckets of shells."

Teachers bring a complementary perspective about a child.

Teachers' perspectives are based on their experiences with the child. They have information about the following areas:

- **Favorite play materials.** "Tanya loves to lie on her blanket and reach for the objects that we hold out to her."

- **Which toys are frustrating.** "Tory isn't ready to do the farm puzzle yet. He chooses the ones that don't have as many pieces."

- **How the child plays with others.** "Janna likes to be next to other toddlers in the area with the large cardboard blocks or at the drawing table. She watches their play while she builds her own structures and draws her own pictures."

- **How the child reacts to changes in the environment.** "Whenever we play music, Mark waves his arms in the air while he lies on his blanket. It looks as though he is dancing."

- **How the child communicates her needs and feelings.** "When Gina is bored, she squirms and then whines and reaches her arms out to be picked up. If I don't get there fast enough, she starts to cry."

- **What the child talks about during the day.** "Carlos is very excited about seeing his cousin, Luis."

- **How the child handles separation from family members.** "Today I heard Malik tell Sandy, 'Mommy come back.' I think that's his way of assuring himself that you will always come back."

As you learn about each family and share information about children, you build positive relationships.

Establishing the Partnership

Families are entrusting the care of their child to you.

Your relationship with a family begins when they select your program for the care of their child. Although they hardly know you, you are the person whom they will trust to care for their child for many hours each week. It is natural for them to want to learn as much as they can about you, the other children in the group, and how their child will spend each day. Tell the family something about yourself and why you enjoy working with children. Share copies of recent classroom or program newsletters and the daily and weekly schedules. Show photographs and describe what you and the children do during a typical day. Explaining your program's philosophy and approach to caring for children and promoting their development and learning will help families know whether your program is right for their child and for them.

Take time to get to know the family members, as well as their children. Find out about their interests, their work, cultural traditions, caregiving preferences, how they feel about leaving their child in the program, and what kinds of stress they might be handling. Discuss ways of sharing information with each other and making decisions together about their child's routines and activities.

Let the family know that you appreciate and will take good care of their child.

At first, you and family members are likely to get to know each other through brief conversations at drop-off and pick-up times. Be friendly and respectful; always greet each family member by name. Share interesting, positive information about their child's day. Let them know by your attitude, body language, and tone of voice that their child is appreciated and well cared for. "Peter coos when I hold him up to the aquarium so he can see the fish." Remember, it is not only what you say and do but how you say and do it that conveys messages to families. Your ongoing communication and the positive feelings behind it build trust and acceptance, which lead to stronger partnerships.

Communicating to Maintain a Strong Relationship

Use multiple ways—written, oral, visual—to communicate with families.

Like other relationships, those you build with families need ongoing communication to grow and thrive. Take advantage of formal and casual opportunities to acknowledge and strengthen your partnerships with families, as well as to share other information about their children and the program. Give examples of how your work together supports children, and invite families to share their ideas. Be willing to ask questions as well as share knowledge, give families plenty of notice about meetings and other events, and remind families that they are always welcome to schedule a time to talk with you. It is important to select ways to communicate that are manageable for you and for the families in your program. To make sure that communication is effective, consider a variety of ways to share news and information.

A program newsletter can provide general information of interest to all families, as well as specific news about each group of infants and toddlers. It might include news, information about coming events, suggested activities for families and children to do at home, information about community events of interest to families, reviews of children's books, and books on parenting and related topics. If you have a digital camera, it is easy to add photos to the newsletter.

Weekly class bulletins are brief notes—with or without photographs—about what happened that week in a particular classroom. They give families a sense of what their children are doing, so they can ask you questions and talk with their children at home.

A mailbox system gives each family a box or pocket where you can place flyers about upcoming events, news bulletins, or notes to individual families. When families speak several languages, some teachers color code the boxes and paper for each language.

Family journals can be sent home with the child and returned the next day. Families can write notes about daily routines or something new or unusual that happened at home. Teachers, in turn, can write notes back and include flyers or notices with the journals.

A family bulletin board can be located in the lobby or inside the classroom near children's cubbies where families will see it easily. Post articles, a calendar of events, reminders of upcoming meetings, the week's menus, and other items of general interest.

Visual displays of what children are learning can include photographs of children involved in routines and activities. Write a brief description of what the children are doing and learning, and include toddlers' writing and artwork.

Pictures of children and their families can be displayed prominently in the classroom along with pictures of the staff. This conveys the message that everyone is part of the classroom community. Include everyone's names so families can begin to identify other children and get to know the other families.

Regular telephone calls to each family are another way to maintain communication. You can share something about their child's progress, express concern if a child is sick, discuss a problem, or invite family members to help with a project. These calls do not have to take a lot of time; perhaps one call a month to every family will be enough.

Computers offer many options for communicating if the families in your program have access to them. You can use e-mail to send general messages and to communicate with individual families. Some programs set up a Web site or an electronic bulletin board to keep families informed. They use digital cameras to post pictures of what different groups of children are doing.

- How do you communicate with families in your program?

- What can you do to make your communication more effective in building strong caregiving partnerships?

what's next?

Skill-Building Journal, section **11-5** (*Learning Activity A*) and section **11-1** (*Feedback*).

LEARNING
ACTIVITY

Learning Activities

B. Resolving Differences

In this activity you will learn to

- recognize when differences with families need to be addressed

- address differences with families in positive ways

High-quality early childhood programs depend on strong partnerships between teachers and families. As in all partnerships, there are bound to be differences in the ways people think and feel. How you deal with differences is important, because a child's development is enhanced when all of the adults who care for her work together.

Sharing care involves deep feelings.

As you work to establish partnerships with families, consider the deep feelings involved in sharing the care of a very young child. The feelings of families and teachers are rooted in their deep attachment to the children in their care. Recognizing both positive and negative emotions can help you build partnerships with families. Imagine the family's perspective and try to understand their feelings about leaving their child at the program. Some parents feel guilty and concerned about not spending as much time with their child as they would like. They might also worry that their child will love you more.

Understanding your own feelings is a vital part of your work, because they influence your responses to children and their families. It is important to consider how you may be conveying your own feelings to the family through your tone of voice, facial expressions, and the kinds of information you share. Be careful not to make assumptions about a family or to judge them.

Addressing Differences in a Positive Way

Differences can be experienced in almost any area, such as ideas about sleeping or toileting patterns or the wisdom of giving candy to children. As a teacher, your goal is not to prevent differences but to be sure that they do not undermine your partnerships with families and your ability to care for children. Sometimes this involves deciding not to create an issue out of a difference. For example, you might be annoyed when a father forgets to return the sheets he took home to wash, but you realize that there is a spare sheet for his child to use. Expressing your annoyance would not be constructive, so you simply remind him casually to bring the sheets back.

When differences begin getting in the way of your relationships with families or your ability to care for children, they need to be addressed. For example, a very experienced teacher once got so upset with parents who were continually late at the end of the day that she stopped communicating with them. Talking with her supervisor helped her understand that her strong feelings were interfering with her ability to get all the information she needed to best meet the child's needs. She also realized that she was not giving the parents an idea of how their child was doing at the program. She made an appointment to talk with the parents and explained the problem. They apologized and made arrangements for an aunt to pick up their child on days they would be late.

Cultural differences can lead to misunderstandings.

Sometimes misunderstandings are caused by cultural differences. For example, a teacher may misunderstand a mother who insists that her infant is toilet trained and sends him to child care without a diaper. The teacher thinks, "Infants do not have the muscle control they need to use the potty. We need to use a diaper until this baby shows signs of knowing she has to relieve herself and signs of being able to use the potty successfully." In the family's culture, however, family members hold babies over the toilet regularly throughout the day and consider these babies to be toilet trained.

A teacher who does not understand the family's perspective might tell the mother that she is wrong, causing the mother to feel angry, confused, guilty or uncomfortable about leaving her child in the care of people with different beliefs. However, a teacher who understands the mother's perspective might say, "I understand that your son doesn't need a diaper at home. However, we are caring for several children here, so we can't take them to the bathroom very often. We wait until they are ready to sit on the potty by themselves. To keep everyone healthy, all the babies need to wear diapers." She knows children understand and can live with differences between how things are done at home and at the program, as long as there is mutual support, and she shares this idea with the family.

Try these suggestions to resolve differences.

Especially when your ideas differ from a family's, keep in mind that you share genuine concern for the child's well-being. The following chart provides some suggestions to help you resolve differences in ways that strengthen your partnership.

Resolving Differences to Strengthen Your Partnership With Families

What to Do	What You Might Say
Learn how the family understands the situation and consider their point of view. Listen carefully to what family members are saying. Ask open-ended questions to gain a better understanding of what they think and feel.	"What are you most eager for your child to learn here?"
Repeat what you think you heard, so the family member can confirm or clarify your understanding.	"You think we should be teaching your toddler how to read."
Be aware of how your feelings about families and sharing care can affect your perceptions and the way you handle differences. For example, if you were unduly pressured to excel in school, you may resent a parent who wants his baby to learn to read. Unless you acknowledge your resentment constructively, it might interfere with your working together.	"Your toddler already likes to explore books. She's turning pages and is fascinated by the pictures. We will have plenty of time to look at them together."
Discuss the situation with someone who is not involved, such as your director or a colleague, to get a more objective idea of the situation.	"I see what you are saying. They want their child to read because they want him to be competent and successful in life."
Explain how you and the program can address the family's concerns and preferences. Share information about child development and your program's approach.	"Many of the things we do here—talking with your child, singing with her, looking at pictures, reading to her, talking about signs we see on neighborhood walks—are helping your child get ready to read."
Discuss ways to work together to meet the family's goals.	"Toddlers love to look at pictures of familiar people and things. We are asking families to bring in a few photos that we may cover with contact paper. We will keep them in a bin on this low shelf for children to enjoy looking at and talking about."
Decide a time to talk with each other about how your plan is going and about making any necessary changes.	"May we set up a time to talk in a month about how things are going? I'll be able to share examples of other things your child does that will help her become a reader. We can also talk about other activities you might like to help with or try at home."

- What kinds of differences have you experienced with families?

- How do you feel when you have differences with families?

- How do you handle your feelings? Who supports you?

Good working relationships help children feel more secure.

Good working relationships require time and effort, but everyone benefits. Parents feel more confident about their parenting skills and freely share the information that you need to help their children develop and learn. You will feel a sense of achievement as you help children, families, the program, and your own skills develop. Infants and toddlers feel more secure when they sense that the important adults in their lives are working together.

what's next?

Skill-Building Journal, section **11-6** (*Learning Activity B*) and section **11-1** (*Feedback*).

LEARNING
ACTIVITY

Learning Activities

C. Offering Ways for Families to Be Involved

In this activity you will learn to

- offer a variety of ways for families to be involved in the program

- help families feel welcome and competent when spending time in the program

Most families want and need to be involved in their children's lives at the program. For some, it is the first time they have left their child in the care of someone other than a family member. For infants and toddlers, their families' presence at the program is the best way to bridge home and program care.

While some families are able to arrange their work schedules to eat lunch with their child, join the group for a neighborhood walk, or assist in the classroom for a morning, most are not able to participate in these ways. They may feel lucky if they have a few extra minutes to spend in the morning and afternoon when dropping off and picking up their children. It is important to offer a variety of involvement options that match families' interests, skills, and schedules, so that families feel welcome and competent when they come. During the enrollment process, let parents know that they are welcome to visit at any time and ask families how they would like to participate.

Families can be involved in many ways.

Tell families how much you value their participation and how it benefits their child and the program. A grandmother who comes to hold her grandson, and who reads and talks with him and another baby, will see how the babies and you appreciate her help. She may even offer to come regularly. The parent who sews two new covers for the bouncing mattress, however, may never see the children use them. Be sure to thank her when she picks up her child in the afternoon. Explain the advantage of having two covers: Now you can wash one while the other is in use. Show her some photographs of a toddler who was extremely excited about jumping on the "new" mattress. Similarly, acknowledge the parent who produces the newsletter by listing his name in every issue. The purpose of your partnership is to support and communicate with families; there is no need to keep track of how much each family participates.

Offer a variety of ways for families to be involved in the program.

Consider some of the following suggestions for involving families in your program:

The job jar. On index cards, list program-related jobs that families can do at home. Parents can select a job from the jar and then talk with you about additional instructions. Jobs could include repairing broken toys, shopping at yard sales for water toys such as measuring cups and spoons, and making books or other materials for the room.

Projects. At an evening or weekend session, families can work together to improve the program by such things as painting walls; making a new, splinter-free sandbox; or preparing a garden plot. Some projects can be completed by families at their own convenience, over a period of time. Celebrate when a project is completed.

Useful junk. Every home has disposable items that the program can recycle as play materials. Empty food containers, ribbons, wrapping paper, and paper towel tubes are among the items an infant/toddler program can put to use. Try asking for one or two specific items at a time.

Book reviews. Invite families to read and review children's books or books on child development and parenting. Provide a book review form to record the title, author, publisher, price, and comments. For children's books, leave space on the form to record the ages for which the book is appropriate, what the book is about, and why they and their child liked it. Use these recommendations to select books for the children. Families can also review music CDs and tapes.

Family dinner night. Plan an event that lets families eat dinner together before going home. Dinner might be a meal planned and prepared with the older children or something simpler, such as pizza.

Family playtime. Open the program for an evening or a weekend afternoon so that infants, toddlers, and their families can experience a special activity or typical daytime routines, including playing and a snack.

A room for families. If space is available, consider creating a resource area for families. Include comfortable places to sit, resources of interest to families, and refreshments. Some programs find that family involvement increases dramatically when families are invited to use the washer and dryer that are reserved for them.

Class photo album. Provide an album and ask a volunteer to insert photographs you have collected. Display the photo album prominently and include a cover page thanking the person who made it. Include it in the family lending library.

Help families feel welcome and competent at the program.

An infant/toddler setting can be an intimidating place for many family members, because the activity and conversation seem chaotic to them at first. Offer an orientation and plan ways to make their experience in the program meaningful for them and their child and helpful to you. When families are encouraged to spend time at the program, they see how you interact with their children and learn new strategies to try at home. You gain extra help, and their presence tells their children, "This is a good place."

Some children behave differently when family members, especially their parents, visit the program. They may act out or insist on their parents' full attention. It is important to prepare parents for these possibilities and to assure them that such behavior is to be expected. Advise them to focus on their children first, although they may also want to be with other children later.

Here are some suggestions to make participation a positive experience for families:

Greet families when they arrive and say goodbye when they leave. Families know they are welcome and important when you acknowledge their presence and departure.

Offer a quick update about their child when family members arrive, to help them relate to their child. When you explain that Sam just came back from a walk to the park, Sam's mother has information about his morning and something to talk about with him.

Give directions when needed, clearly and respectfully. You are responsible for the caregiving setting, and you have an overall sense of what is needed to keep things running smoothly. If two parents who came for lunch are standing in the corner talking with each other while their children are seeking their attention, you might say, "Please join your child in an activity until we are ready for lunch. They are so glad to see you, it's hard for them to wait to show you what they are doing." If visiting siblings start behaving inappropriately, give them each a book to read aloud to some of the children.

Offer concrete suggestions about what families might do when they arrive. "I'm sure Jen will love it if you look at this book with her." "Why don't you join Henry and those two other toddlers playing with the farm animals?" "You look tired. Here's a cup of tea. Sit down and relax."

Explain that lengthy conversations must be postponed until a time when the children do not need your full attention. "Let's set up a meeting to talk about this later. Right now I need to be with the children."

Make the physical environment manageable. Labeling shelves and drawers will help parents find the supplies they need without having to ask you.

Share information about how children develop and learn. Post charts or use a bulletin board display to explain what children are learning. If your curriculum has specific goals and objectives, post them too. They help families and teachers remember what they want children to learn.

Ask for assistance when you need it. If you need help, do not hesitate to ask. "Will you please carry the bag of balls out into the play yard?"

Explain to families how they can support their child—and others—throughout the day. It is very likely that family members will come at different times of the day. To help make their experiences meaningful, consider posting a chart that describes what children might be doing and learning and how family members can help. Your chart might be similar to the one that follows. (For information about hellos and goodbyes, see *Learning Activity E, Providing Support to Families*, "Helping Families and Children Deal With Separations and Reunions.")

Family Involvement in the Classroom

Daily Routine or Activity	What a Child Might Be Learning	How Families Can Help
Changing diapers and helping toddlers learn to use the toilet	Assistance is available to help me stay comfortable. Health practices, such as washing hands, help me stay well. Body parts have names. I feel competent when I use the potty. Toileting accidents are okay.	Follow safe practices, such as never leaving a child on a changing table unattended. Wash your hands often. Play "Where Is Your Tummy?" while changing a baby's diaper. Look for signs that a toddler is ready to use the potty. Explain that "accidents happen" and look together for a dry pair of pants.
Supporting play and exploration	Things look, feel, smell, taste, sound, and behave differently. Things can be used for different purposes. My actions cause effects.	Narrate what children are doing. Sit near a child who is playing. Join in. Offer a toy or suggestion to a child who does not seem to be engaged.
Preparing, serving, and eating snacks and meals; helping children brush teeth after meals	Foods look, feel, smell and taste differently. Foods have names. Some foods are better for me than others. I can control my small muscles. Brushing my teeth after meals helps them stay healthy.	Prepare a favorite family food with two or three toddlers. Help children wash their hands, as necessary. Hold your baby while he drinks or watches older children eating. Invite toddlers to help set the table. Sit and talk with toddlers while they eat. Help children brush their teeth after meals.

Family Involvement in the Classroom, *continued*

Daily Routine or Activity	What a Child Might Be Learning	How Families Can Help
Encouraging children to sleep and take naps	I need to rest when I am tired. Rest time comes after we eat lunch. I can close my eyes and fall asleep. I am safe here. When I wake up, someone will be here to take good care of me.	Bring your child's comfort item and blanket to the program every day. Wash your child's sheet weekly. Explain how you help your child fall asleep at home and what teachers should expect when she wakes up.
Cleaning up	I can help! Particular materials are put in particular places.	When finished playing with your child, put away your toys together. Help clean up if you have time at the end of the day or when visiting during the day.
Taking children outdoors	There are interesting things to smell and see and touch and do. I am safe outside. I like to go outside.	Label your child's outdoor clothing, to make getting dressed easier. Join the class for a neighborhood walk when you can.

what's next?

Skill-Building Journal, section **11-7** (*Learning Activity C*) and section **11-1** (*Feedback*).

Learning Activities

LEARNING ACTIVITY

D. Planning and Holding Conferences With Families

In this activity you will learn to

- prepare for family conferences by reviewing information about each child's developmental progress and experiences in the program

- share information with families and jointly plan ways to support their children's development and learning

In most early childhood programs, teachers meet with families two to three times a year and whenever a special need arises. Together, the teacher and family review progress in all areas of development and jointly set goals for continued growth and learning. Conferences are opportunities to focus on one child and family without any distractions or interruptions. Although much information about the child is shared daily, conferences allow for in-depth discussions. When they are planned carefully, everyone benefits. Families are assured that the teachers really know their child and that their child is developing and learning as expected. Teachers gain new insights about a child's behavior, interests, culture, and experiences and often receive more support from the family. Children benefit from the stronger partnerships that usually result.

Share your observations about all areas of development.

To make the best use of the opportunity to communicate with a family, it is important to be well prepared. Review all you know about their child and prepare a summary of the child's progress to share with the family. If you use a systematic approach to assessing children's development (see module 12, *Program Management*), you will have a wealth of information about what each child knows and can do in relation to the goals and objectives of your curriculum. You will have observed children and kept records of what you saw and heard. You may have a checklist to keep track of each child's progress. You will probably have a portfolio for each child that includes photos of the child engaged in various activities. For older children, the portfolio might include samples of drawings and other creations. If there are concerns about a child's health or behavior (difficulty hearing, for example) these concerns should be documented. Ask other staff members to provide any information they have about the child.

Involve families in planning the conference.

Families are interested in learning as much as possible about their child's daily experiences in the program. For example, Nigel's family might ask, "What does Nigel do after I leave in the morning? What activities does he enjoy? What makes him happy and sad? How do you comfort him?" Make sure your notes include examples that will help the family imagine their child's everyday life in the program and understand how his experiences support development.

When you schedule a conference, ask families when it would be most convenient for them to attend. If possible, offer several options and provide advance notice so they can make plans. Whenever possible, offer child care if conferences are held after normal program hours. Allow enough time for the conference so you will not feel rushed. Explain to families that the conference is an opportunity for each of you to share what you know about their child so you can work together to support the child's development and learning.

Encourage families to share their goals for the conference with you ahead of time. Most importantly, they will want to know that you understand and like their child. In addition, they may have a specific concern they would like to discuss or a suggestion for how they would like you to work with their child. It is also possible that a parent might have a concern about the program's philosophy or a complaint about something you did or did not do. It is helpful to know about these issues ahead of time so you can be prepared to respond to their concerns.

To help families prepare for the meeting, you can provide a simple planning form that explains the general purpose of the conference and the benefits of working together. In addition to stating the date and time, you may also want to remind families to bring photographs, observations (written or oral), and anything else that helps describe their child's recent experiences and development.

Conducting the Conference

Be relaxed and respectful.

At the beginning of the conference, try to establish a relaxed and comfortable tone by allowing time for casual conversation. Offer a snack and confirm how much time you have available. Throughout the conference, show respect for the family's cultural preferences with regard to conversational practices. Maintain an appropriate physical distance, eye contact, and tone of voice; respect individual response times to questions; and use or avoid physical contact, as appropriate. Pay attention to body language, especially signs that a parent might feel tense, hurt, disappointed, or angry.

Here is how a conference might proceed:

Share some examples of the child's explorations and discoveries. A good way to give parents an idea of how their child is developing is to show examples of what she can do. For example, you might share photos of a child playing with water or turning the pages of a book, or you might show samples of a toddler's writing or painting. Explain the aspects of development that each sample documents, e.g., "Remember how Mark used to explore books by chewing on them? Now see how he smiles as he turns the pages of the board book with his thumb and first finger? He is gaining new control over the small muscles in his hands, so now he enjoys taking part in reading by turning the pages of the book. He likes books and being read to. These are important steps in becoming a reader."

Discuss the child's progress and relate it to his daily experiences. Review your summary of the child's progress in each developmental area. Share your program's goals and objectives and point out what the child is learning. Always link the child's new accomplishments to the family's everyday life. For example, when Mark starts to crawl, it is a good time to remind his family to be sure that their home is safe for a mobile child. The family might have new questions about guiding his behavior, because he has started getting into things he could not reach earlier.

Invite families to share their own observations. "What do you think Mark is learning now? What kinds of activities does he do at home?" Record what you learn from families on the form that summarizes your observations.

Bring up any concerns. If you have any concerns, be sure to share concrete examples that illustrate your points. "We've noticed that sometimes we have to call Mark several times before he seems to hear us. A few days ago, he didn't turn when a fire engine passed us. We think it might be a good idea to have his hearing checked."

Discuss specific goals for the child. Use your curriculum goals and objectives to talk about those you think are the most important. "We want to encourage Mark's physical development and to encourage his interest in books and reading." Also invite the family's ideas by asking, "What specific goals do you have for your child?"

Agree on some next steps. At the end of the conference, summarize your discussions and identify the actions you have each agreed to take and how you will follow up. "It would be great if you put big cushions on the living room floor for Mark to crawl over and around. He will have lots of chances to climb and move here, too. Why don't we take a few minutes to look at some books we think he might like? You are welcome to borrow any you want to read at home. Here is the name of an audiologist who specializes in working with young children and who has examined other children in our program. Would you like me to tell her to expect your call?"

Tips for Family Conferences

- **Respect culturally based conversational practices.** Maintain an appropriate physical distance, eye contact, and tone of voice; respect individual response times to questions; and use or avoid physical contact, as appropriate.

- **Ask open-ended questions.** This often elicits more information and extends the conversation.

- **Confirm the partnership.** "It's helpful to know that you hold Mai Le over your leg to burp her. We'll remember to do that here as well."

- **Take notes during the conference.** This is very important if you are discussing a complex or difficult situation. Explain to families that the notes will help you follow up on their concerns and implement their suggestions.

- **Pay attention to body language.** Especially note signs that a parent might feel tense, hurt, disappointed, or angry. Be aware that nonverbal language is sometimes different in various cultures. Be sensitive to the range of emotions that families might experience, even if they do not express them directly. Acknowledge their feelings and respond appropriately.

- **Repeat what you hear.** Restate the family's comments and suggestions, so they can confirm or clarify your understanding. "You are concerned that Maria is tired when she gets home, so you would like us to make sure she naps every day."

- **Offer advice when asked.** Always offer more than one suggestion. "Some families find it helpful to allow their toddler to select his clothes. Others offer a narrower choice, for example, red socks or blue ones." If you do not know an answer, say that you will try to find out and then tell them.

what's next?

Skill-Building Journal, section **11-8** (*Learning Activity D*) and section **11-1** (*Feedback*).

Learning Activities

E. Providing Support to Families

In this activity you will learn to

- recognize signs that families are under stress

- provide support to families to prevent or cope with stress

Many families with infants and toddlers have stressful lives, especially young and first-time parents. Parents can be overwhelmed, trying to balance the demands of a job and family. They may be unsure about sharing the care of their children, and they might not understand changes in their children's behavior. Some families also face the extra challenges of children with special needs. Many families are comfortable about voicing their worries and seeking assistance; others are not. Teachers of young children are often in a good position to support families and to offer help before stress becomes overwhelming.

Sharing Information on Child Growth and Development

You can provide information to families about the typical development of children.

Families sometimes do not know much about typical child development, so they may expect too much or too little of their children. Here are some things you can do to help:

Invite a family member to observe his child with you. Discuss your observations and explain why the child's behavior is typical of a particular developmental stage. Asking family members to imagine their children's perspectives helps them think about what the children experience.

Provide information about parenting workshops on relevant topics. Include topics such as supporting emerging language, adjusting to a new baby, responding to children's growing independence, parenting a child with special needs, and other subjects of interest to families of infants and toddlers.

Include information on infant and toddler development in newsletters and on the family bulletin board. The charts in other *Caring for Infants & Toddlers* modules are useful to families.

Invite families to attend staff workshops about topics of interest. The workshops might be about such topics as first aid, child health, early literacy learning, and adapting environments for children with special needs.

Establish a family lending library. Include books, magazines, and videotapes about child growth and development.

Introduce families who are dealing with, or who have already successfully handled, similar developmental issues and special needs. Be sure that these families have first expressed their willingness to share information.

Helping Families Locate Resources

You can help families find resources in the community.

Much of the time, families simply need to know where they can get help for themselves, their child, or the family. Your director can give you information about parent education opportunities. Here are some things you can do to help:

Encourage connections by introducing families who live in the same neighborhood or who have children of the same age. "Carl, this is Jack Wheeler. He and his wife, Pam, have a son about the same age as your daughter."

Develop a classroom directory so families can support one another by sharing responsibilities and errands such as carpooling, grocery shopping, and preparing meals. "Several families want to start a dinner club."

Point out resources, articles, workshops, Web sites, and television or radio shows on children and families. "Next Tuesday at 8:00 p.m., there's a show on Channel 8 about stepparenting and blended families."

Display books on topics of interest to families. These might include ideas about safety proofing a home, juggling home and work responsibilities, and introducing solid foods. Invite families to borrow them.

Tell parents about services and special programs in the community. Provide as much information as possible: names of contacts, phone numbers, locations, and hours of operation.

Model positive ways to interact with children.

When families are in the classroom, either to participate or just to drop off or pick up their children, you can talk with them, explain your approach to child development, and model positive ways to interact with children. Here are some examples of positive interactions, a family member's concern, and ways to support the family.

Interactions With a Child	A Family Member's Concern	How to Offer Support and Encouragement
You work beside Ashleigh to put away the blocks.	"I can't get Ashleigh to put any of her things away at home."	Explain how you promote children's self-help skills, e.g., "We find that toddlers are more willing to put materials away if we join in the cleanup."
You talk and laugh with Evan as you change his diaper.	"Evan squirms around so much at home that I just want to get his diaper changed as quickly as possible."	Explain how you talk with children during routines and engage their interest. "We talk about how good it feels to be clean and dry. I also describe what we are doing and play simple games like 'Where's Your Tummy?'"
You ask a child about his painting: "Bart, tell me how you made these long, squiggly lines."	"I never know what to say about Bart's artwork. All his paintings look the same to me."	Talk about supporting creativity by acknowledging children's efforts. "I describe what I see and ask questions that help children talk about what they did."

Helping Families and Children Deal With Separations and Reunions

The first few weeks of group care can be very challenging for children, families, and teachers, especially when a child has never been cared for by someone outside of the family. Separations and reunions involve deep feelings for children, families, and teachers. Being aware of your own feelings will help you be sensitive to the needs of children and families. When separations and reunions are handled well, relationships between teachers and families are strengthened.

Explain why it is important to say goodbye.

Because separating can be so painful, some families are tempted to sneak out of the room while their children are looking the other way. Explain to these families that, although leaving without saying goodbye might seem to be the easiest thing to do, they might find it useful to imagine how they would feel if the most important people in their lives disappeared without warning. Point out that saying goodbye gives children the security of knowing they can rely on their families to let them know what is happening. Let parents know that you are there to support them and their child. "I know it's hard to say goodbye to Mark when he is clinging to you and crying. We can help him together. You can give him a big hug and reassure him that you will be back after nap. We'll say goodbye to you, and I'll stay with him until he calms down. You can call when you get to work to find out how he is doing."

Here are some suggestions to help children and families handle separation. (Also see module 8, *Self*, for more information about separation.)

- Encourage families to stay for a few minutes and help their child get involved in an activity. Provide comfortable adult-size furniture so family members can sit.

- Remind parents to let you know when they are getting ready to leave so you can help their children say goodbye.

- Display photos of each child and family in the classroom where children can see them easily.

- Have a "goodbye window" where children can wave to their families as they leave.

- Invite families to send a comfort item for the child from home, such as a stuffed animal or a special blanket.

- Encourage play that helps children gain a sense of mastery over separation. For example, babies enjoy peek-a-boo games, and toddlers like pretend play about going to and coming back from the grocery store and office.

- Provide toys that allow children to express their feelings and feel connected to home, such as puppets and toy phones.

- Read picture books and tell stories about saying goodbye and hello.

Families and children also need support at the end of the day.

Like separations, reunions are sometimes easy and sometimes difficult. Some days, children run gleefully to greet family members who are picking them up. They are happy to see them and ready to go home. On other days, they are upset. They may burst into tears or have tantrums about getting their coats on. Help families understand that this range of emotions is perfectly normal. Children sometimes save their deepest feelings for their families, the people they trust most.

Recognizing When Families Are Under Too Much Stress

Most families can cope with typical frustrations and tension, so stress does not interfere with their work and home activities. Some families, however, are affected over a long period of time by significant sources of stress, such as community violence, homelessness, substance abuse, or lack of basic necessities. The stresses are not caused by single events such as an illness or accident. They are routine, unrelenting, and an integral part of daily life. They may be beyond the control of individual families.

There are many sources of long-term stress.

Long-term stress may be caused by

- unemployment

- lack of food, clothing, transportation, and medical care

- living in overcrowded, inadequate, or temporary housing

- violence or substance abuse in the home or community

- chronic illness or disability of a child or other family member, along with lack of access to needed services and support

- abuse and neglect of a child, spouse, of other family member

- depression or other mental illness of a child or family member

- learning a new language and adapting to a new culture

There may also be other sources that are specific to your community, such as when military personnel are called for duty away from home.

High levels of stress can overwhelm some families.

Regardless of the cause of extreme stress in their lives, families tend to have similar concerns, needs, and behavior. Although many families have the skills and resources needed to cope with stress, some are overwhelmed. When families are overwhelmed, family life suffers and children's behavior is affected.

If family life is unpredictable, unstable, and chaotic because the family moves frequently, children must adapt to new child care programs, teachers, and classmates. Children may have difficulty focusing and lack a sense of order and discipline in their lives.

If adult family members are unable to give their children affection and attention, older children might be expected to assume adult responsibilities such as caring for younger siblings. The children's basic needs might not be met.

If children and adult family members do not have access to adequate food or needed health care, including immunizations, dental checkups, and counseling, children might come to the program hungry, sick, or worried.

If children receive inconsistent, overly punitive, or nonexistent parental discipline, they may not know what is expected of them or how to behave.

Learn to identify the signs of a family's overwhelming stress.

When stress is overwhelming, family members may seem disorganized, frequently forgetting things such as mittens on a cold day or a child's special blanket. A parent might seem frustrated when a child is slow to get ready to go home. A family member might complain to a teacher about the difficulty of handling the child's growing independence. Families under stress might be unwilling to accept help, or they might be more interested in talking about adult problems than their child's experiences.

When you see signs that a family is coping with multiple sources of stress, it is important not to add to them. This is not the time to discuss such concerns as the child's inappropriate behavior or changes in the program's vacation schedule. However, it would be appropriate to share information about their child that will help a family get through the evening. For example, you would let a parent know her child has been tired and cranky all afternoon so you can discuss whether the child might be getting sick. When a family knows the reasons for their child's behavior, they are less likely to be frustrated or angered by crankiness and more likely to comfort the child. They are more likely to interact positively with their child and less likely to lose control.

Involve your supervisor if you think a family needs help.

Your job is to help families get the support they need, not to provide it yourself. Always notify your supervisor when you think families may need professional help. Do not counsel families or refer them to social services or mental health professionals without first discussing the situation with your supervisor.

When families do confide in you, it is essential to maintain complete confidentiality. This means you should not discuss a child with anyone other than your colleagues or the child's family. This is true for information about families as well. You should not share records with anyone who does not have permission to see them, and you should not hold discussions about particular children or families when other children or families are present. Ask your supervisor about your program's guidelines for maintaining confidentiality.

Help families build confidence in their expertise and in their partnership with you.

Families often ask teachers for advice about frustrating or confusing behavior. When this happens, be sure to respond in a way that acknowledges families' skills and helps them feel confident and capable. Remind families that they know more about their children than anyone else. Asking what approaches they use at home helps families discover or recognize what works well for them and their child.

Here are some ways to help families feel confident about your partnership:

Let the family know that you appreciate their child's special characteristics. "Denise always has a smile ready. We all feel good when she smiles at us."

Help families understand that their presence at the program helps their children bridge home and program care. "Mr. Bradley, Jerry is so excited when he knows you're coming for lunch. He really likes it when the other kids talk about your visits."

Wait until you are asked, before offering advice. When you are asked for advice, offer suggestions that allow families to make choices. "Most child development experts say that children Billy's age are usually too young for toilet learning."

Acknowledge life events and transitions. "Congratulations on your promotion. Your husband told me that the whole family had a party to celebrate."

Help families cope when a parent must be away. Suggest sending artwork, photographs, or messages to the parent who is away. Talk with children about their families and look at their photos together.

Maintain communication when a child is absent or ill. "Hello, Ms. Carson. How is Paula feeling today?"

what's next?

Skill-Building Journal, section **11-9** (*Learning Activity E*), section **11-1** (*Feedback*), and section **11-10** (*Reflecting on Your Learning*).

12 Program Management

Overview

Learning About Each Child

Working as a Team to Offer a Program That Meets Each Child's Needs

Evaluating the Program

Managing Your Own Life

Learning Activities

A. Getting to Know Each Child

B. Organizing and Using Portfolios

C. Responding to Each Child's Needs and Interests

D. Working as a Team to Plan and Evaluate the Program

12. Program Management

Teachers plan, conduct, and evaluate the program.

As a teacher, you play many roles. Your most important role is to provide for children's health, safety, and developmental needs. Caring for infants and toddlers also involves supporting families and helping children feel competent and self-confident. With your colleagues, you use managerial skills to ensure the smooth operation of your program.

Many teachers do not see themselves as managers. Your program probably has a director who performs managerial tasks such as preparing budgets, hiring, scheduling, and providing support to teachers. You and your colleagues are also managers. Your managerial role includes planning, conducting, and evaluating the program. As you perform these managerial tasks, you create a supportive learning environment, guide children's learning, and assess their progress.

Teachers use information about each child to plan and evaluate their program.

Effective infant/toddler programs are both developmentally, individually, and culturally appropriate for each child. They are based on knowledge of how young children develop, and they are tailored to respond to each child. Teachers and families share information about each child's temperament, experiences, preferences, abilities, needs, and interests. This team of adults works together to plan a program that supports the development of every child. Then families and teachers continue to share information regularly and work together to offer a program that responds to the children's needs and interests; offers appropriate challenges; and reflects the families' languages, cultures, and talents.

Program evaluation helps teachers decide what changes to make.

As plans are implemented, it is important to review what actually happened each day, each week, and over longer periods of time. Evaluation lets teachers know which approaches and experiences are leading to positive outcomes for children. It also lets teachers know where changes need to be made in the environment, interactions, the daily schedule, and so on.

You can manage your program effectively by

- learning about each child

- working as a team to offer a program that meets each child's needs

- evaluating the program

Learning About Each Child

1. **Communicate with families often, using a variety of strategies.** Learn about each child's family life, culture, home language, and unique characteristics. Use this information to plan learning opportunities and changes to the environment.

2. **Observe each child regularly and note your observations.** Use a notation system that is objective and accurate and that avoids labeling. Include these notes when you analyze portfolio information.

3. **Observe children in different settings and at different times of the day.** "Yesterday I observed Avida when her father was saying goodbye. Tomorrow I'll observe her when she is playing with other children."

4. **Collect examples and photographs that document children's skills, interests, and progress.** Portfolios for each child, which contain these examples and photographs of children's explorations, are useful for documenting each child's progress over time.

5. **Take advantage of everyday routines and interactions to learn about children's interests and abilities.** Make use of everyday opportunities to discover each child's likes, dislikes, strengths, and needs.

Mr. Lewis Learns by Watching

As you read the following story, pay attention to the way Mr. Lewis gathers objective and accurate information about Jessica. Also think about what Mr. Lewis learns about her.

Mr. Lewis: Ready to try some apple butter on your bagel?

Mr. Lewis: I'll pass the apple butter to Lovette, now that you have some, Jessica.

Mr. Lewis (writes): J. used r. hand to hold and use spreader w/ a. butter. Held bowl and then bagel w/ left hand.

Mr. Lewis: How about a bite of bagel with your apple butter, Jessica?

Working as a Team to Offer a Program That Meets Each Child's Needs

6. **Meet regularly with colleagues to plan the program.** Weekly meetings are opportunities to review children's progress, discuss changes to the environment, and decide future activities.

7. **Ensure that curriculum goals are the basis for planning experiences for the children.** "Let's talk about our curriculum goals during our next teachers' meeting. We must make sure that we're offering opportunities for all children to meet those goals."

8. **Use ongoing assessment information to plan for individual children and the group.** To plan the program with your team, review and analyze observation notes, portfolio information, and information from families.

9. **Include each family in planning ways to support their children's development and learning.** Include families in regular planning meetings or provide other opportunities for them to offer ideas.

10. **Use creative thinking skills, such as brainstorming, to plan and to solve problems.** Team members use these skills to develop short- and long-term plans, strategies for guiding children's behavior, and other issues.

11. **Appreciate and use the strengths of all team members, including teachers, families, and volunteers.** "In our planning meeting, we will review our first set of observation notes about children, as well as information families provided at enrollment about their children's interests and strengths."

Three Colleagues Plan as a Team

As you read the following story, pay attention to the way Ms. Bates, Ms. Gonzalez, and Mr. Lewis work together to plan an individualized program. Also think about how the teachers use information from their observations.

Ms. Bates: Let's focus on outdoor time this week. On Friday, we can discuss what we do now and plan new activities.

Ms. Bates: What did you observe this week?

Ms. Gonzalez: Malou sure enjoyed the ball. I think we need some more.

Mr. Lewis: Adam and Ricky like wagons and water play. They could wash the wagons.

Evaluating the Program

12. **Use program goals as a component of program evaluation.** Program or curriculum goals guide teachers' planning and help them assess children's progress.

13. **Identify what is working well and what needs to be improved, every day.** "Our lunch routines are working well, but getting ready to go outdoors is still chaotic."

14. **Use assessment information to plan teaching approaches and to change the environment, interactions, routines, and activities in response to children's individual characteristics.** "Jamie and Sara are fascinated by trucks and backhoes. This week we'll walk by the construction site on our way to the park every day."

15. **Use information about children's use of materials to determine whether changes are needed.** Lack of interest in or misuse of toys can help teachers determine whether they need to put some toys away, add new ones, or display them differently.

Three Colleagues Evaluate Their Program

As you read the following story, pay attention to what information the teachers use to evaluate their program. Also think about what they decide to do on the basis of their evaluation.

Ms. Gonzalez: We have a lot of information to help us. Earlier, we agreed to start by reviewing the developmental summary forms to see what skills the children are using.

Ms. Bates: Let's list their skills in each area of development. Then we can discuss which activities went well and where there were problems.

Ms. Bates: I thought that Ricky would enjoy the new climber, but he didn't.

Mr. Lewis: We need more outdoor space for the children who crawl to explore safely.

Ms. Gonzalez: I also like your idea for changing the schedule.

Ms. Bates: I'm excited about our plans for improving the program!

what's next?

Skill-Building Journal, section **12-2** (*Overview*), section **12-10** (*Answer Sheet*), and section **12-1** (*Feedback*).

Managing Your Own Life

Managerial skills are used at home.

Managerial skills, such as observing, individualizing, and planning, are used at both home and work. For example, you might begin by making a list when you plan a trip to the grocery store. You consider how many people will be eating each meal, what foods each person likes, and the ingredients you will need. You can do this because you observe each member of your household, include them in planning balanced meals, and follow recipes.

When you manage your life outside of work efficiently, you have more time to do things other than chores. The more planning you do together, the more likely you and your family and friends will enjoy spending time together. Think about how careful management improves your use of time and resources.

- You save gasoline and time by doing all of your errands at the same time, rather than making several trips.

- You make sure that you have all the tools and materials you need before you start a project, such as painting a room or repairing a bicycle.

- You keep records of all bills and file receipts promptly.

- You keep emergency numbers posted near the telephone.

- You borrow a folding table and extra chairs from a neighbor when you are having a crowd over for a special meal or a neighborhood meeting.

- You decide what you must do (e.g., have the car inspected), what you would like to do (e.g., get a haircut), and what you can do later (e.g., shop for new running shoes).

- You remember the importance of relaxation, exercise, and spending time with friends and family.

Effective management includes organizing your time and environment to work for you, rather than against you.

what's next?

Skill-Building Journal, section **12-3** (*Managing Your Own Life*), section **12-1** (*Feedback*), and section **12-4** (*Pre-Training Assessment*).

Learning Activities

A. Getting To Know Each Child

In this activity you will learn to

- use multiple sources of information to get to know each child

- take observation notes that are objective, accurate, and complete

Program management involves planning an environment, routines, and activities that are appropriate for individual children, as well as for the group. Planning begins with gathering information about each child. Teachers need information about the typical behaviors and interests of infants and toddlers (see *Learning Activity A*, modules 1–10) and about each child's culture, language, family, interests, skills, needs, temperament, and other individual characteristics.

Assessment information helps you make decisions.

Assessment begins by using formal and informal strategies to learn about each infant and toddler. Different types of assessment serve different purposes. Some programs conduct *health and developmental screenings* at enrollment or soon after. Screening tools provide useful information about the child's development and may identify signs of possible developmental concerns. When concerns arise, teachers and specialists meet as a team to discuss the results and need for a *health or developmental evaluation*. Information from screenings helps the team plan ways to address the child's needs in the program, at home, and through other interventions. Teachers also might conduct *initial developmental assessments* to begin planning for each child and the group. The appropriate use of an initial assessment is to get to know each child, that is, to find out what each child can do and to identify next steps. Then the program can be adjusted to match children's skills, interests, and needs.

Different strategies help you to learn different things about each infant and toddler.

To keep track of and respond to each child's changing skills, interests, and needs, teachers have a system for *ongoing assessment*. You can use a number of different strategies to get to know each child and to track development. Different strategies provide different kinds of information. Informal, ongoing conversations with children's families provide information about children's unique characteristics. Documentation of children's explorations and discoveries, collected over time, also provides useful information about each child's progress. Observation of children during daily routines and play tells you about children's skills and interests, as well as such matters as handling frustration and coping with separation. Observation notes describe the setting and record what children do and say during a brief period of time.

To offer an individualized program, you need to know each child's unique characteristics. You learn a lot about children each day as you observe and care for them, share information with their families, and analyze your observation notes. For example, you might learn that Aimee is starting to roll over, Tony loves filling and dumping containers, Linda comforts herself by hugging her stuffed fish, and Maria's Spanish and English vocabularies are expanding rapidly. Through observations, discussions with colleagues, and conversations with individual children and their families, your knowledge about how children are growing and changing stays current.

Your program's curriculum and assessment system helps you plan for each child and the group.

Your program might use a written curriculum to guide teachers' work with children and families. A developmentally appropriate curriculum includes information about all areas of a child's development: social/emotional, physical, cognitive, and language.[46] The curriculum also includes goals and objectives that are realistic and attainable by most children in the group. It is important that you understand the goals and objectives, as well as how children show progress and mastery.

Assessment that can be used to support learning is linked closely to the goals and objectives of your curriculum. Assessment and curriculum work hand in hand:

- The **curriculum** provides goals and objectives that help you plan your routines and activities, as well as a focus for your assessment of children's development and learning.

- **Assessment** helps you know how each child is progressing toward meeting the goals and objectives.

Observing and Documenting Children's Development

Observation provides information you need to build relationships with individual children.

When you observe children, you watch them in order to learn about their development, learning, and unique characteristics. Observation provides some of the information you need to build positive relationships with individual children and to support their development and learning.[47] Watching and listening to infants and toddlers helps you understand what they are feeling, thinking, and learning.

Being a teacher means being a learner, too. There are always new things to learn about a child, even a child whom you think you know well. You can only begin to understand a child's changing strengths, abilities, and needs by asking questions and by observing a child regularly and purposefully over time. What do you need to know about the children in your care? Observation can help you learn about a child's

- health and physical development

- temperament

- relationships with others

- feelings about himself

- ability to communicate

- cognitive skills

- interests

- culture and home life

- approach to learning

Useful observation notes are complete, accurate, and objective.

The primary purpose of an observation is to collect accurate, useful information about a child. This requires a careful, systematic approach. You and your colleagues need to watch, listen to, and write down what children do and say as it happens, according to a particular method.

To be complete, observation notes must include particular facts.

Facts to Include in Observation Notes

- the child's name

- the observer's name

- the date and time of the observation

- the setting (where the activity is taking place and who is involved, for example, "Linda and Maria sit on the rug, looking at books")

- the child's behavior (what the child you are observing does and says, including descriptions of the child's actions and quotations of the child's language)

- descriptions of the child's gestures and facial expressions

- descriptions of the child's exploration or creation

Observation is an ongoing process.

A single observation does not provide a complete picture of a child. A child, like an adult, does not always behave the same way. Illness, reactions to events at home or the program, and other factors affect what children do and say. Several brief (3- to 5-minute) observations can provide useful information about a child's interests, skills, and needs. You can observe during indoor and outdoor activities, as children arrive and leave the program, as they move from one activity to another, as they participate in routines, and as they interact with other children and adults. Children change over time, so observation is an ongoing process. Work with your colleagues to develop a schedule for conducting regular observations of all the children in the class.

A collection of observation notes completed over a period of time should address all areas of a child's development. A single observation, however, can provide information about several areas at a given time, particularly if the observation is focused on one or more aspects of the child's development. For example, a child might demonstrate cognitive and social skills as you observe a short play period. In another instance, she might demonstrate cognitive and physical skills.

When you have collected several observation notes about a child, you can analyze the information and summarize your findings. For example, you might comment,

> *Jake is an easy-going baby. Because he rarely fusses, I need to be careful not to ignore him.*

> *Caren cries in protest when it is time to say goodbye to her family. Her parents have observed the same behavior at home when they leave her with a babysitter.*

> *Jason is learning the names of colors.*

Write only the facts.

To draw conclusions such as these, you must be sure that your recordings are objective and accurate. Useful observation notes contain only the facts about what you see and hear. Subjective interpretations, impressions, assumptions, and judgments are not included. As you write descriptions of what a child does and says, do not try to determine what the child's actions mean. Interpretive labels, such as *shy*, *aggressive*, or *creative*, do not provide the objective information about the child's behavior that you need for planning. In addition, your observations should be stated positively, and your notes should not include your thoughts about the child's intentions. When you record what a child does and says, write down what you see and hear, not what you think he wants to do or why he is doing it.

Compare the following excerpts from different observation notes about the same situation.

Comparing Observation Notes

Example 1: An Objective and Accurate Observation Note

Tony (30 months) pours the water quickly from the pitcher. The water splashes inside and outside the basin. Some falls on other children's shoes. Tony begins to giggle.

This observation note includes only the facts about what Tony does ("pours the water quickly"), what happens ("the water splashes inside and outside the basin"), and his reaction ("Tony begins to giggle"). The facts about what the child does and says are recorded in the order of occurrence, and information is not omitted.

Example 2: A Subjective Observation Note

Tony (30 months) is a bad boy. He angrily splashes water on the floor and on other children at the water basin. Then he laughs at them.

This is not an objective observation note. A label ("bad") is used, and a judgment is made about Tony's feelings and intentions ("he angrily splashes the water"). Given only what the teacher sees, he does not know why Tony is laughing. A note that he is bad does not tell anything useful about his behavior, because the word means different things to different people.

Example 3: An Inaccurate Observation Note

Tony (30 months) stands at the water basin, looking to see if a teacher is watching him. He giggles and begins to splash water on other children.

In this observation note, a fact is added that is not observed ("looking to see if a teacher is watching him"). A fact is omitted ("Tony pours the water quickly from the pitcher"). Other facts are written out of order ("He giggles and begins to splash water").

Writing an objective and accurate observation note, such as Example 1, requires practice, but there are opportunities to take brief notes throughout the day. With practice, you will become skilled at completing observation notes as you care for infants and toddlers.

How, When, and What to Observe

Use these tips for observing children.

Plan periods in your daily schedule to observe a child, if only for three minutes. Develop a schedule to be sure that you observe each child regularly. Here are some suggestions for observing children effectively:[48]

Focus your observation.

- Think about what you want to know about children, an area, or an activity.

- Watch and listen deliberately for the information you need.

Be prepared.

- Place note-taking materials within easy reach throughout the room (a pen or pencil; index cards, Post-It® notes, or other paper; clipboard).

- Coordinate your observations with other teachers so that they will supervise the children when you want to step back from offering immediate care.

Write accurate and objective recordings.

- Record the facts about what you see and hear, not your interpretation of what is happening.

- Use descriptive words and action verbs, but avoid judgmental words and labels.

- Record events in the order they occur.

- Use abbreviations so that you can write quotations quickly.

- Invent your own shorthand system (e.g., *bl* means *block area*)

- Underline words to indicate emphasis ("She <u>smiled</u> at him.")

- Observe with a partner and compare notes to determine whether you recorded the same information.

To ensure accuracy, compare your observation notes with the notes that colleagues make about the same situation.

It is useful to compare your observation notes about a child to those made at the same time by a colleague. If they are similar, you are maintaining a useful record. If they are different, try to determine why. If the notes differ greatly, your director or trainer can help.

Observation is a vital part of your everyday work.

When you observe, slow down, watch or listen to a child carefully, and pause to reflect for a moment before you respond. Observation helps you build relationships with infants and toddlers because you come to know each child as a unique individual. You can provide the responsive care that infants and toddlers need and deserve only when you know them well.

Some teachers think that observing and taking notes will take away from their time with children. Others resent a colleague's taking a few minutes to step back and observe. However, observations provide information that is essential to meeting the needs of each child. Strategies that allow all teachers to observe and take notes regularly are well worth the time and effort involved. Be sure to organize your notes so that you can refer to them regularly.[49]

what's next?

Skill-Building Journal, section **12-5** (*Learning Activity A*) and section **12-1** (*Feedback*).

Learning Activities

B. Organizing and Using Portfolios

In this activity you will learn to

- document a child's growth and development by creating a portfolio

- use portfolios to share information with parents and to plan and evaluate your program

An important part of a teacher's managerial responsibilities is keeping current records about each child's growing skills, changing interests, and experiences that affect their development. One way to ensure that your program meets every child's needs is to create and use portfolios.

The items in a portfolio are concrete illustrations of a child's growth and development. Portfolios for infants and toddlers include photos of children engaged in daily routines and play. They also include observation notes, notes from parents, developmental checklists, and other items that contribute to an up-to-date portrait of the child. Many teachers of infants and toddlers make scrapbooks or boxes that they give to children and their families at the end of the program year.

Portfolios are records of children's progress over time.

For portfolios, teachers typically collect items that document children's explorations and discoveries. They include such things as photographs of an infant moving around the room (to show his developing large motor skills) or a collection of observation notes about a toddler's language during neighborhood walks (to show her increasing vocabulary). It is important to date each item, so that, taken together, these materials provide a picture of a child's development over time. You can also add a note to help you remember details about particular items or events.

- How do you display examples of children's explorations and discoveries in your program setting?

- What examples might you collect to show what children are learning?

Here are some examples of items that could be included in a portfolio.

Portfolio Items

Samples of the child's explorations and discoveries

- scribbles
- a book made by the teacher and child
- leaves collected on a walk
- list of favorite books

Photographs of the child's explorations

- looking at own hands or reaching for an object
- stacking blocks
- squeezing and poking playdough
- crawling through a box
- pretending to talk on the phone

Photographs showing the child's efforts and accomplishments

- sitting up
- holding a toy
- standing while holding onto a chair
- walking
- doing a puzzle

Photographs showing the child involved in everyday routines and activities

- smiling with a teacher
- patting a bottle
- rubbing the edge of a blanket
- getting dressed to go outdoors
- helping to prepare snack
- listening to a story
- helping to clean up

Written records of the child's interests

- observation notes about the child's favorite toys and activities
- descriptions of drawings and other projects
- notes about the child's responses during a neighborhood walk

Video and audio recordings of a child's communication

- babbling
- pointing or using other gestures
- cooing, singing, telling a story, or playing with others
- engaging in pretend play
- solving a simple problem
- asking a question

A child's portfolio offers a balanced picture of development.

Teachers and families each play a role in selecting items to include in the portfolios. Families might contribute scribbles written at home, descriptions of the child playing with an older sibling, or examples of the child's increasing self-regulation. Teachers might collect items that illustrate the child's creativity, interests, and progress toward developing cognitive, physical, social/emotional, and language skills. The portfolio should present a balanced picture of the child's development by showing the child's experiences in all parts of the program, including routines, transitions, and special activities.

Each portfolio sample provides information about a child's development and learning. You will need a sufficient variety of items to assess the child's growth, but you do not need a large number. To show growth, collect similar samples over a period of time, such as a collection of photographs of a child eating lunch over a period of several months. At the beginning of the year, think of two or three items—such as photographs, drawing samples, and teacher and family observation notes—that would be good for documenting development in particular areas. Set a goal to collect these items 3–5 times throughout the year.

Teachers use portfolios to

- share information with parents ("It's easy to see Jorge's progress when we compare these photos of him. Six weeks ago, he was crawling. Now he is pulling himself up and cruising around our room.")

- review a child's progress, set new goals, and plan strategies for individual children ("This videotape shows Maria pretending to cook dinner. We'll add some new props to help her expand her play.")

- help older toddlers recognize their own growing abilities ("Tell me what you were doing when we took this photograph.")

Portfolios should be organized collections.

Portfolios grow quickly! You will need containers that are large enough to hold the items and a system for organizing them. The containers should fit into the locked storage file or closet where portfolios are kept. Consider using accordion files, magazine files, clean pizza boxes, hanging file folders, pocket folders, X-ray folders, or plastic containers with lids. File the portfolio items by date and group them by categories that make sense for your program. For example, you might group them by time of day, activity, or developmental area.

what's next?

Skill-Building Journal, section **12-6** (*Learning Activity B*) and section **12-1** (*Feedback*).

Learning Activities

LEARNING
ACTIVITY

C. Responding to Each Child's Needs and Interests

In this activity you will learn to

- develop understandings about each child's culture, family, strengths, needs, and interests

- tailor the program to correspond to children's individual characteristics

High-quality infant/toddler programs respond to children's developmental and individual characteristics.

High-quality early childhood programs are based on two understandings: the typical developmental characteristics of young children and the characteristics of individual children. The environment, materials, activities, and interactions between adults and children in such programs are planned according to children's developmental levels and correspond to each child's culture, family, strengths, needs, and interests.

When you know infants' individual eating and sleeping patterns, you can adapt the daily schedule accordingly. When you know individual children's interests and developmental levels, you can offer activities that encourage them to develop new skills. You help children feel competent by including them as partners in daily routines according to their abilities.

To offer an individualized program, you need to know and appreciate what makes each child special. You learn a lot about the infants and toddlers in your care as you live with them each day. For example, you learn that Jon is reserved in new situations, Peter is starting to pull himself up to standing, and Jessica loves cats.

Systematically observing children and taking notes can help you confirm and modify your ideas about each child. Through observations, discussions with colleagues, and one-on-one conversations with older infants and toddlers, your understandings about how children are growing and changing stay current. You can also learn about children's culture, language, and development by talking with their families. As discussed in module 11, families know their children best. By developing partnerships with families, you gain their help in getting to know their children.

Your program may be similar to other infant/toddler programs in some ways, because you do many of the same things, such as taking walks around the neighborhood, preparing and eating snacks, and making playdough. Nevertheless, your program is unique because the children are unique. You and your colleagues might respond to their uniqueness in several ways. For example, you might hang pictures of children's families on the wall, organize nap time so a child's special teacher can rock him to sleep, and listen to a compact disc that a child brings in to share.

Teachers do not have to provide separate materials and activities for each child.

Individualizing the program does not mean that you have to provide a separate set of materials or plan one-on-one activities for each child. You can respond to individual children during your regular activities. To plan this, you and your colleagues review observation notes, examine portfolio samples, reflect on recent events and interactions, and analyze the information you have about each child. Think about what individual children enjoy doing, the materials they use, the skills they are developing, and recent events in their lives. Here is an example of how teachers plan an individualized program.

Ms. Kim says she has observed that 20-month-old Marcus wants to help himself and often refuses help even when he needs it. When using a spoon lately, he spills more food than he eats. He refuses help from an adult, but then he gets very frustrated and sometimes throws his spoon across the table. Ms. Richards agrees. She has also noticed that Marcus attempts new, more complex self-help skills and refuses adult help even when it is needed. They discuss his temperament and agree that his reactions are always very strong. Ms. Kim reviews the observation notes she made last month to assess Marcus's physical skills. Her notes show that Marcus was not using the spoon at all last month. When she talks with his mother, she learns that Marcus insists on feeding himself at dinner and often ends up in tears.

The teachers develop the following plan with Marcus's family, to make mealtimes in the program and at home easier for everyone:

Make mealtime as relaxed as possible. Give Marcus finger foods as well as food he can eat with his spoon. Validate Marcus's feelings about how frustrating it is when his food spills. Explain that everyone spills sometimes. Notice when Marcus begins to get frustrated and try to redirect him to the food he can eat with his fingers.

They also suggest activities to give Marcus practice using his small muscles, such as pretending to feed a doll with a spoon.

In this example, the teachers respond to Marcus by incorporating strategies within the existing schedule. They do not try to teach him directly to eat with a spoon. They plan to observe, to help him feed himself successfully, to work with his family, to offer encouragement, and to build on his interests. All of these strategies contribute to meeting his individual needs.

Individualizing will help you to work with children in groups, as well as one-on-one.

Teachers use various teaching strategies to make sure that they are supporting each child, even when not working with him individually. For example, Ms. Thomas has analyzed assessment information about the children for whom she is primary teacher, so she knows their language skills. Janelle babbles; Tony communicates with word-like sounds, single words, and gestures; and Avida uses simple sentences. As she reads *Goodnight Moon*, Ms. Thomas encourages the children to say, "Shhh." She asks Tony to point to the mouse. Then she asks Avida what the mouse is doing. In this way, each child has a chance to participate in the activity at an appropriate level.

Write a summary of development for each child.

To plan for each child, you must evaluate each child's development in relation to your program's goals and objectives for children. Then you consider appropriate ways to help each child reach the next steps of development. You review the children's portfolios, including your observation notes, to make daily decisions about what individual children need. You also develop understandings about individual children when you summarize each child's development in terms of your goals and objectives for children. Many teachers complete these summaries at least three times during the year and use the information for planning.

It is helpful to have a system for documenting information about each child, analyzing the information to understand each child's strengths and needs, and planning for each child and the group. In the following example, Ms. Kim plans for Marcus.

Ms. Kim has information about Marcus's growing ability to use a spoon, as well as his attempts to put his shoes on and to spread apple butter on a cracker. She and Ms. Richards review the information about Marcus and complete a summary of development that shows his progress in these self-help skills. On the basis of the information in his portfolio, they record the objectives he has met on the program's "Developmental Summary Form." The teachers also have information about Marcus's cognitive, language, and social/emotional development, so they use this information to complete his summary. They also have similar information about all of the children in their group, and they use the developmental summaries when they prepare their weekly plans. (See *Learning Activity D.*)

Meeting the Needs of Children With Special Needs

Including children with special needs is critical to their development and learning.

Many programs include infants and toddlers with disabilities. Disabilities might be developmental, such as having mental retardation; physical, such as having a hearing, visual, or neuromuscular disorder; or language-related. As they do for all children, teachers, families, and administrators work together and with specialists, as necessary, to identify and respond to a child's skills, needs, and interests.

Including children with disabilities in an infant/toddler program can be a very rewarding experience for everyone involved. Inclusion provides an environment in which all children can succeed. It helps children with disabilities gain independence and enables all children to develop comfortable, fair relationships with others. It sets the stage for children to resist stereotypes and name calling. Infants and toddlers with special needs thrive in an environment that accepts differences and where adults strive to meet each child's needs.

Consider your own feelings about persons with disabilities.

To offer a responsive program for a child with special needs, teachers may need to consider their own attitudes and behavior toward persons with disabilities.

Here are some typical responses to children with disabilties:

- avoiding or ignoring the child ("May Carrie be in your group? I never know what to say to her.")

- feeling sad ("Every time I see her walker, my eyes start watering.")

- believing that the disability can be fixed without intervention ("He'll outgrow his vision problems.")

- denying that the child has a disability ("Lots of children don't respond when you call their names.")

Although these are commonly held attitudes and behaviors, they do not benefit children. To support each child's development, teachers must take time to identify, acknowledge, and address their personal feelings.

THINK

- What are the benefits of inclusion for the child with special needs and for the whole group?

- What challenges do you face in meeting the needs of a child with a disability?

- How can you get support to overcome these challenges?

Caring for Infants & Toddlers

Get to know the child and learn about the disability.

When an infant or toddler with a disability enrolls in your program, you need to learn about the child and family, as well as the characteristics, effects, and treatment related to the disability. Here are some sources of information:

The child. Make a home visit and invite the child and his family to visit your program. This will help you get to know the child as a person, rather than focusing primarily on the disability.

The child's family. Meet with the parents and other family members to learn about the child's favorite activities, overall level of development, strengths, and interests. Families are the best source of information about the child's experiences and developmental history and about the best ways to support the child's development and learning.

Doctors, specialists, and previous teachers. With the family's written consent, your program may contact professionals who have provided treatment and supported the child's development. The information they provide will contribute to your understanding of the child. If addressing the child's needs is beyond your expertise and experience, seek advice from these specialists. You are not expected to know about every type of disability.

Professional resources. Use books, journals, Web sites, videos, and other resources to research the range of abilities and needs that a child with a particular disability might have. Remember that the range of individual differences among children with the same disability is as great as the range among children in general.

Contact regional and national support groups and clearinghouses. Your director or trainer can help you identify and contact organizations that can provide information to help you work with children in your care who have special needs. You might want to conduct an online search for these organizations, using keywords such as *disability* or *inclusion*, or the name of a specific condition, such as *muscular dystrophy*.

Once you have an understanding of the child and the disability, you can meet with your colleagues, the child's parents, and specialists to plan an individualized program. In addition, you may need to make accommodations, such as rearranging the environment to make the pathways wide enough for a wheelchair, creating books of textured fabrics to provide tactile experiences, or providing books with large illustrations for a child with a visual impairment. (See module 3, *Learning Environment*, for additional suggestions.)

what's next?

Skill-Building Journal, section **12-7** (*Learning Activity C*) and section **12-1** (*Feedback*).

Learning Activities

LEARNING ACTIVITY

D. Working as a Team to Plan and Evaluate the Program

In this activity you will learn to

- develop daily, weekly, and long-range plans

- evaluate the effectiveness of your plans

Planning helps you prepare well for each day.

Planning involves thinking about what you want to do and how you will do it. It starts by considering children's recent activities and experiences and thinking of ways to build on their interests. You organize materials so you can focus on the children without frequent interruptions. As a result, you are better prepared to support children's learning.

Planning provides you with a sense of order that can be difficult to establish in an infant/toddler program setting. Flexible plans allow you to respond to children's interests and needs. For example, when children are fascinated by the parade of ants that they see during their walk to the store, your daily goals serve as the basis on which to decide whether to postpone going to the store in order to watch and talk about the ants.

Everyone who cares for and interacts with children at the program—teachers, families, and volunteers—can be part of the planning team. Many programs regularly include family members and volunteers in planning and implementing the program. The more all team members are involved in planning, the more likely they are to realize the important role they play in carrying out the plans.

Teaching teams often include individuals with particular strengths, interests, and talents. Ideally, each member's skills complement those of others on the team. One teacher might speak several languages; another might be a gifted storyteller. A regular volunteer might be an artist with the ability to share her talent with others. A parent who is a carpenter can repair some of the program's old equipment. Each member contributes something special to the team.

THINK

- Which people in your program can be involved in planning for individual children?

- What special interests and talents does each person bring?

- How can you involve them?

Long-range planning covers a month or more ahead.

Two types of planning are useful for early childhood programs: long-range and weekly. Long-range planning involves thinking a month or more ahead to consider what materials, activities, and experiences you want to offer the children. For example, if your goal is to engage children in meaningful activities, the planning process might include these tasks:

- Invite a colleague from another room or program to observe and to share her insights.

- Determine which of the toys and materials on display are not being used. Rotate unused toys with toys you have been storing.

- Consider ways to change the environment to create interesting, protected places where children can become engaged in activities.

Long-range planning allows you to respond to changing seasons and to arrange special events such as a family picnic or a visit by a special guest. Planning ahead ensures that special events really take place.

Weekly plans are also needed.

Think about weekly planning as planning for moment-to-moment possibilities. You set the stage for meaningful activities and then follow the children's leads, taking time to enjoy experiences together. Observing and responding to what children do each day is one of the joys of working with infants and toddlers. If your plans are flexible and you feel free to revise them as often as you think best, you are more likely to take advantage of opportunities that arise in the course of daily life at the program.

Weekly plans are more detailed than long-range plans, but weekly planning does not need to be a lengthy process. Nevertheless, it can be difficult to find time to plan. In many programs, teachers who work together hold planning meetings before children arrive, after they leave, or during rest time.

Most programs use a standard format to guide planning meetings and to record weekly plans. However, what works well for one team may not work for another. A good place to start is to ask, "What do we need to plan that will help us be better managers?"

The following considerations may be useful as you plan with your colleagues.[50]

Target goals and objectives. Which goals and objectives are you going to focus on this week with the children and their families? For example, if you are focusing on helping children develop gross motor skills, you will want to offer opportunities and choices for active physical play both indoors and outdoors.

Changes to the environment. Do you need to make any changes? Do you need duplicate materials for toddlers who cannot yet share? Can you minimize organizational problems by creating more storage space? Do you need to rearrange and reorganize existing space or improve your labeling system?

Special activities. What new opportunities can you offer for children to explore and make discoveries? Remember to give children opportunities to choose between activities and to choose materials, equipment, and people with whom to play.

Changes to daily routines. How well are daily routines and transitions supporting the children's development? Are there other ways to include children in daily routines? Are children getting cranky because there is too much waiting time between activities?

Family involvement. Do families feel comfortable in your program? What else can you do to strengthen your partnerships with families to support their children's development and learning?

List of "to do" tasks. What will you need to do in order to carry out your plans? For example, if your plan includes creating a display of dress-up props, someone needs to ask families to contribute to a collection of old hats, scarves, and handbags. Agree upon responsibilities and post a reminder.

Weekly Planning Form

Week of: _10/18_

Changes to the Environment

Create a reading nook with cushions and a hanging book pocket so child can sit and look at books.

Add more blocks so several children can build together.

Add doctor props to pretend play area because Eddie has a series of doctor appointments coming up.

Rotate toys.

Special Activities I Plan to Offer This Week

	Monday	Tuesday	Wednesday	Thursday	Friday
Indoor Opportunities to Explore and Discover	*Serve apple butter— children spread it on crackers*	*Make playdough*	*Playdough*	*Finger painting* *Sing songs about feelings*	*Finger painting*
Outdoor Opportunities to Explore and Discover	*Paint with water*	*Blow bubbles*	*Blow bubbles*		*Walk to library for story time*

Changes to Daily Routines

Make a point of inviting children to help me prepare snacks and lunches and to set the table. See if this helps lunch time go more smoothly.

Family Involvement

Talk with the Curtises, who are concerned about Valisha's hitting other children. Ask them what they do to help Jonisha when her sister hurts her. Share the new article about positive guidance with all families.

To Do

Display the new set of blocks. Copy article on guiding behavior for all families.

Be prepared to adapt your plans as necessary.

When you work with infants and toddlers, you must always expect the unexpected. Each child has a personal style. As you are preparing an infant's lunch, his cries might tell you not to feed him yet because he is too tired or needs a diaper change. Toddlers also have an amazing ability to overturn the best-laid plans. Turn around one moment after fastening the last toddler's overalls in preparation to go outdoors, and you may find her standing in her diaper with her overalls around her ankles and a big smile on her face.

Responding to children often means adapting your plans in some way. Here are some helpful steps:

Each morning, review your plans for the day. Having an idea of how the parts of the day fit together will give you a framework from which to rearrange them.

Assess the realities of the day. Will an infant need some extra time and attention because she is teething? Has a colleague called in sick? Will you need to provide extra support to the children because the substitute teacher is not familiar to them? Did a family bring in fresh apples that tempt you to change your plans for snack? Does finger painting suddenly seem too complicated because you have a headache?

Remember, being responsive is more important than sticking to your plan. Teachers often feel pressured to carry out every detail of their plans. Always keep in mind that your positive interactions with children are more important than particular activities. Playdough or an obstacle course can wait for your attention until another day, but infants and toddlers cannot.

Evaluation is the next step of the planning process.

The word *evaluation* might seem intimidating at first, but on a basic level the process simply means asking, "How are things going?" You probably already evaluate your program as you converse with colleagues and families every day. Talking with each other provides much of the information you need to assess and change your plans.

Your observations over time are also helpful if you take time to think about them. For example, you may discover that lunch became a struggle when it was scheduled half an hour later. The older infants and toddlers were not only hungry but were getting tired after a busy morning. Taking time to think about how things are going is a worthwhile investment in improving the program for everyone.

Modify your plans on the basis of what you learn.

In many early childhood programs, teachers meet at the end of each day to discuss what happened. Questions such as these can guide your discussions:

- What activities interested the children?

- Which materials did the children use?

- What skills did the children demonstrate?

- What worked well? What problems came up?

- How did we welcome and provide meaningful roles for family members who visited the program?

- What changes are needed in

    - the indoor and outdoor environments?

    - materials and equipment?

    - our interactions with children?

    - our interactions with families?

    - small-group activities?

Daily evaluation meetings tend to be short but very effective, because the answers to these questions are fresh in teachers' minds. Planning is an ongoing process. When necessary, the team changes the weekly plan to solve a problem or respond to children's interests. Here are some examples:

Making English muffins pizzas was a popular activity today. The three toddlers who helped felt proud, and we all enjoyed the food. Ms. Thomas and Mr. Lopez will change their plans and offer another food preparation activity later this week.

Linda had a particularly stressful day. She clung to her mother and cried when her mother left this morning. That hasn't happened in several months. Ms. Kim will help her say goodbye tomorrow morning and spend more time with her individually, to see whether she can find an explanation for Linda's distress and help her become engaged in activities.

Several children had trouble using the new climber. Ms. Kim and Ms. Richards will observe its use over the next few days to see if the climber continues to be a source of frustration.

Teachers can use a similar evaluation process when meeting to develop weekly and long-range plans. Analysis of observation notes collected over time is useful for planning. For example, when some toys are not used for several weeks, you can spark children's interest by putting some toys away, adding new ones, or even changing the location of some items. Observation also lets teachers know when a plan is not working. For example, if lunchtime is chaotic, you might decide to serve the food before the children come to the table.

what's next?

Skill-Building Journal, section **12-8** (*Learning Activity D*), section **12-1** (*Feedback*), and section **12-9** (*Reflecting on Your Learning*).

13 Professionalism

Overview

Continually Improving Your Performance

Continuing to Gain New Knowledge and Skills

Behaving Ethically in Your Work

Viewing Yourself as a Professional

Learning Activities

A. Meeting Professional Standards

B. Continuing to Gain New Knowledge and Skills

C. Behaving Ethically in Your Work

D. Talking About the Value of Your Work

13. Professionalism

Overview

You are a member of an important profession.

Teachers are professionals who use specialized knowledge and skills. You work with infants and toddlers when they are developing more quickly than they will at any other period in their lives. You help shape children's first experiences and their understandings about themselves, other people, and the world. Teachers build responsive relationships and provide high-quality programs in which children's individual needs are recognized and met. By helping children gain a positive sense of self during these early years, teachers help assure children's later success in school and life.

Your professional skills also support families. By being aware of the unique and important roles you each play in children's lives and by building partnerships to support children's development and learning, you and families help each other meet your responsibilities.

The early childhood profession sets standards for quality.

Every profession sets standards that guide the practice of its members. There are different types of standards in the early childhood profession. Some address program health, safety, and supervisory requirements and practices. As a professional, you should know what standards apply to you so you can be confident that you are working to achieve them.

Professionals are obligated to act responsibly and ethically at all times. This can be challenging because it is not always easy to know the best decision or course of action in a given situation. A code of ethical conduct guides early childhood professionals in behaving responsibly and resolving difficult problems.

Professionals continue their learning.

In the early childhood field, professionalism means planning and implementing a program that is based on knowledge of children's individual and developmental characteristics and needs. It also means taking advantage of opportunities to learn more about children and to develop and continually improve your skills.

You can maintain a commitment to professionalism by

- continually improving your performance

- continuing to gain new knowledge and skills

- behaving ethically in your work

Continually Improving Your Performance

1. **Try new approaches when current practices are not working with individual children or the group.** "In the last two weeks, I have had to tell children many times not to climb on the sofa. I am going to rearrange our room and put out the climber that is in storage."

2. **Ask for feedback from families, colleagues, and supervisors.** "Mrs. Kendall, what else can I do to help Jason get used to being away from his mom and dad?"

3. **Use professional standards as guidelines for providing high-quality care.** Review the standards that apply to your program, such as NAEYC Center Accreditation Criteria, military child care program standards, your state and local licensing standards, or Head Start Program Performance Standards.

4. **Stay healthy by taking care of your physical, emotional, social, and intellectual needs.** "I am making it a point to get enough sleep at night. Now I have plenty of energy in the afternoon."

Ms. Gonzalez Decides to Organize Her Room

As you read the following story, pay attention to what Ms. Gonzalez does to improve her organizational skills.

Ms. Gonzalez: This morning started smoothly, but everything was crazy by late afternoon.

Ms. Gonzalez: Where are Peter's hat and sweater?

Ms. Gonzalez: I have to organize this room.

Ms. Gonzalez: You seem to be very organized. Will you give me some tips?

Continuing to Gain New Knowledge and Skills

5. **Participate in professional organizations and staff development opportunities.** "I'd like to attend the state conference next month, to learn more about the nutritional needs of infants and toddlers."

6. **Keep up-to-date about ways to build positive relationships with infants and toddlers.** "I just read an interesting article on the ZERO TO THREE Web site that gave me some ideas for responding to children according to their temperaments."

7. **Observe and talk with colleagues to increase your knowledge and learn new teaching strategies.** "How do you keep children safe while also encouraging their explorations and independence?"

8. **Work with families, as partners, to understand and respond to children's skills, interests, and needs.** "What does Leroy like to do on the weekend?"

9. **Work toward a credential and/or teaching degree.** Complete the process of obtaining a CDA credential; enroll in college classes and complete the requirements for certification.

Ms. Bates Conducts Online Research

As you read the following story, pay attention to what Ms. Bates learns that can help her support children's development. Also think about how the teachers help each other continue to learn.

Ms. Collier: This site has directions for making safe toys for infants and toddlers.

Ms. Bates: Thank you for helping me find this. I see several toys that we can make.

Ms. Bates: Here are some sock puppets the young infants would enjoy.

Ms. Gonzalez: Those look great. How did you find these instructions?

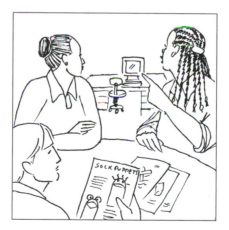

Ms. Bates: Ms. Collier showed me an infant/toddler Web site. It has information on all areas of development.

Ms. Gonzalez: I'm going to look at it during my break. Maybe I can find some new ideas for finger foods.

Behaving Ethically in Your Work

10. **Maintain confidentiality about children and families.** "Children's files are confidential, Mrs. Chin. Only you, her father, and the center staff may read Pam's files."

11. **Treat each child as an individual and show no bias because of culture, language, background, abilities, or gender.** Find out about each child's special interests and family practices and traditions. Plan your program according to what you learn.

12. **Support the use of developmentally appropriate practices and speak out against inappropriate practices.** "We never shame a toddler for having a toilet accident."

13. **Discuss concerns with supervisors and administrators so they can be addressed.** "Billy has a terrible diaper rash that isn't getting better. I've talked with his family about taking him to the doctor, but they don't seem concerned. What else should I do?"

14. **Support colleagues when they need assistance.** "When I first started working with infants and toddlers, I didn't realize that a well-planned room arrangement prevents many problems. If you want to come over, I'll be happy to show you our space and share some ideas."

Responding to Ricky in a Positive Way

As you read the following story, pay attention to what Ms. Bates says and does to uphold professional ethics.

Ms. Bates: I know you like to climb and jump, Ricky, but it's not safe to climb on the shelf.

Ms. Bates: You may jump near the cushions, where it's safe.

Gina's mother: He sure is a wild one!

Ms. Bates: He is learning about his body in space. Now, let me tell you about Gina's day.

what's next?

Skill-Building Journal, section **13-2** (*Overview*), section **13-10** (*Answer Sheet*), and section **13-1** (*Feedback*).

Viewing Yourself as a Professional

Teachers of infants and toddlers have specialized skills and knowledge.

Do you consider yourself to be a professional? Some people think that teachers who work with infants and toddlers are not as professional as those who teach older children. When they see a teacher playing with an infant on the floor, talking with toddlers about a worm, or taking on a pretend role in the dramatic play area, they think that anyone can teach young children. They do not realize that early childhood teachers have specialized knowledge and skills.

Early childhood teachers understand how young children develop and learn and how to meet diverse needs. You work hard to develop this knowledge and specialized skills. When you appreciate your own growing knowledge and skills, you gain confidence in yourself as a professional. You understand not only how to teach, but why you use particular practices. For example, you can explain to family members and visitors that the infant you are singing to is learning to trust others. You can also explain that the infant's enjoyment of the sounds and rhythms of language helps him eventually learn to speak, read, and write. When you make playdough with a group of toddlers, you are helping them learn to take turns, measure ingredients, and notice how things change when they are mixed. People will recognize that you are a professional when you are confident about what you are doing and why.

Each person has special interests and abilities.

Every teacher, like each child, is a unique person. You bring your personality, temperament, interests, and special talents to your work with infants and toddlers.

Do you tend to be outgoing and energetic, or quiet and reserved? Would people describe you as fun-loving or serious? Do you like being in a big crowd or prefer to be with one friend? When you respond to a new challenge, do you like to jump right in or analyze and think about it first? Gaining self-awareness will help you recognize how you respond to the children you teach and their families. Think about the children you relate to most easily and those with whom it is more difficult to form a relationship. How do your own personality and style of relating affect your relationships with children and families?

You also bring special interests and talents to your work with young children. Are you musical?...artistic? Do you love animals? ...like to cook?...enjoy gardening? What are your special abilities and interests? What do you most enjoy? Think about how you can share your passions and talents with young children.

what's next?

Skill-Building Journal, section **13-3** (*Viewing Yourself as a Professional*), section **13-1** (*Feedback*), and section **13-4** (*Pre-Training Assessment*).

Learning Activities

LEARNING ACTIVITY

A. Meeting Professional Standards

In this activity you will learn to

- use the profession's standards to recognize your skills and abilities

- identify the standards that apply to your program

Striving to meet professional standards and taking care of yourself help you provide high-quality care.

Like many other professions, the early childhood field sets standards for practice that all good programs share. These standards are not meant to restrict you but rather to serve as guides to providing high-quality care.

At the same time, your program is unique. This is in large part because of your personality, knowledge, skills, and interests and because of the relationships you build with children and families. Taking care of yourself will help you meet the challenge.

Standards define high-quality care.

A number of professional associations and groups concerned with the quality of infant/toddler group care have established standards. These standards recommend a child-centered approach that allows children to learn through exploration and play. They agree on the importance of basing program practices on what we know about child development and partnerships with families.

Participating in this training program is helping you to meet standards for teachers.

As you participate in this training program, you are becoming familiar with a set of standards that apply to teacher competencies: the *Child Development Associate (CDA) Competency Standards*. Early childhood teachers must demonstrate competence in 13 functional areas. The 13 modules in *Caring for Infants & Toddlers* address these areas. The Council for Professional Recognition is the organization that operates a national credentialing program for early childhood educators. Teachers who demonstrate that they are competent in each of the 13 areas are awarded a CDA credential. This credential is nationally recognized in the field of early childhood education.

Three resources for obtaining copies of standards are listed. Your supervisor may have copies of these documents. If not, you can order your own from the organizations or find them on the organizations' Web sites.

National Association for the Education of Young Children (NAEYC)
1509 16th Street, NW
Washington, DC 20036-1426
800-424-2460 or 202-232-8777
www.naeyc.org

After studying and discussing issues of importance to the early childhood community, the NAEYC leadership writes position statements, by themselves and, when appropriate, in collaboration with other organizations. These statements describe ways to improve program practices with children, public policies affecting early childhood programs, and early childhood professional development and professionalism. You can read a description of each statement and download free copies from the NAEYC Web site (http://www.naeyc.org). Early childhood professionals find the following statements especially valuable

- *Code of Ethical Conduct and Statement of Commitment* (Revised ed.) (1997, 2005)

- *Prevention of Child Abuse in Early Childhood Programs and the Responsibilities of Early Childhood Professionals to Prevent Child Abuse* (1996)

- *Inclusion* (by the Division of Early Childhood of the Council for Exceptional Children and endorsed by the NAEYC) (1993)

- *Violence in the Lives of Children* (1993)

- *Developmentally Appropriate Practice in Early Childhood Programs Serving Children From Birth Through Age 8* (Revised ed.) (1997)

ZERO TO THREE: National Center for Infants, Toddlers, and Families
2000 M Street, NW
Suite 200
Washington, DC 20036
202-638-1144
www.zerotothree.org

ZERO TO THREE is the only national organization dedicated solely to promoting the social, emotional, cognitive, and physical development of children from birth through age three, and to supporting their families and teachers. ZERO TO THREE has developed *Caring for Infants & Toddlers in Groups: Developmentally Appropriate Practice*, to help teachers, families, and others concerned with providing quality child care to our youngest children.[51] It discusses the knowledge and skills that are needed to offer a nurturing group care environment that supports healthy development.

Council for Professional Recognition
2460 16th Street, NW
Washington, DC 20009
202-265-9090 or 800-424-4310
www.cdacouncil.org

The Council operates a national credentialing program for early childhood educators. The Council awards the Infant/Toddler Child Development Associate (CDA) credential, which is the nationally recognized credential for early childhood professionals.

The CDA *Competency Standards* define 13 functional areas in which infant/toddler teachers must demonstrate competence. The competency standards also serve as guidelines for teachers who are not seeking a CDA credential but who want to improve their child care skills. The functional areas serve as the framework for the 13 modules in *Caring for Infants & Toddlers*. The Council publishes guides to the assessment system and competency standards, as well as a newsletter.

what's next?

Skill-Building Journal, section **13-5** (*Learning Activity A*) and section **13-1** (*Feedback*).

B. Continuing to Gain New Knowledge and Skills

In this activity you will learn to

- think about your growth as an early childhood professional

- make short- and long-range professional development plans

Teachers have four stages of professional development.

There is always something new to learn in the teaching profession. Lilian Katz, an early childhood educator, has studied how teachers grow professionally. Her research suggests that teachers pass through four different stages of professional development: survival, consolidation, renewal, and maturity.[52]

Survival

Teachers at the Survival Stage are new to the field and are often insecure. They devote most of their attention to learning the program's daily schedule and activities and performing assigned tasks. This stage is called survival, in part because of the concentrated focus on immediate needs rather than long-range planning. If you are at this stage, you will benefit from a comprehensive orientation to the job and from shadowing or observing an experienced teacher. You may want to join a professional association such as the National Association for the Education of Young Children (NAEYC). Continued training and experience in building relationships with infants and toddlers will help you move to the next stage, Consolidation.

Consolidation

When teachers reach this stage, they are more confident and begin to look beyond simply meeting the basic needs of infants and toddlers. They seek new ways to accomplish everyday tasks, such as helping a group of toddlers get dressed to go outdoors, and to handle problems, such as comforting a baby who cannot stop crying. If you are at this stage, you will find it useful to exchange ideas with other teachers and to become actively involved in a professional association. Informal conversations, group meetings, training sessions, and open discussions will help you grow and move to the next stage, Renewal.

Renewal

During the third or fourth year on the job, teachers may begin to be bored with the daily routine. Their interest often drops, and enthusiasm falls. Teachers in this stage need renewal through new challenges that rekindle their excitement and commitment to teaching infants and toddlers. If you are at this stage, try to attend conferences and workshops and assume a leadership role in a professional organization. Pursue a special interest, such as helping children and families cope with separation or introducing the natural world to infants and toddlers. These professional activities will provide needed stimulation and help you move to the fourth stage, Maturity.

Maturity

Teachers at this stage are committed professionals. They understand the need to seek new ideas and skills and continue to grow professionally. If you are a mature teacher, you can share your knowledge and experience by becoming a mentor for new teachers. You might also gain the skills needed to assume new challenges as a supervisor, trainer, or center administrator.

- What stage of professional development best describes you? Why?

- How can you find the support you need to continue to learn and grow?

Continual learning has many benefits.

No matter how long you have been a teacher or how much you already know, you can continue to learn. It is important to continue to gain the skills and knowledge needed to support the development and learning of infants and toddlers. Continual learning strengthens your professional development:

- A commitment to continue learning can lead to improved performance. Learning may lead to greater confidence, more responsibility, a promotion, and perhaps a salary increase.

- Continual learning helps you recognize your strengths as a teacher. Learning tends to affirm the good work you have been doing and the understandings you have already developed. You might also rediscover ideas to support children's development and learning that you have not thought about in a while.

Even more importantly, your continual learning benefits children:

Use the resources of professional organizations.

- Each article and book you read, every discussion you have, and every conference you attend can give you new insights to help you support children's learning. Because you care about infants and toddlers, you are always alert for new and helpful information relating to their development. For example, when a child with a disability joins your group, you can learn how to adapt the environment so the child can take part in daily activities with the other children.

- Continual learning helps you evaluate and strengthen your practices. You will have new interests to bring to the program and to share with infants and toddlers. When you enjoy learning, you help children enjoy learning, too.

- There is always new information to be learned. All professionals need to keep up with the latest developments in their field. Learning from researchers and from the experiences of other teachers helps you develop more effective strategies for supporting infants and toddlers.

How can you continue growing and learning? In addition to participating in this training program, there are many other ways to continue learning. Here are some suggestions.

Professional organizations help you keep up-to-date about the latest information and current issues related to caring for infants and toddlers. Some have local affiliates that meet regularly. These organizations offer Web sites, online courses, newsletters, books, videotapes, brochures, and other publications with useful information and helpful tips. Attending professional conferences is a way to meet other teachers with similar interests and concerns. The following chart identifies some early childhood professional organizations and the services they offer.

Early Childhood Professional Organizations

Organizations	Services
Association for Childhood Education International (ACEI) 17904 Georgia Avenue, Suite 215 Olney, MD 20832 301-570-2001 800-423-3563 www.acei.org	Provides resources and support for meeting the developmental needs of children from birth through early adolescence worldwide Journals: *Childhood Education* and *Journal for Research in Childhood Education* Annual conference National and international affiliate chapters
Center for the Child Care Workforce, American Federation of Teachers Educational Foundation 555 New Jersey Avenue, NW Washington, DC 20001 202-662-8005 www.ccw.org	Works to improve wages, status, and working conditions of early childhood professionals An e-mail bulletin and other resource materials are available on the Web site
Council for Professional Recognition 2460 16th Street, NW Washington, DC 20009 202-265-9090 800-424-4310 www.cdacouncil.org	Operates a national credentialing program for early childhood educators Publishes guides to the assessment system and competency standards, as well as other professional development resources and a bi-monthly newsletter
National Association for Bilingual Education 1030 15th Street, NW, Suite 470 Washington, DC 20005 202-898-1829 www.nabe.org	Advocates for language-minority students with a variety of programs to support English language learners Publishes *NABE News, Bilingual Research Journal,* and *NABE Journal of Research and Practice* (NJRP)
National Association of Child Care Resource and Referral Agencies (NACCRRA) 1319 F Street, NW, Suite 500 Washington, DC 20004-1106 202-393-5501 www.naccrra.org	A national network of more than 850 child care resource and referral agencies that help families, child care providers, and communities find, provide, and plan affordable, quality child care Provides training and resources, and promotes national policies and partnerships Annual policy meetings and events in Washington, DC
National Association for the Education of Young Children (NAEYC) 1509 16th Street, NW Washington, DC 20036-1426 800-424-2460 202-232-8777 www.naeyc.org	Provides print, video, and Web resources and support on the care and education of children from birth through age eight Journals: *Early Childhood Research Quarterly, Young Children,* and an online resource, "Beyond the Journal" Holds a national conference and a smaller professional development institute each year Has 100,000 members and 360 affiliates at local, state, and regional levels

Organizations	Services
National Black Child Development Institute (NBCDI) 1101 15th Street, NW, Suite 900 Washington, DC 20005 202-833-2220 800-556-2234 www.nbcdi.org	Advocates on behalf of the growth and development of African-American children Focuses on critical issues in early childhood education, child welfare, and health care Quarterly newsletter includes two issues of *Black Child Advocate* and two issues of *Child Health Talk* Annual conference Affiliate chapters throughout the country
National Child Care Association 1016 Rosser Street Conyers, GA 30012 800-543-7161 www.nccanet.org	A professional trade association focused on the needs of licensed, private child care and education programs Quarterly newsletter Annual conference with workshops focused on management issues Credentials for teachers and for administrators
National Clearinghouse for Military Child Development Programs Military Family Resource Center CS4, Suite 302, Room 309 1745 Jefferson Davis Highway Arlington, VA 22202-3424 703-602-4964 www.mfrc-dodqol.org/mcy	Web site contains an overview of the military child development system and information about training materials and opportunities
National Head Start Association (NHSA) 1651 Prince Street Alexandria, VA 22314 703-739-0875 www.nhsa.org	Represents Head Start children, families, staff, and programs nationwide Agency and individual memberships Annual training conferences Quarterly journal: *Children and Families*
Southern Early Childhood Association (SECA) P. O. Box 55930 Little Rock, AR 72215-5930 800-305-7322 www.southernearlychildhood.org	Provides a voice on local, state, and federal issues affecting young children Quarterly journal: *Dimensions of Early Childhood* and other resource materials Holds annual conference
ZERO TO THREE: National Center for Infants, Toddlers, and Families 2000 M Street, NW Suite 200 Washington, DC 20036 202-638-1144 www.zerotothree.org	Provides print, video, and Web resources on the care of children birth through age three, and supports their families and teachers Bi-monthly journal: *Zero to Three* Holds annual National Training Institute

Early childhood professionals can find useful information by using the Internet.

The Internet offers a world of information that is just a mouse click away. As you can see from the chart, most national and regional early childhood organizations have Web sites, as do publishers of resources for early childhood professionals. Educational television shows and museums have companion Web sites. Government agencies, such as the Department of Education and the Department of Health and Human Services, share free publications online and offer legislative updates. In addition, government-sponsored clearinghouses and projects, such as the National Child Care Information Center (www.nccic.org), offer research reports and practical strategies online. Every site has links to other sites, making online sources of information easy to find.

If you are a new to the Internet, you will find helpful guidance on learning to use e-mail, surf the Web, and conduct research on the Community Learning Networks Web site, www.cln.org/guidebooks.html. This site is for K–12 teachers, but the "Beginners Central" provides an excellent orientation on how to use the Internet.

A comprehensive set of links to more than 80 important Web sites for early childhood professionals can be accessed from the Teaching Strategies Web site (http://www.teachingstrategies.com/pages/page.cfm?pageid=116).

Study groups and professional conferences are excellent ways to continue learning.

Study groups are an excellent way to continue learning. They sometimes explore a particular topic, such as ongoing assessment or early literacy. Members agree to read relevant materials (e.g., an article or a chapter of a book) in preparation for each meeting. A study group might form to address an aspect of development, such as supporting children's communication. In a study group, one person should take the lead in facilitating the meetings, and another member should keep notes so that everyone stays informed about the discussions and decisions.

Participants are more likely to attend each meeting when the time and location for the study group sessions are convenient. Consider setting up a study group at your center or in the neighborhood. Talk with the director about allocating time during the workday for these meetings if possible.

Attend professional conferences. The early childhood field offers a wide range of national and local conferences, as indicated in the chart of professional organizations. At these conferences, you often have an opportunity to hear keynote speeches by well-known educators. You can select from a great variety of workshops on a wide range of topics; visit an exhibit hall to browse and shop; and meet with colleagues from the state, the country, and the world.

Attend workshops, take courses, observe colleagues, and share your knowledge.

Participate in training or degree programs. Completing this training program will be a great achievement, but it is not the end. You can continue learning by attending workshops and courses in your area. Local departments of social services, public school adult education programs, the Office of Child Development Services, a county extension office, and other government agencies in your area may offer workshops. In many areas, community colleges offer courses leading to state certification; a CDA credential; and associate, bachelor, and graduate degrees. Individual courses at colleges and universities may also be an option for you. Some courses and seminars are offered by distance learning, through satellite hook-up or Internet-based learning modules.

Observe other teachers in action. You can learn a lot by observing colleagues, a supervisor, or a teacher in another program. Because each teacher has a personal style, you can discover new ideas about, for example, introducing finger foods, guiding toddlers' behavior, and keeping children safe outdoors. Seeing how someone else handles situations similar to yours can offer new insights and expand your knowledge about successful strategies.

Teach something you have learned to someone else. After attending a conference or workshop, you can use your knowledge and skills to lead a training session for your colleagues. This reinforces your learning and contributes to program improvement.

Keep a journal. Like all teachers' days, yours are busy. Nevertheless, everyone needs to take time to reflect on her practices. You can only evaluate your program by taking time each day to think about what you do. Then, if necessary, you can change the environment, interactions, or routines to support even better the infants and toddlers in your care. A journal provides a written record of what you do and what happens as a result of your efforts. You can note questions and challenges that you want to think more about and discuss with colleagues. Recording your successes can help you recognize your growing skills and competence.

Colleagues can help you identify the skills you want to strengthen.

Ask a colleague to help you assess your performance. If you are concerned about your skills in a certain area, ask a colleague to conduct an objective, focused observation. Afterwards, meet to discuss your colleague's notes and exchange thoughts about what was going on. If you identify a problem together, plan ways to improve your skills. Alternatively, you can assess your skills by setting up a video camera in the classroom to record what you say and do and how the children respond. Then view and discuss the tape with a colleague. Identify the skills you want to improve and plan ways to meet your training needs.

Develop plans for continued learning. In addition to identifying resources to help you learn more about young children, it helps to have a plan for using those resources. If you identify your goals and know how you are going to accomplish them, it is easier to take each step and to recognize your achievement when you reach a goal. As you take each step and check it off on your plan, you will know that you are progressing toward your goals.

- What opportunities to continue learning are available to you?

- How can you take advantage of these opportunities?

what's next?

Skill-Building Journal, section **13-6** (*Learning Activity B*) and section **13-1** (*Feedback*).

LEARNING ACTIVITY

Learning Activities

C. Behaving Ethically in Your Work

In this activity you will learn to

- recognize professional and unprofessional behavior

- follow the ethical standards of the early childhood profession

Some decisions require careful thought.

You probably make hundreds of decisions each day about your work with children, families, and colleagues. Some decisions require a lot of thought, such as how to set up your environment, how best to respond to individual children, and how to support children's interest in particular activities. You make other decisions at the moment, such as whether to intervene or stand back, or how to respond to a family's request. Some decisions involve careful thought because they concern core values and beliefs, such as how to respond to a parent who wants you to toilet train a one-year-old, or what to say to a colleague who is sometimes rude in her communication with families.

The Early Childhood Code of Ethical Conduct

The early childhood field, like many professions, has developed a code of ethics to provide educators with a guide for responsible behavior. The code also provides a method for analyzing and resolving ethical dilemmas, situations where just one right answer is difficult to identify. The NAEYC *Code of Ethical Conduct* defines professional responsibilities in four areas.[53]

Ethical responsibilities to children: These include providing safe, healthy, nurturing, and responsive settings for children; supporting children's development with respect for individual differences; helping children learn to live and work cooperatively; and promoting children's health, self-awareness, competence, self-worth, and resiliency.

Ethical responsibilities to families: This section points out that the teacher's role is to work together with families in ways that enhance the child's development.

Ethical responsibilities to colleagues: This section discusses your role in establishing and maintaining settings and relationships that promote the professional work of co-workers and your employer.

Ethical responsibilities to the community and society: This section explains the importance of cooperating with agencies and professions that share responsibility for children, developing needed programs that are not currently available and serving as a voice for children everywhere.

The following chart identifies some ethical standards for teaching young children and provides examples of professional and unprofessional behaviors related to each standard.

Ethical Professional Behavior

Ethics of Teaching	Professional Behavior	Unprofessional Behavior
Treat each child as an individual; avoid comparisons; and show no bias because of culture, language, background, abilities, or gender.	Comforting a child who is hurt or upset. Not comparing one child to another. Including materials and activities that relate to the cultures and backgrounds of all children. "I know that you're feeling sad. Let's sit together in the rocking chair."	Ignoring or teasing children if they cry. Comparing one child to another. Failing to support the cultures and languages of all children. "Why can't you play nicely, the way Timothy does?"
Be honest, reliable, and regular in attendance.	Arriving at work on time every day, ready to perform your assigned duties. "I'll be ready to greet the children after I restock the diaper area."	Talking with colleagues rather than paying attention to children. Calling in sick unnecessarily, arriving late, or not carrying out assigned duties. "You'll have to watch these kids yourself. I have to call my girlfriend to make plans for tonight."
Treat families with respect, even in difficult situations.	Talking privately to a parent who about problems and possible solutions. "Ms. Lowell, our center closes at 6:30. If you can't get here by that time, could someone else pick up Jan?"	Getting angry with a parent who is late. "This is the third time you've been late this week. I need to go home, too, you know!"
Maintain confidentiality about children and their families.	Sharing private information only with persons who have a professional need to know it. "Thank you for telling us why Donna needs extra support right now. We will keep the information confidential."	Talking with other families or acquaintances about particular children or families. "Poor Donna has been so sad since her parents separated. Do you see her in the neighborhood?"
Make sure materials, activities, practices, and routines are developmentally appropriate.	Allowing children to take part in routines according to their personal schedules. "Sure, Randy, you may have a snack now. I'll help you get out the crackers and apple butter."	Making all children do the same activities or follow the same strict schedule. "Wake up, Damian. It's time to eat snack. You've slept long enough."
Be a positive model for learning and language. Never use profanity in front of children and families.	Giving children clear, respectful directions. "We're going to start getting ready to go outside now. It's time for everyone to help pick up the toys."	Speaking rudely to children, using harsh words and a negative tone. "How many times do I have to tell you to clean up? Get busy. Now!"

Ethical Professional Behavior, *continued*

Ethics of Teaching	Professional Behavior	Unprofessional Behavior
Wear clothes that are appropriate for your work. Pay attention to dress, grooming, and hygiene.	Wearing comfortable, clean clothes suitable for playing with and caring for children, bending and lifting, sitting on the floor, and moving quickly when necessary. "I'm most comfortable in a wide skirt or slacks so I can sit on the floor with the children."	Wearing clothes that hinder movement and are inappropriate for a child care setting. "Ask Ms. Peterson to help you. I can't walk on the grass in these shoes."
Maintain accurate, timely, and appropriate records.	Completing an injury report immediately after the incident. "Lori's mother read the injury report about Lori's fall before she went home."	Failing to record information about an injury. "No one ever reads these injury reports. I'm not wasting my time by filling one out."
Advocate on behalf of children, families, yourself, and others. Let others know how children benefit from high-quality early childhood programs.	Sending a letter to a legislator. "I encourage the City Council to continue efforts to improve the safety of our town's parks for young children and families."	Assuming that efforts to influence public policy are futile. "The parks are a mess, but we can't do anything about it."

Situations With Ethical Dimensions

Sometimes there is not a simple right decision or action.

Ethical dilemmas occur when there is not a simple answer about the right thing to do. A lot of different issues may be involved, making it difficult to determine how to respond. The following situation was described in the NAEYC journal, *Young Children*.

> *At a staff meeting, Marla reports her concern that a family with a toddler in her classroom has asked that their daughter be served her food after the male children in the class have been served, as a way to support the family's belief that females should 'learn their proper place' in society.*[54]

If you were in a similar situation, how would you respond? You probably have strong views of your own about gender issues. To determine an ethical response, you could turn to the NAEYC *Code of Ethical Conduct* for guidance.[55] A principle under ethical responsibilities to children is applicable:

> *P-1.2: We shall not participate in practices that discriminate against children by denying benefits, giving special advantages, or excluding them from programs or activities on the basis of their race, ethnicity, religion, sex, national origin, language, ability, or the status, behavior, or beliefs of their parents.*

After reading this principle in the *Code of Ethical Conduct*, you reassure yourself that it is not professionally ethical to treat boys and girls differently. It is also against your personal values. This seems like an easy conclusion, until you look further in the *Code*. Under ethical responsibilities to families, you see two statements of ideals that relate to this situation:

> I-2.3: *To respect the dignity of each family and its culture, language, customs, and beliefs.*

> I-2.4: *To respect families' child rearing values and their right to make decisions for their children.*

This guidance reminds you that families are of primary importance in children's lives and in their development. Does this mean that you must agree to the request of these parents? How do you balance conflicting values and beliefs? Is there a way to show respect for the family's wishes while helping them to understand the reason for program practices? This next principle supports that approach:

> P-2.2: *We shall inform families of program philosophy, policies, and personnel qualifications, and explain why we teach as we do—which should be in accordance with our ethical responsibilities to children.*

To respond to the family responsibly, you must find a way to convey your respect for their beliefs and to reassure them that their practices at home will have a profound influence on their child. At the same time, you will have to explain the reasons for the practices you follow at school.

what's next?

Skill-Building Journal, section **13-7** (*Learning Activity C*) and section **13-1** (*Feedback*).

LEARNING ACTIVITY

Learning Activities

D. Talking About the Value of Your Work

In this activity you will learn to

- share what you know about the needs of infants and toddlers and the early childhood profession

- advocate for high-quality programs for young children

Advocacy is working for change.

Advocacy is working for change, and an *advocate* is someone who works for a cause. Early childhood advocates speak out about issues that affect children and families and their own working conditions because they feel very strongly about them. Often decision makers are not aware of the problems and issues related to providing high-quality child development programs for infants and toddlers. Without awareness and understanding, change is not possible.

It may seem like a lot, to expect early childhood professionals also to advocate for children and for their profession by sharing their knowledge. Advocacy, you might think, is for others, for people who like to speak before groups and who know how to influence the thinking of politicians and the public. However, as an early childhood professional, you are in a good position to help others understand important issues and concerns.

You know a lot about the value of high-quality care and education.

Think about how much you know about your profession. Having taught for some time, and by working through this training program, you have gained a good understanding of the importance of your work. You understand children's developmental needs and the kind of safe, nurturing environments that support growth and learning. You see firsthand the positive impact you have on young children and their families. You also know that infants and toddlers who attend high-quality programs are more likely to thrive in preschool and to succeed in school.

You know a lot about the problems that the profession faces.

Advocates are people who see a problem and care deeply about making a difference. You are aware of how many children and families are not able to benefit from living in a nation that is rich in resources. Many children are growing up in poverty and in families that are also experiencing high levels of stress for other reasons. Early childhood teachers work long hours and usually earn low salaries, even though they provide crucial care and education for children. Some teachers leave the profession because they cannot make enough money to support their families.

Policy makers and the public might care about children, but they do not always understand the difference that a high-quality early childhood program can make. As a result, they have not been willing to allocate the funds that programs need desperately. They must hear from knowledgeable early childhood professionals.

Choose an approach that is comfortable for you.

You do not have to give a speech before a group of people to be an effective advocate. There are many ways to share the value of your work and convince others that investing in programs for young children makes sense. You can have informal conversations with people you know. You can write about your experiences and meet with people who make decisions about public policy and funding. Start with an approach that is comfortable for you.[56]

You might want to begin your advocacy work by talking with colleagues and families.

Share ideas about appropriate practice with other teachers and families.

Explain developmentally appropriate practice to administrators, such as why it is not appropriate to require mobile infants and toddlers to sit together for a lengthy large-group activity. Invite them to observe how you greet children individually in the morning and then encourage group conversations during lunch.

Explain to families why children learn best through play. Invite families to join you in observing their child at play and talk together about what he is learning.

Meet someone new who is interested in early childhood education. Ask him to join a professional group such as NAEYC, NBCDI, SECA, or ACEI.

Persuade colleagues that it is important to work toward NAEYC program accreditation. Then work with your colleagues and families to meet the criteria and to complete the accreditation process.

Then you can find ways to communicate with public policy makers.

Ask a friend to accompany you to community meetings where issues of concern to children and families will be discussed. Make a plan; then take a step together on behalf of children and families.

Work and learn with others to develop a position statement on a critical issue. If you do not know much about a topic, conduct research together.

Speak at a school board meeting. Explain how your program complies with professional standards for early childhood education.

Conduct a local or state survey of salaries in early childhood programs. Explain how salaries are related to the continuity of care that is critical to the healthy development of infants and toddlers.

Represent your professional group in a coalition to speak out about the developmental needs of young children. With families' permission, bring photos and stories from your program to illustrate your points.

Contact your state and federal legislators to learn about current issues and point out needs by sharing your experiences. To learn about pending legislation and to send an e-mail message to a legislator, visit the Children's Champions Action Center on the NAEYC Web site (http://capwiz.com/naeyc/home).

Serve on a legislative telephone tree. Every phone call helps.

Write a letter to the editor of a newspaper or magazine to respond to an article or letter. Use examples from your own experience to clarify and support your key points.

what's next?

Skill-Building Journal, section **13-8** (*Learning Activity D*), section **13-1** (*Feedback*), and section **13-9** (*Reflecting on Your Learning*).

Glossary

attachment

the ongoing mutual relationship that develops gradually between infants and their primary caregivers

autonomy

independence; the developmental stage when children want to make choices and try to control their own actions

body fluids

liquid and semi-liquid substances eliminated by or present in the body, such as blood, lymph, feces, urine, mucus, saliva, digestive juices, and vomit

classify

to group objects or events on the basis of a similar characteristic or attribute

cognitive development

the growth of the ability to think and reason

communication

the act of expressing and sharing ideas and feelings with others

competence

the knowledge and skills that enable a person to do something

concept

an idea generalized from particular instances

creativity

the ability to use one's imagination to develop a new idea or product

daily schedule

the plan for the day's activities (The schedule includes the times and the order in which activities will happen.)

diet

the kinds and amounts of food and drink regularly consumed, or a special selection of food and drink chosen to promote health

disinfectant

a cleanser that destroys harmful bacteria and viruses

emergency

an unplanned or unexpected event that calls for immediate action to prevent or redress harm

emerging literacy

the developmental process through which children gain listening, speaking, reading, and writing skills

environment

the complete makeup of the indoor and outdoor areas used by children (The environment includes the space and how it is arranged and furnished, the schedule and routines, materials and equipment, activities, and the children and adults who are present.)

ethics

a set of principles, standards, or guidelines that direct acceptable behavior and help one decide what is right or good rather than what is quickest or easiest

eye-hand coordination

the ability to direct finger, hand, and wrist movements to accomplish a motor task, such as fitting a peg in a hole, piling blocks, or catching a ball

fine motor skills

movements that involve the use of small muscles, for example, using hands and wrists to pick up puzzle pieces or to cut with a pair of scissors

gross motor skills

movements that involve the use of large muscles, the entire body, or large parts of the body, for example, running, hopping, or climbing

hazard

a source of danger; a condition that may cause loss or harm

hygiene

practices that preserve good health and prevent disease

maintaining confidentiality

sharing information only with people who have a need to know it

networking

communicating with people who perform similar tasks, in order to share ideas, information, and experiences

nonverbal communication

the act of conveying feelings or ideas through gestures, eye contact, facial expressions, body position, and other body language

nutrient

a substance in food that nourishes the body

nutritious

nourishing; providing vitamins, minerals, complex carbohydrates, or protein to the body

object permanence

the understanding that objects have substance, maintain their identities even when they change location, and usually continue to exist when they are out of sight

observation

the act of purposefully watching and listening to a person (The information gained from observation is used to plan a program that responds to each child's needs, strengths, interests, and other individual characteristics.)

open-ended materials

materials and toys that can be used in many different ways, such as blocks, dramatic play props, and art supplies

open-ended question

a question that can be answered in a number of different ways

physical development

the gradual gaining of control over large and small muscles

precaution

a step taken to prevent harm and to promote good

predictable books

those with a lot of repetition, refrains, and/or cumulative text where one sentence is added on each page and the text is repeated (Such books allow children to anticipate the text that comes next.)

problem solving

the process of considering various aspects of a situation and identifying one or more approaches that are likely to lead to solutions

professionalism

a commitment to gaining and maintaining knowledge and skills in a particular field and to using that knowledge and those skills to provide services of the highest possible quality

professional behavior

the consistent, complete application of knowledge, skills, and ethics

risk

the possibility of loss or harm

risk management

taking action after considering the likelihood of injury or loss and the possible consequences for individuals or an organization

routines

events that take place every day, such as meals, naps, diapering and toileting, washing hands, and getting dressed

safety

freedom from danger, harm, or loss

self-esteem

a sense of worth; a feeling about one's abilities and accomplishments (Someone who feels connected to others, respected, valued, and able to do things successfully and independently is likely to have positive self-esteem.)

sense of self

understanding who you are; how you identify yourself in terms of culture, environment, physical attributes, preferences, skills, and experiences (Development of a sense of self begins in infancy and evolves throughout life in response to experiences and interactions with others.)

sensory awareness

seeking information through sight, sound, touch, taste, and smell, for example, by smelling spices or turning in the direction of a voice

separation

the process by which a child understands himself as an individual and the process through which a child becomes independent of his parents (In the second sense, children often have strong feelings about separating from their families, and caregivers can help children understand and express those feelings.)

sodium

a mineral normally found in seafood, poultry, and some vegetables; one of the components of table salt

starch

a carbohydrate substance found in such foods as potatoes, rice, corn, wheat, cassava, and many other vegetables

Sudden Infant Death Syndrome (SIDS)

the unexpected death of a seemingly healthy infant during sleep that remains unexplained after a thorough investigation of investigation of possible causes (SIDS is the leading cause of death of children 1–12 months of age.)

temperament

the nature or disposition of a child; the way a child responds to and interacts with people, materials, and situations

trust

assured reliance; the developmental stage at which infants develop deep feelings of comfort and confidence because their basic needs are met promptly, consistently, and lovingly

verbal language

a system of words with rules for their use in speaking, listening, reading, and writing

References

1   National Association for the Education of Young Children. (1997). *Code of ethical conduct and statement of commitment: Guidelines for responsible behavior in early childhood education* (p. 5). Washington, DC: Author.

2   American Academy of Pediatrics & American Public Health Association. (2002). *Caring for our children: National health and safety performance standards: Guidelines for out-of-home child care programs: A joint collaborative project of American Academy of Pediatrics, American Public Health Association, and National Resource Center for Health and Safety in Child Care* (2nd ed.). Elk Grove Village, IL: The Academy.

    Dombro, A. L., Colker, L. J., & Dodge, D. T. (1999). *The Creative Curriculum® for infants & toddlers* (Rev. ed., pp. 122–123, 349–353). Washington, DC: Teaching Strategies, Inc.

    For more information about product safety standards, visit the ASTM Web site, (www.astm.org) or contact ASTM Customer Service (service@astm.org). For Annual Book of ASTM standards volume information, refer to the standard's Document Summary page on the ASTM Web site.

3   Aronson, S. (2004). *Reducing the risk of SIDS in child care.* Elk Grove Village, IL: American Academy of Pediatrics. Retrieved March 7, 2005, from www.healthychildcare.org/pdf/DrSueNAEYC.pdf

    National Institute of Child Health and Human Development, National Institutes of Health, Department of Health and Human Services. (2000). *Babies sleep safest on their backs: African American outreach brochure* (03-5355). Washington, DC: U.S. Government Printing Office.

4   Dombro, A. L., Colker, L. J., & Dodge, D. T. (1999). *The Creative Curriculum® for infants & toddlers* (Rev. ed., pp. 123). Washington, DC: Teaching Strategies, Inc.

5   Aronson, S. (Ed.). (2002). *Healthy young children: A manual for programs* (4th ed., pp. 37–46). Washington, DC: National Association for the Education of Young Children.

6   From *Caring for Our Children: National Health and Safety Performance Standards: Guidelines for Out-of-Home Child Care Programs: A Joint Collaborative Project of American Academy of Pediatrics, American Public Health Association, and National Resource Center for Health and Safety in Child Care* (2nd ed., p. 424), by American Academy of Pediatrics and American Public Health Association, 2002, Elk Grove Village, IL: The Academy. Copyright 2002 by AAP, APA, and NRCHSCC. Reprinted with permission.

7   Ibid. (p. 424).

8   Ibid. (p. 23).

9   Ibid. (p. 226).

10 Shonkoff, J. P., & Phillips, D. A. (Eds.). (2000). *From neurons to neighborhoods: The science of early childhood development.* Washington, DC: National Academy Press.

11 American Academy of Pediatrics & American Public Health Association. (2002). *Caring for our children: National health and safety performance standards: Guidelines for out-of-home child care programs: A joint collaborative project of American Academy of Pediatrics, American Public Health Association, and National Resource Center for Health and Safety in Child Care* (2nd ed.) Elk Grove Village, IL: The Academy.

    Dombro, A. L., Colker, L. J., & Dodge, D. T. (1999). *The Creative Curriculum® for infants & toddlers* (Rev. ed.). Washington, DC: Teaching Strategies, Inc.

12 From *Caring for Our Children: National Health and Safety Performance Standards: Guidelines for Out-of-Home Child Care Programs: A Joint Collaborative Project of American Academy of Pediatrics, American Public Health Association, and National Resource Center for Health and Safety in Child Care* (2nd ed., p. 97), by American Academy of Pediatrics and American Public Health Association, 2002, Elk Grove Village, IL: The Academy. Copyright 2002 by AAP, APA, and NRCHSCC. Adapted with permission.

[13] Ibid. (p. 98).

[14] Rings, bugs and handwashing. (2003, September). *Child Health Alert, 21.*

[15] From *Caring for Our Children: National Health and Safety Performance Standards: Guidelines for Out-of-Home Child Care Programs: A Joint Collaborative Project of American Academy of Pediatrics, American Public Health Association, and National Resource Center for Health and Safety in Child Care* (2nd ed., pp. 94, 99), by American Academy of Pediatrics and American Public Health Association, 2002, Elk Grove Village, IL: The Academy. Copyright 2002 by AAP, APA, and NRCHSCC. Adapted with permission.

[16] Ibid. (pp. 93–94).

[17] Pennsylvania Chapter, American Academy of Pediatrics, Early Childhood Education Linkage System. *ECELS: Preparing for illness.* Retrieved March 8, 2005, from www.paaap.org/mod.php?mod=userpage&menu=800&page_id=11

[18] From *Caring for Our Children: National Health and Safety Performance Standards: Guidelines for Out-of-Home Child Care Programs: A Joint Collaborative Project of American Academy of Pediatrics, American Public Health Association, and National Resource Center for Health and Safety in Child Care* (2nd ed., pp. 124–125), by American Academy of Pediatrics and American Public Health Association, 2002, Elk Grove Village, IL: The Academy. Copyright 2002 by AAP, APA, and NRCHSCC. Adapted with permission.

[19] Occupational Health and Safety Administration Regulations (Standards – 29 CFR, 1910.1030).

[20] National Clearinghouse on Child Abuse and Neglect Information. (2004). *Child abuse and neglect fatalities: Statistics and interventions.* Retrieved March 8, 2005, from http://nccanch.acf.hhs.gov/pubs/factshetts/fatality.cfm

[21] Koralek, D. G., Colker, L. J., & Dodge, D. T. (1995). *The what, why, and how of early childhood education: A guide for on-site supervision* (2nd ed.). Washington, DC: National Association for the Education of Young Children.

Bronson, M. B. (1995). *The right stuff for children birth to 8: Selecting play materials to support development.* Washington, DC: National Association for the Education of Young Children.

[22] Wortman, A. M. (2001, July/August). Preventing work-related musculoskeletal injuries. *Child Care Information Exchange, 140.*

[23] American Academy of Pediatrics. (1998). *Caring for your baby and young child: Birth to age 5: The complete and authoritative guide* (4th ed., pp. 186, 206–207, 243, 273, 312). New York, NY: Bantam Books.

[24] Torelli, L. *Suggestions for set-up of Early Head Start classrooms.* Washington, DC: Early Head Start National Resource Center at ZERO TO THREE. Retrieved August 28, 2004, from http://www.ehsnrc.org/InformationResources/ResourceArticles/ftsetup.htm

[25] American Academy of Pediatrics. (1998). *Caring for your baby and young child: Birth to age 5: The complete and authoritative guide* (4th ed., pp. 186, 206–207, 243, 273, 312). New York, NY: Bantam Books.

[26] Shonkoff, J. P., & Phillips, D. A. (Eds.). (2000). *From neurons to neighborhoods: The science of early childhood development* (p. 149). Washington, DC: National Academy Press.

[27] Hart, B., & Risley, T. R. (1995). *Meaningful differences in the everyday experiences of young American children.* Baltimore: Paul H. Brookes Publishing Co.

[28] American Academy of Pediatrics. (1998). *Caring for your baby and young child: Birth to age 5: The complete and authoritative guide* (4th ed., pp. 186, 206–207, 243, 273, 312). New York, NY: Bantam Books.

American Speech-Language-Hearing Association. (2004). *How does your child hear and talk?* Retrieved September 15, 2004, from http://www.asha.org/public/speech/development/child_hear_talk.htm

[29] Isenberg, J. P., & Jalongo, M. R. (1997). *Creative expression and play in the early childhood curriculum* (2nd ed., p. 7). Upper Saddle River, NJ: Merrill.

Kellogg, R. (1970). *Analyzing children's art.* Palo Alto, CA: National Press Books.

[30] Kohl, M. F. (with Ramsey, R., & Bowman, D.). (2002). *First art: Art experiences for toddlers and twos* (pp. 12–14). Beltsville, MD: Gryphon House Inc.

[31] Erikson, E. H. (1994). *Identity and the life cycle.* New York, NY: W. W. Norton & Company.

[32] Gadzikowski, A. (2003). *It's the little things that count.* Young Children, 58(4), 94.

[33] From "Attachment and Bonding," by Center for Early Education and Development (CEED), University of Minnesota, 1991, *Early Report: Winter 1991, 18*(2), p. 14. Copyright 1991 by Regents of the University of Minnesota. Reprinted with permission.

[34] American Academy of Pediatrics. (1998). *Caring for your baby and young child: Birth to age 5: The complete and authoritative guide* (4th ed., pp. 186, 206–207, 243, 273, 312). New York, NY: Bantam Books.

[35] Shonkoff, J. P., & Phillips, D. A. (Eds.). (2000). *From neurons to neighborhoods: The science of early childhood development* (p. 180). Washington, DC: National Academy Press.

[36] Ramsey, P. G. (1991). *Making friends in school: Promoting peer relationships in early childhood* (p. 31). New York, NY: Teachers College Press.

[37] Shonkoff, J. P., & Phillips, D. A. (Eds.). (2000). *From neurons to neighborhoods: The science of early childhood development* (p. 166). Washington, DC: National Academy Press.

Ramsey, P. G. (1991). *Making friends in school: Promoting peer relationships in early childhood* (p. 31). New York, NY: Teachers College Press.

[38] Shonkoff, J. P., & Phillips, D. A. (Eds.). (2000). *From neurons to neighborhoods: The science of early childhood development* (p. 166). Washington, DC: National Academy Press.

Ramsey, P. G. (1991). *Making friends in school: Promoting peer relationships in early* childhood (p. 33). New York, NY: Teachers College Press.

[39] Ramsey, P. G. (1991). *Making friends in school: Promoting peer relationships in early* childhood (p. 33). New York, NY: Teachers College Press.

[40] Shonkoff, J. P., & Phillips, D. A. (Eds.). (2000). *From neurons to neighborhoods: The science of early childhood development* (p. 166). Washington, DC: National Academy Press.

[41] Ramsey, P. G. (1991). *Making friends in school: Promoting peer relationships in early* childhood (p. 33). New York, NY: Teachers College Press.

Shonkoff, J. P., & Phillips, D. A. (Eds.). (2000). *From neurons to neighborhoods: The science of early childhood development* (p. 166). Washington, DC: National Academy Press.

[42] Shonkoff, J. P., & Phillips, D. A. (Eds.). (2000). *From neurons to neighborhoods: The science of early childhood development* (p. 166). Washington, DC: National Academy Press.

[43] Lerner, C., & Dombro, A. L. (2005) *Bringing up baby: Three steps to making good decisions in your child's first years* (pp. 33–45). Washington, DC: ZERO TO THREE Press.

[44] Project ETC, Greater Minneapolis Day Care Association and Portage Project. (1989). *Special training for special needs: Module 5, Program implementation.* Minneapolis: Portage Project.

[45] Brazelton, T. B. (1992). *Touchpoints: Your child's emotional and behavioral development.* New York, NY: Perseus Books.

[46] Bredekamp, S., & Copple, C. (Eds). (1997). *Developmentally appropriate practice in early childhood programs* (pp. 20–21). Washington, DC: National Association for the Education of Young Children.

[47] Jablon, J. R., Dombro, A. L., & Dichtelmiller, M. L. (1999). *The power of observation.* Washington, DC: Teaching Strategies, Inc.

[48] Koralek, D. (1999). *Classroom strategies to promote children's social and emotional development* (p. 30). Villanova, PA: The Devereux Foundation.

[49] Jablon, J. R., Dombro, A. L., & Dichtelmiller, M. L. (1999). *The power of observation.* Washington, DC: Teaching Strategies, Inc.

[50] Dombro, A. L., Colker, L. J., & Dodge, D. T. (1999). *The Creative Curriculum® for infants & toddlers* (Rev. ed.). Washington, DC: Teaching Strategies, Inc.

[51] Lally, J. R., Griffin, A., Fenichel, E., Segal, M., Szanton, E. S., & Weissbourd, B. (2003). *Caring for infants and toddlers in groups: Developmentally appropropriate practice* (2003 ed.). Washington, DC: ZERO TO THREE Press.

[52] Katz, L. G. (1995). Teachers' developmental stages. In *Talks with teachers of young children* (pp. 7–13). Norwood, NJ: Ablex Publishing Corporation.

[53] National Association for the Education of Young Children. (1997). *Code of ethical conduct and statement of commitment: Guidelines for responsible behavior in early childhood education.* Washington, DC: Author.

[54] Brophy-Herb, H. E., Kostelnick, M. J., & Stein, L. C. (2001). A developmental approach to teaching about ethics using the NAEYC Code of Ethical Conduct. *Young Children, 56*(1), 80–84.

[55] National Association for the Education of Young Children. (1997). *Code of ethical conduct and statement of commitment: Guidelines for responsible behavior in early childhood education.* Washington, DC: Author.

[56] From *Speaking Out: Early Childhood Advocacy* (pp. 14–15), by S. G. Goffin and J. Lombardi, 1988, Washington, DC: National Association for the Education of Young Children. Copyright 1988 by National Association for the Education of Young Children. Adapted with permission.

Resources

It is impossible to list all of the excellent resources for early childhood professionals. Here are some favorites, both old and new. The first category lists items that are relevant to all modules. Additional materials are listed for specific modules. Many could be listed in more than one category. You can purchase items marked with an asterisk (*) and review additional books and videos through the Teaching Strategies Web site (www.teachingstrategies.com).

General

1,2,3…The Toddler Years: A Practical Guide for Parents and Caregivers, 2nd edition, Irene Van der Zande (Santa Cruz, CA: Toddler Center Press, 1993). Written with the staff of the Santa Cruz Toddler Care Center, this easy-to-read, practical book gives a clear picture of the characteristics of toddlers and strategies for living with and caring for them.

Ages and Stages: Developmental Descriptions and Activities, Birth Through Eight Years, Karen Miller (Marshfield, MA: TelShare, 2001). This clearly written guide describes the stages of children's physical, emotional, and intellectual development. Descriptions of children's behavior are accompanied by suggestions of ways teachers can respond to encourage growth and development.

Bringing Up Baby: Three Steps to Making Good Decisions in Your Child's First Years, Claire Lerner and Amy Laura Dombro (Washington, DC: ZERO TO THREE Press, 2005). This book does not tell how to raise a child, but it explains how parents become aware of their traits and their child's traits and how to use that awareness to make decisions that work for both.

Caring for Infants & Toddlers in Groups: Developmentally Appropriate Practice, 2003 edition, J. Ronald Lally, Abbey Griffin, Emily Fenichel, Marilyn Segal, Eleanor Szanton, and Bernice Weissbourd (Washington DC: ZERO TO THREE Press, 2003). This book is a guide to the special knowledge and program design necessary to address the unique developmental characteristics of children during the first three years of life.

The Creative Curriculum® for Infants and Toddlers, Revised edition, Amy Laura Dombro, Laura J. Colker, and Diane Trister Dodge (Washington, DC: Teaching Strategies, Inc., 1999). This is a comprehensive curriculum for planning and implementing a developmentally appropriate program for infants and toddlers.

Developmentally Appropriate Practice in Early Childhood Programs, Revised edition, Sue Bredekamp and Carol Copple, Eds. (Washington, DC: National Association for the Education of Young Children, 1997). This revised edition of an industry standard on appropriate practice devotes a chapter to exploring the needs of and appropriate caregiving responses to children from birth through age three.

Developmental Profiles: Pre-Birth to Eight, 4th edition, Lynn Marotz and K. Eileen Allen (Albany, NY: Delmar Publishers, Inc., 2003). Included in this helpful book are a discussion of child development principles and concepts and chapters devoted to each age group.

Infants, Toddlers, and Caregivers, Janet Gonzalez-Mena and Dianne Widmeyer Eyer (Mountain View, CA: Mayfield Publishing Company, 1997). This book gives a wonderful overview of infant/toddler development and quality infant/toddler child care. It emphasizes respect for the individual child and helps caregivers focus on the relationships they build with children. It addresses multicultural issues facing caregivers, such as bilingual communication and culturally appropriate curriculum.

In Time and With Love, Caring for Infants and Toddlers With Special Needs, Marilyn Segal, Wendy Masi, and Roni Leiderman (NY: Newmarket Press, 2001). This book offers practical suggestions for carrying out routines and fostering the learning of children with special needs. Although it was written for parents, much of the information can be used to adapt child care settings.

Prime Times: A Handbook for Excellence in Infant and Toddler Programs, Jim Greenman and Anne Stonehouse (St. Paul, MN: Redleaf Press, 1996). This book helps readers understand and meet the needs of children under age three, their families, and their caregivers.

Simple Steps: Developmental Activities for Infants, Toddlers, and Two-Year-Olds, Karen Miller (Beltsville, MD: Gryphon House, Inc., 1999). Most of the suggestions in this book do not require special materials or equipment. The activities support development in all domains.

Safe and Healthy

Caring for Our Children: National Health and Safety Performance Standards: Guidelines for Out-of-Home Child Care Programs: A joint collaborative project of American Academy of Pediatrics, American Public Health Association, and National Center for Health and Safety in Child Care, 2nd edition, American Academy of Pediatrics and American Public Health Association (Elk Grove Village, IL: American Academy of Pediatrics, 2002). This volume defines the standards for ensuring children's health and safety in child care programs and explains the rationale for each. It is available on the Web (http://nrc.uchsc.edu) and in paperback.

Healthy Young Children: A Manual for Programs, 4th edition, Susan S. Aronson (with Patricia M. Sphar) (Washington, DC: National Association for the Education of Young Children, 2002). This comprehensive manual includes three separate chapters devoted to maintaining a safe environment, promoting transportation safety, and handling emergencies.

Model Child Care Health Policies, 4th edition, Pennsylvania Chapter, American Academy of Pediatrics, (Washington, DC: National Association for the Education of Young Children, 2002). These model policies provide an excellent starting point for writing health policies.

Learning Environment

Caring Spaces, Learning Places: Children's Environments That Work, Jim Greenman (Redmond, WA: Exchange Press, Inc, 1988). This excellent book shows how to create environments that make use of space creatively, with attention to children's developmental needs. A separate chapter on infant and toddler environments includes wonderful ideas illustrated with photographs and diagrams of indoor and outdoor spaces.

The Complete Learning Spaces Book for Infants and Toddlers, Rebecca Isbell (Beltsville, MD: Gryphon House, 2003). The author presents ideas for creating and evaluating 54 different areas for infants and toddlers in child care settings. Illustrations make the ideas clear for readers.

Designs for Living and Learning: Transforming Early Childhood Environments, Deb Curtis and Margie Carter (St. Paul, MN: Redleaf Press, 2003). The hundreds of beautiful color photographs in this book will inspire teachers to evaluate and reinvent their child care settings. The book covers settings for infants through school-age, but the principles of designing appropriate environments apply to any age group.

The Outside Play and Learning Book, Karen Miller (Beltsville, MD: Gryphon House, 1989). A comprehensive and creative collection of outdoor activities, this book offers practical suggestions for making good use of the outdoor environment in all seasons.

The Right Stuff for Children Birth to 8: Selecting Play Materials to Support Development, Martha B. Bronson (Washington, DC: National Association for the Education of Young Children, 1995). This book is a thorough guide to appropriate play materials. There are separate chapters for young infants, older infants, young toddlers, and older toddlers. Each chapter describes typical developmental characteristics of the age group and suggests materials to encourage different kinds of exploration.

Physical

Caring for Your Baby and Young Child, Birth to Age Five, American Academy of Pediatrics (New York: Bantam Books, 1998). This book offers answers and advice that will help families and caregivers understand growth and development and address child-rearing concerns.

Experiences in Movement: Birth to Age 8, 3rd edition, Rae Pica (Clifton Park, NY: Delmar, 2003). The author shares ideas for offering a program based on movement activities and for weaving movement activities into daily activities for children from infancy through school age.

Why Motor Skills Matter: Improving Your Child's Physical Development to Enhance Learning and Skills, Tara Losquandro-Liddle (Lincolnwood, IL: NTC Publishing Group, 2003). The author, a pediatric physical therapist, explains how physical development affects other areas of development and learning. She suggests ways to integrate touch, movement, and body awareness during play with infants and toddlers.

Cognitive

Building Your Baby's Brain: A Parent's Guide to the First Five Years, Diane Trister Dodge and Cate Heroman (Washington, DC: Teaching Strategies, Inc., 1999). The first five years of life are critical for brain development. This clearly written booklet, full of illustrations and helpful charts, explains what scientists know about brain development. It shows how parents and teachers can make a big difference.

Your Child's Growing Mind: A Practical Guide Brain Development and Learning from Birth to Adolescence, Jane M. Healy (New York, NY: Doubleday, 1994). This clear guide explains brain development research in practical terms. The author explains in detail how children develop language and memory, and she addresses academic learning: reading, writing, spelling, and mathematics. This book provides solid advice about how to promote (not push) children's readiness, motivation, and problem-solving skills.

Creative

The Bilingual Book of Rhymes, Songs, Stories and Fingerplays, Pam Schiller, Rafael Lara-Alecio, and Beverly J. Irby (Beltsville, MD: Gryphon House, Inc. 2004). This anthology offers 450 choices in English and Spanish.

Creative Expression and Play in Early Childhood, 3rd edition, Joan P. Isenberg and Mary Renck Jalongo (Upper Saddle River, NJ: Prentice Hall, 1999). Grounded in the authors' experiences teaching teachers, this book offers strategies and activities to stimulate readers' ideas for promoting young children's play and creativity.

First Art: Art Experiences for Toddlers and Twos, MaryAnn F. Kohl (Beltsville, MD: Gryphon House, Inc. 2002). Each of the six chapters in this book focuses on a different type of art exploration for children ages one through three. The activities include paint, dough and clay, making marks, sticking and gluing, and prints. A final chapter includes directions for items that toddlers and adults can make together.

Communication

Building Literacy With Love, A Guide for Teachers and Caregivers of Children From Birth Through Age 5, Betty S. Bardige and Marilyn M. Segal (Washington, DC: ZERO TO THREE Press, 2005). Teachers and caregivers will find a clear explanation of how literacy development is rooted in caring relationships with infants and toddlers, as well as practical information about fostering literacy through typical daily routines and activities.

How Babies Talk: The Magic and Mystery of Language in the First Three Years of Life, Roberta Michnick Golinkoff and Kathy Hirsh-Pasek (New York: Plume, 1999). This book explores how babies learn language and the ways in which parents and caregivers can enhance interactions to nurture children's communication skills during the first three years of life.

Learning Language and Loving It, Elaine Weitzman (Toronto, Canada: The Hanen Centre, 2002). This practical resource reflects the strategies used to implement an on-site training program for early childhood staff members. The author reviews language learning from birth through the preschool years. The examples, illustrations, and graphics are extremely clear and readable.

*Learning to Read and Write: Developmentally Appropriate Practices for Young Children, Susan B. Neuman, Carol Copple, and Sue Bredekamp (Washington DC: National Association for the Education of Young Children, 2000). Teachers can be assured that this approach to fostering early literacy development is developmentally appropriate and based on research about the most effective ways to help young children gain language and literacy skills. Strategies are illustrated through numerous photographs and examples of children's work.

Much More Than the ABCs: The Early Stages of Reading and Writing, Judith A. Schickedanz (Washington, DC: National Association for the Education of Young Children, 1999). This updated version of an early literacy classic explains how young children learn about reading and writing. The final chapter offers ideas for organizing an environment that supports children's language and literacy explorations.

*Reading Right From the Start, Toni S. Bickart and Diane Trister Dodge (Washington, DC: Teaching Strategies, Inc., 2000). This easy-to-read, richly illustrated booklet shows parents how they can help their children (birth to age five) gain the language and literacy knowledge necessary to become readers and writers. Teachers can use this book to help parents feel more confident about what they can do at home.

Story S-t-r-e-t-c-h-e-r-s for Infants, Toddlers, and Twos, Shirley Raines, Karen Miller, and Leah Curry-Rood (Beltsville, MD: Gryphon House, 2002). This book begins with a discussion of emergent literacy and the important role of children's books. Separate chapters focus on books for infants, toddlers, and twos, and they describe simple activities to build on the topics and themes of the books.

Young Children and Picture Books, 2nd edition, Mary Renck Jalongo (Washington, DC: National Association for the Education of Young Children, 2004). Readers learn what to look for in the text and illustrations when selecting high quality books for children of different ages. Lists of recommended books help teachers make selections.

Self, Social, and Guidance

The Emotional Life of the Toddler, Alicia F. Lieberman (New York, NY: The Free Press, 1995). Offers numerous examples and vivid cases that will help teachers and parents better understand the ever-changing emotions of toddlers.

Everyday Goodbyes: Starting School and Early Care (A Guide to the Separation Process), Nancy Balaban (New York: Teachers College Press, in press). This book is the second edition of Balaban's book *Starting School* (see below). Addressed to both teachers and parents, this revised edition includes a more extensive discussion about separation for infants and toddlers.

First Feelings: Milestones in the Emotional Development of Your Baby and Child, Stanley Greenspan (New York: Viking Penguin, USA, 1994). Dr. Greenspan, child psychiatrist and author, reviews the stages of normal emotional development for children. He offers suggestions for parents about how to handle typical problems and challenges. Teachers can adapt these strategies in their work with young children.

Meeting the Challenge: Effective Strategies for Challenging Behaviors in Early Childhood Environments, Barbara Kaiser and Judy Rasminsky (Ontario, Canada: Canadian Child Care Federation, 1999). Available from NAEYC, this book presents an overall approach that helps teachers observe and reflect on children's challenging behaviors. The authors also provide practical strategies for helping individual children learn appropriate ways to express their strong feelings and learn to behave in acceptable ways.

Me, Myself and I: How Children Build Their Sense of Self, 18 to 36 months, Kyle D. Pruett (New York: Goddard Press, 1999). Written for parents, this book provides a comprehensive look at the social and emotional development of toddlers.

Secure Relationships: Nurturing Infant-Toddler Attachment in Early Care Settings, Alice Sterling Honig (Washington, DC: National Association for the Education of Young Children, 2002). Secure attachments and consistent care are key to helping young children form meaningful relationships. Teachers of infants and toddlers play an important role in supporting attachment and establishing responsive relationships.

Starting School: From Separation to Independence, Nancy Balaban (New York: Teachers College Press, 1985). This book explains how children experience and cope with separation and provides practical suggestions for supporting children. A revised edition, *Everyday Goodbyes*, is in press (see above).

Toilet Learning: The Picture Book Technique for Children and Parents, Alison Mack (New York: Little, Brown, and Company, 1983). With separate sections for adults and children, this book offers information that helps the toilet learning process go smoothly.

Touchpoints: Your Child's Emotional and Behavioral Development, T. Berry Brazleton (NY: Perseus Books, 1992). The author, a renowned pediatrician, shares information about key milestones in development and the behaviors that are typical before each milestone is reached.

Families

Partnering With Parents to Support Young Children's Development, Jeree H. Pawl and Amy Laura Dombro (Washington DC: ZERO TO THREE Press, 2001). This book is a valuable resource for supporting the lifelong parent-child relationship. It includes real-life vignettes and exercises to help teachers of infants and toddlers become more aware of how their own beliefs and values shape their relationships with families.

Parent-Friendly Early Learning: Tips and Strategies for Working Well With Parents, Julie Powers (St. Paul, MN: Redleaf Press, 2005). Offering insights about the perspective of parents, this book is a thoughtful and practical resource for helping classroom teachers create positive and meaningful relationships with the parents of young children.

*A Parent's Guide to Infant/Toddler Programs, English and Spanish editions, Diane Trister Dodge, Amy Laura Dombro, and Laura J. Colker (Washington, DC: Teaching Strategies, Inc., 1998). This booklet shows parents how warm and responsive care at home and in child care helps shape the development of infants and toddlers and their ability to learn. It outlines what and how children learn during those crucial years and suggests ways that caregivers/teachers and parents can work together.

Program Management and Professionalism

Advocates in Action: Making a Difference for Young Children, Revised edition, Adele Robinson and Deborah R. Stark (Washington, DC: National Association for the Education of Young Children, 2002). The authors of this revised edition provide practical ideas and strategies for advocating for the care, education, and support of young children and families. New material explains the legislative process.

The Power of Observation, Judy R. Jablon, Amy Laura Dombro, and Margo L. Dichtelmiller (Washington, DC: Teaching Strategies, 1999). The authors share their experiences and those of many others to illustrate the vital connection between observing and effective teaching.

Relationships, the Heart of Quality Care: Creating Community Among Adults in Early Care Settings, Amy C. Bakler, and Lynn A. Manfredi/Petitt (Washington, DC: National Association for the Education of Young Children, 2004). This book focuses on the importance of supportive, collegial relationships between teachers and other staff in early child care settings and how these relationships support young children.